Conflict Management for Managers

The Instructor's Guide for *Conflict Management for Managers* includes two sets of PowerPoint slides, one for undergraduate and another for graduate courses, as well as an explanatory guide from the author for the professor.

The Instructor's Guide is available free online. If you would like to download and print a copy of the Guide, please visit: www.wiley.com/college/raines

Conflict Management for Managers

Resolving Workplace, Client, and Policy Disputes

Susan S. Raines

JOSSEY-BASS
A Wiley Imprint
www.josseybass.com

Published by Jossey-Bass
A Wiley Imprint
One Montgomery Street, Suite 1200, San Francisco, CA 94104-4594-www.josseybass.com

Cover design by Adrian Morgan
Cover photography © Gandee Vasan | Getty (RM)
Author photo by David Caselli

Jossey-Bass books and products are available through most bookstores. To contact Jossey-Bass directly call our Customer Care Department within the U.S. at 800-956-7739, outside the U.S. at 317-572-3986, or fax 317-572-4002.

Wiley also publishes its books in a variety of electronic formats and by print-on-demand. Some material included with standard print versions of this book may not be included in e-books or in print-on-demand. If the version of this book that you purchased references media such as CD or DVD that was not included in your purchase, you may download this material at http://booksupport.wiley.com. For more information about Wiley products, visit www.wiley.com.

Library of Congress Cataloging-in-Publication Data

Raines, Susan.
  Conflict management for managers : resolving workplace, client, and policy disputes /
Susan S. Raines.— 1st ed.
    p. cm.— (The Jossey-Bass business & management series)
  Includes bibliographical references and index.
  ISBN 978-0-470-93111-0 (pbk.)
ISBN 978-1-118-41842-0 (ebk.)—ISBN 978-1-118-41548-1 (ebk.)—ISBN 978-1-118-43354-6 (ebk.)
  1. Conflict management. 2. Interpersonal relations. 3. Personnel management—
Psychological aspects. 4. Customer relations. 5. Conflict management—Case studies.
I. Title.
  HD42.R35 2013
  658.4′053—dc23

                                                       2012039946

Printed in the United States of America
FIRST EDITION
HB Printing 10 9 8 7 6 5 4 3 2 1

The Jossey-Bass Business & Management Series

CONTENTS

FIGURES AND TABLES

FIGURES

TABLES

ACKNOWLEDGMENTS

I would like to offer my deep thanks to my research assistants, Erin A. Exum and Haley Everson, for their endless enthusiasm, support, and assistance during this project. Others who helped and supported this research include Jennifer Victor, Dr. Mary Lou Odom, Adam Blaschke, Dr. Trina Cyterski, Thomas Sclefani, and Hayley Lester. Feedback on the first draft was provided by professor Wallace Tanksley, graduate students taking "Conflict Management for Managers" at Kennesaw State University in Georgia, and four anonymous peer reviewers.

Thanks also go to my husband, children, and coworkers, who displayed great patience when I devoted much time to this endeavor.

INTRODUCTION

Learning Objectives

- List and describe the most common sources of conflict faced by managers in the public and private sectors.

- Describe and analyze the costs of unproductive conflicts within organizations.

- Describe the financial and nonfinancial benefits of being a proactive conflict manager versus a reactive conflict manager.

A TALE OF TWO MANAGERS

John and Elise are managers who strive to apply the principles and practices of conflict management in their everyday working environments. They come from vastly different organizations yet both recognize the importance of proactively addressing conflict. By observing them we can see the techniques from this book at work.

Meet John, Director of the State Bureau of Reclamation

Almost every day, John dreads coming to work. As soon as he walks through the door to the State Bureau of Reclamation, his administrative assistant practically tackles him and regales him with the emergency du jour. It is these constant interruptions and daily emergencies that keep him from doing his real job, which is shaping and leading his department so that it can fulfill its regulatory mandate in an efficient and productive manner. What are these "daily emergencies"? They tend to fall into one of three categories.

Workplace Problems   Inevitably someone on John's staff calls in sick or announces that she or he is leaving for a position in private industry. Staff

Note: These narratives are based on an amalgamation of real managers at real organizations and are not based on any one individual or organization.

members cannot seem to work together well. They compete over scarce resources, blame each other for missed deadlines, or avoid talking altogether even when they are supposed to work on team-based projects. Occasionally employees file union grievances or discrimination complaints with the Equal Employment Opportunity Commission (EEOC). John's organization "wins" nearly all of these cases but the paperwork and drama wear him down and cost his agency tens of thousands of dollars per year.

Customer Complaints   John's agency is part of the state's Department of Natural Resources. Specifically, the Bureau of Reclamation issues licenses for coal mines and ensures that all coal mines operating in the state are doing so within the bounds of applicable state and federal environmental regulations. Because the turnover in John's department is fairly high, it is difficult to meet deadlines for issuing permits and conducting mandatory audits. Sometimes his department loses applications altogether or makes mistakes in the paperwork so the applicant has to start the process over again. Every day that a mining company cannot work because of a missing license application means idle and unpaid employees as well as lost tax revenue. Calls come in nearly every day from citizens and companies who believe that the bureau is not doing its job well enough or quickly enough. When the call comes from a state legislator's office John knows things have really gotten bad.

Regulatory Challenges   On really bad days, one of the mining companies will be in the news for some environmental mess they created or other violation of the state or federal laws that John's agency is supposed to enforce. The alleged violator will likely feign ignorance of the broken rule or law and try to avoid taking responsibility for the damages caused. The violator's legal counsel might threaten to sue the agency. Lawsuits are inevitable and unavoidable. If John does his job right, then the corporations he regulates want to sue him for his overzealous enforcement of state and federal mining laws. If he backs off a bit, then citizens' groups sue him for not adequately enforcing the laws. It is a no-win situation. No wonder turnover and absenteeism is so high in his department.

Something Has to Give   John has passion for the mission of his organization and he views himself as a committed public servant with good people skills who knows the mining industry inside and out. This should be the perfect job for him. So why is it that the bureau has not improved since he assumed command six months ago? John got this job by sharing some of his ideas for improvement with the agency's director, who quickly recognized John's passion and competence. So far, none of those ideas have been implemented due to the nonstop crisis management style in which the bureau seems to function. How can John focus on "fire prevention" when he is so busy "putting out fires" every day?

MEET ELISE, FOUNDER AND CEO OF MAIN STREET BAKERIES

Elise started with a good idea: provide local, organic, fresh foods to people in a café-bookstore atmosphere. Customers buy freshly prepared foods, healthy groceries, and gourmet items, get one-on-one consultations from certified nutritionists, and listen to guest speakers on various topics. Her stores have become gathering places and focal points for the communities in which they operate. Her company is widely reputed to be environmentally friendly and socially conscious, a reputation gained through innovations in environmental management and significant charitable giving. She started in the early 1980s in California and has ridden the green wave into the twenty-first century by expanding from one shop to 425 stores throughout the United States and Canada. Elise plans to expand into European markets next year as well. Her company is consistently rated as one of the best places to work by *Fortune* magazine and *Working Mother* magazine. *Consumer Reports* rates Main Street Bakeries as having the highest customer satisfaction of any grocery store chain.

Does Elise love her job? Definitely. How does she do it? How did she create a workplace environment in which employees are generally happy, customers are satisfied, and the relationships with regulatory agencies are collaborative? More important, how can we learn from her example and improve our own companies?

Throughout this book we will return to John and Elise to see how Elise created and sustains a company with satisfied, dare I say, happy employees and customers. We will watch John as he transforms his workgroup into one that is less riddled with unproductive conflict and more successful at accomplishing its regulatory mission in spite of the ever-present shortage of resources common to public agencies. We will read other examples as well, including some from the nonprofit sector and from organizations of all sizes. Through these examples you will see the pitfalls of organizations that poorly predict, prevent, and manage conflict, as well as learn from contrasting positive examples of collaboratively and wisely managed organizations. By implementing the processes, strategies, and techniques in this book you will learn the skills necessary to be a proactive conflict manager.

THE GOAL OF THIS BOOK

You are reading this book because you are, or you hope to become, a manager who productively manages conflict to the benefit of your organization, your career, and let's face it—your sanity. Whether you acknowledge it or not, all managers are conflict managers. Whether you work in the private, public, or nonprofit sector, you are likely to spend the majority of your day dealing with conflicts between employees; disputes with clients, suppliers, or vendors; or managing relationships with myriad regulatory agencies that influence or shape your organization's work.

The question is not *if* managers deal with conflict but *how* managers deal with conflict. Those who do not recognize it, analyze it, and design better methods for conflict prevention and management end up like John at the Bureau of Reclamation (but there is still hope for John, so don't quit reading now). The goal is to become adept at fostering and facilitating collaboration within your work teams and organizations so as to proactively avoid destructive conflict and harness the power of constructive change. "Conflict brings change and collaborative leadership is the ultimate political transformer" (Adler & Fisher, 2007, p. 21).

This book will provide readers with a knowledge base and a set of skill-building opportunities so they can reclaim their time and make their workplaces enjoyable, productive, mutually supportive, and where people want to work. Even in difficult economic times, during mergers and acquisitions and as leadership changes at the top of the organization, there will always be organizations or departments in which employees are happy, customers and clients are satisfied, and the problems that inevitably arise are handled efficiently and collaboratively. Managers in thriving workplaces are able to poach the best employees from other companies or agencies because their organizations have reputations as great places to work.

INTENDED AUDIENCE

This book is for managers and future managers whether you are reading this book as part of a university course or independently or as a manager seeking to improve his or her organization; or whether your organization is a small business, a department within a large organization, or a nonprofit group engaged in public service. Workplaces of all types and sizes deal with issues of organizational culture, personality conflicts, struggles over scarce resources, the need to create and sustain successful teams, and the need to design solution-oriented processes to the inevitable conflicts that will arise.

You need not be the CEO, like Elise, in order to make changes within your own work unit, as we will see from John's example. Managers at any level can change the way they operate for the betterment of their employees, themselves, and their organizations. The costs of unproductive conflict are too high to remain unaddressed for too long. Look at your most successful competitors and you are likely to find that they have put into place systems and people who manage conflict and collaboration well.

Public Sector Managers

"Yeah, but the public sector work environment is nothing like the private sector environment," some people say. Although differences certainly exist, managers across sectors have more in common than not. They all need to be attentive to the organization's cultural norms, keep customers and those in powerful positions satisfied, solve problems efficiently when they arise, design and use tools to track progress toward goals, give and receive feedback effectively, lead productive meetings, coach and mentor employees, and be strategic about fostering a collaborative team environment. Managers in large unionized corporations may have more in common with public sector managers than they have in common with small businesses. And yes, public sector managers sometimes face problems or environments that are more rule bound and more open to public scrutiny, and they must do it with more accountability than some private sector managers.

Regulatory agencies are usually a part of the executive branch of the government at the federal or state level, and they have statutory authority to perform their functions with oversight from the legislative branch. Regulatory authorities are commonly set up to enforce standards and safety, regulate commerce, and oversee public goods such as national defense or clean air. Regulatory agencies deal in the area of administrative law—regulation or rule making. A **public good** is something that, by its nature, is either supplied to all people or to none, regardless of whether or not each individual has paid his or her fair share for the enjoyment of that good. For example, national defense, clean air, public roads, and public libraries are all public goods: if they exist for anyone, then they exist for everyone. The problem with public goods is that many people try to gain the benefit of the goods without paying their fair share (via taxes, usually). Also, because they are owned by everyone and no one, they may not be adequately supplied or protected without governmental action. Regulatory agencies have historically had adversarial relationships with the organizations subject to their authority but this leads to unproductive conflict and often to suboptimal outcomes for the public.

It is undeniable that government workers (i.e., public sector employees) face some challenges that are slightly different from those working in commercial enterprises (i.e., private sector employees) or for nonprofit organizations. For an organization to operate efficiently, its managers need to develop strategies and skills for collaboratively managing relationships with the overlapping levels of regulatory authority they face as well as with myriad vendors, suppliers, and others within the supply chain. This book will help you map out those necessary relationships for the success of your unit, your organization, and ultimately your career, regardless of the size or type of work in which you find yourself.

Private Sector Managers

The private sector is far from monolithic. Managers in small companies face challenges at a different scope and level than managers in *Fortune* 500 organizations. Small companies are more nimble and open to changing as needed, whereas large ones seem slow to turn around even when big changes are needed. Examples throughout the book are used to illustrate the ways in which the techniques and ideas may be applied in varying contexts—from huge US-based airlines to a family-owned restaurant. Most of the material presented in this book can be applied to businesses of all sizes but the relative costs of implementation for some interventions may be proportionately higher in small organizations. When this is the case, it will be noted and ideas for overcoming or reducing costs will be discussed.

Nonprofit Sector Managers

Nonprofits often combine the biggest challenges from the other two sectors. Like the private sector, nonprofits can be as small as a one-employee shop or as large as Blue Cross Blue Shield Association, with tens of thousands of employees within and across the United States. Similar to the private sector, nonprofits generally must find streams of revenue to support their work, often through grants, government contracts, and fund-raising events. The persistent state of budgetary uncertainty is a source of stress among employees and can lead to burnout and departure for one of the other two sectors. Similar to public sector organizations, nonprofits are generally involved with supplying public goods or private goods for which the market is not well suited (e.g., health care for the poor, emergency housing, humanitarian relief, transportation for the disabled or elderly). The importance of the mission means that most nonprofit employees care deeply about those served by their organization, yet employees may disagree strongly about the best way to serve their clientele and use limited resources. Nonprofits must keep their administrative costs down and their brand name sparkling if they are to compete for scarce funds—thereby increasing the importance of intraoffice collaboration and the need to reduce the costs of conflict. Case studies and illustrations from the nonprofit sector are used throughout the book to show how collaboration and conflict management can be applied in these challenging and diverse environments.

Not a Manager Yet?

What if you are not a manager yet? The material contained in this book will assist you as you improve your communication and customer service skills and interact with your coworkers and supervisors. As you rise in your career, you can use the material contained in these pages to improve collaboration among your peer group and to use feedback for your continued skill development. When you become a manager, you will be ahead of the pack, having already gained much of the knowledge needed to successfully lead your team and organization.

If you are reading this book as part of a university course, you will likely have opportunities to discuss and apply the skills and concepts herein. If you are reading the book on your own, I encourage you to seek out one or more managers either within your company or outside of it in order to fully benefit from many of the skill-building exercises, role-plays, surveys, discussion questions, and goal-setting tasks supplied at the end of each chapter and with the online teaching supplement. Old habits die hard and practicing your new skill set will improve your ability to transfer these practices from the book and classroom into the boardroom and break room.

ORGANIZATION OF THE BOOK

The book is organized into four parts, each with a brief introduction of its own. Part One introduces the primary concepts and practices of conflict management on which the following parts depend. Part Two examines sources of conflict internal to an organization, meaning employment disputes, turnover, dysfunctions within a team, working with union leaders, and so on. These are the sources of conflict that eat up managers' days, leaving them less time to build their businesses, respond to customers, and mentor their employees. Part Three examines conflicts external to an organization, meaning those involving clients, customers, patients, vendors, and so on. This part include case studies of organizations across sectors from which we can gain valuable insights into systematic methods for achieving higher levels of satisfaction for our customers, clients, or constituencies. Finally, Part Four examines the sources of friction as well as potential collaboration between regulators and the regulated. This part includes detailed information about how to lead efficient meetings and decision-making processes, regardless of whether these involve five or five hundred participants.

The first chapter helps managers better understand their own conflict management style and habits as well as the impact of those habits on their managerial efficiency. Once managers understand their own preferences and habits in response to conflict, it becomes easier to be strategic in responding to or preventing conflict. Next, we examine the root causes of conflict and how it escalates and de-escalates, using specific communication and conflict management techniques. This knowledge of conflict theory and basic concepts will serve as the foundation for many of the subsequent chapters. Chapter Three introduces the core concepts and skills of negotiation. Managers negotiate every day—with vendors and suppliers, with disgruntled customers or employees, with those up and down the chain of command (not to mention our spouses, children, and neighbors!). A firm grasp on the skills of negotiation will significantly improve your ability to achieve desired outcomes at work and elsewhere. The final chapter in this part, Chapter Four, introduces and defines common processes used to address disputes that arise in order to avoid costly litigation, such as mediation, arbitration, peer review, and so on.

In Part Two we examine internal sources of organizational conflict, meaning employment disputes. Employment disputes often lead to high employee turnover (Chapter Five) and poorer mission achievement. Chapter Six shares best practices for building and sustaining creative, collaborative, and productive teams even in difficult times such as during mergers and acquisitions. Chapter Seven examines the unique processes found in unionized workplaces as well as sharing innovative methods for moving beyond the worn-out dichotomy of "us versus them" frequently found in labor-management negotiations and contracts. Chapter Eight presents methods for designing systems of conflict prevention and management within organizations. This information is useful to resolve employment disputes as well as disputes with clients and customers, as seen in the next part.

Part Three investigates the best practices for creating positive, stable, mutually beneficial relationships with customers, clients, and vendors. In Chapter Nine we examine the methods used by organizations across the spectrum to enhance customer acquisition, retention, and satisfaction — including methods for resolving customer complaints. Customer satisfaction systems *are* inherently conflict management systems. Chapter Ten presents numerous case studies of customer satisfaction innovations from organizations of various sizes and missions.

Part Four examines methods for creating and sustaining collaborative relationships and participatory decision making among public sector regulators, private sector business, and nonprofit sector civil society organizations. When all three sectors come together to share information and resources, brainstorm policy solutions and implementation methods, and search for solutions that meet the needs of all stakeholders, then amazing things can happen. Chapter Eleven examines innovative applications of conflict management in the public policy arena, including highlights from exemplary efforts. Chapter Twelve walks you through the process of designing and facilitating effective large-group processes such as public hearings, board meetings, shareholder gatherings, and deliberative democracy initiatives. These tools are helpful to leader managers who are called on to facilitate decision-making and change-management processes within and between organizations.

The book concludes with some next steps for the reader to take to improve personal management practice and is then followed with a glossary of key terms and the references for further reading and research.

Each chapter begins with a fictional illustration of the challenges facing two very different organizations — the Bureau of Reclamation, headed by John, and Main Street Bakeries, led by Elise. These examples are used to illustrate common sources of conflict faced by managers and then show how the concepts and tools from each chapter are applied to those scenarios in order to address the challenges. The learning objectives at the beginning of each chapter serve to outline the concepts and skills covered as well as to cue the reader as to the chapter's foci. Teachers may wish to come back to these at the end of each chapter or class to evaluate the extent to which learning objectives have been achieved and determine where further elaboration or clarification is in order. Case studies presented throughout the book are used to show either best practices or worst-case scenarios to avoid.

THE COSTS OF CONFLICT

In organizations, "the typical manager may spend 25% of his time dealing with conflicts" (Bass & Bass, 2009, p. 319). The costs of conflict include the obvious expenses of legal fees and settlements but also include the costs of lost customers, employee turnover, and damage to the reputation of the organization and the brand name. **Alternative dispute resolution (ADR)** refers to a host of processes that serve as alternatives to costly adversarial litigation, including mediation, arbitration, peer review, the use of an ombudsman, and others. According to Europe's leading ADR organization, conflicts costs British corporations more than thirty-three billion pounds per year (fifty-two million US dollars). To give some perspective, if this sum were a country, it would be the fifty-seventh largest economy in the world. Of this amount, only about 22 percent comes from legal fees, with 78 percent stemming from lost business due to customer dissatisfaction (Amble, 2006). A 2008 study showed that US employees spent an average of 2.8 hours per week dealing with overt conflicts, which equals about $359 billion dollars' worth of average hourly wages. This amount equals approximately 385 million days of work (Hayes, 2008). It is likely that this number is underestimated because many people do not accurately recognize or label conflict when it occurs, preferring not to acknowledge its presence. For managers, conflict takes up even more time, with one survey showing it takes about 42 percent of the average manager's day (Watson & Hoffman, 1996) and with *Fortune* 500 executives devoting 20 percent of their time explicitly to litigation. Unfortunately, these statistics are not trending in a positive direction. In 2010, the EEOC reported a record high number of lawsuits (Equal Employment Opportunity Commission, 2010).

Numerous studies detail the costs of high employee turnover. Studies peg the costs of hiring and training a new employee to be between 75 percent and 150 percent of the employee's annual salary. According to the US Bureau of Labor Statistics, 23.7 percent of Americans voluntarily quit their job in 2006 (Allen, 2008). Let's do the math for a moment: for an organization with one hundred employees, with a relatively low turnover rate of 15 percent per year and an average salary of $50,000, this turnover rate means costs of $562,000 to

$1,125,000 every year! If that much money could be saved by mechanizing or changing a manufacturing process most managers would jump at the chance to reap this much in savings. Unlike changes to the assembly line or cutting back on technology purchases, many managers feel helpless to reduce employee turnover, improve morale, or change company culture. The good news is these can be changed and at relatively low cost.

Unfortunately, many managers view employee turnover as inevitable, like the weather—something that must be endured because it cannot be changed. Yet some organizations and some managers have realized that managing conflict is crucial to retaining employees and thriving as an organization. A growing body of research links high turnover rates to shortfalls in organizational performance and low customer satisfaction. "For example, one nationwide study of nurses at 333 hospitals showed that turnover among registered nurses accounted for 68% of the variability in per-bed operating costs. Likewise, reducing turnover rates has been shown to improve sales growth and workforce morale" (Allen, 2008, p. 5).

Spotlight: Turnover Is Tougher on Small Organizations

The loss of key employees can have a particularly damaging impact on small organizations:

- Departing workers are more likely to be the only ones possessing a particular skill or knowledge set.

- A small company's culture suffers a more serious blow when an essential person leaves.

- There is a smaller internal pool of workers to cover the lost employee's work and provide a replacement.

- The organization may have fewer resources available to cover replacement costs.

Source: Allen (2008, p. 5).

Organizations that have high rates of employee turnover also have related problems with high levels of absenteeism, low employee commitment to the organization and its mission, employee tardiness, and overall low worker productivity (Allen, 2008).

It is a myth that employees leave primarily for higher-paying jobs. The primary drivers of employee turnover include the relationships experienced on the job (between coworkers and between employees and managers), the work environment, the quality of communication within an organization, and job characteristics such as the opportunity to advance and develop professionally (Allen, 2008). Even in a tight budget climate, when raises are hard to dole out, conflict savvy managers can increase employee retention and productivity gains. This book will examine thoroughly the ways in which managers, owners, and employees can create the kind of workplace where people feel valued, they enjoy their work, and those conflicts that will inevitably arise from time to time are handled smoothly, collaboratively, and result in strengthened rather than weakened relationships.

Keeping employees happy is closely related to keeping customers and clients happy. Companies with high levels of employee satisfaction consistently produce high levels of customer or client satisfaction (Zondiros, Konstantopoulos, & Tomaras, 2007). In addition to lost productivity at work and high employee turnover, an organization's reputation and brand name suffer due to litigation over unresolved conflicts. A study in the *Journal of Financial Economics* (Baghat, Brickley, & Coles, 1994) showed that the stock value of large firms drops an average of 1 percent on the announcement of a lawsuit against the company whereas the stock of the plaintiff's company does not increase at all. Stock prices tend to rebound when an out-of-court settlement is announced. One percent may seem small but for the companies analyzed in this study the overall drop in stock value was equal to $21 million.

According to the Centre for Effective Dispute Resolution (CEDR), Europe's largest dispute resolution organization, the majority of managers state they have not been adequately trained to handle the conflicts they encounter. In CEDR's survey of conflict among managers, more than one-third of managers claimed they would rather jump from a plane in a parachute for the first time than address a problem at work! The desire to avoid confronting problems results in wasted opportunities for improved performance on the part of employees and the entire company but apparently it bodes well for the parachute business.

Gerzon (2006), a leadership researcher, emphasizes that "leading through conflict involves facing differences honestly and creatively, understanding their full complexity and scope, and enabling those involved to move beyond the powerful, primordial responses to difference that result in an 'us versus them' mentality. It requires capacities that many leaders have never developed, bringing to bear both personal and professional skills that turn serious conflicts into rewarding opportunities for collaboration and innovation" (p. 4). Conflict can be positive or negative, depending on how it is handled. By handling conflict efficiently you can harness its creative power for positive change and avoid the negative elements that give it a bad reputation.

Collaboration and collaborative management are evolving as the dominant forms of leadership but we are not there yet. With an educated, creative, and capable workforce, dictatorial, oppressive leaders are increasingly seen as dinosaurs from the era of factory-style production. With an economy focused on knowledge-creation and service industries, management styles must change to reflect the evolving nature of work itself. Barbara Gray (1989) defines **collaboration** as having four distinct parts:

- Interdependent stakeholders (i.e., those affected by a decision)
- The ability to constructively address differences
- Joint ownership of decisions
- Collective responsibility for the future of the partnership

Collaboration is different from *cooperation* or *coordination* because these "two terms do not capture the dynamic, evolutionary nature of collaboration. Collaboration from this perspective is best examined as a dynamic or emergent process rather than as a static condition" (O'Leary & Blomgren Bingham, 2011, p. 5).

Conflict management (CM) refers to the systematic prevention of unproductive conflict and proactively addressing those conflicts that cannot be prevented. Every workplace has existing conflict management methods but these methods may have developed in an ad hoc fashion without explicit discussion. As a result the existing methods may need to be examined and (re)designed for maximal efficiency and user satisfaction. According to Adler and Fisher (2007), two visionaries in the field of conflict management, "By necessity, leaders must be many things: strategists, warriors, moralists, peacemakers, artisans, technicians, managers, and more. Sometimes a leader becomes an 'undercover mediator' within his organization or at the negotiating table" (p. 21).

Nonprofit organizations and government agencies are not immune from the high costs of conflict mentioned already, including costs related to employee turnover problems and dissatisfied clients, customers, and citizens. For example, in 2005 the four largest counties in California paid $79.2 million in litigation costs (Citizens Against Lawsuit Abuse, 2007). Although some of this litigation may be unavoidable, these costs could undoubtedly be reduced through the judicious use of ADR processes as well as systems to solve problems in their earliest stages.

Many organizations have learned the hard way that unproductive conflicts and poor management methods hurt the bottom line. Unproductive conflicts can result in costly and unpleasant relationships between companies and regulatory agencies such as the Department of Labor, the EEOC, the Occupational Safety and Health Administration (OSHA), and so on. But you do not have to take my word for it. Luckily there are numerous examples of companies that have turned things around by making changes to their management of conflict as well as examples of those who have experienced huge costs from not learning those lessons early enough.

Through the systematic analysis of the sources and types of disputes, organizations can engage in a process called **dispute systems design (DSD)**. DSD is a process for assisting an organization to develop a structure for handling a series of similar recurring or anticipated disputes more effectively. These can be internal employment disputes or disputes with external conflicts with clients, customers, or regulators (e.g., EEOC complaints within a federal agency or environmental enforcement cases with polluters). Chapter Eight will help you with the process of assessing the disputes facing your organization and then designing processes to prevent and limit the costs from those disputes.

CASE STUDY IN UNMANAGED CONFLICT: WALMART

Walmart Corporation has been in the news on and off for more than a decade concerning gender and racial discrimination charges. Although a recent Supreme Court decision means that women who want to sue Walmart for gender discrimination will need to do so individually rather than as a class action, the bad press and damage to their brand has been significant. According to the *New York Times*, plaintiffs cite significant differences in pay and promotion by gender, with women in salaried jobs earning on average 19 percent less than men in similar jobs. Men at Walmart are 5.5 times as likely as women to be promoted into salaried, management positions. Even in hourly positions, women earned on average 5.8 percent less than their male counterparts. Women were disproportionately hired as cashiers and less often in higher-paying hourly jobs (Greenhouse, 2010). Disparities in pay were also found between black and white employees, although the differences were smaller. A subsequent analysis done by a statistics expert from California State University at East Bay in 2001 found a 26 percent difference in salaries by gender and a 6 percent difference for hourly workers. In 1995, Walmart hired an outside law firm to examine potential litigation liabilities related to gender discrimination complaints. In that report, the law firm of Akin Gump Strauss Hauer & Feld found widespread disparities in pay and promotion by gender and estimated Walmart's legal exposure to a class-action suit at $185 to $740 million dollars (Greenhouse, 2010).

What does this have to do with conflict management? Many companies struggle with issues of diversity and the need to effectively implement nondiscriminatory hiring and promotion policies. Walmart is not unique in that it has received gender discrimination complaints and other types of discrimination complaints. If nothing else, because of its size and the sheer number of employees, we could predict that each year there will be some number of employee complaints lodged against Walmart with the EEOC. But it is not the existence of complaints that indicate whether a company is managing conflict well—although the proportion of complaints can certainly be an indicator that room for improvement exists. Instead of the existence of complaints, it is how those complaints are handled or ignored that indicates whether an organization has a healthy system for resolving disputes early and before large litigation costs and damage to the organization's image have occurred.

Among other changes, the Akin Gump report recommended that Walmart set up an internal mandatory arbitration system for employment claims (Greenhouse, 2010). If Walmart had followed the recommendations found in the report by the Akin Gump group, they could have saved themselves millions in lost revenue due to damage to their brand name, cascading lawsuits, and customer boycotts.

CASE STUDY IN POSITIVE CHANGE: AMERICAN HOME SHIELD

Managers at American Home Shield knew they had a problem with employee turnover. With about 1,500 employees, the company was experiencing rates of turnover as high as 89 percent in some departments, which was estimated to cost the company more than $250,000 in the direct costs of hiring and training new employees (Allen, 2008). To better understand why employees were leaving, the company instituted a systematic survey of former employees and those currently leaving the company. These surveys indicated that employees left out of concerns about inadequate supervisor availability: they could not access their supervisors to ask for help when they needed it. Employees also felt they needed more job training and that the organizational system for communication was insufficient to accomplish work-related tasks. The survey information was used to make changes in the company's procedures, resulting in a 35 percent decrease in turnover in the first year alone (Allen, 2008).

As you proceed through this book you will learn strategies and techniques for reducing unproductive conflict within your organization and with customers as well as techniques for improving your ability to communicate positively and to respond to problems that arise. You will learn how to design policies and procedures to effectively handle disputes that are inevitable and how to use alternatives to litigation to save yourself and your organization money, time, and emotional energy. Exercises, scenarios, and analytical tools will be presented to help you practice these new skills so that you can develop the habits of effective conflict management.

CONCLUSION

Knowing there is a problem is only half the solution. After reading and practicing the skills contained in this book, you will better understand the sources and solutions to conflict in the working lives of managers. The next step is the hardest one: changing knowledge into action. Managers skilled in the art and science of collaborative problem solving will bring the specific skills of mediation, facilitation, process design, and visionary leadership to their work teams and organizations. The days of hierarchically organized, authoritarian rule by organizational leaders are fading fast. Dynamic, successful leader managers of today and tomorrow will act as catalysts for collaboration, maximizing performance by drawing on the individual strengths of team members and fostering firm commitment to a shared mission accomplished through a supportive, humane, energizing work environment. If you are reading this book, you have the ability to make these changes happen.

KEY TERMS

Alternative dispute resolution (ADR)
Collaboration
Conflict management (CM)

Dispute systems design (DSD)
Public good
Regulatory agencies

DISCUSSION QUESTIONS

1. What are the sources of employee turnover in your organization? How might a collaborative manager reduce employee turnover?

2. What are the current methods for addressing conflicts with customers and employees in an organization with which you are familiar? How satisfied are the users of those processes from what you can tell?

3. How collaborative is your organization? Why? How might it benefit from a more collaborative approach?

4. Does your organization have an ADR system? Why or why not?

EXERCISES

1. Analyze the conflict management system(s) within your current or a past work environment. How are workplace disputes prevented, tracked, and managed? What about disputes with clients or customers?

2. How much of your day is spent in dealing with disputes with employees or customers? Can you estimate the costs of unproductive disputing for your organization?

Conflict Management for Managers

PART ONE

Conflict Management Knowledge and Skills

Before you can begin to catalog, analyze, and address the sources of conflict in your organization, you need to gain a solid grounding in the theories and practice of conflict management and alternative dispute resolution.

Chapter One will help you become more aware of your own tendencies and habits in responding to conflict: Are you a conflict avoider, a scrappy conflict-a-holic, or something in between? Once you become cognizant of your own patterns of response to conflict, you can improve those responses and choose among a menu of possible responses in order to solve problems more efficiently and humanely. You will learn that nearly every individual and every organization has a pattern of responses to conflict and by predicting and explaining those patterns you will be able to become proactive rather than merely reacting to conflicts that arise. You will learn how to communicate effectively with people who prefer to respond to conflict in ways that are very different from your own. You will learn their language of conflict so you can better understand one another and work together productively. Moreover, by analyzing the strengths and weaknesses in your current managerial skill set, you will be able to set goals for improvement and become the manager that other departments wish they had!

Once you gain a more complete understanding of your own management style, Chapter Two will examine the root causes of conflict, study the typical paths of conflict escalation, and introduce foundational theories of conflict prevention and resolution. An understanding of basic conflict theory will serve as the cornerstone for the practices introduced later in the book and will provide us a cognitive framework with which to understand and organize the material presented in subsequent chapters. The theories presented in Chapter Two will begin at the most basic level — explaining conflict using evolutionary, anthropologic, and biologic research. To be human is to experience conflict within ourselves, between individuals, and among groups. Chapter Two presents common explanations for conflicts at all levels, from the psychological processes that lead us to distrust those who are different from us all the way to explanations that draw on political science and economics to describe competition over scarce resources including power, wealth, and influence. Chapter Two will equip you with much of the terminology to understand why, how, and when conflict arises in organizations and between individuals.

Chapter Three is designed to sharpen a key skill needed by all managers: negotiation. Most managers negotiate every day — deadlines, salaries, and access to needed resources are commonly negotiated by managers. Beyond the workplace applications, good negotiation skills also serve us well in our civic and family lives. We need to negotiate not only to accomplish our individual goals but *how* we negotiate tells a lot about us as people. Chapter Three provides the knowledge and skills necessary to leave your negotiations with a sense of accomplishment and enhanced relationships that will serve you and your organization well in all the negotiations yet to come.

There are many different processes commonly used to avoid litigation and solve problems with employees and customers. Chapter Four introduces each of the most common alternative dispute resolution processes, including mediation, facilitation, arbitration, and others. Knowledge of these processes will be helpful in subsequent chapters when readers will learn how to analyze their organizational environments and design dispute prevention and management systems to reduce costs and increase employee and customer satisfaction levels.

These four chapters lay the conceptual groundwork that will allow the reader to understand the subsequent sections on preventing and resolving internal conflicts (i.e., employment), preventing and resolving external conflicts (i.e., with customers and clients), and collaboration and conflict management between regulators and the regulated.

Manager Know Thyself

Learning Objectives

- Identify and describe the five most common reactions to conflict, known as *conflict styles*.
- Identify and describe the costs and benefits of each of the five conflict styles.
- Demonstrate understanding of your own habits when responding to conflict, along with the pros and cons of your habitual responses to conflict.
- Identify and understand the approaches to conflict used most often by your coworkers and superiors in order to tailor your responses accordingly.
- Demonstrate the process of altering your habitual responses to conflict as needed to increase the likelihood of productive conflict resolution.
- Identify those situations that call for active listening and those that do not.
- Demonstrate changes in improved listening skills.

RESPONDING TO CONFLICT AT THE BUREAU OF RECLAMATION

John Smith is not happy with his administrative assistant, Maria. On the days when John needs her most, she calls in "sick." Today John is scheduled to begin holding the one-one-one meetings required for staff performance reviews. John is supposed to meet with each of his twenty employees to share his ratings of their performance over the past year. Any deficiencies in performance must be discussed and, unfortunately, there are plenty of deficiencies to discuss. Although John has not administered performance reviews at this agency before, he has heard that it is typically a painful process with lots of hurt feelings and even occasional resignations. Because Maria is not here, John will have to find all the files himself, answer calls during the meetings with staff members, and try to keep on schedule without the benefit of his assistant who should strategically buzz him to let him know when his next appointment has arrived. Maria left a message on John's answering machine saying that she feels that helping him manage the review process is "above her pay grade." She said that she is happy to work on other tasks but won't participate in the review management process. John is wondering what he should do about this problem and then it hits him: he will send out an e-mail to all of his staff, including Maria, to tell them that the performance reviews are being postponed until Maria is feeling better. That will buy him at least another day or two so he can get some work done before having to get sidetracked with the drama that will likely result from the performance reviews and from dealing with Maria. He hopes she will take the hint and "get over herself."

Once John understands the five common approaches to conflict, he will be better able to predict and respond effectively to this type of situation.

RESPONDING TO CONFLICT: FIVE COMMON APPROACHES

Conflict is neither inherently positive nor negative. Instead, it is our reaction to conflict that determines whether it is constructive or destructive. Conflict presents an opportunity for positive change, deepening relationships, and problem solving. How you treat the other party or parties in conflict is highly predictive of the strength and duration of the relationship in the future. As Mary Parker Follett (1942) wrote nearly one hundred years ago, "All polishing is done through friction." Tjosvold's work (2008) shows us that organizations that encourage constructive debate and the open expression of disagreement among team members can greatly improve their effectiveness, creativity, and efficiency. Nevertheless, when most people use the term *conflict* there is an implied negative connotation. Is your reaction to conflict generally constructive or destructive? How do you feel after you address a problem with employees, your boss, or your clients? That postconflict feeling can tell us a lot. Does conflict make you want to fight or take flight?

Before reading further, please read and complete the conflict style assessment in Figure 1.1. Please select the answer that best corresponds to your preferred methods for addressing conflict in the two situations.

The **conflict styles inventory (CSI)** is a questionnaire that is used to assess an individual's habits in response to conflict. As the CSI indicates, there are five primary responses to conflict: avoidance, accommodation, collaboration, compromising, and competing. Each of these responses is appropriate in some circumstances and inappropriate or ineffective in others. You might have assumed that the **collaborative style** is the best of the five conflict styles because this is a book on the subject of collaboration. Surprisingly, that is not the case at all. Instead of pushing you toward the use of one of these conflict styles over the others, this book will argue that competent conflict managers are adept at analyzing problems and consciously choosing the style that is most likely to produce the desired results. Sometimes accommodation is called for, whereas other situations call for compromise, and so on. Each conflict presents an opportunity for the parties to consciously articulate their goals in the interaction and choose the best conflict style response to achieve those goals. Sometimes preserving or enhancing the relationship is the ultimate goal and in other cases your goal may be to avoid a no-win situation or make a quick and fair decision. Matching the conflict style to the particular dispute or decision-making opportunity is an important skill at work and in our civic and personal lives.

Most people will notice higher scores in one or two categories and significantly lower scores in other categories. This reflects a tendency for one to react with one predominant response to conflict, regardless of the type of problem at hand. For example, one may be conflict avoidant even when the problem would be more effectively resolved through direct action. The next section will help you understand each of the possible responses to conflict and when to employ each one most effectively.

It can be problematic that most of us predominately use only one or two of these conflict styles when we unconsciously respond to problems as opposed to analyzing situations and choosing the style that best matches the problem at hand. The best conflict management works something like good health care. When health problems are avoidable they should be avoided through preventive measures, such as good eating habits. When problems arise in spite of our preventative efforts, they must be diagnosed and then treated based on that diagnosis. So it should be for conflict. However, even the most stressful

Figure 1.1
Conflict Styles Inventory

Styles

Think of two different contexts (A and B) in which you have conflict, disagreement, argument, or disappointment with someone. An example might be a work associate or someone you live with. Then, according to the following scale, fill in your scores for situation A and situation B. *For each question you will have two scores.* For example, on question one the scoring might look like this 1. 2/4.

Write the name of each person for the two contexts here:

Person A_____   Person B_____

1 = Never   2 = Seldom   3 = Sometimes   4 = Often   5 = Always

Person A/ Person B

1. __/__ I avoid being put on the spot; I keep conflicts to myself.
2. __/__ I use my influence to get my ideas accepted.
3. __/__ I usually try to split the difference in order to resolve an issue.
4. __/__ I generally try to satisfy the other's needs.
5. __/__ I try to investigate an issue to find a solution acceptable to us.
6. __/__ I usually avoid open discussion of my differences with the other.
7. __/__ I use my authority to make decisions in my favor.
8. __/__ I try to find a middle course to resolve an impasse.
9. __/__ I usually accommodate the other's wishes.
10. __/__ I try to integrate my ideas with the other's to come up with a decision jointly.
11. __/__ I try to stay away from disagreement with the other.
12. __/__ I use my expertise to make a decision that favors me.
13. __/__ I propose a middle ground for breaking deadlocks.
14. __/__ I give in to the other's wishes.
15. __/__ I try to work with the other to try to find solutions that satisfy both our expectations.
16. __/__ I try to keep my disagreement to myself in order to avoid hard feelings.
17. __/__ I generally pursue my side of an issue.
18. __/__ I negotiate with the other to reach a compromise.
19. __/__ I often go with the other's suggestions.
20. __/__ I exchange accurate information with the other so we can solve a problem together.
21. __/__ I try to avoid unpleasant exchanges with the other.

Figure 1.1
(continued)

22. __/__ I sometimes use my power to win.
23. __/__ I use-give-and-take so that a compromise can be made.
24. __/__ I try to satisfy the other's expectations.
25. __/__ I try to bring all our concerns out in the open so that the issues can be resolved.

_____

Source: Reprinted with permission of McGraw-Hill, from Wilmot and Hocker (2001).

conflict provides you with an opportunity to showcase your conflict management skills and communicate the importance you place on treating others fairly and respectfully, even when you disagree about the outcome of a dispute.

THE FIVE CONFLICT STYLES

There are five predominant styles for dealing with conflict (see Figure 1.2). Most of us habitually use only one or two of these styles. Your choice of preferred styles likely depends on the culture in which you were raised and the way your family of origin dealt with conflict. Knowing your own style tendencies will help you improve your own response to conflict and also deepen your understanding of those around you—especially if their preferred style is different from yours. Rather than vilifying those who seem to fight every fight or those who behave with passive aggression, you will come to understand why people exhibit different habitual responses to conflict and how to work successfully with others who may not share your preferred conflict style.

Conflict Avoidant Style

It does not take an expert in conflict theory to realize the **avoidant style** is the approach to conflict being employed by John and Maria in the scenario at the beginning of this chapter. Clearly, John is avoiding dealing with performance reviews and he previously avoided addressing the absenteeism problem with Maria. He has rationalized his avoidance with the thought that he has not been on the job very long and maybe Maria's performance over the long term will improve. Avoidance becomes the preferred conflict management style for individuals who

---

Figure 1.2
Scoring the Conflict Styles Inventory

Scoring: Put your total for each question and each person on the lines and then add together on the blank lines at the end.

A/B	A/B	A/B	A/B	A/B
1. __/__	2. __/__	3. __/__	4. __/__	5. __/__
6. __/__	7. __/__	8. __/__	9. __/__	10. __/__
11. __/__	12. __/__	13. __/__	14. __/__	15. __/__
16. __/__	17. __/__	18. __/__	19. __/__	20. __/__
21. __/__	22. __/__	23. __/__	24. __/__	25. __/__
__/__	__/__	__/__	__/__	__/__
A/B	A/B	A/B	A/B	A/B
Avoidance totals	Competition totals	Compromise totals	Accommodation totals	Collaboration totals

Source: Reprinted with permission of McGraw-Hill, from Wilmot and Hocker (2001).

---

have had highly negative experiences with accommodating or competing styles of conflict management. If avoidance is your preferred approach, then it is likely that you view conflict as a win-lose situation and you believe you are likely to come out on the losing end more often than not. People in low-power positions, those from cultures that prioritize social harmony above all else, and those with lower verbal and social skills are likely to rate high on conflict avoidance.

John is not in a low-power position, so why did he use the avoidance response? In this particular case, he may perceive that his power to influence Maria's behavior is relatively weak. Of course, as any psychologist will tell you, we can only control what we think, do, or say—but we cannot control what others think, do, or say. If Maria wants to use her sick leave, the organization's policies allow her to do so. The fact that she uses it at the worst times doesn't change the policy. However, John does have some tools at his disposal and so far, avoidance hasn't really solved this recurring problem. We will read more about the changes he decides to make in his response to conflict but by the end of the chapter he will realize that avoidance will not achieve the results he desires in this case.

As previously discussed, conflict avoidance is not always a bad or irrational response when faced with a daunting problem. In fact, avoidance is the right approach in some situations. Specifically, if a problem is small and likely to go away on its own, then avoidance may be called for. When we fight every fight we expend energy that might be better used to address the most important problems. It is important to pick your battles. If you scored low on this style (below three), then you might want to be more judicious at picking your battles so that you can save your energy for problems that are more central to the mission of your work unit or to your career goals. If you scored high on this style (seven or above), then you might want to work on your framing and problem-solving skills (covered in Chapter Four) so that you feel confident in your ability to proactively address problems.

For many problems, avoidance only works temporarily and can often make matters worse in the long run. Conflict avoiders tend to let things go repeatedly until something snaps and they explode—sometimes over a relatively small infraction. I call this *the volcano effect* (see the following for more information on volcanoes at work). Large organizations are better at conflict avoidance than smaller organizations. In large organizations, if one person procrastinates about addressing a problem, then maybe someone else will take charge and deal with the issue. In smaller organizations there are fewer people onto whom we can push our problems. Do not confuse *conflict prevention* with *conflict avoidance*. **Conflict prevention** occurs when an individual or group examines the sources of predictable and recurring problems and then takes reasonable steps to address the root causes of those problems so that they do not occur or recur. Examples of conflict prevention within organizations may include changing overlapping job descriptions so as to have greater role clarity and accountability. However, **conflict avoidance** occurs when an individual or group has evidence that a problem currently exists or will soon exist but no steps are taken to acknowledge and address the problem. Conflict avoiders refuse to acknowledge the problem exists, in the hope it will just go away. This may work for small, nonrecurring problems but is unlikely to work for systemic, recurring, or large problems.

One can see clear connections between some conflict avoidant behaviors and the psychological phenomenon of *denial*. Like avoidance, **denial** occurs when an individual or group refuses to acknowledge a reality that is highly unpleasant. Denial is a protective mechanism that comes into force when reality is so overwhelming that to acknowledge its truth could result in a psychological or physical breakdown, for example, when an organization announces it is downsizing and your unit will be entirely eliminated. Yet you refuse to look for other work until the doors officially close because you keep hoping some miracle will occur and the decision to close will be reversed. Denial protects the individual from the shock that reality poses to his or her psyche.

If you are conflict avoidant, how did this pattern develop? Perhaps you have had traumatic experiences with conflict in your family or in your work environment. Perhaps you feel a sense of hopelessness or powerlessness to positively affect decisions and to fix problems. Perhaps you have a shy personality and prefer not to engage in the long conversations often needed to solve problems productively. The first step to becoming a more proactive and successful conflict manager is to understand why you tend to want to avoid conflict. The next step is to work on your conflict management skills so you can feel confident in your ability to proactively affect conflicts and solve problems. The third step is to develop a plan and a timeline for improving your ability to proactively address problems as they arise (see the goal-setting section at the end of this chapter).

In the meantime, when you push yourself away from the default style of conflict avoidance you may fear that you are being too confrontational with others or taking on too many problems. This is rarely the case with someone who scored high on avoidance (or, coincidentally, on accommodating, too). As long as you are not acting out of anger when you address problems with other people and you use tactful and constructive language, then you are much more likely to see positive results and be viewed as a problem solver. Note that conflict avoiders are nearly nonexistent in upper level management of successful and dynamic organizations.

Accommodation

The **accommodative style** occurs when individuals have a preferred outcome but are willing to sacrifice their preferences so the other negotiators can realize their own, conflicting preference, thereby ensuring no harm comes to the relationship between the two. Conflict accommodators care deeply about the feelings of others and they seek to maintain harmony in their relationships and their work environment. If you scored high on this style (seven or higher), then you may believe it is frequently necessary to place your own wishes or preferences as secondary to those of others in order to maintain positive relationships. Although this belief is certainly true in some situations, a high score here may indicate that you are, believe it or not, "too nice." You may seem too indecisive when difficult decisions need to be made at the management level. Your desire to please others and to be liked by them may mean that some people take you for granted or take advantage of you, with suggestions like "Ask Barbara to work late, she never says no." Or "Try to get Jose to work that holiday because you have plans. He is such a nice guy." Although everyone needs to "take one for the team" now and then, accommodating people tend to sacrifice more than their fair share. But why not, because it does not seem to bother them? Yet constant accommodation does bother them; they have learned to keep their opinions and preferences to themselves. Accommodators sometimes experience negative health or psychological effects from holding in their frustration and bottling up their emotions.

Conflict accommodators have difficulty openly sharing their ideas, feedback, and concerns for fear that they may harm the feelings of others. As a result, the team often misses out on the full contribution that these team members could be making. Their ideas do not surface. Accommodators also have difficulty delegating work to subordinates, which is a recipe for disaster in a manager's career. The ability to delegate reasonable tasks to others using clear direction is crucial for maintaining efficient work flow and for reserving the manager's time for true management-level decisions.

By contrast, if you scored low on this measure (three or lower) then you may want to consider being a bit more flexible, accommodating, and making concessions to others occasionally so that you are viewed as more of a team player and to show that you care about the needs of others. Those who seldom act in an accommodating manner are typically viewed as pushy, selfish, and not a team player.

When is accommodation the best approach to conflict? When an individual is in a low-power situation, with little hope of achieving the preferred outcome, then accommodation may be the best choice. Also, when an issue is of relatively little importance to you but the other person has a strong preference or need. For example, your colleague wants to reschedule your meeting with him from Tuesday to Wednesday. The change is only a minor inconvenience to you but it allows your colleague to meet an important family obligation. Accommodating others in this fashion allows for a reasonable give-and-take between interdependent team members and builds good will. Next time you need to reschedule a meeting, you hope your colleague will return the favor. However, if you find that you repeatedly accommodate others and it is becoming frustrating to you, then you may not be adequately communicating or asserting your own needs to others. Most accommodators see conflict as a win-lose situation, believing that if they win it might come at the cost of the relationship. Positive movement would include changing the vision of conflict to one in which all persons can win sometimes, particularly considering their pressing needs and a fair give-and-take among colleagues and friends.

Collaboration

A high score in the collaboration category indicates a preference to work together with others to achieve outcomes that meet the needs of all. Collaboration occurs when two or more individuals work together to share information and make joint decisions. If you scored low on this measure (three or lower), then you may have trouble delegating and sharing decision-making authority with others, even when their buy-in is crucial to the implementation of decisions. If you scored high on the collaborative style (seven or higher), you likely view conflict as an opportunity to solve problems by working positively with others. Some have called this the win-win viewpoint, meaning that for one person to win in a negotiation or conflict the other person's needs must also be met (meaning they must also win). You are not willing to win at the cost of the relationship, but you believe that by putting your heads together, you can generally find mutually acceptable solutions to the problems at hand.

Collaboration is important in work teams. According to a recent study, workplace teams with cooperative approaches to conflict management, as opposed to competitive approaches, exhibited higher levels of trust among team members (Hempel, Zhang, & Tjosvold, 2009). Chan, Huang, and Ng (2008) found that managers with a cooperative style also showed more concern for their employees as people and that this concern fostered more trust. The deeper levels of trust between cooperative managers and their employees led to greater deference to those same managers when difficult decisions had to be made or when the manager intervened to resolve conflict.

So why is this not the best style of conflict management? Not all problems call for collaboration. Imagine the following scenario. At a daylong meeting of one hundred employees you decide to use a collaborative approach to decide whether to order sandwiches, pizza, or fried chicken for lunch. After an hour of unsuccessful consensus seeking you would likely abandon this approach and switch to making an authoritative decision more closely associated with the competitive style. There are times when a quick decision by our leaders is called for and times when it is not. Collaboration takes time. When time is short, leaders must act swiftly and decisively. In other situations, the decision is not important enough to justify bringing together everyone to jointly reach a decision. If you have laid the groundwork by building strong relationships with others in your organization, then they will typically trust your judgment when decisions must be made quickly or do not warrant the time it takes to engage in collaborative decision making.

The larger the group, the harder it will be to obtain 100 percent consensus on any issue. Imagine trying to get one hundred people to agree on whether to order Chinese or Mexican food for lunch. This would not be a good use of time and may result in more conflict rather than having someone make an executive decision on the matter. Although an open and collaborative discussion of issues is often warranted, sometimes it is necessary to adopt a decision rule that allows for something less than 100 percent consensus, especially in large groups. Requiring 100 percent consensus gives extraordinary power to potential spoilers who enter into a process with the intention of derailing it or stalling as long as possible. If the decision is made to use a collaborative style, it will be helpful to clarify the decision-making parameters at the outset. For example, will the manager seek input and brainstorming from the group but then retain final decision-making authority? Or will the manager defer to the expressed preferences of the group? If the latter route is adopted, will decisions require 100 percent consensus or something less, such as a simple majority vote, a supermajority vote, consensus minus one or two, and so forth? Voting is a process that matches the **competitive style** of decision making yet it can be combined with participant input, dialogue, and collaboration to create a process deemed fair, participatory, and efficient.

As a manager, you cannot seek consensus on every decision. Employees do not want to be bothered for their input on issues they view as noncritical or decisions they feel should be reserved for managers. The more they trust their managers, then the less they will feel their input is needed on smaller decisions. The tricky part is for managers to have a good understanding of where these lines are drawn. Sometimes a collaborative manager should seek input from one or more employees by asking whether this is a decision in which they wish to be involved. Sometimes they will say, "No, thanks. I trust your judgment on this one." In that case, your inquiry has signaled that you value their feelings and that you understand the decision will likely affect them and their work. Reserve the use of collaborative decision making for the following instances: when others have the information needed to make a good decision, when buy-in will be needed in order to effectively implement the decision, when there is likely to be push back if input is not sought, when there is adequate time for input and discussion, and when you seek to build or repair relationships with others.

Compromise

The **compromising style** indicates a preference for splitting the difference between the negotiator's positions. Compromise can be a quick, efficient way to reach a solution. For example, in hiring negotiations, an employer offers the prospective employee a salary of $60,000 and she counters with a request for $70,000. The two quickly decide the most efficient and fair outcome would be to settle at $65,000. Both got part of what they wanted and left the negotiation feeling that the process was fair. The negotiation was relatively short and painless. The compromising style is appropriate when a decision is not highly important, the time for negotiation and discussion is relatively short, and the process needs to be viewed as fair to all parties. One risk of using compromise is that value might be left on the table so to speak. For example, what if the employee offered to take on additional duties that would have otherwise required the hiring of a part-time employee in exchange for the previously requested $70,000 salary? By engaging in discussions to learn more about each negotiator's needs, it may be possible to reach a solution that is better for everyone. Compromise often misses these opportunities.

One of the most widely known stories of compromise comes to us from biblical and Koranic lore: the story of wise King Solomon. In the story, a mother had accidentally rolled over on her own baby, killing it as they both slept. In her grief she stole another woman's baby and claimed it as her own. The two women came before King Solomon, asking him to determine the true mother of the infant. In his wisdom, Solomon stated the he intended to use a sword to cut the baby in half so that each mother could lay claim to half the child (an example of the compromising style). One of the mothers cried out that she would give up her claim to the baby and allow the other mother to have the child. Solomon knew this was the baby's true mother and awarded the baby to her.

This story illustrates the largest flaw in the compromising style. It focuses on creating a fair process (you each get equal amounts) but can ignore even better solutions that lie unexplored. The compromising style encourages game playing rather than the open and sincere expression of needs, goals, and limitations. It encourages parties to "start high" instead of telling each other what is really desired and why. It sometimes leads negotiators to miss opportunities for joint gains that might occur if a more collaborative style were used. To return to the earlier salary negotiation example, the employer may have been willing to go as high as $80,000 but the potential employee started low so as to make it look like she was "being nice." Although the higher salary of $65,000 was appreciated, what if the job applicant really wanted a flexible work schedule and was willing to sacrifice some pay in order to obtain that type of schedule? Perhaps this would have been acceptable to both sides in the negotiation, yet the needs that lay underneath the monetary amounts were not fully discussed, so they walked away with an agreement but not one that met all of their needs as fully as a collaborative negotiation could have accomplished.

If you scored high on compromising (seven or above) and on accommodating, then you may leave negotiations feeling a bit disrespected or taken advantage of. You generally start off your negotiations using the compromising style because you see it as fair, but if the other side is a tough negotiator, you give in rather than risk the chance of hurting the other person's feelings or damaging the relationship.

What to do to improve? Choose carefully among the different conflict styles so as to use the one that best matches your needs in any particular situation. Be sure you have a number (or other end result) in your head that is your bottom line before you enter the negotiation and only change that bottom line if new information comes to light during the negotiation that justifies reconsideration. We will discuss negotiation at greater length in subsequent chapters as well. Communicate to the other party about *why* you are asking for *x* or *y*. Invite the other party to brainstorm solutions that are mutually satisfying in regards to solving the problem or reaching a negotiated agreement. If the other person is unwilling to engage in this type of conversation or unwilling to reach what you view as a fair compromise, consider walking away from the negotiation and telling him or her you need time to think about it. This may make the person reconsider his or her willingness to compromise or to engage in collaboration with you.

Competition

The competitive style indicates a preference to win as much as you can, even at the expense of the other side or damage to the relationship between negotiators. You have probably heard the cliché that individuals tend to have either a fight or flight response to conflict. Of course, the responses we are examining here are much more nuanced and varied. However, if the avoidant style represents flight, then the competitive style represents fight. High scores on this style (seven or higher) tend to reflect individuals with strong opinions with a tendency to make decisive unilateral decisions. These individuals often correspond to a Type A on a Myers-Briggs assessment and are commonly found in leadership roles or sales positions. They tend to communicate directly and are more concerned about the outcome of a decision than they are concerned about the feelings of others. We call this a focus on task over relationship. These individuals may also err in believing that many interactions are competitions with zero-sum outcomes, when in reality the situations are more amenable to negotiations that yield joint gains for both parties, effecting win-win outcomes. Individuals scoring high on the competitive style are often viewed by others as overly assertive, pushy, or insensitive. Individuals who scored low on this style (three or lower) tend to score high in either the accommodating or avoiding conflict styles. As a result, these individuals are often seen as pushovers who will not advocate for themselves or their team even when it makes sense to do so.

When does a competitive response to conflict make sense? Some situations, such as elections or sporting events, are inherently structured as competitions and they call for competitors. However, many organizations inject competition into the workplace in ways that result in unintended negative consequences. For example, an internal sales competition may result in attempts to steal clients from other team members rather than from other firms or organizations, or to sabotage the efforts of team members in order to win. The trick with the competitive spirit is to harness its energy in positive directions and remember to correctly identify those areas in which competition results in the best possible outcomes. When done correctly, competition can result in increased productivity and healthy camaraderie. When done poorly, competition pits team members against each, leading to hard feelings and negative outcomes.

A competitive style of decision making is called for when a unilateral, swift decision is needed because time is short and you, as a manager, believe that your preferred outcome is the only one that is acceptable or in the best interests of the company. It is better to be transparent about this assessment than to pretend to engage in collaboration or compromise, knowing that in the end your decision will be final.

CHOOSING AMONG THE CONFLICT STYLES

As a child you began learning about conflict management by watching your family members and others in your environment. You may have adopted the conflict techniques exhibited by one or more of your family members or you may have developed a style that is opposite because you determined theirs to be dysfunctional. Whichever style(s) you adopted, you have had many years to develop your current conflict habits. Changing habits feels awkward at first and mistakes or backtracking is to be expected. Eventually, with practice and reflection, choosing the best style or approach will become habitual. Until then, it helps to ask yourself some explicit questions about the problem, decision, or conflict in question:

How important is this issue?

Is there passion around this issue among my employees, superiors, or clientele?

What will likely happen if no action is taken or if action is delayed?

How soon is a decision needed?

Who will be affected by the decision and who will be tasked with implementing the decision?

Would a decision that had the input and expertise of other stakeholders likely be a better substantive decision for addressing the problem?

Do I have the information I need to make a good decision?

How much buy-in will be necessary for the decision to be implemented smoothly?

Do I have the power or authority necessary to make a unilateral decision?

How will a unilateral decision be received by others?

Do others in my organization trust that I will make the best decision possible, even if they are not particularly happy with the outcome of the decision?

How are my preexisting conflict management habits biasing my answers to these questions?

Choosing the Best Response to Conflict

- Is this a no-win situation due to a power asymmetry that is working against you? If so, consider choosing the avoidant style.
- Do you need buy-in from those affected by a decision in order to get it implemented? If so, consider using the collaborative style.
- Does a quick, authoritative decision need to be made? If so, consider the competitive style.

(continued)

(*continued*)

- Does your colleague care passionately about this issue although it is of minor or moderate importance for you? If so, consider the accommodating style.

- Is time short? Do you need a fair process that allows you and the other negotiator to both get something out of the deal? If so, then consider a compromising style.

It is also important to note that your choice of a specific conflict management response will need to take into consideration the context of the dispute, its importance to the organization and individual employees, whether the conflict or project is in its early or late phases, and the preferred style or approach of those with whom you work.

As you strive to be more analytical and proactive in your approach to dealing with conflict, do not be too hard on yourself or on those around you. You are developing a deeper cognitive framework for understanding conflict and its management, but changing patterns of behavior takes time and practice. Allow yourself a "do-over" when you catch yourself falling back into old, destructive patterns of communication or decision making. If you are explicit with others about your desire to improve these skills, you are likely to find that your colleagues and employees are not only open to working *with* you, but they will also appreciate that you are trying to develop your abilities in these areas. At the end of this chapter, check out the goal-setting section to get started on making improvements in your conflict management habits.

THE LANGUAGE OF CONFLICT

We learned how to manage conflict the same way we learned language—by watching and listening to those around us. Our conflict management style(s) is likely to be either a close replica of one we learned at home or it was adopted as a reaction against what we learned there. The way in which we communicate our approach to conflict includes verbal and nonverbal signals that we give to others, either purposefully or subconsciously. Just as every spoken language has rules of grammar and punctuation, so does the language of conflict. However, for most people the unspoken rules or norms of conflict management, also known as *the language of conflict*, have never been explicitly discussed except at the most obvious level, with statements such as "Tommy, we don't hit" or "We have a zero tolerance policy for bullying." The rules vary within each family or organization and within each of the five conflict styles discussed in this chapter. When individuals exhibit a conflict style that is different from that of the group (such as at work or with in-laws), it seems as if they are breaking an unwritten and unspoken rule, one that everyone should know. Because we learned our language of conflict through the osmosis of watching the world around us, we implicitly believe that everyone saw the same world that we saw and therefore they should have learned the same lessons. When someone's communication mode or approach to problem solving really irritates you, ask yourself, "What approach to conflict is he using and how different is it from my preferred mode?" You may find that it is the difference in styles that is the obstacle to smooth interactions more than the preferred outcomes voiced by each party to the conflict.

By way of example, let's revisit the scenario at the beginning of this chapter with John and Maria. At the Bureau of Reclamation, Maria has previously called in sick when she was dreading her work more than usual. Annual review day definitely falls into that category. John has not complained before and therefore Maria concludes that it must not bother him too much when she calls in sick. In Maria's family people communicate very directly and they tend to fall more into the competitive conflict style. The rules for communicating under this style tell us that if someone has something to say, then she should say it regardless of the other's feelings. If people do not come forward to tell others they have a problem, then either they do not have a problem or they aren't playing by the rules.

Communication Rules in Aggressive Organizations

- Practice the rules of survival of the fittest.
- Be blunt and to the point, no matter if it hurts someone's feelings.
- Stake out your positions early and don't compromise.
- Have an audience when you engage someone in conflict.
- People who don't engage this way are weak.

John, however, comes from an avoidant and accommodating conflict culture in which emotion is typically conveyed indirectly. Rather than verbally expressing a problem, in John's family they might slam doors, pout, give the silent treatment, or avoid each other until the problem blows over. In competitive conflict environments this would be considered a violation of the unwritten rule of the conflict language. Therefore, it does bother John that Maria calls in sick so much when she is not really sick. But he believes she should be able to pick up on his anger through the indirect signs he sends her, such as how he tries to avoid her when she returns to work while he calms down. John is conflict avoidant, so he has not said anything to Maria before about this problem, but he has had all he can take. He has put up with this behavior for too long already and this is the proverbial straw that broke the camel's back. In a fit of frustration, John calls Maria and yells into the receiver, "If you value your job, you will be back here tomorrow morning at 8 AM sharp and ready to do your part with the performance reviews! Good-bye!" This is what I call the *volcano effect*. Like volcanoes, John's anger and frustration has been bubbling below the surface for a long time, yet on the outside he has appeared placid and calm. Then, something seemingly small has triggered a reaction, or even an overreaction, and his anger can no longer be contained. He lets his temper get the best of him and he erupts like a volcano. This time he lashed out at Maria, the source of his frustration. But sometimes when his temper erupts, his anger spills out to hurt innocent bystanders or even follows him home. It isn't helping his health either because he keeps needing to increase his dose of antacids.

Communication Rules in Conflict Avoidant Organizations and Individuals

- Walk away from conflict whenever possible.
- Don't express strong feelings.
- Sulking, snide comments and the silent treatment are acceptable means of expressing dissatisfaction.
- Others should be able to tell when something is bothering you.

John and Maria communicate in very different ways. John prefers to avoid conflict until it can no longer be avoided. By contrast, in Maria's family if someone is feeling hurt or upset he or she directly tells the other person what is on his or her mind. For example, Maria's husband recently asked her what she wanted for her birthday and she said, "Nothing, really. Just let me go twenty-four hours without cooking or doing laundry" and she meant it. There was no gift she was secretly wanting, no surprise party in the back of her mind. Not so for John's wife. John's wife communicates indirectly, like John does. If she says she does not want anything for her birthday, what she really means is that he should know what she wants without her having to tell him. Because John knows his wife so well, he knows that she will be offended if he does not get her a nice gift for her birthday, so the goal is to surmise what it is she really wants. By spending time with her and investing in their relationship, he is able to pick up on her subtle cues. Or, perhaps he will call one of her girlfriends to see if she might have a gift idea to share.

In collaborative organizations and families, individuals share their concerns and preferences tactfully and openly. They listen to one another, convey empathy, and seek out mutually acceptable solutions to problems. They do not yell or throw temper fits. They do not avoid one another when a problem exists, sulk, or use the silent treatment. They express confidence that the problem can be solved through respectful and considerate dialogue, taking turns, and sharing in the costs and benefits of any eventual decisions.

Rules in Collaborative Organizations and Individuals

- Have regular meetings to discuss challenges and make decisions together.
- The expression of strong feelings is allowed but sulking and passive aggression is not.
- Good listening and framing skills are used by all.
- Strong relationships are built through shared activities and time spent together.

CONFLICT, COMMUNICATION, AND CULTURE

On a related note, many cultures have a preference for nonverbal and indirect communication. For indirect communication to work well, the communicators need to build deeper, longer-term relationships that provide the context needed to correctly decode nonverbal or scripted communications. **Nonverbal communication** includes many contextual cues that convey acknowledgment of power dynamics and emotional ties or lack thereof between individuals or groups. Nonverbal communication is conveyed through vocal tone, body language, eye contact, and even such things as clothing, hairstyles, and demeanor, which communicate relative social status and dominance or submission within a chain of command.

All cultures communicate through the use of scripted conversation, which is one in which both parties to the conversation understand what they are expected to say because of prevailing cultural norms that dictate appropriate and inappropriate responses during the conversation. When a US worker asks a casual coworker, "How are you?" there is an implicit understanding that this question really means "hello" and is used to create a friendly tone of greeting rather than as a sincere inquiry into the health or emotional status of the other person. The responder knows that only a few kinds of responses are considered appropriate to this question, with the best one being something akin to, "Fine, thanks. How are you?" However, in some communication cultures, there are many more scripts that cover the acceptable conversations between a supervisor and employee or between casual acquaintances. In these cultures, context and power relations are key to understanding the meaning that the speaker wishes to convey. Context can include the known power dynamics between the communicators as well as the place or timing of the communication.

High-context cultures for communication are those in which the majority of meaning is conveyed via nonverbal means such as eye contact, tone, the use of silence, and scripted conversations. *High context* refers to the degree to which one must understand the context of the conversation in order to understand the intended meaning. In high-context cultures the burden of understanding falls to the listener, not the speaker. If the listener understands the context well enough and has nurtured a strong relationship with the speaker, then she will understand the intended meaning of the communication. Relationships are attended to first and tasks or activities second. High-context cultures tend to be more rigidly hierarchical and homogeneous, which allows for the development of shared norms governing communication. Typically, social harmony is highly valued, which means that conflicts are often addressed indirectly through informal mediators or emissaries rather than directly. High-context communication cultures developed in relatively isolated and homogenous societies with low levels of immigration (e.g., Japan, Finland, and Hawaii). This isolation facilitated the development of shared norms of behavior in various settings. Avoidance and accommodation are more common styles in these cultures than competition or compromise. The United States is considered to be a **low-context culture** in which most of the meaning is conveyed in the explicit verbal conversation as opposed to being implied through the context, nonverbal cues, or the use of scripted conversations. In low-context cultures the burden of understanding falls on the speaker. If the speaker is clear enough, then the listener will likely understand the intended meaning. Low-context cultures developed at societal crossroads, in regions with high levels of immigration, or in cultures prone to imperialism, which brought them into frequent contact with foreign cultures (e.g., Great Britain, France, New York City). Low-context cultures tend to score higher on competitive and compromising styles than high-context cultures. It is important to note that an individual's cultural context as well as his or her individual personality traits go a long way to explaining preferred communication and conflict styles. Be sure to avoid stereotyping individuals from cultures different from your own. Individuals may not always exhibit the communication tendencies of their broader cultural group.

HIRING, MANAGING, AND CONFLICT STYLES

Once you have done the work or have been lucky enough to benefit from the work of your predecessors, and your organization exhibits healthy responses to conflicts and problem solving, then ongoing maintenance of that environment is required. Small work units or organizations are highly susceptible to small changes, whereas it takes larger changes to affect huge bureaucratic organizations. One new employee who exhibits destructive communication patterns can be devastating to team productivity and morale in a small team environment.

Hiring employees who share your team's approach to problem solving will be critical to maintaining a positive and productive work environment. You may decide to use tools like the CSI or other assessment tools to help you understand the conflict management habits and approaches of applicants before they are hired. Second, you will want to have explicit discussions with new (and even with existing) employees to share your organization's expectations regarding the handling of inevitable problems that will arise as well as expectations regarding preferred interaction among team members. For example, you might tell new employees they are highly encouraged to constructively share their feedback, ideas, and concerns with their colleagues and managers. Once that input is received, decisions will be reached that take into account that information as well as other sources of information and the needs of the organization as a whole.

Much of an organization's culture is learned through osmosis, meaning that it permeates the organization's methods of communication and decision making but is not explicitly stated. Every organization has written (e.g., policies) and unwritten ways of doing things. This is especially true of communication styles. Learning the cultural norms of the organization as well as the expectations of its team members will be furthered by lots of professional and social interaction among team members. Getting to know one another deeply will help to facilitate the smooth functioning of an organization and form a reserve of good will to be called on in difficult times. It is the manager's job to encourage, promote, and create opportunities for relationship building between employees in order to make this happen. Great managers foster an environment in which great things happen. They hire hard-working yet personable employees, create policies and procedures that are rational and reward positive behaviors and achievements, and they set the stage for team building and camaraderie, which creates a happy work environment, reduces turnover, and shows employees they are valued and appreciated. Learning more about your own conflict style will help you as you work toward constant improvements in your decision-making and communication skills.

EMOTIONAL INTELLIGENCE AND THE COLLABORATIVE MANAGER

Emotional intelligence (EI) refers to the ability to perceive, control, and evaluate emotions in oneself and others (see Cherry, 2012; Salovey & Mayer, 1990). Emotional intelligence can be further broken down into four factors: the perception of emotion, the ability to reason using emotions, the ability to understand emotion, and the ability to manage emotions. Individuals vary in their ability to correctly perceive the emotional states of others through the interpretation of body language, tone, and facial expressions. Emotion plays an important role in the prioritization of tasks or determining the importance of different events or activities. Some individuals are better at using emotion for these purposes than others. In addition to correctly perceiving emotion, individuals need to be able to connect the dots to correctly link up the causal factors leading to particular expressions of emotion. For example, your employee may be agitated because it is time for her performance review or because she just found out she is being audited by the Internal Revenue Service (IRS). The manager's reaction to the employee would be different for these two events. Finally, individuals differ greatly in their ability to manage their emotional states or react to the emotional states of others. This is particularly important in the field of management because supervisors and managers are asked to respond to crises, make decisions that affect many people, and communicate the reasons behind those decisions to affected populations.

There is some debate as to whether emotional intelligence is fixed at birth or whether it can be learned. In either case, knowing your own strengths and weaknesses in emotional intelligence can equip you to ask better questions, direct more of your attention to the emotional states of others or yourself as need be, and monitor your own response to emotions. Hypothetically, understanding EI should help you during the processes of hiring and team formation. One would predict those with greater EI would work better with others, whereas low EI might indicate a need to place an employee on tasks that can be accomplished more independently. However, research into EI remains in its early stages and support for the linkages between EI scores and leadership abilities have not been proved (Harms & Credé, 2010). As this research evolves, what we can say from anecdotal evidence is that managers with good emotional control and empathy tend to create more stable and pleasant working environments. Employees or managers who struggle with emotional outbursts or insensitivity to the emotions of others can create difficult working environments.

CONCLUSION

The first step in improving your managerial skills is to take stock of them. Understand how you communicate and respond to conflict. Know your own level of emotional intelligence and find strategies to compensate for areas of weakness (e.g., using listening skills more purposefully, wording comments constructively, etc.). Understanding common responses to conflict will help you to choose among those responses more explicitly when problems arise.

Look around your organization or your competitors. Describe the skill sets of the best managers—those with low turnover, high productivity, and employee-client satisfaction levels. How do they communicate with their employees, peers, and superiors? How do they respond to problems that inevitably arise? Managers who understand themselves will be better able to understand and respond to others.

JOHN AT THE BUREAU OF RECLAMATION

What can John do? Can he control whether or not Maria calls in sick? No, but he can communicate his needs in a way Maria will understand as well as creating and enforcing incentives for productive workplace behaviors. When Maria called in sick before, John might have considered having a one-on-one discussion with her in order to learn more about her concerns, to convey his own concerns to her, and to let her know that he wants to work with her to make her work environment as positive as possible. In order to address this problem as a proactive conflict manager, John called Maria back and said, "I know that some days are harder than others around here. I am dreading these reviews myself, but without your help, I do not think I can get them done at all. What can we do together to make the hard days easier for both of us? How can we work together as a team to handle problems or challenges that might be too much for one person to handle individually? Can you recommend any changes for me to consider so that this process (or others) can be made better for all of us? In the future, when you feel that sense of dread coming on, can you discuss it with me so we can try to get to the root of the problem? Although I can't fix everything, there may be ways we can make improvements so that we both look forward to working here." These are examples that accomplish three things: (1) convey a sense of understanding and sympathy for Maria's feelings, (2) clarify John's needs and concerns in a neutral way, and (3) invite Maria to engage in joint problem solving with John. Although John retains the final decision-making authority as the manager, he has made it clear that he is open to Maria's ideas for ways to improve things at work and that he cares about her as an employee and as a person.

KEY TERMS

Accommodative style

Avoidant style

Collaborative style

Competitive style

Compromising style

Conflict avoidance

Conflict prevention

Conflict styles inventory (CSI)

Denial

Emotional intelligence

High-context cultures

Low-context cultures

Nonverbal communication

SUGGESTED SUPPLEMENTAL READING

Avruch, K. (2003). Type I and Type II errors in culturally sensitive conflict resolution practice. *Conflict Resolution Quarterly, 20*, 351–371.

Brackett, M. A., Rivers, S. E., & Salovey, P. (2011). Emotional intelligence: Implications for personal, social, academic, and workplace success. *Social and Personality Psychology Compass, 5*, 88–103.

Jameson, J. K. (2001). Employee perceptions of the availability and use of interest-based, right-based, and power-based conflict management strategies. *Conflict Resolution Quarterly, 19*, 163–196.

DISCUSSION QUESTIONS

1. What personal qualities or behaviors make for a great manager? What behaviors or qualities make for a horrible boss?

2. It is likely that different managerial styles work best in different environments. What kind of manager succeeds in your organization and which kind fails to thrive? Why?

3. How can you use the Conflict Styles Inventory outside of work, to improve your family or civic life?

EXERCISES

1. Think about a current or previous problem or conflict in your work environment. Which of the five conflict styles best describes your approach to that conflict? Which style best describes the style(s) used by others in

the conflict? Was the conflict or problem successfully resolved? Why or why not? In groups of two to five, share your stories. What might have happened if you used one of the other conflict styles? Analyze these questions collectively and individually.

2. Although the CSI was developed as an individual-level tool, we often see analogous behaviors within work teams (e.g., departments or units) as well as entire organizations. Which style best describes the unit in which you work or manage? Why? Which style best describes your organization as a whole? How does your individual style fit in with those in your work environment? Discuss.

3. Either individually or in small groups, develop a list of interview questions that you will use for potential new hires. These questions should give you a sense of how this person responds to conflict and how well she or he will fit into your team's environment. In addition to designing appropriate interview questions, what other sources of information will provide clues as to how this person deals with problem solving and teamwork?

4. Think of a current problem or pending decision at work, at home, or in your civic life. Use the questions found in the section "Choosing Among the Conflict Styles" to determine which style is the most likely to achieve a successful resolution to the problem.

5. Choose the best style of decision making for these scenarios: in the last month three out of ten of your employees have come to you to complain that one of their coworkers is shirking responsibility by coming in late, leaving early, leaving his work for others to finish, and so on. You were hoping this employee would take the hint from his coworkers and start to do his fair share of the work but this has not happened. What would it look like if you addressed this situation using each of the five conflict styles discussed in this chapter?

GOAL SETTING

You now have a better understanding about your own conflict management habits and tendencies. How are these working for you? Is there room for improvement? Are you able to consciously choose the best style for each problem you encounter? If not, ask yourself this question: "On a scale of 0 to 10, where 0 equals a conflict management train wreck and 10 equals masterful conflict management, where do I fall?" Now imagine what behaviors you would need to change in order to move your score up by only one or two points. Write down those behavioral changes as goals to pursue this week. Revisit this question next week and see if you have made any progress and whether new goals are appropriate. Sample questions may include the following:

- How well do I delegate work that can and should be delegated?
- How clearly do I communicate my expectations to my subordinates?
- How clearly do I communicate my needs to my superiors?
- How efficiently do I deal with problems that arise rather than putting off addressing them as long as possible?
- How well do I communicate to my employees that I care about them as people?
- How well do I create opportunities for my employees to get to know each other and develop strong interpersonal relationships?
- How well do I analyze the extent to which a decision should be reached unilaterally versus through a collaborative process?
- How well do I really listen to others?
- How well do I make decisive decisions when they are called for?

Theory to Practice

The Root Causes and Cures of Conflict

Learning Objectives

- Demonstrate an understanding of the root causes of unproductive conflict.
- Diagnose the causes of unproductive conflict within an organization.
- Explain the differences among key conflict theories such as attribution theory, procedural justice theory, conflict ripeness, and others.
- Describe the differences between structural and nonstructural sources of conflict.

ELISE AND UNPRODUCTIVE CONFLICT AT MAIN STREET BAKERIES

This morning Elise got a call from Ben, her director for human resources (HR). Ben told her he has been asked to find yet another assistant manager for store number seventy-five because the one they had just resigned. This makes four assistant managers in less than two years. The turnover level for the other employees at store number seventy-five is 65 percent higher than for the rest of the company. In general, Main Street Bakeries holds onto its employees for many years so it is surprising to see this level of turnover. Ben wanted to bring this issue to Elise's attention and he recommends that either he or Elise should visit this store (more than one thousand miles away from the corporate office) in order to find out what is happening there. Elise agrees and decides that Ben should do the initial digging and make recommendations back to her about possible next steps.

There are many ways to think about the origins of conflict and theories of conflict resolution with research coming from diverse areas of the behavioral sciences, social sciences, and physical sciences. A brief examination of some of these key theories is indispensable to a manager's ability to predict, diagnose, and intervene successfully in conflicts. This chapter begins with explanations of conflict's origins, which come from the physical sciences, and then progresses to social science explanations of intrapersonal, interpersonal, and intergroup conflict. These theories are linked to managerial conflict resolution through examples and illustrations throughout the chapter. Once managers understand the root causes of conflict, they are better able to find creative and constructive approaches to managing conflict at work.

BIOLOGICAL, PHYSIOLOGICAL, AND EVOLUTIONARY THEORIES OF CONFLICT AND RESOLUTION

Since about 2000, research has yielded great insights into the biological, physiological, and evolutionary sources of human behavior. Scientists are learning more every day about what makes us tick, including common sources of and responses to conflict and cooperation.

The Evolution of Cooperation and Conflict

Good managers understand how to motivate their employees to perform at a high level and to cooperate with each other successfully. By understanding the mechanisms through which cooperative behavior in humans has evolved, managers are better able to harness motivating forces in the service of conflict prevention and early resolution.

In order for human beings to live and work successfully in groups, we have had to develop the ability to differentiate those who will likely cooperate for mutual gain from individuals who will seek individual gain at the group's expense. Game theorists label this latter group as *defectors*. Game theory uses a combination of mathematics and economics to predict human behavior in circumstances with varying incentive structures (see von Neumann, 1944). For example, how can managers discourage shirking in group environments? One lazy worker can drive a small office crazy as the sense of unfairness rises among those who have to pick up the slack. Game theorists have much to tell us on this issue.

Game theorists as well as evolutionary biologists have long sought to uncover the mysteries that explain why we do what we do. For example, being nice made evolutionary sense when we lived in small bands surrounded by relatives because helping them helped our genes survive. And we had a direct incentive to be fair to people who would later reciprocate kindness or punish selfishness. But why even consider returning a stranger's wallet you find in a taxicab? Why leave a tip in a restaurant you'll never visit again? (Tierney, 2010)

Yet people do. Most people are honest and try hard to be good public and corporate citizens even when there is little overt incentive to do so. However, how do we explain and deal with the occasional individual who claims the work of others as his own or fails to deliver on deadlines and promises, leaving others to hold the bag?

Game theorists have learned that cooperative individuals are better off if they can find other cooperative people with whom they can trade, unite for mutual defense, reproduce, and otherwise work with for mutual gain (Vogel, 2004, February 20). The work of biologist William Hamilton (1964) shows us that humans and other animals cooperate with family members, even at their own individual expense, in order to ensure that their gene pool is passed on to future generations. Robert Trivers (1971) took this research to the next step by showing how cooperation with unrelated individuals can benefit the altruist as long as one's cooperative or altruistic acts can be expected to be reciprocated in the future. In common terms, this is akin to "what goes around comes around"; doing good works now will allow you to reap rewards later in a society in which reciprocity and reputation are valued.

Taking this concept even further, Nowak and Sigmund (2005) have developed a theory called *indirect reciprocity*, which predicts that people are willing to help a stranger as long as others witness the helpful act, thereby enhancing the altruist's reputation as a cooperative, generous person in the community. This reputation effect works to increase the likelihood that others will be willing to cooperate with the altruist in the future.

Yet an unscrupulous individual could take advantage of a group of collaborators by feigning cooperation, only to dupe them in the end and abscond with benefits beyond what they are due. Human societies have generally established social rules that reward cooperators and punish defectors through ostracism or by other means (for example, think of tax evaders, thieves, and so on). Once defectors are identified, they are typically punished and often banished from the group. Ostracized or banished individuals are less likely to survive and less likely to reproduce. Therefore, individuals with tendencies toward cooperation and collaboration are able to more effectively reproduce and form societal majorities, and defectors make up a relatively small percentage of individuals in any society. According to scientists, as cooperators pass on their genes, and defectors do so less frequently, our world is evolving into one where cooperation is increasingly common and defection is increasingly less common. Believe it or not, violent crime has gone down in the United States since the 1980s and fewer people are dying from war worldwide than in any previous century.

So why do some individuals fail to cooperate? Neuropsychologists are doing pathbreaking work on the connection between biochemistry and aggression versus altruism in humans and nonhuman animals. When individuals act altruistically, the parts of the brain responsible for human bonding and positive feelings are stimulated. In sum, altruistic acts *feel good* at a biological level in biologically normal people. Similarly, the strength of this response varies among individuals, making some more likely to behave altruistically than others (Vedantam, 2007). Literally, some people are born "helpers." On the other end, multiple studies (Gunnar & Fisher, 2006; University of Chicago Medical Center, 2000) have concluded that levels of cortisol, a hormone in the brain, rise when animals are under stressful conditions in order to help them cope. Chronically low levels of cortisol are correlated with aggressive and antisocial behaviors in human beings, meaning that some people cope more poorly with stress and are prone to act on violent impulses in reaction to stress, particularly children (University of Chicago Medical Center, 2000). Cortisol levels likely have some genetic influence but also can change because of the environment and exposure to chronic stress during pregnancy, infancy, and childhood, when the brain is developing (Gunnar & Fisher, 2006). Children who have been abused or neglected have a higher likelihood of experiencing chronically low levels of cortisol, resulting in antisocial and aggressive tendencies (Gunnar & Fisher, 2006). Some forms of autism have been correlated with unusual levels of cortisol (Brosnan, Turner-Cobb, Munro-Naan, & Jessop, 2009).

Biologists have uncovered important information about the role that oxytocin plays in increasing empathy and trust between individuals or, by contrast, the role it plays in the absence of empathy and trust.

> Researchers found that genetic differences in people's responsiveness to the effects of oxytocin were linked to their ability to read faces, infer the emotions of others, feel distress at others' hardship and even to identify with characters in a role-play exercise. (Angier, 2009, p. D2)

In fact, individuals with one type of oxytocin receptor (type A) are more likely to display signs of autism and poor parenting skills than those with the other type of receptor (type G) (Angier, 2009). So at a very basic level, some individuals are hormonally predisposed to be more or less trusting and empathetic than others. This does not explain trust and empathy in all situations, of course, but it does lay the groundwork for a deeper understanding of these issues. Indeed, some individuals are simply more willing to trust than are others.

For managers this means that some employees and customers will simply be more difficult to deal with than others because they are inherently more aggressive, impulsive, antisocial, or untrusting than others. Rather than taking this behavior as a personal affront to the manager or others, it can be helpful to remember that each person has a different biological endowment that may result in varied coping abilities. Some employees may be better at working collaboratively with others in high-stress environments, whereas some employees may need to have greater isolation from stress or work more independently. This information has many potential implications in the workplace.

Although this summary of evolutionary and biological explanations of trust and cooperation is necessarily short, it indicates that there are likely physical and biological differences that explain why two people react differently to the same situation. This may help us to depersonalize conflict when it occurs, meaning that we need not attribute aggressive or antisocial behaviors as signs of personal affronts but instead understand the myriad reasons why an individual may struggle to behave constructively in difficult situations.

This does not definitively answer the nature-versus-nurture question but it does indicate that the role of nature is likely stronger than previously believed. Understanding the evolution and science of aggression and cooperation is a crucial step for successful conflict management interventions. Although science is just scratching the surface of the nature-nurture debate, this information helps us to better understand that some individuals are simply better at dealing with stress and social interactions than others. Regardless of an individual's natural endowment in these areas, these skills can be increased and improved through a variety of interventions discussed in this book.

The good news is that human beings are significantly more likely to cooperate with others than to take advantage and that cooperation feels "right" to most humans. Cooperation and helping others are the norms, not the exceptions. For individuals with abnormally poor social skills or maladaptive behaviors traceable to a medical condition, treatments may be available now or in the near future that will help them improve their ability to interact and cope successfully with stressful situations, particularly when combined with training designed to enhance these skills and abilities. Hiring managers may wish to develop and use scenario-response questions designed to determine how well potential applicants work with others, deal with stress, trust others, are trustworthy, and so on. This information can help ensure an appropriate match among employees, job duties, and team members.

PERSONALITY AND INDIVIDUALLY BASED CONFLICT THEORIES

Individual personalities and previous life experiences may create fertile ground for misunderstandings and conflict. When managers equip themselves with an understanding of the interplay between personality characteristics and conflict behaviors, they can use this information to depersonalize the behaviors of others, to gain a deeper understanding of the motivations underlying those behaviors, and to develop customized approaches for working successfully with individuals displaying a variety of personality traits. We started this discussion in Chapter One with an examination of the conflict styles inventory. In this chapter we will extend this understanding of individual-level responses to conflict including need theories, psychodynamic theories, and other theories.

Need theories refer to those explanations for human behavior, including conflict, based on the unmet needs of individuals. More than fifty years ago Abraham Maslow articulated a theory of human motivation that remains crucial to our understanding of conflict today (see Figure 2.1). According to Maslow (1954), people seek to meet their needs but some needs take precedence over others. To be more specific, physiological needs must be met first, meaning food, water, air, reproduction, sleep, and so on. Safety needs must be met next, meaning freedom from violence, access to employment, security of property and one's family's needs, and so on. Third, humans need to feel that they are loved and have a sense of belonging with family and friends. Fourth, people are motivated to have a sense of positive esteem about themselves and to hold others in esteem. The fifth motivational factor is the desire to be "self-actualized," meaning that people wish to fulfill their potential as creative, moral, intelligent beings. Maslow later added a sixth level of self-transcendence, dealing with an individual's need to understand God, his or her place in the universe, and so on. This last level has not been as well received and accepted as the first five, on which we will focus our attention.

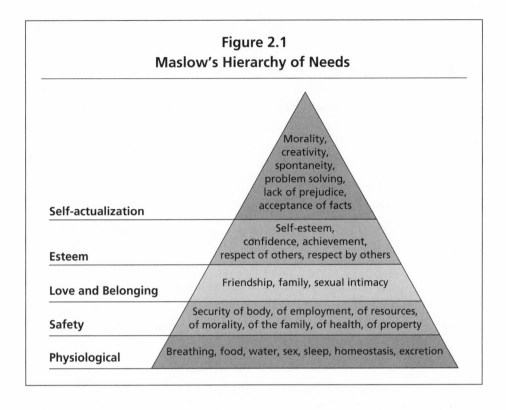

Figure 2.1
Maslow's Hierarchy of Needs

Self-actualization — Morality, creativity, spontaneity, problem solving, lack of prejudice, acceptance of facts

Esteem — Self-esteem, confidence, achievement, respect of others, respect by others

Love and Belonging — Friendship, family, sexual intimacy

Safety — Security of body, of employment, of resources, of morality, of the family, of health, of property

Physiological — Breathing, food, water, sex, sleep, homeostasis, excretion

It should be noted that some have criticized **Maslow's hierarchy of needs** out of a belief that it is less accurate when applied to collectivist rather than individualist societies (Cianci & Gambrel, 2003). In **collectivist societies**, the needs of the group generally come before the needs of any individual. These cultural differences are reflected in laws and social norms that give priority to the best interests of the group above those of individuals. "Among collectivists, social behavior is guided by the group. Along with group membership come prescribed duties and obligations. Among individualists, one's behavior is guided by one's personal attitudes, motivations, and internal processes" (Neuliep, 2009, p. 46). Therefore, in collectivist societies, Cianci and Gambrel (2003) and others have argued that Maslow's hierarchy would reflect greater emphasis on group belonging, gaining the respect of others, and meeting group needs than on meeting individual needs. Conflicts in collectivist societies are likely to occur more often at the group level rather than between individuals. When individuals experience conflicts in collectivist societies they are more likely to express them more indirectly and collectively through a web of social alliances and ties designed to enforce norms of expected behaviors and reduce overt conflicts that threaten intergroup and intragroup harmony. We will continue to use the original figure and ideas developed by Maslow and note that outside of a Western cultural context or when applied to individuals from subcultural groups within Western societies, this hierarchy might need to be amended.

How does Maslow's hierarchy of needs help us understand the origins and escalation of conflict for managers? The lower an issue falls on this hierarchy, the more fiercely people and groups will fight for their preferred outcome. For example, union members might enjoy professional development courses as part of their benefits package but they will fight much harder for wages and guarantees of employment because these fall on the lowest rung of the needs hierarchy. Voters may be for or against nuclear power but when the power company tries to locate a new reactor in their neighborhood, they become motivated to organize and lobby for their preference, generally along the lines of "not in my back yard" (also known as the *NIMBY problem*) because local residents fear for their physical safety as well as economic security related to falling property values. When an employee or customer is fighting tooth and nail for a preferred outcome, ask yourself, "What need is motivating this behavior?" Is this a matter of survival (e.g., a job is on the line or one's health is threatened)? Has someone's pride been hurt or is there a potential loss of face at issue? Once you understand the unmet need, then it is possible to better understand the range of potential solutions available to meet that need. Understanding the underlying needs of any party in conflict is the first step to resolution.

PSYCHODYNAMIC THEORIES OF BEHAVIOR AND CONFLICT

This bundle of theories deals with the intrapsychic processes used by individuals to make sense of reality. Originally developed by Sigmund Freud, these theories and concepts have been repeatedly amended by his followers, including Carl Jung and Erich Fromm, among others (Sandy, Boardman, & Deutsch, 2000). For example, people develop control and defense mechanisms designed to "control their impulses, thoughts, actions and realities so that they won't feel anxious, guilty or ashamed. If their controls are ineffective, they develop defensive mechanisms to keep from feeling these disturbing emotions" (Sandy, Boardman, & Deutsch, 2000, p. 290). When a conflict feels overwhelming, individuals may rely on one or more control and defense mechanisms to control their own potentially negative behavior and to deal with feelings of anxiety that occur when involved in conflicts.

There are a number of common defense mechanisms that even armchair psychologists have typically heard of. Denial occurs when the reality of a situation is so overwhelming that it potentially causes an emotional breakdown. To avoid this potential, one refuses to acknowledge the reality of a situation in order to allow it to sink in slowly, if at all, rather than all at once. Those scoring high on avoidance as a preferred response to conflict (see Chapter One) *may* be prone to more frequent bouts of denial than others. One chooses what one sees by ignoring evidence that possibly contradicts one's preferred vision of the world or of events. By improving one's conflict management skills, it is possible to become more conflict competent, thereby making denial and avoidance less common or less severe. Projection is related to denial and involves projecting one's own characteristics onto another as a defensive behavior. By focusing oneself on the faults of others, one does not need to address them in one's self. **Displacement** involves changing the topic to avoid dealing directly with a problem or acting upset about one issue when it is really a different issue that has caused one's upset (Sandy, Boardman, & Deutsch, 2000). Another way to avoid dealing directly with a problem is to minimize its importance and downplay its significance. **Disassociation** occurs when individuals are emotionally overwhelmed by a situation and therefore have difficulty focusing on that situation. Their minds may wander to more attractive thoughts, such as where to go on vacation or even drift toward making a mental grocery list—anything seen as safe or pleasant. In common terms, they daydream. Overall, people have developed myriad ways to procrastinate in dealing with overwhelming problems, if not to avoid addressing them altogether. If you or your negotiation partners are becoming defensive, it is helpful to determine the true source of the anxiety and work together to address any perceived threats. Defensiveness makes problem solving quite difficult. As discussed later in this chapter, it can be helpful to step back and focus on finding an appropriate process with which to address the problem in order to learn more about the needs of each party and meet those needs through a fair, respectful process. A good process usually ends with a good outcome and can help reduce various forms of denial because it changes the focus away from a potentially feared outcome.

Why do managers need to be aware of various forms of denial? There are common scenarios addressed by managers that are likely to evoke some level of denial, such as layoffs, mergers, poor performance reviews, or any source of large-scale change. Managers themselves may fall victim to denial when confronted with proof that a trusted employee has violated a deeply held norm. When a valued employee, peer manager, or supervisor has engaged in embezzlement, sexual harassment, or other inappropriate behavior the first impulse is to think, "That can't be possible," even in the face of incontrovertible proof. No one is immune to the pitfall of denial when faced with devastating news.

ATTRIBUTION THEORY AND OTHER COGNITIVE BIASES

When trying to determine a fair outcome, individuals are generally unaware of the many forms of cognitive bias that hamper one's ability to process information efficiently and objectively. **Cognitive bias** is a pattern of deviation in judgment that leads to inaccurate conclusions, distorted perceptions of reality, illogical interpretation of facts or events, and often irrational behaviors or thought patterns (Kahneman & Tversky, 1972). The way our brains process information can lead us to err or exhibit unrecognized biases when making decisions. Cognitive biases often serve as shortcuts to reaching the conclusions necessary to make decisions but the shortcuts may lead to poorer decision making in some circumstances. The first step in conflict management is to heighten your awareness of the existence of common cognitive biases. Acknowledging and addressing these cognitive biases will help us correctly diagnose the sources of conflict as well as identify elements necessary for conflict resolution.

To understand the origins of conflict and its escalation, we must first understand how we attribute motivations to behaviors. When we give someone the benefit of the doubt we assume good intentions or reasons for observed behaviors, thereby making us less likely to become confrontational and more likely to work together to solve problems. Sometimes the opposite occurs. **Attribution theory** explains the ways in which cognitive biases hinder our ability to accurately understand the motivations behind the behaviors of others. There are a host of specific cognitive biases falling under the headings of *attribution theory* or *attribution errors*. **Fundamental attribution errors** occur when we incorrectly attribute someone's behavior to their dispositional or personality characteristics rather than attributing it to a situational factor. For example, imagine that your least favorite coworker arrives late for a Monday morning meeting. In your mind you think, "Apparently she isn't willing to make an effort to be here on time because she is an inconsiderate person." Later in the day you find out that her car was rear-ended on the way to work. This form of fundamental attribution error is called **accuser bias**, which is "the tendency for an observer negatively affected by an actor's behavior to attribute the behavior to causes under control of the actor" (Allred, 2000, p. 244). You attributed her lateness to her disposition (that is to say an inconsiderate personality) rather than to a situation beyond her control (the auto accident). Research shows individuals are more likely to make a negative attribution error when they have had a negative relationship with the other party, when they are total strangers, and when they come from different cultural groups. Attributing someone's negative behavior to circumstances within his or her control generally results in anger toward that person and conflict escalation. Once angered, parties become less effective at problem solving because high emotions interfere with rational thinking as well as reduce ability to sympathize with others (Allred, 2000).

However, we are more likely to give the benefit of the doubt to people with whom we have a positive relationship history or cultural commonality (e.g., they are part of our in-group). We are most likely to encounter cognitive biases when we seek to understand or explain our own behaviors. Our tendency to downplay our own poor decisions or actions, while attributing them to circumstances beyond our control, is called *bias of the accused* (Allred, 2000). This is akin to what psychologists label *rationalization* or denial, meaning that individuals find rational reasons why their own behaviors make sense under the prevailing circumstances that were beyond their control. "I had to eat that cookie in spite of my diet. I was starving!" If you were the one coming in late to the meeting you would most likely blame it on bad traffic or other causes beyond your control—even if you hit the snooze button on your alarm clock four times that morning.

In other words, every fact that we see (for example, someone is late for the meeting) gets filtered through our preexisting cognitive biases when we take that naked fact and attribute meaning to it. The fact is placed in situational and relational contexts so we can derive its meaning and relevance. Sometimes our preexisting biases drive us to interpret facts incorrectly or jump to conclusions prematurely. In conflict escalation and resolution, it is the perceptions surrounding facts that are keys to understanding the roots of the problem at hand. A negative attribution of a fact is likely to result in an angry response that will make escalation more likely and successful resolution less likely. Awareness of the existence and functions of cognitive biases can help managers prevent, explain, and diffuse conflict situations when they occur.

THE SEVEN DEADLY COGNITIVE BIASES OF NEGOTIATION

You will read more about negotiation theory in Chapter Three but for now it is helpful to give a brief overview of Bazerman and Neale's (1992) list of seven common decision-making biases that interfere with one's ability to correctly calculate one's own best interests in negotiation or decision making.

The Seven Deadly Cognitive Biases of Negotiators

- Irrational stubbornness
- Zero-sum thinking
- Unduly influenced by an anchoring number
- Framing bias
- Satisficing
- It's all about me
- Overconfidence

The first mistake is to irrationally stick to an initial course of action, even once it becomes clear that this course is no longer the optimal position. This is a classic mistake made in labor-management negotiations. The union makes a public statement proclaiming that nothing short of a 6 percent raise will be accepted and then has difficulty backing down once managers provide data showing their competitors are paying their workers less or that the profit margins simply won't sustain a 6 percent raise. Related to this error is the human tendency to seek out information that confirms our preexisting beliefs and to filter out information that runs contrary to those beliefs (closely related to attribution bias previously discussed). In our labor-management example, this means that union negotiators will have a tendency to discount or disbelieve facts presented by management that bode poorly for their hopes for a 6 percent raise whereas they seek out data and information that substantiates the need for the requested raise. We'll label this mistake *irrational stubbornness*. It has also been labeled *irrational escalation of commitment* in negotiation literature. This bias also explains why individuals tend to read, watch, or listen to news sources that reflect their own political leanings, thereby reaffirming their existing worldviews and filtering out contrary ideas or interpretations of events. This tendency leads to further polarization and poor decision making.

The second common mistake is zero-sum thinking and it occurs when one assumes that any gain made by the other party in a negotiation must come at your expense, thereby missing opportunities for joint gains that could come from working together in creative problem solving. A variation of this is the tendency to assume there is a competitive situation when, indeed, collaboration may be the best route. A great example of this comes from the holy grail of conflict management literature, *Getting to Yes: Negotiating Agreement Without Giving In.*

> In 1964 an American father and his twelve-year-old son were enjoying a beautiful Saturday in Hyde Park, London, playing catch with a Frisbee. Few in England had seen a Frisbee at that time and a small group of strollers gathered to watch the sport. Finally . . . one Britisher came over to the father: "Sorry to bother you. We have been watching you a quarter of an hour. Who's winning?" (Fisher & Ury, 1981, p. 148)

In many situations, it is possible to accommodate the needs of all parties without necessarily meaning that someone must sacrifice his or her individual goals. Assuming otherwise is a common cognitive error.

The third error is to anchor one's judgments of a "good" or "bad" offer based on the initial offer made instead of linking one's judgment to some objective criteria. You've seen this technique before ... when the car salesman throws out a wildly high number so that the next number offered seems much more reasonable. The buyer can leave the lot believing she has talked him down to a great extent when the salesman never believed he would achieve success with his initial offer.

More specifically, the first number rendered in a negotiation is called an *anchoring number* and it tends to become the reference point for all future offers. For example, if I offered to sell you my used car for $20,000 but later came down in my demand to $8,000 you might think you were getting a good deal because you are mentally comparing $8,000 to $20,000. But what if the true value of the car was really only $6,000? Clearly, it is unwise to anchor one's judgment of an outcome to arbitrary figures solely because those figures were used at the early stages of bargaining or decision making. Getting unduly influenced by an anchoring number is a common cognitive bias.

The fourth common mistake is to be positively or negatively influenced by the framing or language used by the other party. The **framing effect** is a cognitive bias that occurs when the same option is presented in different formats or with different phrasing (i.e., it is framed differently) and the choice of format or phrasing unduly influences one's opinions or preferences on the matter (Druckman, 2001). This bias is difficult to avoid because a nice person with a bad offer remains harder to refuse than a rude person with a good offer. The framing of an offer may be akin to "putting lipstick on a pig," but sometimes our minds focus more on the lipstick than the pig—making this a particularly humbling cognitive bias. We'll call this the *framing bias*.

The fifth bias is the overreliance on information that is readily available, even first impressions, rather than doing the digging necessary to get the best data possible. Accepting readily available information saves time and makes sense when a decision is relatively unimportant. However, for important decisions, such as whom to hire or promote or which production method is best, gathering and analyzing information becomes quite important. There are no perfect shortcuts to sound decision making. This tendency was labeled as *satisficing* by Herbert Simon many years ago. This means people tend to take the first acceptable option that comes along rather than do the homework necessary to find the best option. This is a perfectly rational choice when faced with an overwhelming amount of data or information—taking the first good option alleviates the need to sift through a large amount of information. Yet it is important to note that satisficing may not always lead to the most efficient outcome possible.

The sixth bias occurs when the decision maker fails to take into consideration the other's needs and viewpoints. This leads to suboptimal decisions based on false assumptions about the motivations of the other side. In a negotiation, you cannot get what you want unless the other side agrees to it. Unless your proposal meets his needs, your negotiation partner won't agree to anything. Failing to acknowledge the interdependence of negotiators is a cognitive bias that results frequently in **impasse** (also known as *stalemate*). As a result, no agreement is reached. We'll call this bias *it's all about me*.

The seventh and final common cognitive error made by decision makers is simply overconfidence. Study after study has shown that attorneys generally overestimate their chances of winning at trial and this tendency can be found in many other forms of decision making. It is difficult to be objective about our own behaviors or chance of winning. Overconfidence leads to a lack of preparation and effort, including a reduced willingness to seek out new information that contradicts what you think you know or to try to understand the other side's views or needs. Most likely, this bias is related to the psychological concept of denial, mentioned previously. Focusing on the possibility of losing is unpleasant, so individuals overestimate their odds of winning an argument, a legal case, or a negotiation.

SOCIAL LEARNING THEORY

Social learning theory posits that humans are not innately aggressive but that they learn to behave aggressively or peacefully based on observing others in their social environment. People respond to the expected consequences of their behavior, which are learned from experience or observation (Sandy, Boardman, & Deutsch, 2000). For example, if managers in company x speak rudely to their subordinates yet they experience no negative repercussions from above, then other managers learn this is acceptable behavior. If an employee sees her colleague coming in late and leaving early with no negative consequences, then she will learn that punctuality is not rewarded in this organization. Positive behaviors also prove instructive. If managers are rewarded for keeping morale high by developing positive relationships with their employees, then others will mimic this behavior as long as they have the intellectual and practical ability to do so.

Using this approach to understanding organizational conflict management, one would observe the behaviors occurring in the workplace, track the consequences of those behavioral choices, and then make changes as necessary to ensure that desired behaviors lead to positive reinforcement and undesirable behaviors lead to negative consequences. This alignment of behaviors and outcomes should occur in ways that allow others in the organization to learn through observation and official policy rather than trial and error.

The theory of social learning means that we must address negative behaviors in the workplace because they have an infectious tendency that can lead to real changes in workplace culture. Yet managers are often hesitant to confront unproductive or noncollaborative workers. "If we want to have an honest conversation with someone about a problem," Kenneth Cloke and Joan Goldsmith (2003) write, "we need to confront it. If we want to stimulate a significant personal, organizational, societal, or political change, we need to create a minimal level of impoliteness, discourtesy, and unpleasantness. . . . No one learns to confront someone else unless they are willing to make an effort and face the consequences. By not trying, we allow inappropriate behavior to negatively impact everyone within its reach" (p. 196). Employees watch other employees for cues about what behavior is expected or allowed. Failing to intervene with a difficult, abusive, or shirking employee leads to widespread problems within the work unit, as predicted by social learning theory. Therefore, managers need to learn the skills necessary to successfully address these problems: coaching skills, the authority to create incentives for improvements, and negative sanctions for continued poor performance or negative behaviors. Managers may need to terminate or demote an employee who has clearly crossed a line into inappropriate behaviors or after repeated attempts to improve the employee's performance have failed. When managers work proactively to address negative workplace behaviors or attitudes, they need to feel rewarded for that proactive intervention. Unfortunately, many organizations reward conflict avoidance—allowing an employee to continue to violate norms or policies rather than take affirmative action for change. When this happens, other employees realize the "smart guy" is the one who comes late, leaves early, and misappropriates organizational resources (e.g., uses the work vehicle for personal errands or brings office supplies home). Because honest employees are not rewarded and dishonest employees are not punished, the organization's culture may begin a downward spiral if these behaviors are not address by proactive managers. Using the tools in this book, managers will be better equipped to work with "challenging" employees and colleagues, to give them the coaching and skills they need to succeed, and to develop techniques for making difficult decisions in the rare cases in which these skills are insufficient to turn around a poorly performing or misbehaving employee.

In social learning models, "realistic encouragement to achieve ambitious but attainable goals promotes successful experience, which in turn, aids developing the sense of self-efficacy. Social prodding to achieve unattainable goals often produces a sense of failure and undermines self-efficacy" (Sandy, Boardman, & Deutsch, 2000, p. 300). This means that managers can learn a lot from the field of coaching. Players respond better when coaches offer encouragement and specific advice. Coaches who yell insults at their players or who don't take the time to get to know their strengths and challenges are less effective at setting realistic goals.

FRAMING TOWARD A COLLABORATIVE PROCESS

Framing error was discussed previously. **Framing** refers to the ways in which facts or perceptions are defined, constructed, or labeled. "Framing is a process whereby communicators, consciously or unconsciously, act to construct a point of view that encourages the facts of a given situation to be interpreted by others in a particular manner. Frames operate in four key ways: they define problems, diagnose causes, make moral judgments, and suggest remedies. Frames are often found within a narrative account of an issue or event, and are generally the central organizing idea" (Kuypers, 2006, p. 7).

How a situation is labeled has a great influence on how people behave. For example,

> in a laboratory setting, when people worked on an activity labeled as an assessment activity (a test of their ability to perform on the task), they were more anxious, and produced lower-quality work and a small quantity of it compared to people who worked on the same activity when it was labeled as a self-development or learning activity. (Katz & Block, 2000, p. 280)

This is an example of the framing effect in action, yet this same cognitive bias may be used to prevent conflict and solve problems constructively. One's perceptions of a situation are directly linked to one's behaviors in response to that situation. For example, if individuals perceive that a situation calls for competition rather than cooperation, then they are likely to behave in ways that are more egocentric, even selfish.

Whether a situation is framed and perceived as one of competition versus collaboration is important in any negotiation—and most conflicts or problem-solving sessions involve negotiation at some level. By framing the situation as calling for joint problem solving (collaboration) rather than a winner-take-all situation (competition), negotiators are often able to think creatively, build and enhance relationships, and work together to reach a more optimal outcome.

Situations can be framed as either competitive or collaborative opportunities. In most negotiations, especially those with ongoing relationships between the negotiators (as in most workplace settings), a collaborative style tends to be better than a competitive style. Situations may be framed in ways that focus on the process or the outcome of the negotiation. "A process orientation (as compared to an outcome orientation) is likely to lead to more interest in the task, greater effort, less anxiety in the face of challenge, better performance, and higher self-esteem" (Katz & Block, 2000, p. 280).

Process orientations tend to result in greater collaboration whereas a focus on outcomes over process tends to produce competitive orientations. Let's use the process of performance reviews to illustrate this difference. Feedback from one's boss can focus either on the employee's performance relative to others in the organization (a competitive orientation) or it can examine changes or improvements in the employee's own performance. Feedback that compares an employee to others in the company does not necessarily provide the information needed for improvement. "Be more like Bob or Mary" is less effective than specific suggestions about to how to improve one's skills or performance. As the previous quotes from Katz and Block (2000) indicated, framing this feedback as a learning opportunity rather than as a competition with other employees is likely to result in greater improvement.

This principle also applies to goal setting. When employees are given process-related goals their performance improves more than when they are assigned task-related goals. As Katz and Block (2000) note, "People who are oriented toward an outcome goal mainly concentrate on the final result or outcome; as a consequence they are preoccupied with their position [or their demand]" (p. 283). The more individuals feel a need to clarify, reiterate, or reassert their own positions, the less time they spend trying to meet the underlying concerns of the other party. When people focus instead on a process goal, they devote their energy to developing a mastery of that process, which usually leads to a more successful resolution of the conflict or problem (Fisher & Ury, 1981; Katz & Block, 2000). Think of Google's instructions to its employees: "Take risks, make mistakes." Rather than telling employees that they must generate a specific level of profit or develop new products at a certain rate, they are given a process goal that encourages them to experiment and think creatively.

In another example, a company that sells cell phones and cell minutes on a pay-as-you-go model noted their Hispanic employees had consistently higher sales than the nonbilingual employees. All Spanish-speaking callers were automatically routed to Spanish-speaking employees, so this was not a linguistic barrier.

Managers thought that perhaps the Spanish-speaking customers were just more free spending than the English-speaking customers. To test this hypothesis, some of the Spanish-speaking (bilingual) sales representatives were offered overtime to take extra calls with English-speaking customers. To the managers' surprise, sales to English-speaking customers increased significantly when they were given a bilingual sales representative. Why the difference? Because all the sales calls are recorded, the managers began poring over the calls and comparing the data. It turns out that the Spanish-speaking and bilingual sales reps spent slightly more time on each call—getting to know their customers. This allowed them to build rapport as well as better understand the products and services that would best serve them. This slight increase in call length was more than made up for in profits from increased sales. In the end, it was a difference in cultural tendencies that resulted in greater profits generated from the Hispanic sales reps. Based on this information, the company managers decided to give greater training to their English-speaking reps. That training included a process orientation with specific information about how the call center employees can build relationships with their customers, listen to them, and thereby improve their individual sales as well as customer satisfaction with the sales experience. Employees were encouraged to try various techniques as a learning exercise in order to see which ones worked the best for them as individual sales reps. Sales soared.

PROCEDURAL JUSTICE AND THE PROCESS FOCUS

When customers, clients, or employees experience conflicts they often claim the status quo isn't fair or that they aren't being treated fairly. **Fairness** can be defined as the quality of being just, equitable, impartial, or evenhanded. Fairness can refer to the process through which decisions were made and the outcome of those decisions. There may be many contradictory viewpoints about what comprises a "fair" outcome depending on one's preference for equity, equality, or need-based outcomes. Concepts of justice and fairness are central to our understanding of conflict and are keys to its resolution. Humans and other primates have an innate sense of fairness and react negatively when they feel they are being treated unfairly (Markey, 2003). An interesting example of the deep roots of our need for fairness comes from a study of capuchin monkeys by the Yerkes Primate Research Center at Emory University (2003). Capuchin monkeys were trained to give a researcher a pebble in return for a small piece of food, usually a slice of cucumber. However, capuchin monkeys prefer grapes to cucumbers. Researchers placed pairs of capuchins next to each other so they could watch the exchanges taking place between their neighbor and the researchers. The first monkey was given a grape in reward for handing over a pebble. The next monkey was given a piece of cucumber as a reward for handing over the pebble. This equates to equal work (giving a pebble) for unequal pay (grape versus cucumber). The capuchins receiving cucumbers instead of grapes reacted by either throwing their cucumbers back at the researchers or simply refusing to eat the cucumbers. Capuchin pairs who saw only cucumbers exchanged for pebbles ate their cucumbers happily (Markey, 2003). This research demonstrates that humans and other animals have developed understandings of fairness that have enabled them to work together successfully in groups. Fairness matters. A perceived lack of fairness leads to anger, resentment, and conflict within human and primate groups.

The **theory of relative deprivation** explains the fairness concerns held by the capuchin monkeys in our previous example. The capuchins were perfectly satisfied with exchanging the pebbles for cucumbers until they saw another capuchin receive a grape for the same service. The theory of relative deprivation states that a sense of injustice can arise when one compares one's distribution to others in a competitive environment and sees that others are receiving more. In modern society this has led to competitive materialistic pursuits often called the need to "keep up with the Joneses." This explains why many private employers ask their employees to avoid discussing their individual pay rates with one another. For public sector employees, wage rates and salaries are public record—making these discussions about relative pay more frequent and giving rise to frequent discussions about fairness.

Yet fairness can mean different things to different people and is influenced by situational factors. Would the capuchins react differently if the grapes were given to mothers with small offspring and the cucumbers were reserved for those without dependents to feed? In order to better understand what we mean by fairness we must examine the concepts of procedural and distributive justice.

Procedural justice refers to the fairness of the process used for reaching a decision or resolving a conflict. Individuals tend to perceive that a process is fair when it is transparent, respectful, and allows them to be heard during decision making:

> One wants procedures that generate relevant, unbiased, accurate, consistent, reliable, competent, and valid information and decisions as well as polite,

dignified, and respectful behavior in carrying out the procedures. Also voice and representation in the processes and decisions related to the evaluation are considered desirable by those directly affected by the decisions. (Deutsch, 2000b, p. 45)

Think of this example: your boss issues a memo to all employees that details a new dress code that he has devised for the entire organization. This new dress code will require some minor changes and a slight expense to you personally. How do you feel about this decision? What if the memo stated the new dress code was created by a committee composed of five employees and three managers from different parts of the organization? What if the memo reminded you that those delegates were chosen by a vote from each employee group? Does this change how you feel about the decision? Typically individuals can accept, abide by, and even help implement a policy decision they do not like as long as they feel the process used to reach it was fair, transparent, and they had a reasonable opportunity to participate. Therefore, between the two types of justice, attention to procedural justice concerns typically increases the likelihood that parties will accept and support decisions.

Distributive justice refers to the criteria that lead people to feel that they have received a fair outcome. Perceptions of distributive justice generally hinge on one of three criteria for determining the fairness of an outcome: equity, equality, or need (Deutsch, 2000b). The **equity principle** denotes that benefits should be distributed based on each person or group's contribution; those who worked harder or contributed greater expertise to a project should receive disproportionate amounts of the payout. The **equality principle** states that all group members should receive equal amounts of any good or benefit that comes from the labors of the group. Under this version of fairness, all employees would receive the same pay. The **need principle** asserts that more of the goods or benefits should go to those who need more. Therefore, a parent with three young children might receive greater pay or fewer taxes than someone with no children at all. These principles can be seen as the organizing principles underlying the capitalist, socialist, and communist economic and political systems, respectively. In practice, capitalist societies still pay some attention to need-based distributive principles through the provision of social welfare policies, such as food stamps or housing assistance, but they do so to a smaller extent than in socialist or communist societies. Based on your individual political culture, you will be prone to believe that one of these is more efficient and morally correct than the others in the majority of situations. According to Deutsch (2000b), the equity principle is most often called on when the goal is economic productivity. Workers have greater incentive to work hard when hard workers receive more pay than shirkers and when they know there are few government services to guarantee their livelihoods otherwise. The equality principle is used in situations in which social harmony and positive social relationships are the highest goal. The need principle is followed when the most important goal is ensuring human welfare.

In any particular situation, individuals rely on one of these definitions of outcome fairness to support their argument for a different outcome distribution than they are slated to receive. "Officer, it is not fair that I get the speeding ticket! That car ahead of me was going much faster than my car" (appealing to the equality principle). "Officer, I should not have to pay such a huge speeding fine. I won't be able to make my rent payment" (appealing to the need principle).

When examining competing claims of fairness, it is helpful to dig more deeply into the underlying definitions of fairness by asking each party (or ourselves if we are a party), "What makes you say it is fair or unfair? What criteria are you using to determine fairness in this situation? What would a fair outcome look like and how could it be attained?" It can be helpful to be metacognitive with the parties, meaning that you take the time to explain to them the various types of fairness and ask them to analyze their own claims to see which type of fairness undergirds them. This allows space to build an understanding that people can hold differing preferences for an outcome but both outcomes can be defended as fair under the equity, equality, or need principle. This lays the groundwork for a respectful discussion of possible outcomes that does not privilege one viewpoint over another or dehumanize one negotiator as patently unconcerned with fairness.

How do theories of distributive and procedural justice affect conflict and its resolution for managers? Clearly, feelings of injustice and unfairness give rise to much of the world's conflict. Decision-making procedures that lack transparency and do not allow participatory input from stakeholders or fail to uphold procedural rules often result in a backlash. When managers are acting as mediators between two employees in conflict or when they facilitate a decision-making meeting, it can be helpful to use a process-focused approach, similar to that used by mediators: "The mediator can encourage the sides to focus on such processes as finding common ground, developing mutual understandings, empowering one another, and understanding each other's needs and emotions.

Doing so encourages using fair tactics and constructive strategies to resolve the conflict" (Katz & Block, 2000, p. 285). Although it is counterintuitive, it can be helpful to remind employees that they are more likely to reach their preferred outcome if they focus instead on walking through a thoughtful and fair process of discussion and information sharing. This process focus, rather than an outcome focus, is most likely to build and enhance working relationships and achieve outcomes that meet their needs.

Distributing Raises Fairly

Recently, a high school principal at a private school asked a conflict management consultant to conduct an assessment to determine the reasons why her staff seemed frequently disgruntled. That assessment revealed, in part, that teachers were dissatisfied because the merit bonuses were distributed in ways that seemed unfair. Teachers with seniority wanted their loyalty rewarded. Teachers who worked a lot of overtime to improve and update their lectures and materials wanted their efforts recognized. Teachers whose students scored highest on standardized tests wanted recognition for this achievement. Young teachers who had student loans to repay stated a greater need for the merit pay increases. With so many competing criteria, the principal had been distributing raises without any clear criteria to define *merit* or *fair*. Each teacher defined a fair distribution in ways that privileged his or her own situation, giving rise to a no-win situation for the principal. How should the principal proceed?

CONCEPTS OF FAIRNESS ACROSS CULTURES

In addition to the three types of fairness defined previously, it should be noted that different cultural groups tend to exhibit generalized preferences for one of the three types. This means that individuals within a cultural group will continue to exhibit individualized differences in the type of fairness they prefer but the majority in each cultural group will tend to prefer one of these three types of fairness over the others.

Individualistic societies are those in which the needs, rights, and responsibilities of the individual are prioritized above those of the group or community.

In these societies, it is generally considered positive for individuals to stand out from their peers through individual achievements, whereas in collectivist societies it is less appropriate for individuals to stand out from the crowd. In individualistic societies, members are encouraged to be independent from others, support themselves financially, make decisions for themselves, and deal with the outcome of their decisions, whether it is good or bad. Individualists believe that people are largely in control of their own fate and through hard work nearly any goal can be achieved. This closely matches the definition of a concept known as *locus of control* from the field of psychology. An **internal locus of control** means that individuals believe they are in control of events that affect themselves, rather than being controlled by external forces such as God, the environment, or those in powerful positions. Individuals with an **external locus of control** believe that they are controlled by factors external to themselves such as a higher power, the environment, political forces, and so on. Individualists put their faith in individuals' abilities to master their environment and make decisions or take actions that result in positive outcomes for the individual. Therefore, it follows logically that in individualistic societies, distributions based on need are less supported than other definitions of fairness and the equity principle is typically preferred. Because individuals are thought to be able to control their environments through good decision making and hard work, an equity distribution makes the most sense.

In collectivist societies, in which individual identities are based on ties to the group or community, it is more common to share resources based on equality or need. In collectivist societies, belief in an external locus of control is more common. For example, in Russia, Liberia, or China an individual's fate might have more to do with the family one is born into or the political climate (e.g., whether your family is politically well connected or whether there is peace and stability or war). Even getting to work on time might have more to do with luck than individual choice because the public buses might be unreliable or run off schedule. In truth, in developing economies or in war-torn regions, it is likely more true that an individual's fate lies more heavily with factors beyond his or her own control due to societal inequity, random violence, and corrupt political systems. Collectivist societies tend to believe that it is fair to distribute the costs of education, health care, parenthood, and so on across society as a whole rather than to allow persons to shoulder these burdens individually. They may use a web of social relationships to get ahead but rarely do they believe individuals will succeed or fail solely based on their own efforts.

As a manager in a multicultural workplace it is important to understand why employees behave as they do. The locus of control concept helps us understand why employees may have culturally based differences in their concepts of fairness. It also helps us to understand preferences for team-based or individually based assignments. Individuals from each different perspective tend to get frustrated in dealing with the other: those with a high internal locus of control find their opposites to be indecisive and slow to act. Those with a high external locus of control find their opposites exhibit a high degree of hubris or consider them egotistical. Understanding these different worldviews and views of self can be helpful in finding fair and productive ways to work together.

In sum, our cultural affiliations and identities shape how we see the world and how we view fairness. Managers need to take the time to ask their colleagues and employees about their perceptions and to explain their own. Workplaces develop their own cultural norms as well. Having a fair, transparent, and participatory process to make joint decisions, when appropriate, can provide an opportunity to build deeper relationships and understandings among those with whom we share our work lives.

POWER IN THEORY AND PRACTICE

Traditionally, power has been defined as the ability to accomplish one's goals over the objections of others if necessary. Powerful people were those who had the ability to force their will on others. In a modern managerial setting, *power* can be defined as the ability to act effectively (Folger, Poole, & Stutman, 2000). This definition means you have the ability to communicate your vision for the organization or your unit, solicit buy-in for that vision, and empower your employees and teams to work effectively toward a shared goal.

Power structures in most organizations are evolving from strict hierarchical designs into systems with disbursed power centers, delegated decision-making authority, and collaborative work products. Bill Ury, in an introduction to Mark Gerzon's book *Leading Through Conflict*, writes, "A generation or two ago, it is fair to say, most decisions were made hierarchically. The people on the top gave the orders and the people on the bottom simply followed them. That is changing. Nowadays, leaders increasingly cannot simply give orders and expect them to be carried out" (Gerzon, 2006, p. xi). As Cloke and Goldsmith (1997) note, "There is a clear evolutionary pattern of movement from management based on authoritarian principles to leadership based on democratic values" (p. 161). Understanding the evolving nature of power is central to effective managers in the twenty-first century.

Increasingly, power over others has been replaced by power with others. "Social power stems from relationships among people" (Folger, Poole, & Stutman, 2000, p. 120). Managers are able to exercise their power and authority when others view their exercise of power as legitimate and useful. In effect, they endorse the manager's power. Building positive relationships with one's subordinates, peers, and supervisors is crucial to building and maintaining power as a manager. Positive relationships mean that others are likely to give you the benefit of the doubt when difficult decisions need to be made. Managers who abuse their power or authority by treating people disrespectfully or by repeatedly making decisions that are contrary to group expectations and preferences are likely to lose power, especially their ability to convince others to support and implement their decisions.

A host of resources come together to determine one's power: access to resources, knowledge, special skills, access to professional contacts and networks, control over rewards or sanctions, communication skills including persuasiveness, empathy, and even one's personality can contribute to one's power. These facets of power are often conditional and change from one setting to another. A three-star general can move armies at work but may not be able to win every argument at home. Even dictators can be toppled by a coup. The best managers have power because others in the organization want to please them, employees want to help them enact their vision for the organization, and they have built a reputation for fairness, collegiality, and effectiveness. Not only is power *with* others more successful than power *over* others, it also feels better.

When deciding which battles to fight and which to let go, it is helpful to engage in a brief analysis of the contextual power dynamics of the situation. Who has the most power? How important is this issue to him or her? How much power do you have to affect the outcome? This assessment includes the power of your connections with others and your access to resources, including knowledge. What are the costs versus the benefits of your preferred outcome compared to other possible outcomes? And finally, is there a high-quality process that the decision makers might follow to allow them to arrive at the optimal outcome? Would it be helpful to have the decision-making group brainstorm all possible actions and weigh the costs and benefits? Should stakeholders be involved in the decision-making process? You might be surprised and find out that you change your own mind about the preferred outcome once you engage in a clear problem-solving process that includes an analysis of power.

THE TIMING OF CONFLICT INTERVENTIONS

When should managers or neutral conflict resolvers (for example, mediators, facilitators, or others) intervene in conflicts to seek a resolution? Timing may not be everything but it certainly is important. Intervene too early and there may not be enough information to tell you who the parties are and what the problem is really about. Intervene too late and tempers have already grown hot and hard feelings may make resolution difficult. Conflict managers call this the problem of *ripeness*.

Figure 2.2 displays the spiral of unmanaged conflict. Although originally developed to explain public policy disputes, the concepts are also well applied in the workplace. Intervene too early and no one wants to participate. Intervene too late and it is difficult to undo the damage already done by the conflict.

Once sides have formed, positions begin to harden. Cognitive biases, including attribution bias, work to filter out information that runs contrary to our own view of the problem or the other parties. Eventually, we refuse to communicate with the other side. Once communication stops, we are more likely to fall prey to attribution bias. At this point, parties often expend resources to hire an attorney or build their case against the other side. They take the conflict outside the immediate parties by telling their story to others, looking for allies elsewhere in the organization or the broader community, or even going to the press or using a hotline to report complaints. Perceptions of the dispute and of the other parties become distorted by the lack of information flowing between them. At this point, if not earlier, a sense of crisis emerges and one or more parties comes to believe that a resolution is needed right away. They want to be proved right, make the other side pay for what they have done, and so on. This need for revenge, justice, and resolution means that they are now willing to pay whatever it takes, or whatever they can pay, to get it resolved. Ironically, intervention at this stage is likely to be less successful than intervention at an earlier stage, before significant resources were committed and communication stopped. The trick for interventionists, including managers, is to allow the dispute to ripen enough to increase the chance of successful intervention, but not so late that the dispute has gotten highly escalated.

Figure 2.2
The Spiral of Unmanaged Conflict

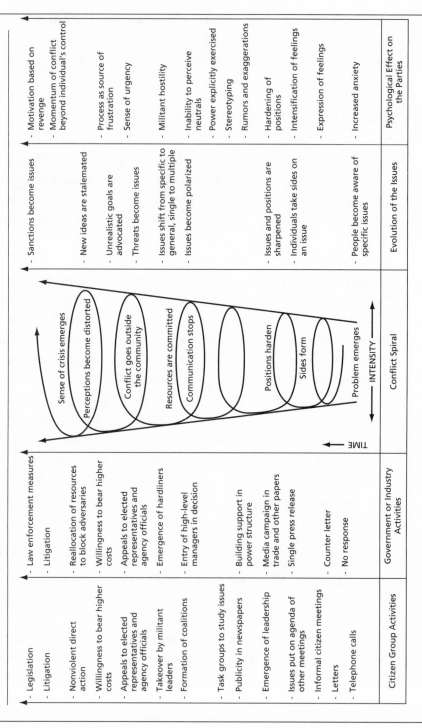

Citizen Group Activities	Government or Industry Activities	Conflict Spiral	Evolution of the Issues	Psychological Effect on the Parties
- Legislation	- Law enforcement measures		- Sanctions become issues	- Motivation based on revenge
- Litigation	- Litigation			- Momentum of conflict beyond individual's control
- Nonviolent direct action	- Reallocation of resources to block adversaries	Sense of crisis emerges	- New ideas are stalemated	- Process as source of frustration
- Willingness to bear higher costs	- Willingness to bear higher costs	Perceptions become distorted	- Unrealistic goals are advocated	- Sense of urgency
- Appeals to elected representatives and agency officials	- Appeals to elected representatives and agency officials	Conflict goes outside the community	- Threats become issues	
- Takeover by militant leaders	- Emergence of hardliners	Resources are committed	- Issues shift from specific to general, single to multiple	- Militant hostility
- Formation of coalitions	- Entry of high-level managers in decision	Communication stops	- Issues become polarized	- Inability to perceive neutrals
- Task groups to study issues				- Power explicitly exercised
- Publicity in newspapers	- Building support in power structure			- Stereotyping
				- Rumors and exaggerations
- Emergence of leadership	- Media campaign in trade and other papers	Positions harden	- Issues and positions are sharpened	- Hardening of positions
- Issues put on agenda of other meetings	- Single press release		- Individuals take sides on an issue	- Intensification of feelings
- Informal citizen meetings		Sides form		- Expression of feelings
- Letters	- Counter letter			
- Telephone calls	- No response	Problem emerges	- People become aware of specific issues	- Increased anxiety

TIME → INTENSITY

Source: From Carpenter and Kennedy (2001), p. 12. Used with permission.

In a managerial setting, it can be helpful to allow employees some time to attempt to resolve their own interpersonal conflicts before intervening. When employees reach their own resolution and handle their own conflicts, it can (re)build relationships and increase their conflict resolution skills. Yet, conflicts between two employees can quickly become a conflict among ten employees when others take sides or the problem morphs from an interpersonal conflict to an intergroup conflict. In conflicts between customers and clients and employees, it is best to allow employees some specific remedies they can offer in order to resolve the dispute at the lowest level possible. This means the unsatisfied customer needs only to speak with one employee rather than be transferred to a manager. Both customers and employees tend to be happier when small problems can be resolved at the lowest levels without taking a disproportionate amount of time.

STRUCTURAL VERSUS NONSTRUCTURAL SOURCES OF CONFLICT

When people experience conflict at work or with clients, they tend to blame it on the other person's personality flaws or otherwise chalk it up to causes beyond their own control (review denial and attribution bias covered previously in this chapter). Often the conflict is attributed to a personality conflict. To become adept at managing collaboration and conflict you must develop the ability to diagnose the sources of conflict in much the same way that a physician diagnoses the cause of an illness. Information about the root cause of a dispute can be indispensable in crafting an effective response. The first step in the diagnostic process is to determine whether the source is structural or nonstructural. **Structural sources of conflict** include unfair, unclear, or inefficient policies, procedures, organizational cultures, or ingrained practices that repeatedly give rise to disputes irrespective of personnel changes. High levels of employee and customer dissatisfaction are nearly always indicators of structural sources of conflict within an organization. A few examples will help to illustrate the most common structural sources of conflict within an organization:

- Overlapping job descriptions that create turf battles or conflict between employees who are left unclear as to which tasks are to be accomplished by themselves or others
- Organizational cultures that encourage or fail to punish racism, sexism, harassment, bullying, or other recurring negative workplace behaviors

- Rewards for individual achievement that encourage no-holds-barred competition between members of the same team such as stealing clients from one another or sabotaging the work of one's colleague in order to increase one's chance of winning the monthly sales competition

- Failures to recognize and reward desired behaviors among individual employees and teams

- Incentives to use or lose one's sick time or vacation time resulting in mass absenteeism near the end of the year

- Unrealistically high performance goals or objectives

- Performance goals or policy changes that are not communicated clearly along the entire chain of command

- Any policy, procedure, or cultural norm that misaligns the needs of the individual and the needs of the whole organization

- An absence of mechanisms for informal employee or customer dispute resolution, thereby incentivizing formal actions, such as litigation, as the only venue for redress

Understanding structural conflicts is all about understanding incentive structures. Sometimes organizations create policies or procedures that have unintended consequences. To elaborate, let's look at an entire subset of conflict based on poor procedures, policies, and practices: those that misalign the good of the individual and the good of the organization. For example, in order to save money, an organization may create a policy stating that all sick leave or vacation time must be used by the end of the year and will not roll over. This gives employees the incentive to use it or lose it, even if this means the organization is understaffed near the end of the year and employees call in sick when they aren't really ill.

A second example: imagine a company that installs and services burglar alarm systems for corporations and government offices. In order to respond quickly to customers, the technicians are told they must reply to e-mails or voicemails within ten minutes. In order to avoid reprimands from their managers, technicians are taking calls and answering e-mails while driving between customer sites. In order to abide by the new policy, they must violate the state's driving laws and common sense. This increases the number of car accidents, worker's compensation claims, and overall liability for the entire company. Even if the company terminates the employment of those with two or more accidents or traffic citations, the policy provides negative incentives for all the technicians to continue these conflict-causing behaviors.

In nearly all cases, high employee or client turnover can be traced to structural sources of conflict. If your organization has terminated the "bad apples" and the problem remains, then the source of the conflict is likely structural rather than due to a few bad personalities. Sabotage, theft, and apathy that are widespread within a company indicate a need for cultural change rather than simply terminating individual employees. Structural sources of conflict mean the conflict will recur repeatedly until the source of the conflict is addressed.

Nonstructural sources of conflict happen one time or rarely, occurring as isolated events that could not have been predicted or avoided. These are usually resolved by taking action to address the individual problem rather than creating or changing policies across the organization: the employee who can't show up on time or does not treat his coworkers appropriately even after retraining or coaching, the two team members who simply cannot get along with each other but who seem to work well with others. In these instances retraining, discipline, or termination may be in order.

When dealing with nonstructural (i.e., individual) sources of conflict, don't fall into what I label the *elementary school discipline trap*. For example, when one child misbehaves or lollygags in the halls during a trip to the restroom, the principal changes the rules so that individuals can no longer make these trips on their own. Instead, each classroom is assigned two times during the day when they are allowed to use the restroom together as a group. Everyone is punished for the misbehavior of one or a few members rather than dealing directly with those who misbehave. Large organizations tend to do this rather than respond as needed to misbehaving individuals. Ironically, this stems from a desire for conflict avoidance — rather than deal directly with the wrongdoer, the organization creates a blanket policy for the whole organization.

Training for Everyone!

A male employee was accused of sexual harassment by three different female employees on three or more separate occasions. Each female employee

(continued)

(*continued*)

thought she was the only woman being harassed by this offender. Rather than disciplining or terminating the offender, the company hired a sexual harassment trainer and required that all employees, including the three victims and the offender, attend this training together. During the training, the women shared their experiences and realized they had similar experiences. In the end, the harasser was left undisciplined and the entire workforce sat through a training that most of them didn't need. The victims felt further victimized by being forced to take this training, as if they had done something wrong. They filed a joint suit against the company, costing more than $200,000 in claims and legal fees. A year later, two additional women left the organization after being sexually harassed by the same male employee.

CONCLUSION

This brief introduction to the theories and terminology of conflict management was designed to present the conceptual frameworks and ideas that will make sense of the chapters to come. These theories are organized from those existing within one's own mind all the way to intergroup conflict. Although a diverse array of theories was presented, in my experience, these are the most indispensable theories for understanding and intervening in destructive conflict within and between organizations. Before managers can create methods to prevent or resolve unproductive conflict they first need to know why and how it arises, evolves, and dissipates. When managers understand the biological and evolutionary sources of conflict and cooperation, they see the root causes of human behaviors and learn to depersonalize challenging behaviors from employees or customers. When they understand procedural justice they gain critical insights about the procedures for gaining buy-in for important decisions that will need to be implemented by employees across the organization. When managers understand differing worldviews and definitions related to fairness, they learn there are many fair ways to distribute resources or solve problems and that communicating these perspectives can lead to deeper understandings between employees and better relationships. Through an examination of the evolving nature of power relations between managers and employees, collaborative managers learn how to motivate people through cooperation, mutual respect, and genuine understanding—the ultimate source of power for leaders. When managers act as diagnosticians who see conflict as a symptom of a deeper problem, they become able to diagnose and change the underlying structures that give rise to unproductive and recurring conflicts.

ELISE AND MAIN STREET BAKERIES: BEN'S TRIP TO STORE NUMBER SEVENTY-FIVE

As Ben boards the flight to deal with the problem at store number seventy-five, he is already building a list of likely causes in his head: Janice, the manager of that store, may be driving other employees away. The last two times Ben has called Janice he has left voicemail messages because she was too busy to talk to him and she did not bother calling him back. She is probably avoiding him. Ben hates it when others treat him disrespectfully. No matter how busy she is, she could at least call him back. Store number seventy-five is taking up more of his time than the other stores. That is not fair to those managers who are seeking more training, advice, or other resources from HR.

When Ben arrived, he contacted the last two assistant managers who quit and arranged to meet them for coffee. He asked them, "What would make store number seventy-five a better place to work? What would make it a place where people like you would want to build your careers?" Both assistant managers told the same story. Janice, the store manager, works herself to death. She is so afraid the assistant managers won't make the right decisions that she refuses to delegate anything. The assistant managers are treated like glorified cashiers. The assistant managers are told what to do and how to do it but their input is never sought. Janice won't take the time to listen to their ideas for improvement. When changes are made, the assistant managers are not informed about the reasons for the changes, nor are they informed about policy changes coming from corporate headquarters. There is a lack of communication from the top down and certainly from the bottom up. Assistant managers want to be problem solvers but their scope of authority is so limited they end up frustrated—always needing to go to the manager to get problems solved. The assistant managers are unclear about their full job descriptions or the ways in which their performance will be evaluated.

When it comes time for the manager to distribute merit bonuses, the assistant managers both claim that Janice does this in an unfair manner that lacks transparency. No one knows why some employees get more than others and they suspect favoritism. Some employees wonder if it is because the manager seems to get along better with those employees who are most like her (e.g., gender, race, religion, etc.). Additionally, the store lacks a friendly, collegial atmosphere. Employees at store number seventy-five come to work and leave eight hours later. They do not build relationships or support each other as colleagues and friends. The environment is lonely and frustrating, so most assistant managers do not stay long.

KEY TERMS

Accuser bias	Framing effect
Attribution theory	Fundamental attribution errors
Bias of the accused	Impasse
Cognitive bias	Individualistic societies
Collectivist societies	Internal locus of control
Disassociation	Maslow's hierarchy of needs
Displacement	Need principle
Distributive justice	Need theories
Equality principle	Nonstructural sources of conflict
Equity principle	Procedural justice
External locus of control	Rationalization
Fairness	Structural sources of conflict
Framing	Theory of relative deprivation

SUGGESTED SUPPLEMENTAL READING

Axelrod, R. (1984). *The evolution of cooperation*. New York: Basic Books.

Birke, R. (2010). Neuroscience and settlement: An examination of scientific innovations and practical applications. *Ohio State Journal on Dispute Resolution*, *25*(2), 477–529.

Elangovan, A. (1998). Managerial intervention in organizational disputes: Testing a prescriptive model of strategy selection. *International Journal of Conflict Management*, *9*(4), 301–335.

Jones, W., & Hughes, S. H. (2003). Complexity, conflict resolution, and how the mind works. *Conflict Resolution Quarterly*, *20*, 485–494. doi: 10.1002/crq.42.

DISCUSSION QUESTIONS

1. How useful (or not useful) is a knowledge of conflict theory for managers? What is the connection between these theories and your practical management decisions?

2. Think of a conflict that has been in the news recently. Which of these theories best explains why the conflict arose or the choices parties to the conflict have made? Discuss the pros and cons of different theories as explanations for these events.

EXERCISES

1. First, go to "Elise and Main Street Bakeries: Ben's Trip to Store Number Seventy-Five" at the end of this chapter. Go through each paragraph and identify every form of cognitive bias or conflict theory you can find. Then develop a list of possible remedies that Ben can recommend to Elise that will reduce the sources of unproductive conflict. Remember—getting rid of the manager is not the first or only option on this list.

2. Think of a performance-review process you have experienced, either as the reviewer or as the employee being reviewed. How would it have been different if it took a collaborative and procedural orientation? Brainstorm questions for a performance review that encourages employees to compare their current performance to past performance and set future goals for improvement tied to current and past performance rather than being tied to a comparison of other employees in the company. You can do this individually or in small groups.

3. You are the manager of your work unit and you just learned that you must lay off one of your ten employees. You are not part of a unionized workplace and you have full discretion to decide whom to let go. Which standard of fairness will you use and why? Which factors will you include in your decision-making process and which will you exclude? Discuss this among others to see how many fair decision-making criteria you can come

up with. What kind of fairness does each criterion speak to? Why would different managers come up with different criteria?

4. Imagine you are a manager for a corporation, government agency, or nonprofit organization (pick whichever applies to you). You need to speak to an employee who is underperforming. How would you frame the situation to maximize the employee's chances for improvement? How might you create goals and measure progress toward those goals using a collaborative process orientation rather than a competitive orientation?

5. Alex, Pat, and Sandy own a consulting business together. They just completed a job that brought in $2,400 to their company (after expenses). Alex is a semiretired former executive. His contacts brought the business to the company but he only worked six hours on the project. Pat is single and has no kids. She worked twelve hours on the project. She has much less experience in this area than Alex. Sandy is a single parent with three kids and a lot of student loans. Her hectic schedule meant that she could only work six hours on the project. Like Pat, she has much less experience with this work than Alex. How should the money from this project be distributed and which definition of fairness does your preferred outcome represent? Once completed, analyze your answers to see which definition of fair you used (T. K. Hedeen, personal conversation, 2011).

GOAL SETTING

For the next week, make some notes about the conflict you have. Which conflict style did you use to address the conflict and which theories explain how the conflict arose and progressed. Then, set one goal for the upcoming week that you believe will help you more efficiently match your conflict response to the conflict itself. Try to address the conflict before it gets too high on the spiral of unmanaged conflict and see what earlier resolution can achieve. Set some goals that specifically incorporate your new knowledge of conflict styles and conflict theories.

chapter THREE

The Power of Negotiation

Essential Concepts and Skills

Learning Objectives

- Demonstrate an understanding of the role of negotiation in managerial life.

- List, describe, and apply common negotiation concepts and skills.

- Demonstrate an understanding of when to avoid negotiating.

- Demonstrate an understanding of the differences between distributive and integrative bargaining.

- List and describe the steps of the integrative bargaining negotiation process.

- Analyze and identify the interests that underlie positions.

- Demonstrate an understanding of the ethical implications of negotiation decisions.

- Demonstrate an understanding of strategies to prepare for planned negotiations.

- Demonstrate an understanding of the role of trust building and repair in negotiations.

ELISE AND MAIN STREET BAKERIES

In recent years, the price of flour has risen dramatically. At the same time, the country has suffered an economic downturn, resulting in increased bargain hunting by consumers and reduced profits for many boutique food outlets such as Main Street Bakeries. Elise and her company have weathered the storm relatively well by negotiating long-term, fixed-price contracts with organic farmers and mills around the country. These contracts mean Elise and her team do a lot of negotiating. Elise has a meeting this afternoon with a young farmer named Jacob who wants to sell his organic crops to Main Street Bakeries. She hopes she can strike a good deal because she is trying hard not to raise her prices in this economy. If she does not reach a deal with Jacob, then her only alternative would be to continue looking for additional suppliers. Because prices are going up quickly, the longer she waits to conclude a deal, the higher the price she will likely pay. If she simply cannot afford to buy local wheat, then she could buy wheat from outside the United States. This is not ideal because her shop always has little notes on its products, stating where the ingredients came from—her customers want locally grown, organic food whenever possible.

When was your most recent negotiation? If you cannot remember, then you may have too narrow a definition of negotiation. You began negotiating as a small child, wheedling your way into a later bedtime, a cookie before dinner, or the cereal with the best toy inside the box. Today you may have negotiated with a roommate or spouse about household chores, negotiated with the police officer who pulled you over for speeding, negotiated with your colleagues about the division of labor on a project requiring teamwork, negotiated with your supervisor to let you out early so you could get to class on time, and negotiated with your professor to grant you an extension on your paper due date. In the news, we see attorneys negotiating plea bargains, members of Congress negotiating trade bills, government agencies negotiating with the businesses they regulate, large businesses negotiating tax incentives for relocation, and public employee unions negotiating new contract terms. Nearly all collaboration or teamwork requires some level of negotiation. Whether negotiations are formal or informal, they are all around us.

MANAGERS AS NEGOTIATORS

The first step to improving your negotiations is to recognize when a negotiation is under way. **Negotiation** occurs between two or more interdependent parties who have a perceived conflict between their needs and desires yet believe a negotiated outcome is superior to what they could achieve unilaterally. The parties are interdependent by definition or they would not be negotiating with one another; neither person can achieve his or her goals without the other's cooperation. If any party to the negotiation can accomplish her goal unilaterally, then she can do so without any negotiation. Parties to a negotiation may not be equally dependent on one another in a negotiation—dependence may be asymmetric. Yet some interdependence exists or there would be no need to negotiate.

Wanted: A Professional Negotiator

Melissa was looking for her first management job. She recently completed her master's degree with an emphasis on negotiation and dispute resolution but she could find very few job titles with the word *negotiator* or *dispute resolver* in them. Then she found the ad for her dream job: supply chain manager. The successful applicant would be responsible for managing all of the vendor contracts for one of the largest nonprofit hospital chains in the United States. In addition to securing agreements over price and quantities, the supply chain manager was responsible for getting feedback from end users of these products, such as nurses and doctors, in order to seek changes and improvements to the products. *Relationship management* was listed as a job duty. After all, the hospital cannot find itself without bandages due to a business dispute. In this organization, all the supply chain managers had been either attorneys or hospital administrators. During the interview, Melissa successfully argued that this position needed an expert in negotiation and problem solving rather than someone versed in the law or medical knowledge. The hiring team hadn't really thought of this work as being negotiation but that is exactly what it was. Melissa has since become the most successful supply chain manager in the history of the organization.

Understanding the dynamics of negotiation will help you navigate performance reviews, advocate for your department or organization as it competes for limited resources, and resolve conflicts that arise with customers, employees, and members of the regulated community or with regulators, as the case may be.

DISTRIBUTIVE VERSUS INTEGRATIVE BARGAINING

Negotiations can be **zero sum** or nonzero sum. In **zero-sum** situations, also called *distributive negotiation* situations, there is only one winner at the end of the negotiation. Each gain made by one negotiator comes at the expense of another negotiator. In **distributive bargaining** situations, resources are fixed and cannot be increased. Distributing bargaining situations typically involve only one issue in the negotiation (e.g., price) rather than multiple issues under negotiation. In contrast, nonzero-sum negotiations, also called *integrative bargaining*, are those in which negotiators can achieve their goals without necessarily leaving the others worse off and in which multiple issues are at stake (Lewicki, Barry, & Saunders, 2010).

We know that negotiators often assume a situation is distributive and therefore competitive when indeed it is not necessarily so (Deutsch, 2000). In the classic negotiation primer, Fisher and Ury (1981; and an earlier version from Mary Parker Follett [1942]) give the example of two individuals fighting over a small number of oranges. Each needs the oranges for worthwhile purposes and there is no way to obtain additional oranges. The negotiators begin using competitive strategies—trying to convince each other to give up or sell the oranges. Because their claims on the oranges were assumed to be mutually exclusive no deal could be reached—more oranges for one negotiator meant fewer oranges for the other. Then they changed to an integrative bargaining strategy. They sought to learn more about each other's needs with the goal of helping each other meet their needs. In the end, they realized that one negotiator needed the juice of the orange and the other needed only the rind. Their needs were not mutually exclusive yet a traditional distributive bargaining approach would have resulted in an impasse. A collaborative approach resulted in a mutually beneficial outcome.

In many bargaining situations, it is possible to expand the pie, meaning to find ways to create value rather than compete over an existing fixed pie, or a nonexpandable resource. In **creating value**, the negotiators work together to ensure that their needs are met by expanding existing value through collaboration, increased efficiency, or creativity. In distributive bargaining situations, negotiators are focused on **claiming value** for themselves. This means they are competing to claim something they both value. The more one claims, the less that will remain for the other. It is not uncommon for negotiations to include distributive and integrative characteristics. One key skill for successful negotiators is to correctly identify the nature of the situation.

Steps in Distributive Bargaining

At its core, distributive bargaining involves either the seller or the buyer throwing out the first number (called the *anchoring number*) as a proposal and the other side responding with a counterproposal. The negotiators may then share information about why their number is supported by the "facts" as the negotiators' initial offerings move closer together. If a deal is to be reached, they typically reach agreement on a number that is somewhere between the buyer's and the seller's initial proposals. This is an appropriate process for negotiating in some circumstances: when the time for negotiating is short, when the outcome is not crucial to either party, when the relationship between the negotiators is not harmed by this process, and when the deal leaves no value unclaimed. This is not an exact science, but the more of these conditions that apply, the more likely distributive bargaining does no harm.

Although distributive bargaining has become the default approach used by many negotiators, it is not necessarily the best choice in the majority of circumstances. Imagine you ask your boss for a raise of $4.00 an hour. He counters with a proposal for $2.00 an hour and you both eventually settle on a $3.00 per hour raise. No harm done but value might have been left unclaimed. Why were you seeking the raise? Was it to help pay the costs of tuition for the graduate school you attend in order to move up in your career? What if there was a tuition remission policy at the company about which you were unaware? You both might have been better off by sharing more information during the negotiation and trying to create value rather than to claim value.

A distributive approach encourages game playing by the negotiators; you must start high so that when you meet somewhere in the middle, you still achieve your desired target. Instead of sharing your true target point (see the following for a definition), you give a different number with the idea that some haggling will occur and you will need to come down to a lower number in order to reach agreement. Each party may share information to support his or her proposals but rarely does each fully disclose the reasoning behind his or her choice of a specific target point. What if you were seeking the raise because you found out that your colleague earned more than you earn? If equity was your primary concern, then perhaps your boss could have made sure you knew that your colleague already has his master's degree and that is the reason for his higher salary.

The biggest downside to distributive bargaining is that bargainers may get exactly what they have asked for, yet still not have what they need. This happens because the negotiator makes a demand (also known as *stating a position*) and this demand may not contain information about why the demand is sought. A joke illustrates:

Wife: You really need to stop working so many nights and weekends. I just wish you wouldn't work so much.

Husband: You have been saying this for a while so I have good news to announce: I have told my boss that I won't work any more weekends for the rest of the summer. Instead, I joined a traveling golf league that plays in a different city each weekend. I can't wait to get started! Why do you look so upset? You are getting exactly what you asked for: I am working less.

Steps in Integrative Bargaining

In 1981 Roger Fisher and William Ury wrote a book entitled *Getting to Yes: Negotiating Agreement Without Giving In* and it spent years on the *New York Times* and other best-seller lists. It has been called negotiation's holy book because it has been around a long time, sold millions of copies, and given us rules to live (and negotiate) by. Fisher and Ury promoted a new way to think about and carry out negotiations. Using their prescriptions, one could be a world-class negotiator and still go to bed each night with a clear conscience. The steps in their model have been adapted into many decision-making and problem-solving processes, including most formal mediation programs in Western societies. By understanding the basic steps in the integrative negotiation process (also known as *win-win*), you can greatly improve your negotiation outcomes and also your relationship with your negotiation partners.

Integrative bargaining integrates the needs of both parties into any agreement. Because all negotiators exhibit some level of interdependence, one is most likely to reach an agreement by focusing not only on meeting one's own needs but also by focusing on meeting the needs of those with whom you are negotiating.

The first step to accomplishing this goal is to "separate the people from the problem" (Fisher & Ury, 1981, p. 16). Every negotiation can be broken down into two main categories: substance and relationships. Negotiators are people first—people with egos, desires to save face, and needs to feel treated fairly and respectfully. Negotiators often mistake substantive comments by the other negotiator as personal affronts. A manager may observe, "We are behind on this project." Although it is a factual statement, some employees may take it as an attack on their work ethic or efficiency. Once someone feels they have been treated rudely or unfairly, then the problem grows instead of getting settled. Defensive behaviors lead to counterproductive negotiation tactics. Fisher and Ury recommend dealing with the people problem explicitly and separately from the substantive problem. That means negotiators need to make statements to the other side that address relationship and psychological needs rather than sticking only to the substantive issues.

To address the people problems, negotiators need to keep three categories in mind: "perceptions, emotion, and communication" (Fisher & Ury, 1981, p. 22). It is important to understand how the other negotiators view the problem and any potential solutions. Often, it is the way one views or perceives a problem that causes obstacles to settlement more than any possible objective reading of the facts. "Facts, even when well established, do nothing to solve the problem" (Fisher & Ury, 1981, p. 22). It may be helpful during the negotiation to have each negotiator summarize the other's perspective. This reflection does not mean the two sides have reached one shared understanding of the problem or possible solution, only that they have both heard and registered each other's viewpoints. This perspective taking can be an important step in putting together the pieces of the negotiation puzzle and in building the rapport necessary to build and sustain agreements.

For example, in a dispute between two employees who share an office space, one might consider the other rude for never inquiring into her health or her family's well-being. The other employee might consider herself polite for not prying into the personal life of her workmate. Learning about the other's perspective can be a prerequisite for problem solving.

If you believe the other negotiator has a negative impression of you, then it may be worth trying to behave in a way contrary to expectations. For example, if you are perceived as stubborn, you could offer an unexpected concession. If you are considered too loud or domineering, you might let them speak first and without interruption. Ask for their ideas, thoughts, and input. Behaving in ways contrary to their perceptions may help them realize their perceptions could be inaccurate.

If an individual or group is likely to be strongly affected by a decision you make or a decision that results from your negotiation, be sure to include that person or group in the discussions. If people perceive that a decision is being forced on them, then they will be less inclined to support and implement it (read more about procedural justice in Chapter Four). If parties perceive a fair process, they may be more tolerant of an unattractive outcome.

Difficult negotiations are emotionally challenging. They make us feel worried, fearful, anxious, angry, or even guilty. Don't ignore these emotional reactions in negotiations. Acknowledge the difficulty of the situation and explain how you're feeling. Inquire about how others feel. Normalize and legitimize these feelings — if these negotiations were easy, they would have been resolved already, right? Allow negotiators to let off steam through the use of breaks and by allowing people to vent and talk about their concerns. If a negotiator yells or gets angry, consider sitting patiently and quietly — urge her to say all she needs to say. Do not get defensive or shut down the expression of emotions. Be sure to include relationship-building functions in the negotiations: eat together, recreate together, and share family photos. If you take part in an ongoing or long-term negotiation, develop rituals and social exchanges that help keep the group bonded together over time, such as by celebrating birthdays and milestones together. These experiences remind negotiators they have a lot in common, even if they disagree or struggle with the negotiations. They build trust and rapport that will be necessary for any eventual agreement.

Communication problems can make the negotiations turn personal and lead to attacks on the people instead of the problem. Be sure to avoid statements that indicate the other side is to blame for the problem. Do not personalize the problem in that way. Instead, try adopting this worldview: you and I will work together as a team against the problem. Instead of trying to win at the other's expense or attacking the other person for his or her view of the problem and solution, seek to work together to solve the problem and reach agreement. Talk about how you feel, what you need, and how you see the problem. Even if you feel the other person is 100 percent to blame for the problem, you might consider using a future-focused statement designed to invite the other person to work with you toward a solution, such as "regardless of how we got here, let's talk about how we can fix this problem going forward."

Now that you know how to separate the people from the problem, let's talk about the next step in the integrative negotiation process, focusing on "interests, not positions" (Fisher & Ury, 1981, p. 40). The concept of interests versus positions is the core contribution of *Getting to Yes*. Whereas distributive bargaining focuses almost exclusively on the trading and amending of bargaining positions, integrative bargaining looks at the interests that underlie positions. Think of **positions** as demands: *I demand a raise! Not in my backyard! Turn down your music!* Instead, **interests** tell us of the needs that underlie the positions: "I want to feel that my contribution to this business is fully recognized," "I am concerned for the safety of my children if the dump is built too close to our subdivision," and "I need to be at work very early and cannot sleep with the noise" (see Table 3.1). Positions, by definition, have only one way to be met: you can grant the raise, avoid placing the dump in her backyard, and turn down the music. Positions lead to win-lose outcomes in which one party's gain comes at the other party's expense. By contrast, interests can be met in multiple ways. There are many ways to help other parties meet their need to feel respected, safe, or rested. Understanding the underlying interests of each party allows the negotiation to move away from a zero-sum discussion to one in which all parties leave the negotiation better off than they would be through the use of distributive bargaining techniques.

Although interests give negotiators much more to work with, people generally begin their negotiations with positional statements, out of habit if not for another reason. Before you enter into a planned negotiation, take some time to outline your own positions and interests as well as those you might predict for the other negotiators. Once the negotiation starts, be sure to get a full understanding of the other negotiators' interests. If they state or restate their positions, ask them why or how they arrived at that position. What need does that position meet for them? How did they arrive at that number or demand? Tell them you want to better understand their needs and goals for the meeting to increase chances for reaching an agreement that works for everyone.

The best managers and negotiators inquire about the needs and interests of their employees, customers, and negotiation partners. By seeking to meet those needs it may be possible to get one's own needs met as well. Interests focus the negotiators on working together to solve problems rather than assuming an adversarial stance.

The third step is to "generate options for mutual gain" (Fisher & Ury, 1981, p. 56). This can be done through the process of brainstorming. When faced with conflicts or problems, people tend to leap to diagnosing the causes and solution for a problem before they have fully heard the other perspectives and ideas. We also tend to search for a single solution or assume a competitive rather than creative problem-solving posture. Sometimes people feel like a problem affects

Table 3.1
Positions Versus Interests

	Positions	Interests
What the statement type communicates	Demands	Needs
Options for resolution	Only one way to meet a position	Many ways to meet an interest
Statement's effect on negotiation	Positions often terminate negotiations.	Interests usually open up discussion.
Examples:	"I demand a raise!"	"I want to feel that my contribution to this business is fully recognized."
	"Not in my backyard!"	"I am concerned for the safety of my children if the dump is built too close to our subdivision."
	"Turn down your music!"	"I need to be at work very early and cannot sleep with the noise."

them but it is someone else's job to solve. This kind of conflict avoidance can mean negative outcomes for organizations and individual careers.

After thoroughly brainstorming as many solutions as possible to a problem, there are multiple paths forward. Sometimes the best solution will be clear to everyone at the end of the brainstorming session. If not, it may be time to create a package of trade-offs or work together to expand available resources.

The last step is to generate and use objective criteria by which to evaluate settlement terms whenever possible. For example, if you are engaged in salary negotiations, it will be helpful to benchmark salaries for similar positions at similar or competing organizations or for the same position within your organization. If you are selling a house or business, you get an appraisal. This information provides some objective measure of the value of that house or business. Your objective criteria may include reference to precedent, professional standards, market values, past practice, equity, or other criteria deemed appropriate by the negotiators (Fisher &

Ury, 1981). The goal is to ensure that agreements are not arbitrary but are fair to all parties and supported by objective criteria whenever possible.

In modern organizations, how you treat people matters. Your choice of negotiation strategy will affect your reputation as a manager, as a neighbor, as a citizen, and as a person. Although integrative bargaining may be overkill at the local farmer's market, it will likely be the most useful strategy to use in negotiations where relationships matter. Even when you are unlikely to see your counterpart again, integrative negotiation can achieve agreement when distributive bargaining often fails. Mastering the techniques of win-win negotiating will help you to solve problems and advance in your career.

NEGOTIATION TERMS AND CONCEPTS

Whether you are entering into a distributive or integrative negotiation, the following terms and concepts are helpful to understand negotiation and maximize your success in negotiations.

Anchoring Number

The anchoring number is the first proposal made during the negotiation. It tends to create a cognitive anchor against which all subsequent offers are judged. As long as there is enough information on which to create an anchoring number, the negotiator who makes the first offer has the advantage of creating the frame or boundary in which the negotiation will occur. For example, if I am the seller, I may make a wildly high initial offer. By doing so, any eventual agreed-on amount will then seem like a significant concession on my part. However, if I am negotiating in an unfamiliar environment or have little information on which to make an initial offer, it may be best to allow the other side to throw out the anchoring number. If the other side gives the anchoring number, it may be helpful to remind all parties in the negotiation that this number need not become the focus around which the negotiations occur, especially once information is shared that makes it possible to evaluate the fairness or feasibility of that first proposal.

When negotiators throw out an anchoring number that is purposefully overstated, they are using a distributive bargaining technique. Being able to spot this strategy will enable the integrative bargainer to label it as such and then engage in a discussion about the merits of integrative bargaining over distributive bargaining in most situations. If the negotiation continues in the distributive vein, then understanding this and the subsequently examined techniques will help maximize one's success within that bargaining style.

Asking Price

The **asking price** (also called *initial offer*) is the first proposal shared by each party in the negotiation. Each negotiator has an initial offer or asking price but the negotiation as a whole only has one anchoring number. Deciding on one's asking price can be tricky. Start too high and you may offend or alienate the other negotiator. If your initial offer is so high that the other side quickly reaches the conclusion that no deal will be made, then he or she may walk away prematurely. Start too low and you end up a "sucker," having received less value than you might have won with a higher initial offer. Whenever possible, do your homework in advance of the negotiation so as to craft an initial offer that is benchmarked appropriately. What is the going price in the marketplace? What has the buyer or seller paid before to others? How does the quality of your good or service compare to that of your competition? What can you offer to sweeten the deal? For example, perhaps you can deliver the item faster for a higher price. It is difficult to choose an appropriate initial offer or asking price without this kind of information. In the absence of this information, you run the risk that your initial offer will be inefficiently high or low, resulting in an increased chance of impasse (i.e., failure to reach an agreement) or you may simply strike a poor bargain.

Target Point

A **target point** is the negotiator's end goal or preferred outcome for the negotiation. Depending on the strategies used by negotiators, they may or may not directly share this information. One's target point may take into account many factors: the cost of the item under negotiation plus some reasonable profit margin; elements of supply and demand, such as the relative scarcity of the item; the desire to continue a long and profitable relationship with one's bargaining partner so as to maximize long-term rather than only short-term profits; and so on. As information is shared during the negotiation, one's target point may change. Occasionally a negotiation will exceed negotiators' expectations and they are able to reach a settlement point that surpasses their target. This outcome generally means that the original target point was based on incomplete information about the other side's circumstances or the nature of the good or service at stake in the negotiation.

Resistance Point

If the target point is the goal, the **resistance point** is the bottom line. For example, if a merchant purchases his stock wholesale at a cost of $5.00 per unit, his resistance point generally will be somewhere above $5.00. The resistance point is the smallest amount he will settle for and is sometimes referred to as the *reservation price* (Lewicki, Barry, & Saunders, 2010).

The **settlement range**, or the zone of agreement, is the space between the two resistance points. For example, the buyer's initial offer is $5,000 and her resistance point is $8,000 and the seller's initial offer is $9,000 but his resistance point is $6,000, so the settlement range will be between $6,000 and $8,000. Barring communication problems or emotionally based obstacles to settlement, these negotiators can be predicted to strike a deal between the settlement range of $6,000 to $8,000. This zone may change during the negotiation itself, especially if the parties engage in integrative bargaining, which may result in the creation of value or sharing of information that allows for a more efficient solution to become apparent to all (see Figure 3.1).

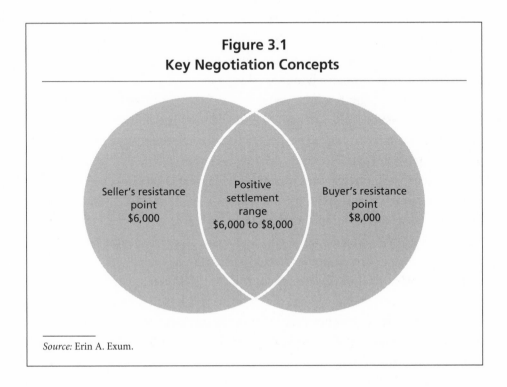

Figure 3.1
Key Negotiation Concepts

Seller's resistance point $6,000

Positive settlement range $6,000 to $8,000

Buyer's resistance point $8,000

Source: Erin A. Exum.

KEY NEGOTIATION CONCEPTS

A negative settlement range is one in which there is no overlap between the lowest amount the seller is willing to take and the highest amount the buyer is willing to pay. Unless something changes the mind of the buyer or seller, then no agreement will be reached. A positive settlement range indicates overlap between the acceptable outcomes for the buyer and the seller. Although one likely comes into a negotiation with target and resistance points in mind, in most negotiations these are somewhat fluid as information is shared and a greater understanding is reached by all parties as to the nature of what is possible and mutually advantageous.

The **settlement point** is the spot within the settlement range at which the negotiators reach agreement on settlement terms. The goal in distributive bargaining is to reach an agreement that is as close to the other side's resistance point as possible.

Transaction Costs

Every negotiation entails **transaction costs**, which include the time, energy, and money necessary to facilitate the negotiation and the deal itself. For example, every hour that the people on the union's negotiation team are tied up in contract discussions is an hour they are not working on the factory floor. In fact, for negotiations with relatively minor consequences, the transaction costs may exceed the value of the resource under discussion. It is therefore important to minimize transaction costs when possible and correctly identify those situations in which the transaction costs make negotiation a losing proposition. For example, when holding a long staff meeting, the manager may decide not to ask whether those present prefer pizza or sandwiches for lunch. If a large number of employees are present for the meeting, the negotiations over lunch will simply take too long, making an executive decision superior to a negotiation.

Hiring attorneys, financial advisors, or other experts increases the negotiation's transaction costs. When hiring experts to assist with any negotiation, each party must decide whether the added transaction costs of doing so will be outweighed by the better outcome assumed to occur as a result of this expert help. This decision is a bit of a gamble because one cannot know the outcome of the negotiation until it is over. Yet engaging in complicated negotiations without legal or financial expertise can also be costly.

Contingent Agreements

Sometimes the future is uncertain. Each negotiator may have a different prediction for the future. For example, Elise thought the price of flour was unlikely to rise beyond x but the farmer disagreed. It can be difficult to reach an agreement when the future is uncertain and the agreement binds one or more of the negotiators to a promise that may, in fact, become impossible to execute. In this type of situation, it can be helpful to create **contingent agreements**. These agreements tend to take this type of format: if x happens by (insert date), then we both agree to do y. If x does not happen by this date, then we agree instead to do z. This allows both parties to react to changing future circumstances without needing to renegotiate the contract.

A good example of a contingent agreement comes from the nonprofit field. Humanitarian relief organizations and governments must plan for possible natural disasters such as floods, droughts, earthquakes, tornadoes, wildfires, and so on. Yet, with luck, these disasters may not materialize. Disaster relief organizations often hire and train local employees and volunteers on a contingency basis. For example, an employee's contract might state something like this: "Mary Jones agrees to be available to work up to sixty consecutive days per year with two days of notice. If called on to work, Mary Jones will receive $500/day. If not called on to work within any calendar year, Mary Jones will receive $3,000." Contingent agreements, such as this, are helpful when the future is uncertain and the transaction costs make frequent renegotiation undesirable.

BATNA is an acronym that stands for *best alternative to a negotiated agreement*. Sometimes one or more negotiators realize they can better meet their goals by entering into negotiations with a different business partner or by pursing their end goal without the benefit of the negotiation. A BATNA is not a fallback offer. A **fallback offer** is the offer made once the initial offer is rejected. It is somewhere between the initial offer and the resistance point, and it may lead to an agreement. Instead, a BATNA is something negotiators can do unilaterally to accomplish their goals better than the current negotiation. A strong BATNA gives the negotiator a strong bargaining position. For example, you want to ask your boss for a raise. You already have a job offer from a competing organization. If your boss is unable or unwilling to come close to the other offer, then your BATNA is to change organizations. Your chances of achieving your target point are now higher than if you went into these salary negotiations with a weak or nonexistent BATNA.

When negotiations concern specific disputes, the BATNA may be to go public with the dispute or to go to court. These are actions that any side can do on its own, without the permission of the other side. A BATNA can be strong or weak. A strong BATNA gives the negotiator the ability to walk away from a negotiation without assuming large risks—another, better deal can be found elsewhere. Perhaps there is another supplier to whom you can turn or maybe you have stockpiled your supplies and can go a long period of time without needing to reach a deal. Prior to entering into a planned negotiation, take some time to think through your alternatives to an agreement. What can or will you do if the negotiations result in impasse or the other side refuses to enter into a negotiation? You will likely have a list of alternatives, perhaps including to do nothing. The key is to be clear in your mind about your *best* alternative to reaching agreement. All potential offers will be weighed against this benchmark. When your BATNA exceeds the best offer from the other side, then it is time to end the negotiation with no agreement. Whenever possible, make your BATNA stronger. A weak BATNA significantly reduces your chances of attaining your preferred outcome (Magee, Galinsky, & Gruenfeld, 2007).

IMPASSE AND OBSTACLES TO SETTLEMENT

Impasse is reached when the parties are unable to strike an agreement that is superior to their BATNAs so they terminate the negotiations without agreement. Sometimes an impasse is temporary and lasts only until the obstacles to settlement are removed. Impasses occur for various reasons, including those cases in which no settlement range exists or overlap exists (e.g., party A cannot pay more than $7,000 but party B cannot sell for less than $8,000). Sometimes an impasse results from communication problems, insufficient time to negotiate, or counterproductive psychological barriers such as anger or frustration. In these cases it is important to go back to the steps of the integrative bargaining process to ensure that all of the interests have been examined and all possible solutions have been brainstormed. When you get stuck, go back to these two earlier phases to see if a step was missed or if some important information was missed. If the barriers to settlement seem to arise from differences in communication style, aggressive behaviors, or personality differences, consider bringing in a mediator (i.e., a neutral third party to assist with the negotiations). When dealing with a hardnosed bargainer or a difficult personality, the important thing to remember is to focus on what *you* do and say in the negotiation rather than trying to control the other person.

Personal Attacks or Offensive Behavior

What if the other negotiator uses language you find offensive or speaks to you in a disrespectful way? Although these behaviors may seem uncommon, they can happen when customers or clients feel mistreated or have lost control of their tempers. It happens most frequently in dysfunctional workplace cultures but it can happen even in a relatively positive workplace climate. The first step to addressing inappropriate expressions of anger, frustration, hostility, contempt, and so on is to try to diagnose the root cause (refer back to the materials in Chapter One). If it seems like a large amount of anger in a small situation, then it is possible the negotiator is actually angry about something else but the outlet for this anger has become the present negotiation. Alternatively, the negotiator's view of the problem may be quite different, resulting in a belief that the problem is very serious. Use your active listening skills (see Chapter Four) to better understand how the other negotiator perceives the problem, its origins, and any possible solutions. Let him or her know you are there to really listen and understand concerns, even if the negotiator perceives that you are the root of the problem (that is to say, he or she received bad customer service or a poor performance review and so on).

The key is to avoid letting the other negotiator's anger or outburst trigger a fight or flight response in you. If someone yells at you, do not yell back. If a negotiator uses bad language, do not respond in kind. Remember, you control only what *you* think, say, and do. When someone verbally attacks you, a counterattack may be understandable but it is indeed not necessary. If the goal is to solve the problem, let the individual vent for a few minutes. Invite him or her to share criticism and make specific suggestions for improvement. If the negotiator is unable to think about constructive solutions because of his anger, consider suggesting a short cooling off period. The following are examples of some verbal exchanges you might hear in an organizational setting.

With customers or clients:

Customer: This is the worst rip-off ever! I paid good money and the item I received is worthless. I want my money back!

Manager:	I am so sorry to hear that you had problems with our product. Can you tell me more specifically what the problem was? I will do all I can to fix the problem with you.

In work teams:

Manager:	I told you I needed that report last week! Was I unclear?! What do I need to do around here to see that the work gets done on time?!
Employee:	I agree, this situation can't continue. I want to meet deadlines and do good work. Can we talk through some changes that might help?

In a more formal negotiation, it can be helpful to agree on ground rules in advance to avoid behaviors that might alienate or anger some of the negotiators. If ground rules cannot be made in advance, it is still possible to discuss and agree on ground rules once the discussion has begun. This can seem awkward or preachy. It may help to normalize this—act like ground rules are an important part of all the problem-solving discussions that occur with your organization. Ask for all parties to contribute ideas to the ground rules. Post them on the wall or on a piece of paper in the center of the table for everyone to see. Acknowledge that these decisions and negotiations can be difficult and that everyone's patience may be strained at some point in the discussions. Normalizing these feelings can help parties to understand what to expect and what is expected of them.

"Recast an attack on you as an attack on the problem" (Fisher & Ury, 1981, p. 109). Let upset individuals know you understand they have been disappointed by your product, service, staff member, and so on. Invite them to work with you to solve the problem. Do not fall back on defending yourself or launching a counterattack. Although such tactics may feel good in the short term, they will not help solve the underlying problem and they will likely escalate the situation further up the chain of command. One of the best compliments a person can give to your organization is to say that when a problem arose, it was handled professionally, efficiently, and fairly.

Hardnosed Negotiator

Public employees union representative:	We won't settle for less than a 4 percent raise and one additional vacation day!

Agency negotiator:	Can you tell me more about how you arrived at that proposal? Or could you tell me what need that proposal will meet for you?
Public employees union representative:	It will meet my need for a 4 percent raise!!

What if you are attempting to hold an interest-based negotiation but your counterpart insists on reiterating positions rather than addressing the needs and interests that underlie his position? In *Getting to Yes*, Fisher and Ury (1981) discuss the concept of "negotiation jujitsu" (p. 108). Like the martial art, negotiation jujitsu does not meet an attack with a counterattack. Using power against power may not be as successful as stepping back or aside. When hardnosed positional negotiators reiterate their position, take it as one possible option. Let the other side know that their position is indeed one possible outcome but that you would also like to examine all other possible options before reaching an agreement. Ask questions to better understand how their position meets their needs. "Could you tell me how this amount will be used?" or "Would $25,000 completely solve the problem or would an amount higher or lower perhaps be appropriate?"

Rather than defending your position against theirs, take some time to invite criticism and feedback about your position: "I understand that our offer of a 1 percent raise is not satisfactory for your group. Please tell me more about why this doesn't meet your needs." By inviting criticism, you avoid triggering the fight or flight response and signal that you truly want to understand the other side's needs. Sometimes the why question can trigger defensive responses. If this seems likely, consider using other open-ended questions, such as "*What* raise were you seeking and *how* does that number meet your needs?"

Be sure to frame your comments as questions rather than statements. "If we agreed to the 4 percent raise and added a vacation day, would that be more similar to what our competitors pay? Can you tell me your thoughts about how it would affect our competitiveness as a company?" It is easier to attack a statement than a question. Questions invite analysis and discussion, whereas statements can seem more adversarial. Do not be afraid of silence. If you ask a difficult question, the other side may pause or seem unwilling to answer. Silence can be a useful tool when posing difficult questions (Fisher & Ury, 1981). Try to use questions to turn hardnosed bargainers away from their positional tactics.

The Spotlight Is Too Bright

When a negotiation occurs in a public space, especially when the media is present, negotiators tend to resort to more confrontational behaviors, including posturing and positional statements. These are intended as much or more for their constituents as for their negotiation partners. This is why most diplomatic negotiations have formal sessions in which all parties state their positions and ask general questions in the presence of the press or other observers. The real work of diplomats occurs behind closed doors, away from the prying eyes of the public. Keep this in mind when planning public meetings and decision-making processes. Although some sunshine laws (see Chapter Eleven) require meetings to occur in public, and for good reason, it is important to understand that the behaviors of negotiators, as well as their willingness to speak frankly, differ with the presence of an audience.

Emotional Investment

When someone sells a used car, the seller typically overestimates its value. The buyer will typically underestimate its value. Cognitive biases standing in the way of an objective assessment of the car's value on both sides. To make matters worse, suppose the buyer and seller had a long-standing grudge against one another—perhaps they fought for a girl's attention back in their school days. They may decide to call off the deal altogether. Then, each would be worse off, not because a deal was against their best interests but because their emotions worked to sabotage a deal that could have benefitted them both. That is why Fisher and Ury (1981) strongly recommend "separating the people from the problem" (p. 17) whenever possible. Be careful when negotiating with someone who raises an emotional response in you, whether positive or negative. Strong emotions will cloud judgment, making it difficult to objectively evaluate the other side's proposals.

Related to this issue is the way in which we as negotiators show or hide our desire to reach an agreement with the other party. Even if you are desperate to get the job, acting desperate at the interview may result in a lower rate of pay once the job is secured. When selling a used car, the seller need not come down in price by much if the buyer makes it clear he or she loves the car and has had difficulty finding one like it. Lesson: when negotiating in a distributive bargaining situation, it is important to know when to keep your "poker face." (This is a reference to a card game in which bluffing is a key strategy. When the player has been dealt a good hand of cards, it can be important to keep this to one's self if the others are to be enticed to place bets.)

Time Pressure

"Act fast, only two left at this price!" Creating the appearance of a crisis is one of the oldest tricks in the book. When your negotiation partner pressures you to commit and threatens to revoke the offer soon, try to pause for a moment. Evaluate the situation to determine if there is indeed the need for a quick decision. "The higher the other party's estimate of his or her own cost of delay or impasse, the weaker the other party's resistance point will be" (Lewicki, Barry, & Saunders, 2010, p. 41). If there is no urgent need to close the deal, then slow the negotiation down. Let your negotiation partner know that you will take whatever time you need to evaluate the costs and benefits of the proposal. However, you may be tempted to use this strategy yourself—create a false sense of urgency in order to close the deal. Before pursuing this strategy, think about any possible ethical implications, including the impact on any future relationship. This strategy is unlikely to work repeatedly with the same partner.

Absent Decision Maker

Sometimes the people who arrive to participate in the negotiation are not the ones who truly have the authority to reach a deal. This situation is particularly likely in the case of negotiations between government agencies and large businesses. In these cases a mid- or higher-level employee may arrive to represent the agency but in the end it is discovered that the only person with the authority to sign off on a deal is the agency's director. It is unrealistic to believe that the director will attend every negotiation, mediation, or settlement conference in which the agency participates. Therefore, it will be crucial for the person representing the agency to be authorized with a reasonable amount of authority to settle. Typically, organizational leaders will authorize a specific settlement range within which their representative can strike a deal. This works best for distributive bargaining situations. What happens in integrative bargaining situations, during which the participants are able to come up with creative, unanticipated settlement terms? In these situations it is important for the negotiators to be able to reach the ultimate decision maker by phone in order to gain new settlement authority.

If you are attending a negotiation on behalf of your organization, be sure to clarify the limits of your settlement authority in advance of the session. Ensure that your superior(s) will be available by phone during the negotiation in case you need to request different or additional settlement authority. However, if your negotiating partner sends a representative to negotiate on his behalf, be sure to inquire about that person's settlement authority and procedures to secure additional or different settlement authority as needed. Otherwise, you may spend hours in a tough negotiation only to discover the person with whom you have been negotiating lacks the ability to commit to any agreements.

Situations wherein parties send a representative to negotiate on their behalf tend to cause increased use of two particular negotiation strategies. If your negotiation partner has sent a representative in his or her stead, be on the lookout for stalling and good cop–bad cop. First, the negotiator may have sent the delegate purely as a stalling tactic—as a last resort the representative can claim to need more time to check with his or her boss. If you believe the other side has incentives to stall for time, you may want to insist that the decision maker participate directly. Second, the representative can play good cop–bad cop in order to manipulate concessions from other negotiators. The representative might say, "I think your offer is reasonable, but I have to sell it to my boss, and he already told me that I would not have the authority to settle at that amount." Be cautious when negotiating with representatives in the absence of the authoritative decision maker to ensure the absence is not used strategically.

BRING IN A THIRD PARTY

If the negotiations are not making progress or if the negotiators have become too heated to carry on a productive and civil negotiation on their own, it may be time to bring in a third party. This third party can be a neutral person, such as a mediator, facilitator, ombudsman, or arbitrator. If the negotiation is internal to the organization, rather than with a customer or client, then the neutral may be a higher-up manager, someone from HR, or someone from elsewhere in the organization. This person needs to be someone whom each negotiator trusts as well as someone who is able to maintain his or her temper, listen well, and help the parties resolve the problem productively and maintain or enhance their working relationships. As Chapter Four shows, there are many different types of problem-solving processes on which you may wish to draw when the negotiators are unable to reach agreements on their own.

NEGOTIATIONS TO AVOID

There are numerous reasons why today may not be the right time to negotiate. First, what if you have not had time to prepare for the negotiation? If so, it may be better to postpone if possible. Sometimes you may wish to put off a negotiation because stalling for time only improves your strength in the situation by raising the value of what you bring to the table or creating an urgent need on the other's side. If you are feeling apathetic to the potential outcome of an issue, then the level of impact may simply be too small to warrant the time and energy you would spend on negotiation. When you are rushed, take a step back from the abyss. Don't forget that one common strategy in the negotiation playbook is to create an artificial deadline or perceived state of urgency: "If you don't scoop up this deal right now, somebody else will," says the used car salesman.

Some situations are no-win situations that should be avoided. For example, when the power dynamics between the parties are highly asymmetric and you are on the low end, your chances of achieving your goals may be too low to make it worthwhile to engage in the negotiation. In other instances, that little voice inside you tells you something about this negotiation or this negotiation partner is not quite right. If a negotiation's outcome could harm parties who are not present or if your negotiation partner is someone you cannot trust to fulfill her end of the bargain, then forgoing the negotiation may be your best bet. A manager's reputation takes years to build and only minutes to be destroyed.

TRUST BUILDING AND TRUST REPAIR IN NEGOTIATIONS

Friedlander (1970) determined that initial group trust is more predictive of later group success than is initial group effectiveness, showing that trust has important implications for predicting how well teams may work together. The same can be said for negotiators. Taking steps to build up trust is important so that negotiations proceed more smoothly, and when disagreements arise, they are handled more collaboratively. Hempel, Zhang, and Tjosvold (2009) argue that conflicting viewpoints are inevitably present in work teams and certainly in negotiations. However, as with conflict itself, differing views need not lead to reduced levels of trust. It is the management of those differences that result in either higher or lower levels of trust among teams and negotiators.

One thing negotiators can do to build trust is to share information. Sharing information is a sign of trust and also works to build additional trust between negotiators. Moye and Langfred (2004) investigated the role information sharing has in group conflict and success. The authors write that prior research indicates information sharing may increase group efficiency and improve decision making. Sharing information works to build trust and relationships, which help negotiators reach and implement sound agreements.

There are two main types of trust: identity-based trust and calculus-based trust. The best manager negotiators understand how and when to use each type of trust and related trust-building measures (Lewicki, 2006). Identity-based trust (IBT) comes from the strength of the relationship between the parties or through trust in shared social networks. When negotiators have strong IBT, they follow agreements because they do not want to let each other down. They know and trust each other because of their past relationship or because they are tied together in a web of relationships with others. For example, you ask your brother, a plumber, to fix your best friend's kitchen pipes. Your friend knows that the plumber will do a good job and will not overcharge her because he is her friend's brother.

Likewise, two police officers who have worked well together as a team for a decade are likely to trust one another because they have built up trust from previous shared experiences. Additionally, reputations are important to IBT. A negotiator with a reputation for fairness is more likely to have your trust than one with the opposite reputation.

How do you use identity-based trust to improve your negotiations? See what you can learn about the negotiator or collaborator before the negotiations or collaborations begin. What is the strength of his or her reputation? Spend some time getting to know your negotiation partner. Look for any common friends or acquaintances you may have who can share information about each of you to the other or to whom you can go if the negotiation runs into problems. Having a mutual acquaintance who can put in a good word about you or help act as an intermediary may be important in the future. Don't get right down to business. First, go out to lunch or spend time getting to know each other. In work teams, it is crucial not only to build rapport through shared social experiences during the early phases of the collaboration but also intermittently throughout the partnership (for more on this see Lencioni, 2002). Some negotiators may balk that this is nonwork time but if you begin to see it as an essential part of the negotiation process, your negotiations will achieve better results. Additionally, if you run into problems during the implementation of the agreement, you will have developed a relationship on which you can draw to address these unexpected problems. Once you get to know the other person well, you are less likely to fall prey to negative cognitive biases, such as attribution errors, that make negotiations difficult.

What if there has been a breach of trust and the relationship has been harmed by the breach? In these cases you have two options: rely on calculus-based trust (CBT) or take steps to rebuild the relationship, thereby increasing IBT. Repairing a breach of trust will likely require frank discussions between the parties so that each is aware of the other's concerns and perceptions. If one of the negotiators admits intentionally breaching trust, apologizes, and is willing to take affirmative steps to regain trust, then there is a chance of restoring IBT. If the negotiators view the situation quite differently or fail to understand why the other feels harmed by the behavior, it can be helpful to ask a neutral third party to assist with these discussions. This assistance can come from an ombudsman, a higher-level manager, a professional coach, or even a counselor. In the end, if the IBT is not restored, it is likely that any agreements between the parties will need to rely on CBT.

With CBT the parties can be trusted to abide by their agreements because the incentives for doing so are written into the agreement itself. For example, imagine a business-to-business dispute between a hospital and a vendor of medical supplies. In the past, the vendor has not met contracted delivery dates, causing significant shortages for the hospital. The hospital did not trust the vendor to meet future delivery dates based on their poor performance record, resulting in a deteriorating relationship between the two organizations and their managers. As part of their contract renegotiations, the vendor agreed that delivery of any late supplies would mean that the supplies would be free. After six months of on-time performance, the sanction for late delivery would become a 25 percent penalty rather than free supplies. Now, the hospital is confident the supplies will arrive on time and is therefore willing to continue to work with this vendor. For CBT to work, the penalty has to be high enough to motivate each negotiator and the certainty of the penalty's enforcement must be clear to all.

CONCLUSION

Managers negotiate every day, either formally or informally. Mastering the concepts and skills of negotiation will ensure the most fruitful outcome possible. Skilled, interest-based negotiation not only leads to better outcomes, but it also generally feels better because the process respects the needs of all participants and does not require misleading others to achieve one's preferred outcome. Understanding the key terms and concepts in distributive bargaining remains important because this type of negotiation remains common, like it or not. Negotiation skills will serve you well at work and also in your civic and personal lives. Whether you are planning your wedding, buying produce at your local farmer's market, or deciding where to go on your next family vacation, there is no shortage of opportunities to practice these skills. Every negotiation presents you with an opportunity to enhance your relationships with others and achieve your substantive objectives.

ELISE AND MAIN STREET BAKERIES

Elise met with Jacob, the organic wheat farmer. They began their meeting over breakfast and a walking tour of his farm. It turns out that Jacob knows a few other farmers who supply goods to Elise's company and that is how he heard about this opportunity.

Last year the price for a bushel of organic wheat was about $9.00 but this year it has jumped to almost $11.00 per bushel. With such huge fluctuations it has become difficult to maintain stability in the prices charged to customers. Elise prepared for this meeting by thinking about the maximum amount she would pay for a one-year contract ($10.75) but she hoped to strike a deal closer to $9.75. She decided to make an initial offer of $9.00. Although she would prefer a contract period of three to five years, most small farmers are unable or unwilling to do that considering the volatility in the commodity price for wheat lately. She hates to renegotiate contracts each year because of the time and expense. She has more than one hundred farmers around the country to work with, so if she is not careful, she could spend all her time doing nothing but negotiating contracts. She likes to meet personally with each supplier during the initial contract negotiations. If all goes well, other members of her staff will negotiate contract updates or changes as needed.

When she met with Jacob he had some surprising news. He was willing to enter into a five-year contract, but it would not involve his farm alone. He has banded together with five other organic farms in his region. Each of the farms grows wheat and at least one other crop.

They would agree to a multiyear contract at a fixed price but with some special agreements to help address the risk of unknown future conditions. His initial offer was for fifty thousand bushels per year at $10.25 per bushel as long as the average price of wheat on the market does not rise above $11.00 per bushel. If it rises above that price, then Jacob and his farmers would receive $10.75 per bushel. Additionally, they would supply bell peppers, onions, and broccoli as well through a separate contract. In the end, they settled on a price of $10.00 per bushel in a regular market and $10.50 in an inflated market. By agreeing to a longer-term contract, taking into account some future uncertainty, and adding additional products for sale, they both came out ahead. Now, Elise has fewer individual contracts to negotiate: a real win-win outcome.

KEY TERMS

Asking price
BATNA
Claiming value
Contingent agreements
Creating value
Distributive bargaining
Fallback offer
Integrative bargaining
Interests

Negotiation
Positions
Resistance point
Settlement point
Settlement range
Target point
Transaction costs
Zero sum

SUGGESTED SUPPLEMENTAL READING

Fisher, R., Ury, W., & Patton, B. (2011). *Getting to yes*. New York: Penguin.

Myers, S. L., Rosenberg, M., & Schmitt, E. (2012, January 11). Against odds, path opens up for U.S.-Taliban talks. *New York Times*. (Originally published in 1981.)

DISCUSSION QUESTIONS

1. What was your most difficult negotiation and why? What went well and what didn't?

2. Do you look forward to negotiations or avoid them? How does this align with your conflict styles inventory exercise from Chapter One?

3. Who is the best negotiator you know and what techniques does she use?

EXERCISES

1. Think, pair, share: think back to a negotiation in which you participated or witnessed. Was it a distributive or integrative negotiation? How could you tell? Apply the following terms to an analysis of that negotiation. Was value created, claimed, or both? What were the interests, positions, and BATNAs of each party?

2. Similar to the previous question, review the scenario between Elise and Jacob and label their position, interests, BATNAs, settlement zone, resistance points, and so on.

3. Use a story from the newspaper to analyze a contemporary negotiation, labeling the positions, interests, and BATNAs, and apply other course concepts. Was the negotiation interest based or distributive in nature?

GOAL SETTING

Think of an upcoming negotiation in which you will participate. Prepare for the negotiation by determining your target point and resistance points. What are your interests and what is your BATNA? How will you react to positional bargaining by your counterpart? What can you do to ensure an interest-based negotiation? Carry out your negotiation, then engage in reflective practice. What worked well? What can be improved for future negotiations?

chapter FOUR

The Alternative Dispute Resolution Process Continuum

Learning Objectives

- Demonstrate an understanding of the differences among alternative dispute resolution (ADR) processes such as facilitation, mediation, case evaluation, arbitration, and others.

- Analyze dispute characteristics in order to match the dispute with the appropriate ADR process.

- Demonstrate an understanding of the benefits of active listening and list the behaviors of an active listener.

- Describe the duties, qualifications, and benefits of an organizational ombudsman.

- Describe the purpose and techniques used in performance coaching.

JOHN AT THE BUREAU OF RECLAMATION

Today has been a frustrating day. John spent much of last week interviewing internal applicants for an open position in mid-level management. He feels he chose the best person for the position but there were at least three other applicants who were also well qualified and would likely have done well in the position. Now, one of those applicants (Dorys) has filed a complaint with the EEOC, claiming discrimination based on race and gender. The organizational ombudsman has approached John to see if it is possible to resolve the dispute through a less costly, less adversarial process. John is open to any and all ideas because he has learned that these EEOC complaints can take years to reach resolution. The ombudsman recommends . . . [you will be able to fill in the blank after you read this chapter].

The purpose of this chapter is to introduce a variety of processes used to solve problems without resorting to the courts and the process of adversarial litigation. These processes have the potential to reduce costs and the time necessary to resolve disputes. They also have the potential to address legal and nonlegal disputes and improve rather than worsen the relationships between the parties. After introducing these processes of alternative dispute resolution (ADR) we will undertake a discussion of communication skills and listening, which is especially foundational to conflict prevention and management. Each of the ADR processes covered in this chapter requires the use of communication skills but most especially mediation, coaching, and the work of organizational ombudsmen. For this reason, listening skills are covered in this chapter although arguably they could be included elsewhere in the book and will be frequently referred to in subsequent chapters.

THE ADR CONTINUUM

Figure 4.1 shows the ADR processes commonly used in internal workplace disputes. Typically, these are conflicts between employees holding different

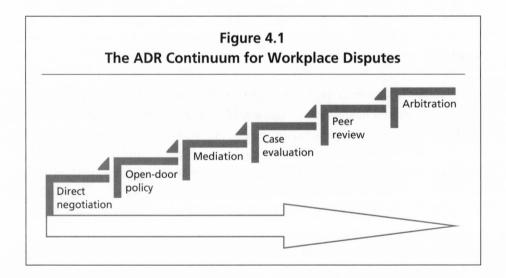

Figure 4.1
The ADR Continuum for Workplace Disputes

positions within the hierarchical structure of an organization, such as between a supervisor and a rank-and-file employee. However, they could also occur between peers. On the continuum pictured in Figure 4.1, the amount of control that a third party has in the outcome increases as the dispute moves up the steps. The first step, direct negotiation, leaves all the control over the outcome of the dispute with the parties themselves. The last step on the continuum, arbitration, takes control of the outcome away from the parties and places it entirely with the arbitrator. Adjudication is not included on this continuum because ADR is meant to be the alternative to going to court but it is similar to arbitration in many ways. The lower the step on the ADR continuum, the fewer expenses will be incurred during the dispute resolution process for most cases.

Direct Negotiations

The first step in resolving nearly any workplace dispute is to encourage direct discussions between the disputants themselves. If an employee has a complaint with her supervisor, then she should first go to that supervisor and attempt to have a productive discussion about her concerns and explore the possibility of an informal resolution to the problem. Employee training can be useful to develop the needed framing and communication skills that will increase the likelihood of a successful interaction when these difficult conversations occur.

Open-Door Policy

An **open-door policy** means that any employee with a problem can go to any manager in the organization for help in solving that problem. Although there is usually a preference to start low on the chain of command and work upward as **needed**, ultimately an open-door policy means the employee can choose which manager to approach for help with a problem.

In our continuum, if the direct negotiation did not succeed, then the next step is to use the open-door policy by speaking to the supervisor of the party involved in the conflict. All supervisory employees should be trained in the basic skills of listening, framing comments constructively, giving and receiving feedback, and so on. An open-door policy can mean anything or nothing, depending on the organization's culture. Some organizations claim to have a policy of open communication, but when employees come to their supervisors with a problem, the supervisor claims to be too busy to listen to them or clearly displays a conflict-avoidant disposition. For an open-door policy to work, all supervisors and managers must be trained and acculturated to take it seriously and gain the skills they need to truly be open to hearing about the needs and concerns of their own employees as well as employees from other units. Employees must believe there will be no reprisals if they seek out the help of a manager to help solve a workplace problem or problems with a customer.

Mediation

If an employee has tried to speak to his or her boss as well as use the open-door policy, yet the problem remains unresolved, the next step on the continuum is mediation. **Mediation** is a process of facilitated negotiation in which the mediator does not act as a judge but instead assists the parties as they strive to engage in a civil, productive conversation about how to resolve the dispute and rebuild relationships if a continuing relationship is to exist. Mediators typically allow each party to state his or her view of the dispute, they draw out information about the parties' needs as they relate to the dispute process and outcome, they jointly engage in the brainstorming for resolution options, and they work with the parties to enforce ground rules and overcome obstacles to settlement. If the parties reach an agreement, the mediator generally drafts a memo outlining the terms of the agreement. Sometimes the agreements reached in mediation deal with nonlegal matters. For example, "the parties agree to speak directly to each other when a problem exists instead of sharing their complaints with others at work." More commonly the terms of the agreement can form the basis of a binding contract that is enforceable in the courts. If the mediation is related to ongoing litigation then the agreement will usually be filed with the court to be reviewed by a judge and, once signed by the judge, it becomes an order of the court. For example, if the employer agrees to reinstate the employee immediately and pay $40,000 in back pay no later than November 1, then these terms form the basis of a binding contract or an out-of-court settlement.

Mediation is a problem-solving process rather than an adversarial process. In court (also known as *adjudication*), each side argues to the judge about why their side is right and the other is wrong. In mediation, the parties work together to try to craft solutions to the problem(s) that brought them to the table. In mediation the parties work *with* one another instead of *against* one another in order to find a solution that is acceptable to both.

There are many approaches to mediation (Moore, 2003). The traditional model of mediation is one in which mediators play a facilitative role; they encourage the parties to come up with the solutions to their dispute themselves, they do not tell them what a judge would likely do in their case or evaluate who has the stronger legal arguments. Mediators guide parties through the mediation process, help them create and enforce ground rules related to civility, and assist them with the drafting of the resulting agreement. In this style of mediation, the mediator truly has no impact on the outcome of the case. Mediators do not pressure the parties to settle when they prefer not to do so, nor do they impose or recommend particular settlement terms. The parties retain full power over the outcome of their dispute.

Evaluative or directive mediation is a style more akin to case evaluation or nonbinding arbitration (to be discussed soon). In this model of mediation, mediators tell parties what a judge or jury might decide in their case. They evaluate the strengths and weaknesses of their arguments or evidence and render nonbinding decisions. The parties use this information to inform their settlement negotiations either inside or outside of mediation. Additionally, mediators work to persuade the parties to step away from unrealistic demands and apply gentle or moderate pressure on them to compromise and reach a resolution. Party satisfaction with this style of mediation tends to be lower than for facilitative mediation, but in some types of cases settlement rates may be higher with this style of mediation, particularly those cases in which the parties will not have an ongoing relationship.

In the transformative model of mediation mediators seek to enhance the parties' abilities to maintain or improve their relationship. Mediators seek to capitalize on moments of empowerment and recognition. They work to empower the parties to come up with their own resolution to the dispute while also striving to enhance their dispute resolution skills through the modeling of those skills. Mediators seek to create and highlight opportunities for the parties to recognize the validity of the others' interests and viewpoints, which allows parties to rehumanize each other in the conflict rather than tear each other down. By recognizing the humanity and inherent value of the other person in the conflict, parties are able to have a genuinely open and productive dialogue, with settlement being only one resulting benefit. Because of the emphasis on relationship building and improved communication skills inherent in the transformative mediation model, the United States Postal Service (USPS) and the United States Transportation Safety Administration (USTSA) have adopted the transformative style of mediation for their workplace mediation programs.

Satisfaction with mediation programs tends to be significantly higher than with other forms of dispute resolution such as arbitration and adjudication. In a study of court-connected general civil case mediation in nine Ohio courts, Wissler (2002) found that "litigants had highly favorable assessments of the mediation session and the mediator" (p. 5). The majority thought that the mediation process was very fair (72 percent) and would recommend mediation (79 percent). In the USPS mediation program, 90 percent of the complainants (the case filers) were either highly or somewhat satisfied with the mediation process, with respondents (the supervisors and managers) having a 93 percent satisfaction rate (Bingham, Kim, & Raines, 2002). Similarly, 91 percent of EEOC complainants say they would participate in mediation again if faced with another complaint and 96 percent of respondents concurred (McDermott, Obar, Jose, & Bowers, 2000). As an interesting side note, those complainants who brought attorneys with them to USPS mediations were significantly less satisfied than those who brought no representative with them (Bingham, Kim, & Raines, 2002). Although various explanations for this exist, the strongest explanation is that parties are allowed to speak for themselves and tell their own story when they come to mediation without a representative. This is an important element of procedural justice (see Chapter Two) that should be part of any dispute resolution process. Being heard during the dispute resolution process is directly tied to participant satisfaction rates in all processes, including arbitration, peer review, and adjudication. In voluntary processes such as mediation, coaching, or working with an ombudsman, when disputants feel their voice is not being heard, they are more likely to terminate their participation in the process or to negotiate less productively (Duffy, 2010).

In addition to mediation using an externally contracted neutral professional, many managers conduct informal managerial mediation as part of their regular duties. **Informal managerial mediation** occurs when a manager acts as an informal mediator between two or more employees, supervisors, or managers in dispute. As informal mediators, managers listen to each party and encourage both to listen to each other. They engage the parties in a problem-solving discussion with the goal of reaching an agreement that meets the needs of all parties and is superior to continuing the dispute via more formal channels.

Case Evaluation

The next step on the continuum is the case evaluation step. **Case evaluation** is a process in which a neutral expert is hired to evaluate the strengths and weaknesses of each side's case and predict for the parties what would happen in court. In this way it is similar to evaluative mediation, except the case evaluator does not then work with the parties to try to negotiate agreement in the case. A case evaluator is usually someone with substantive expertise in the issue of the dispute (such as medical malpractice, personal injury, sexual harassment charges, and so forth) and is usually either a retired judge or a lawyer. Case evaluation can be more costly than mediation because each side must have fully researched its case, prepared documents to support its claims, and because case evaluators charge more than mediators. Case evaluation is a settlement tool because it gives each side more information on which to make or accept an offer of settlement. Sometimes a party is hesitant to take his or her attorney's advice about a settlement offer but hearing the same thing from a neutral expert can help break the impasse and get one or both sides moving toward needed compromise.

Peer Review

Peer review is a process most commonly used within organizational settings to deal with internal employment disputes such as claims of discrimination, wrongful termination, demotions, claims of favoritism or nepotism, or employee appeals of other disciplinary actions. Peer review processes are generally not used to address decisions made through downsizing, workers' compensation claims, unemployment or Social Security benefit claims, health insurance claims or other employee benefits, severance package agreements, or company policies and business decisions related to corporate strategies.

Although many variations exist, at its core the peer review process is designed to allow employees to decide whether their peers are being treated fairly by the organization and its managers or supervisors. One example of the peer review process comes from the United Parcel Service (UPS). In this process, the employee chooses two members of the panel from a roster of employees and the company chooses the third member of the panel. Peer reviewers cannot work in the same unit as the employee under review or be part of that employee's chain of command. Peer reviewers are generally employees from a similar job type but in a different location or department so as to avoid bias. Some organizations may prefer to have a five-member review panel. Any size will work as long as there is an odd number. The larger the panel, the higher the costs because employees are taken away from their primary tasks to sit as panel members.

Peer reviewers are briefly trained about the process prior to engaging in the peer review session. The training teaches them to maintain neutrality, develops their questioning skills, and demonstrates how to review written statements by the parties. During the peer review process, the reviewers ask both sides any questions they may have about the issue or behavior that forms the heart of the complaint. After the process, the panel meets to discuss the session and reach a decision about the panel's findings. The panel then drafts a written finding that is shared with both sides in the case. In some organizations, the findings of the peer review panel are binding on both the company and the employee. In others, the findings are nonbinding on both parties but are advisory. Peer review panels generally can offer the same remedies that would occur through other processes such as arbitration or EEOC adjudication such as reinstatement, back pay, compensation for harm including pain and suffering, and so forth. Although some companies may hesitate to place this much power in the hands of their employees, it is a sign of confidence that the organization believes that it treats its employees fairly and wants to address any potential errors fairly. Organizations with peer review panels have generally found them to be a useful way to communicate a positive organizational culture; peer employees are no more likely to reward shirking or negative behaviors than are managers because these behaviors place a heavy toll on hard-working employees.

Arbitration

Arbitration is an ADR process in which the parties hire a neutral, expert third-party decision maker to act as a private judge in their dispute. Arbitration is commonly used to resolve disputes in unionized workplaces, and arbitration decisions can serve as precedents for future similar cases within a union contract. Arbitration rulings do not set a legal precedent in the courts and cannot generally be appealed there except in cases of arbitrator misconduct. An arbitrator is simply a private judge. So why hire a judge when it costs relatively little to file your case in court? First, the parties can jointly select an arbitrator with subject-matter experience to decide their case. In court, a judge may hear a divorce case, a commercial dispute, and a probate matter all on the same day. By contrast, parties wanting an expert decision maker can hire an arbitrator who has years of experience in labor law, environmental policy, special education, or other fields. Second, parties can get to an arbitrator faster than they can get on the court docket. With court dockets often crowded and slow, arbitrations can usually be scheduled within two weeks if necessary. Third, the outcome of arbitration as well as the arbitration proceedings can be private. Organizations and individual parties often do not want to air their private matters in a public setting for fear of attracting negative attention from the media. Fourth, parties have much more control over the process itself. Parties can agree to a one- or two-day arbitration or longer. They can reach agreements about what kind of evidence will be allowed. For example, will there be live witnesses or only depositions? These decisions can affect the cost of the arbitration and also the strategies of the attorneys and parties involved. Finally, arbitration rulings are generally not subject to an appeal. If a party wins in court, the other side can appeal to a higher court, thereby lengthening the dispute's lifespan and increasing costs and uncertainty. The US Supreme Court has been extremely supportive of mandatory arbitration clauses in consumer and employment contracts. Grounds for appealing an arbitrator's decision are generally limited to claims of arbitrator bias or malpractice, with few exceptions.

The main form of arbitration is binding arbitration, which means that all parties agree to be bound to the arbitrator's findings. A less-common form of arbitration is nonbinding arbitration. This process is exactly the same, except the arbitrator's ruling is advisory rather than binding. Parties use the ruling as a settlement tool to promote further dialogue and negotiation rather than as a final decision. In these ways it is similar to case evaluation except that the arbitrator's decision may include less information about why the arbitrator decided as he or she did.

Adjudication or Court Action

The purpose of ADR is to avoid the costs, delay, and publicity of going through costly litigation that ends in a trial or hearing before a judge. An added benefit of many ADR processes is that they involve collaborative rather than adversarial methods for resolution, which can be helpful if the parties will continue to interact with one another. In order to understand the attractiveness of ADR processes it is helpful to review the costs and benefits of using the courts to solve problems.

Litigation is the process of filing a court case and taking the necessary procedural steps to prepare that case for adjudication. **Adjudication** is the formal process through which a judge renders a decision in a case before the court. Adjudication is the most costly option but remains the best choice when one seeks to set a legal precedent or bring media scrutiny to a serious injustice that affects a large group or the public at large. Employment cases that reach the level of a civil suit, with a judge adjudicating the dispute or a hearing with an administrative law judge adjudicating for the EEOC or other body, are incredibly costly in terms of money, time, and emotional energy for all involved—especially for the employee. Although the company continues on with its mission, the employee in litigation may remain unemployed, may be paying unaffordable sums to an attorney, and is the most harmed by a case that drags on indefinitely. For workers currently employed while they proceed with a discrimination or harassment complaint, tensions can be high, resulting in increased use of sick leave and health benefits, with lower overall productivity. To reiterate, litigation and adjudication are not ADR processes on the continuum because they are the default processes when parties fail to resolve their problems using ADR.

Most employees cannot navigate the litigation process on their own and need an attorney to represent them. Many of these employees are fighting to reverse what they believe to be a wrongful termination, meaning they are unemployed and have no income. This is a bad time to try to hire and pay a lawyer. Howard (1995) reports that the results of a survey of 321 National Employment Lawyers Association members indicate that nineteen out of twenty employees (95 percent) seeking to hire legal counsel cannot get an attorney to take their case. Attorneys know these cases are difficult to prove and they are usually paid on a contingency fee—if they do not win, they do not collect their fee. Therefore, only the most egregious cases, those with lots of evidence to support the complainant's case, are likely to be represented by counsel.

Adjudication may not be a viable option for many employment complaints. For example, the EEOC only brings about .005 percent of the cases filed to trial because discrimination charges are patently difficult to prove at the level required to stand a chance of winning (Hippensteele, 2009). In addition to the difficulty of finding and paying for an attorney, if employees hope to get relief through the EEOC process, they had better be patient. Staff shortages have led to excruciatingly long waits for a case to be processed and eventually dismissed, settled, or adjudicated. The Center for Public Integrity (2008) reports that the EEOC had 2,158 employees at the end of 2007, which means there has been a 22 percent decrease since 2002. The backlog of cases increased 38 percent between 2005 and 2007. The average case takes approximately one year to get through the investigation stage with the EEOC. Illinois Legal Aid (2010) warns charging parties about the likely timeline for litigation:

> Going to court may take at least two and possible five or more years. This is a lengthy and costly process for many people. Even if you win at the end,

the amount may seem like too little, too late. In other words, just because a settlement is not perfect is no reason to think that a court will necessarily provide you any better remedy. (p. 2)

In employment discrimination suits that use the court system instead of the EEOC process, the median case-processing time (filing to disposition) varies between eleven and thirteen months (Kyckelhahn & Cohen, 2008). It is highly likely that the case will be dismissed. The percentage of civil rights cases (employment cases usually fall under this category) dismissed from US district courts in 2006 was 72 percent (Kyckelhahn & Cohen, 2008). Only about one-third of these cases that made it to trial were found in favor of the plaintiff, with 42 percent reversed on appeal (Clermont & Schwab, 2003).

Unfortunately, the media tend to highlight those employment cases in which the employees win at trial much more frequently than those cases in which the employer wins. They also emphasize the large awards that are outliers, leading employees to have false beliefs about their chances of winning and winning big, called the *jackpot syndrome*. In their study of adjudicated cases followed by the media and in which a victor was announced, Nielson and Beim (2004) found that plaintiffs prevailed in 85 percent of the cases. This rate of plaintiff victory is dramatically higher than the actual 32 percent plaintiff win rate in US district court cases during the same time period.

Additionally, the average size of awards covered by the media was thirty times higher than the average actual awards. This skewed representation of case outcomes can cause employees to inflate their chances of winning and the size of any eventual award.

For all of these reasons, adjudication is simply not a good option for most employment cases. Resorting to an ADR process is much more likely to be done *pro se* (without an attorney) and on a shorter time horizon, with less expense for all involved.

Does resorting to an ADR process mean parties are losing their access to justice? This has been a hotly debated question. The good news is that satisfaction with most ADR processes is higher than satisfaction with court processes. With adjudication, even the "winner" often leaves feeling dissatisfied, unheard, and frustrated. Of all the possible ADR processes, mediation has been the most studied, and we can compare the costs of mediation versus court. Mediation is typically faster and less expensive than litigation and court action. For example, according to McEwen (1994), the average time from filing the charge to completing mediation was 67 days as compared to 294 days to complete the traditional EEOC process. At the EEOC, from 1999 through 2008, almost 111,000 mediations were held and over 76,000 charges, or 69 percent, have been successfully resolved (Equal Employment Opportunity Commission, 2009). That means 69 percent of the plaintiffs agreed to some form of settlement in mediation. Considering the 32 percent of plaintiffs receiving a full or partial award, as mentioned previously, minus the one-third or more that most attorneys would require to take on an employment law case, it would seem that most employees have a better chance of receiving relief in mediation compared to proceeding with litigation. Discrimination and harassment charges are simply difficult to prove with the level of evidence needed to win. Yet for 69 percent of the defendants in mediation, settlement was preferable to continuing the long and costly EEOC process, even though they know their chance of winning at the hearing state is quite high.

All of these statistics regarding the EEOC and civil suit process leave one to wonder why employers settle these cases out of court rather than go all the way to trial. We know employers have a much better likelihood of (1) being represented by attorneys, (2) having the case dismissed with no finding of fault against the organization, and (3) employers usually winning if it goes to trial. So why should managers take part in an ADR process aimed at settling the case? Why aren't employers free to treat employees any way they want because employees will have great difficulty mounting, fighting, and winning a legal case against their employer?

First and foremost, organizations that treat their employees well are more likely to flourish in the marketplace — happy, satisfied employees are the first step to having happy, satisfied customers and clients. Second, who wants to work in or even lead an organization where people are treated poorly? At the root of many of the discrimination cases that get dismissed by the EEOC or the civil courts you will find an employee who has been genuinely mistreated. The employee may not be able to prove his or her case or the mistreatment might not be covered by law but that does not mean that the employee was not mistreated. Companies that develop a positive organizational culture designed to prevent avoidable disputes and fairly manage those disputes that do occur will have a more productive workforce with fewer complaints and lower employee turnover. If winning costs tens or even hundreds of thousands of dollars in legal fees, not to mention lost productivity for managers and others needed to testify during the process, then winning is actually losing. "A 1992 study, for instance, found that 21 federal departments paid $139 million simply to process the 6,883 [sexual harassment] complaints filed with the EEOC the previous year" (Larson, 1996). Additionally, many victims of sexual harassment leave their jobs, call in sick, or experience reduced productivity, all of which affect the organization's productivity.

In spite of all this bad news, adjudication is certainly the right process for some disputes. Sometimes a legal precedent needs to be set or the glare of the media spotlight needs to find its way to corporate or individual wrongdoers. For example, *Brown* v. *Board of Education* was the case that led to school desegregation in the United States. If that case had gone to mediation, the parents of the children involved might have reached an agreement they found acceptable for their children but it would not have affected children in other school districts. Additionally, the courts are entrusted with protecting the rights of less-powerful groups in society. Sometimes, individuals or groups need to resort to the courts to have their rights established and protected. It is important to remember, however, that the vast majority of cases decided by the courts do not set any legal precedents. Instead, they involve individuals and organizations who cannot solve problems or collaborate successfully, so they seek the services of a third-party neutral decision maker to do so. The good news is that many ADR services will help parties to meet these needs at a lower cost and allow the limited resources of the courts to be focused on those cases that establish precedents, clarify or establish legal rights, and bring public scrutiny to bear on issue of public interest.

OTHER ADR PROCESSES

The ADR processes just discussed are the most commonly used for employment cases. However, there are other process options that fall off the ADR continuum that merit presentation as well.

Ombudsman (Ombuds)

An **ombudsman (ombuds)** is an organizational conflict management specialist who works to resolve either internal disputes with employees or external disputes with customers, clients, vendors, or business partners. The ombudsman is an organizational conflict management expert who works to help the organization prevent unproductive conflicts and efficiently manage those disputes that do occur. The term *ombudsman* is Swedish in origin and is gender neutral in that language. Unfortunately, when used in English it has a masculine connotation, so some in the United States have shortened it to the term *ombuds*, but they mean the same thing and either one is correct.

Ombudsmen are usually trained by the International Ombudsman Association. Ombudsmen work independently of other departments or functional units within the organization; they are not part of the legal department or HR or departments such as those. Some ombudsmen have investigatory functions but others do not in order to maintain confidentiality. They report directly to the organization's leadership, such as the director, board, or chief executive officer. This independence allows the ombudsman to maintain confidentiality and to avoid pressures that might come from hearing complaints from someone along his or her own chain of command. The ombudsman maintains confidentiality by not revealing the names of those who have used his or her service or any information about the substance of the dispute unless the party has agreed that it can be shared. The ombudsman's job is to see that unnecessary conflict is avoided and that inevitable conflicts are handled fairly and efficiently for all involved.

What do ombudsmen do? They are available to consult with employees (or customers, clients, and vendors) who have a problem or complaint. The ombudsman can provide information to individuals to help them solve their own problems, such as information on policies and procedures. The ombudsman can coach individuals by helping them practice negotiation or communication skills that they will then employ with the hope of resolving the dispute or improving their skills so that future disputes are less frequent or severe. The ombudsman can facilitate conversations between individuals in dispute or informally mediate between conflicting individuals or groups as long as the individuals agree to have the ombudsman do so. The ombudsman can refer parties to external mediators, arbitrators, or other dispute resolution processes that may be useful and appropriate. Ombudsmen can provide training in conflict management or any other specific skill that they deem helpful for the prevention of future disputes. They can design new ADR procedures and policies in conjunction with key stakeholders within and possibly outside of the organization. And crucially, ombudsmen can advise the organization's leadership about suggested changes that might be made in order to better handle the organization's conflicts. Those changes can include mandatory training, performance coaching, new or different policies and procedures, efforts to change organizational culture, and other suggestions. Basically, the ombudsman is the in-house specialist in handling conflict in an appropriate, constructive, and generally less costly manner.

Organizations using the services of an ombudsman often see a decrease in litigation costs, reduced employee turnover, and improved morale. For example, in

2000, Coca-Cola Enterprises reached an out-of-court settlement for $192.5 million dollars to settle claims of employment discrimination. Part of the terms of settlement required the company to create an ombudsman office in the hope that such claims and organizational culture problems could be better prevented and resolved more quickly in the future. Ombudsmen are tasked with helping build and maintain a corporate culture that values ethical, fair treatment of employees, clients, and customers. In addition to Coca-Cola, other large corporations with corporate ombudsmen include UPS, BP America, Dell, General Electric, Shell Oil, New York Life, Mars Inc., Halliburton, Eaton Corporation, American Express, Putnam Investments, Chevron, Bristol-Myers Squibb, Scotiabank, The Hartford, United Technologies, Tyco, National Public Radio (US), The World Bank, most United Nations organizations, and thousands of universities around the world.

Ombudsmen can be promoted and trained from within the organization or brought in from outside. Internally hired ombudsmen have the benefit of already understanding the organization's culture, norms, policies, and mission. The person needs to be someone whom others look up to and respect as well as someone deemed likely to keep confidences and deal fairly with others. Externally hired ombudsmen lack the organizational knowledge held by insiders but they may be seen as more objective and less likely to have preexisting alliances that will get in the way of their new duties. External ombudsmen are more common when an organization has a history of systematic discrimination or trust violations and only an outsider is likely to be an acceptable choice to all involved. Inside hires will need to be sent for special training and credentialing and may need more mentoring to get up to speed in their new role, whereas external ombuds can be hired with this training and experience already on their résumé.

Facilitation

Facilitation is a group process in which either an inside or outside person leads the discussions in a neutral manner in order to assist in promoting an efficient and civil process that stays on track. "A meeting without a facilitator is about as effective as a team trying to have a game without a referee" (Bens, 2005, p. 7). According to Ingrid Bens (2005), a facilitator is someone "who contributes structure and process to interactions so groups are able to function effectively and make high-quality decisions. A helper and enabler whose goal is to support others as they pursue their objectives" (p. 5). Unlike mediation, the goal of a facilitation process may or may not include reaching a written agreement. Instead, many facilitations are designed solely to increase the group's understanding of a problem or improve intergroup relations. Facilitation may be used simply to lead contentious business meetings within an organization or work unit. Many organizations offer facilitation training, including the International Association of Facilitators.

Facilitation of focus groups is one way to gain feedback from external stakeholders regarding the quality of the organization's products or services. Internal focus group facilitation can be used to brainstorm solutions to problems, manage change, and gather information about newly implemented policies and procedures. Facilitation skills, including framing and questioning, are useful tools for all managers to master. Facilitators believe that people have the power to make good, fair decisions for themselves and that two heads (or more) are better than one when making complex decisions. By helping the parties to create an efficient and fair process, facilitators take leadership of the meeting and leave the parties to determine the content of any decision or discussion.

Frequently, managers will be called on to use their facilitation skills in those situations when group input, buy-in, or information sharing are called for. Facilitation is a way to help ensure a high-quality outcome through a fair process that gives everyone a chance to be heard. "Facilitation is a way to provide leadership without taking the reins" (Bens, 2005, p. 7). Sometimes employees or colleagues come to the manager to ask for advice or a decision. There are times when it makes more sense for the manager to facilitate a process through which these people reach their own conclusions rather than to make a decision for them. Manager facilitators might lead organization members when they engage in strategic planning, create goals and objectives, conduct program reviews or assessments, build relationships across or within teams, share feedback for performance improvements, or conduct focus group meetings to gather needed information to improve products or processes.

Facilitators have a number of tools and skills they use repeatedly: staying neutral, managing time, creating and developing an agenda, questioning skillfully, summarizing and paraphrasing, listening actively, convening the right players for each gathering, helping parties to test their assumptions and think creatively, playing devil's advocate when needed, brainstorming, helping parties think analytically, and prioritizing. Some of these specific skills are discussed in the following sections. The best managers and leaders are skilled facilitators who know when to use these skills.

Summary Jury Trials

Summary jury trials (SJTs) are when parties try the case in front of a judge and usually a mock jury. In advance of the mock trial, the attorneys and parties in the case reach agreements related to the types of evidence to be admitted, the length of the trial (usually one to three days), and whether the verdict will be binding or advisory. If the process is advisory, it is used as a settlement tool to enable both sides to see the weaknesses in their case and get the jury's objective perspective on the matter. SJTs are most useful for cases that are complex and would take weeks or months to try in court. This process allows both sides to pick the judge and hear how their case plays out with a jury. If both sides had agreed that the verdict would be binding, the jury is thanked (and generally paid) for their service and dismissed. If the process was advisory, after the jury renders its verdict both sides can pose questions to learn more about which elements of their argument were persuasive or unclear. Sometimes a twelve-person jury is divided into two groups. Each group deliberates separately and renders its own verdict. This method can provide useful information, and it is not uncommon for two juries to render opposite verdicts. Such is the nature of juries and it can be helpful for parties and their attorneys to get a preview of what could happen in court.

Summary jury trials remain an expensive dispute resolution option. Attorneys spend significant resources preparing their case, conducting depositions, selecting the judge, and composing the jury. Expert witnesses are sometimes hired and paid for their work on a case and for their testimony. So why would parties in dispute use a minitrial? Parties often want to avoid the publicity of a real trial and shorten the length of the trial.

Imagine the following scenario. A company accidentally spills chemicals that find their way into the local water supply. Experts disagree as to the level of toxicity of the chemicals that were spilled and disagree about the possible health effects. To make matters worse, the company tried to cover up the spill for forty-eight hours, making the locals suspicious and angry. The effected neighbors are suing via a class action in civil court, claiming wide-ranging health problems all the way from infertility to arthritis, insomnia, cancer, anxiety, and depression. The judge in the case fears that it will take up to three months to try this case, and others pile up on the already-crowded docket. Combined legal expenses for the two sides has already amount to more than $3 million. The judge has asked the parties to consider using a minitrial and they agree. After a two-day trial, with videotaped witness statements, the two juries, each with six participants, deliberate for about three hours before returning opposite verdicts. One jury returned a verdict in favor of the plaintiffs for almost $12 million. The other jury returned a verdict in favor of the defense, giving nothing to the plaintiffs. The attorneys for both sides used their discussions with the jury to advance their settlement negotiations and reach an out-of-court settlement, thereby saving themselves and the public the cost of a long trial.

Public sector managers and companies facing class action or multimillion dollar claims might consider the benefits of a summary jury trial but only if less expensive options such as mediation or arbitration have failed or are unacceptable to the parties.

Coaching

We all know what coaches do. They help players improve their performance, thereby making the team better as a whole. Executive or performance coaching within a workplace is used for two main purposes: to improve the performance of managers who are underperforming or to maximize the performance of managers who are already doing well. The field of executive coaching is booming, with approximately two thousand full-time professional coaches working in the United States in 1996, at least ten thousand in 2002, and fifty thousand were estimated to be working by 2007 (Jones & Brinkert, 2008). Clearly, organizations and individual managers have realized the benefits of using coaches to improve managerial performance. Diedrich argued that executive coaches were best used to "modify an executive's style, assist executives in adjusting to change, help in developmental efforts, and provide assistance to derailed executives" (Jones & Brinkert, 2008, p. 6). In addition to executive coaching, other forms of coaching commonly used are life coaches and career coaches. The former assist individuals as they consider various life choices and critical decisions and the latter does the same during career changes or transitions.

Coaches use a host of diagnostic tools and communication skills to assist managers in assessing their own job performance and create paths to improvement. Jones and Brinkert (2008) define **conflict coaching** as "a process in which a coach and client communicate one-on-one for the purpose of developing the client's conflict-related understanding, interaction strategies, and interaction skills. Coaches help clients to make sense of conflicts they experience, help them learn to positively manage these conflicts, and help them master specific communication skills and behaviors" (pp. 4–5).

In addition to using a coach to improve their own performance, managers can also serve as coaches with their employees by helping them to see the areas in which they need to improve and working on the skills that will get them there. Coaching is a process focused on empowerment. Those being coached are encouraged to examine their assumptions, their desire for change, and the obstacles to improved outcomes, and then to develop paths forward. The coach asks questions, practices communication skills with clients, and supports clients as they work toward achieving the goals set during the coaching sessions. Coaches provide assessment tools to better discover the answer to these questions as well as to assess progress toward goals.

To be more specific, Tidwell (1997) developed a model of conflict coaching (called *problem-solving for one*) that involves six basic steps:

- *Preamble and introduction:* The coach describes the coaching process, discusses the confidential nature, shares information about the general costs and benefits, and asks for clarification of the participant's expectations.

- *Storytelling:* The participant shares the reasons why he or she is participating in the coaching process, shares information about any specific problem or conflict that has precipitated the desire to meet with a coach, and shares other relevant background information.

- *Conflict analysis:* The coach works with the participant to deeply examine the problem by specifying its origins, parties, issues, dynamics, and possibilities for resolution.

- *Alternative generation and costing:* The participant brainstorms possible solutions and the costs and benefits associated with each proposed solution. If more information is needed, the coaching session can recess while the participant researches this information.

- *Communication strategy development:* The coach works to help the participant identify and develop the communication skills and strategies necessary to implement the identified solution(s).

- *Restatement of the conflict-handling plan:* The facilitator and the client develop a plan for moving forward, with any new coaching sessions focused on tracking progress toward the goal or resolution.

Clearly, this type of coaching process has management applications. Managers are frequently faced with employees or colleagues needing help to navigate conflicts at work or needing to improve their communication or collaboration skills. This basic process outline offers a path forward so managers can act as coaches and facilitators that empower people to solve their own problems and develop the skills necessary to do so independently in the future.

Coaches need to have good communication skills, including those covered in the following skills section. They also need to be able to train individuals in these skills as needed to help them overcome the communications-based obstacles to better performance. Explaining the five conflict styles (covered in Chapter Two) or working on active listening skills can be an important step to improved managerial performance. Coaches need to master conflict and communication skills and be able to teach them to their coaching clients, who are often their employees or colleagues.

ADDITIONAL PROBLEM-SOLVING TECHNIQUES

Timing is critical for good decision-making and problem-solving processes. If tempers are high, we know that individuals and groups have difficulty processing complex information and making good decisions. At the opposite end of the spectrum, if an issue is not considered important, those affected by the decision or problem will not want to get involved and contribute to its solution. So, ripeness is key.

Before participants can engage in problem solving it is important for all parties to use active listening skills in order to better understand each other, to understand the problem or issue, and to build rapport among those who must work together toward resolution. Although active listening is a necessary precursor to problem solving, these listening skills will be called on at various phases of the problem-solving process.

Brainstorming is an important part of a problem-solving process. During brainstorming all parties agree to think broadly about any and all possible solutions to the problem at hand. It is critical to the success of the brainstorming process that the participants agree to separate the process of generating options from the process of evaluating those options. Imagine that one employee proposes a creative solution to the problem and from across the table another person says, "That's the craziest idea I ever heard!" Who would want to throw out the next idea for slaughter? The brainstorming will quickly come to an end. Therefore, the manager as process facilitator can gently remind everyone about the importance of separating the process of generating ideas from the process of evaluating them.

Backcasting is a problem-solving technique in which the facilitator, mediator, or manager asks the parties to envision a future in which the problem is solved or the relationship is repaired. The parties are asked to describe what that looks like or feels like. Then, the parties are asked to describe the steps that each of them would need to take in order to reach that ideal future state. The parties are asked to focus on the actions that they can take themselves rather than focusing on the actions they wish the others would take.

Through the choice of the appropriate ADR process, active listening, and problem solving, most managerial conflicts can be handled early, before they grow to threaten the health of the organization.

KEY SKILLS FOR MANAGING COLLABORATION AND CONFLICT

In addition to the ADR processes just covered, managers need to develop foundational conflict prevention and management skills such as active listening and questioning.

Listening

Few managerial skills are as neglected as listening skills. Listening skills are the foundation for most forms of collaboration, problem solving, and dispute resolution. Everyone can improve personal listening skills, and when you work on these, people notice. Most managers believe they already have good listening skills, but would their employees agree?

In a typical conversation in English-speaking countries, there is an overlap of one to two syllables that occurs when the speaker slows down and the listener jumps into the conversation, thereby becoming the next speaker (see Figure 4.2). Culture influences speech patterns; therefore not all English speakers will conform to this pattern, although it will apply to the majority of English speakers. Two problems arise when this listening pattern is used. First, there is an overlap during which time the person who is supposed to be listening starts to speak before the speaker has completed his statement. Second, instead of listening to understand, the listener listens to respond, especially in conflict situations. This means the listener is preparing a rebuttal, an evaluation, or a question of interest to the listener rather than focusing on what the speaker is

Figure 4.2
Common English Speaking–Listening Pattern

Speaker A - - - - - - - -   - - - - - - - - - -   - - - - - - - - - - - -

Speaker B   - - - - - - - - - - -   - - - - - - - - - -

saying and any emotional needs that underlie his or her speech. The first step to solving problems is to understand the nature of the problem and the various parties' perspectives and views of the conflict. By **listening to respond**, people generally listen to figure out when they can jump into the conversation and get out their view, opinion, thoughts, and so on. Instead of listening to respond, the first step in a problem-solving conversation is listening to understand. **Listening to understand** requires listeners to suspend judgment and their own need to drive the conversation. Instead of listening for the moment to jump into the conversation, the goal of listening to understand is to allow the speaker to completely share his or her thoughts, concerns, or emotions with the listener, uninterrupted. This calls for active listening.

Active listening occurs when listeners give the speaker all of their attention, listen to understand the speaker's meaning, in content and in import, and confirm the meaning has been understood through summarizing back what has been said. Active listening serves multiple purposes: increased understanding on the listener's part, building rapport and relationship between the speaker and listener, and making space for speakers to share something they consider important. The term *active listening* is also called *reflective listening* in the literature on conflict management and communication. Although the terms are interchangeable, we will use the term *active listening* because it includes giving reflections back to the speaker as well as many other behaviors related to attentiveness, eye contact, avoiding distractions, and so on. Active listening is called for when the speaker has a high level of emotional energy, which can be positive energy such as excitement or joy or it can be negative energy such as frustration, sadness, or anger. The first step to problem solving is to allow speakers to vent, that is to say, to let them release some of the energy and calm down. If a problem exists that needs to be solved, that phase will come after active listening. Problem solving requires that each party has had a chance to release some energy by speaking to an active listener. Sometimes speakers only need someone to listen to them; they are not trying to engage in a problem-solving process with you. They simply want you to listen so they can get something off their chest or so they can process their emotions themselves. Some people think through their problems by talking them out. Others simply need to know that you care about them and their problems. Giving someone our full attention as a listener is one of the best ways to show we care and helps build strong relationships.

When someone comes to you with high energy and she needs you to listen, the first step is to put down your smartphone! Really, the hardest thing to do sometimes is to stop paying attention to other important tasks, and take a few moments to focus solely on listening. You may be someone who is great at multitasking. You feel you can listen and check e-mail at the same time. You may be right but you cannot convey to someone that you care about them by checking your e-mail while you listen to them vent. If someone needs you to listen actively but you are in the middle of an activity that cannot wait, try saying something like, "I want to give you my full attention. Can I come down to your office in five minutes, after I make this urgent phone call?" Although the brief delay might be frustrating, the speaker will likely receive the message that his concern is important to the listener and the listener will make time to hear it very soon—free from distractions.

Keys to Active Listening

- Avoid distractions.
- Make eye contact (when culturally appropriate).
- Use open body language.
- Listen to understand.
- Use conversation starters and openings.
- Summarize what you've heard.
- Avoid judging what you hear (positively or negatively).
- Avoid trying to solve problems.
- Avoid statements that take the focus away from the speaker.

Once you are away from distractions and in a private setting, make sure you look the person in the eye and, when possible, sit or stand so that you are on a level plane. This assumes a Western context, where eye contact is a sign of respect. In many Asian and Latin American contexts, direct eye contact is inappropriate from a subordinate. This will also help you observe the speaker's body language and nonverbal emotional cues. Use positive or neutral body language by positioning your chair and body to face the speaker. Do not cross your arms, glance at your watch, tap your pen nervously, or otherwise send the signal that you are impatient.

When listening, try to avoid mental distractions, such as unrelated thoughts or mentally composing a response. Use conversation openers such as "What is going on?" or "Please tell me about your concern." It is important for the speaker to be able to tell his whole story without interruption. Some speakers will feel guilty about taking your time and you may need to give them a door opener. This door opener lets her know that you are still listening and she can continue as long as she needs. Try nodding your head or saying something like "uh huh." One recipe for a door opening is to briefly summarize back what you have heard, focusing on the emotional meaning or content: "Sounds like you are really frustrated." Be sure to avoid statements that convey empathy but derail the speaker or put the attention on the listener instead of the speaker. For example, "That happened to me once . . ." or "Why did she do that?" Also, seek to avoid making positive or negative judgments such as "You had every right to feel angry." Judgmental statements have four negative effects. Negative opinions may have a chilling impact on the speaker, making him or her afraid to fully share his or her story or concerns. Second, they can derail the conversation by taking it in a different direction than the speaker was headed. Third, they put emphasis on the listener's opinions rather than the speaker's story. Fourth, if the speaker is a manager or other potential problem solver, it leads to premature judgments before all parties have been heard. Instead, the listener may convey empathy with statements such as "I can tell this has been hard on you" or something similar that reflects back the emotions communicated by the speaker.

Why would a book on conflict management suggest that listeners avoid trying to solve problems? Good conflict managers have one fatal tendency in common. We tend to be fixers. We want to help others to fix their problems by imposing our solutions on them. Sometimes this is necessary and appropriate. Fixing the speaker's problem is rarely, if ever, appropriate at the active listening stage. If need be, the time for fixing the problem may come later, after deep listening has occurred. Additionally, there will be times when it is most appropriate for parties to generate their own solutions to the problems they face. They will usually be more satisfied with solutions they generate themselves—even if it is the same exact solution you would have recommended or imposed (review the procedural justice discussion in Chapter Two). The time to worry about problem solving is after all parties have had an opportunity to listen actively to each other and to their manager or colleague.

Once the speaker is finished and has said all she needs to say, summarize back what you heard. Your summarization should include not only a brief summary of the facts conveyed but also the meaning that the facts or events have had for the speaker—the emotional content. For example, "If I understand you correctly, you're frustrated because Bob has been put on your project and the two of you have had problems working well together before. You're not sure how to make this project turn out better than it did last time you two worked together. Is that accurate?" If you have clarifying questions, this is the time to ask them. Be sure that your questions are not carefully disguised judgments or evaluations, such as "Did you know Mike would get angry when you did x?" Coming to a shared understanding of the problem is the first step in problem solving, *if* that is the next appropriate step in the conversation.

It is important to note that not all conversations need to involve active listening. If you and a friend are discussing the movie you just watched, active listening would be overkill. The purpose of such a conversation is intrinsic rather than instrumental. An intrinsically valuable conversation means that sometimes we talk mostly for the joy of having a pleasant conversation. We also are able to build up shared experiences and solidify positive relationships this way, but that is not the main purpose—the main purpose is just to have fun and share experiences. An instrumental conversation is one with a specific purpose such as venting, information sharing, or problem solving. Showing someone that you care about his or her feelings and needs is also an instrumental function of active listening. By eliminating distractions by silencing your phone or closing your door, you show someone that you care and that he or she is important to you. The following are some statements that do not necessarily lead to active listening:

"Bob, where did you put that report?"

"What date do you return from the training?"

"What are you doing this weekend?"

Because you are not actively listening does not imply that you are not listening at all but it means you are not inviting the speaker to get it all out by shutting off all distractions during the conversation and then **summarizing** back what you have heard. These are not particularly emotional conversations. At work or with customers, you might hear these statements, indicating a need for active listening:

"The product arrived but I am not satisfied with it."

"I can't believe how she talks to me!"

"I got a negative performance review. This is totally unfair!"

"I can't work with him. He drives me crazy."

"This deadline (or goal) is unattainable."

Opportunities for active listening occur regularly but we tend to miss them. Look for high emotional energy on the part of the speaker: excitement, frustration, anger, weariness, or anxiety. Try to identify these opportunities and you will see noticeable improvements in your relationships and problem-solving abilities.

Listening as a manager may indeed be somewhat different than listening to your peers or with friends outside of work. As a manager, people come to you to solve problems and make decisions. Yet before you have the information you need to do so, you need to listen fully to what the speaker has to say and reflect back what you have heard to ensure complete understanding and to build rapport with the speaker. Once these listening tasks have been accomplished, it makes sense to engage in a conversation about the best role for the manager in this issue: should you intervene in some way or simply coach the speaker so he can resolve the situation successfully himself? Is a unilateral decision needed from you as the manager or should you consult others on your team before making any decisions? Be sure that you and the speaker leave the conversation with the same understanding of your role so as to avoid any later confusion.

Questioning

Whether you are acting as a facilitator or an informal mediator or simply trying to better understand a problem or person, questioning skills are critical for good communication. The first step in selecting the appropriate question is to consider the question's purpose. Questions may be used to elicit information, to promote reflection or analysis, or to challenge the speaker. The next step is to select a question type: "general (open-ended), opinion seeking, fact finding, direct-forced choice, or leading questions" (Hughes & Bennett, 2005, p. 95).

To elicit the most comprehensive information, general open-ended questions may be the most useful (see Figure 4.3). An open-ended question asks speakers to share any information they deem useful with which to answer the question, for example, "Please tell me how this problem started and evolved?" An example of an opinion-seeking variety of open-ended question might be "What kind of solutions would you like to see?"

When more specific information is needed, questioners may turn to fact finding (slightly more general) for forced-choice (more specific) questions. For example, a fact-finding question would be, "What kind of employment information did you include on your application?" A similar question posed as a forced choice would be, "Did you tell us of your previous termination on your employment application?" These questions provide precise information needed to better understand the problem. These tend to be relatively low-risk questions, but expect defensiveness to decrease as openness of the question increases.

Questions designed to promote reflection or analyses are used to get speakers to think through the consequences of potential solutions or to better understand their own role in the problem or solution. These are often phrased as opinion-seeking questions, such as "If we moved Bob to another team, would your team be short-handed?" or "Can you think of any options or changes that you can make which would lead to a better outcome than before?" Depending on how they are phrased, questions demanding reflection and analysis can be incredibly useful during a problem-solving or decision-making process. It is important for questioners to have developed rapport and trust with the speaker so that they do not become defensive during the use of these questions.

Questions that challenge the speaker are the most risky of all. They are not truly part of a problem-solving or decision-making process but are instead used to express frustration or judgment by the questioner. These are often leading questions that are an indirect way for the questioner to make a statement rather than ask a question. Such a question might be, "Don't you think you overreacted?" Or, the famous standby, "When did you stop beating your wife?" A leading question can be difficult to answer without sounding defensive or guilty. In general, leading questions are not commonly used in problem-solving processes.

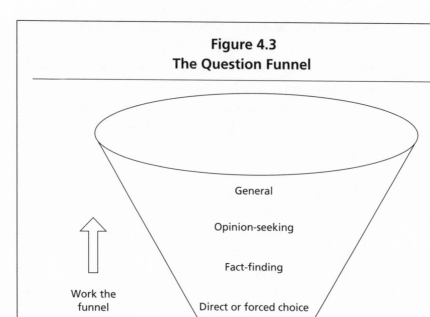

Figure 4.3
The Question Funnel

General

Opinion-seeking

Fact-finding

Work the
funnel

Direct or forced choice

Leading

Source: Hughes and Bennett (2005, p. 95). Reprinted with permission of the National Institute for Trial Advocacy.

Leading questions lead us to the important issue of framing and reframing. As Chapter Two described, the framing effect is a cognitive bias that occurs when the same option is presented in different formats or with different phrasing (i.e., it is framed differently) and the choice of format or phrasing unduly influences one's opinions or preferences on the matter (Druckman, 2001). Therefore, framing refers to the language used to put one's thoughts into words. During conflicts or tense decision-making processes it is important to choose your words carefully. The wrong word choice can lead parties to question the neutrality of the mediator or facilitator. The words used to describe a thought or situation can reveal implicit judgments or biases that influence the course of a conversation or conflict. Additionally, individuals generally seek to avoid losses more than they endeavor to seek out equivalent gains. People tend to avoid risk when a negative frame is presented but seek risks when a positive frame is presented (Tversky & Kahneman, 1981). For example, if the organization's leaders are seeking to solidify employee support for a proposed merger, they might focus on the risks to the company's survival if they remain small and less competitive in an increasingly globalized world. Framing also speaks to the procedural justice issues raised in Chapter Two. For example, a facilitator at a contentious zoning meeting might avoid this framing, "Where will the big-box stores be built?" and instead ask participants, "What is your vision for the economic future of our town?"

Reframing refers to the language used to summarize, paraphrase, and reflect back what a party has said but using a different frame than originally intended with the goal of altering the course of the communication between two or more parties. For example, if two employees come to their manager with complaints about how the other isn't doing her fair share of work on a joint project, the manager might begin to reframe the discussion to refocus on the importance of teamwork by saying, "I can tell that getting the work done well and on time is important to you both. What ideas do you have for improving your teamwork?" The manager is beginning her interaction by reframing the dispute as an opportunity for collaboration rather than competition. If taken to extremes, this technique runs the risk of being seen as manipulative or putting words into the mouths of others, so use caution when reframing the words of others.

Facilitators, mediators, and conflict managers often use reframing techniques when creating an agenda based on the expressed positions or concerns of the parties. For example, if a party says, "I'll agree to her demands over my dead body!" a neutral reframing might be, "I can tell you have strong feelings about this. Please tell me more about why you feel this way." Reframing can be used to move parties from a past to a future focus, to depersonalize comments away from a personal attack to an attack on the problem, or to redirect parties from an adversarial to a collaborative focus. There are ethical implications of reframing because it can be used to manipulate a party's statements or to put words in their mouths. When used correctly, reframing helps refocus a conversation from a destructive to constructive focus.

CONCLUSION

This chapter has served as a brief introduction to the many ADR processes being used to address complaints within and sometimes external to organizations. In addition to explaining the differences between processes such as mediation, facilitation, and arbitration, we discussed the role of the organizational ombudsman and other neutrals such as performance coaches. Additional techniques for problem solving were examined such as brainstorming and backcasting. Finally, we delved into the communication skills necessary to make all of these processes work smoothly: active listening, questioning, framing, and reframing. In order to efficiently resolve disputes, managers need knowledge of these processes and the communication skills that make them work.

JOHN AT THE BUREAU OF RECLAMATION

The last thing John needed was to have to respond to an EEOC complaint. He had heard about the endless paperwork and lengthy delays that are common with this kind of process, plus he resented the accusation that he had discriminated against anyone during the hiring process.

After meeting with the organizational ombudsman, John decided to invite Dorys to take part in mediation, using an outside neutral mediator. Dorys agreed to give mediation a try after the ombudsman explained the process. At the mediation, John explained that he was not allowed to share private personnel information about the other applicants with anyone but he was able to share with her the criteria on which he based his decision. Dorys met the minimum qualifications for the position and had performed well while at the bureau but John explained he was looking for someone with more experience in dealing with budgets and overseeing staff. He explained to Dorys the way in which he assigned point values to various elements he was looking for, such as education, specific types of experience, and seniority. He also asked Dorys to share her concerns with him. Why did she believe she had been discriminated against? John learned Dorys was concerned because there were no mid- or upper-level managers within the bureau who were Hispanic and there were very few women at the highest level of the organization. John agreed this was a problem that needed further examination.

As a result of the mediation the following agreement was reached: John would recruit a diverse set of employees from different levels within the organization to develop proposals for increasing diversity at the middle- and upper-management levels. Dorys would meet with the human resource manager for one-on-one coaching about how to be more competitive for any future promotions. Dorys would drop the EEOC action.

KEY TERMS

Active listening

Adjudication

Arbitration

Backcasting

Brainstorming

Case evaluation

Conflict coaching

Facilitation

Informal managerial mediation

Listening to respond

Listening to understand

Litigation

Mediation

Ombudsman (ombuds)

Open-door policy

Peer review

Reframing

Summarizing

Summary jury trials (SJTs)

SUGGESTED SUPPLEMENTAL READING

Kent, J. C. (2005). Getting the best of both worlds: Making partnerships between court and community ADR programs exemplary. *Conflict Resolution Quarterly*, *23*, 71–85.

Kuttner, R. (2011). Conflict specialists as leaders: Revisiting the role of the conflict specialist from a leadership perspective. *Conflict Resolution Quarterly*, *29*, 103–126.

Szmania, S. J., Johnson, A. M., & Mulligan, M. (2008). Alternative dispute resolution in medical malpractice: A survey of emerging trends and practices. *Conflict Resolution Quarterly, 26,* 71–96.

DISCUSSION QUESTIONS

1. Who is the best listener you know and what makes them so skilled?

2. Share any experiences you have had with alternative dispute resolution. What worked or didn't work well?

3. Think of a conflict in your work environment or in the news. Which ADR process would have been best to address this conflict and why?

EXERCISES

1. In groups of three, practice being the speaker, the listener, and the observer. Have the speaker tell a short story about some problem or concern he or she has had in a past or present work environment. The listener should use the skills described in this chapter, including the use of a summary statement at the end. The observer will provide feedback about the listener's eye contact, body language, use of door openers, ability to refrain from judging or evaluating, and the summarization at the end. Rotate roles every five to seven minutes. Discuss these debriefing questions: how did it feel to be the listener? How did it feel to be the speaker? Which skills do you need to practice more?

2. Sometime this week, find an opportunity to engage in active listening at work, at home, or in your civic life. After the listening episode, analyze your performance using Figure 4.2. Which of these skills were you able to employ well? With which skills do you need more practice? Did the speaker notice your active listening? What was the impact of this listening episode on your relationship with the other party, if any?

3. If your organization has been involved in litigation, can you think of an ADR process that would have been worth trying before going to court? Analyze the situation to see which ADR processes would or would not be applicable in that situation.

4. Make a list of the sources of recurring, predictable conflict within your organization or with its customers or clients. Which skills or processes could be applied to reduce the negative effects of those conflicts and resolve them at the lowest possible level?

5. Think of a challenging relationship in your work life or a persistent unresolved problem at work. Now, imagine that two years have passed and this relationship or problem has reached an ideal state. What actions would you need to take now to reach that ideal state in two years? (Engage in backcasting.)

GOAL SETTING

On a scale of one to ten, how good a listener are you? Consider asking a trusted coworker or family member to rate you as well. Then choose one skill or technique from this chapter to employ so as to raise your rating by at least one point on the scale.

PART TWO

Preventing and Resolving Internal Conflict

Some of the most frustrating challenges faced by managers are those related to employee disputes. The chapters in this part examine different facets of conflict internal to organizations rather than those dealing with external parties such as customers or vendors. The first step in preventing unproductive workplace conflict is creating policies and procedures that encourage constructive and collaborative behaviors from employees at all levels of the company.

Good customer service nearly always begins with creating a positive, friendly, and rewarding environment for workers. Toward that end, Chapter Five examines the root causes and cures for employee turnover. Using the information found there, managers can redesign their workplaces to improve productivity and also improve employee satisfaction.

Chapter Six leads the reader through the process of building and managing teams. Managers can play important roles in hiring with team performance in mind, assigning existing employees to compatible teams, using performance reviews to pinpoint areas of growth for each employee, and help their organizations navigate the challenges encountered during mergers and acquisitions.

In Chapter Seven we will uncover the unique conflicts and dispute resolution procedures frequently used in unionized environments. From the steps commonly found in the union grievance process to the application of arbitration in baseball disputes, this chapter provides specific advice for managers seeking to improve the morale and collaboration found in their organizations.

Chapter Eight examines methods for designing disputing systems for organizations large and small. By cataloging the sources and numbers of disputes and designing systems and policies to prevent or manage them, organizational leaders can vastly reduce the costs of dispute resolution and improve employee satisfaction and morale. The ideas and methods presented in this chapter will be revisited in the next part when we apply them to track and improve customer dispute prevention and management.

chapter FIVE

Causes and Cures for Employee Turnover

Learning Objectives

- Demonstrate an understanding of the impact of high employee turnover on organizational productivity.

- Demonstrate an understanding of the links between conflict management and employee satisfaction.

- List and describe the causes of high employee turnover and low morale.

- Demonstrate an understanding of the techniques used to diagnose the causes of employee turnover and low morale.

- Describe techniques for reducing employee turnover and raising morale.

- Explain techniques for dealing proactively with difficult employees.

- Identify workplace bullying and appropriate methods for addressing bullying behaviors.

- Identify and explain the characteristics of a great boss or a great manager.

ELISE AT MAIN STREET BAKERIES

In Chapter Two Elise had sent Ben, her director of HR, to store number seventy-five to learn more about the relatively high rate of employee turnover experienced at the store. In general, turnover in Main Street Bakeries is low, approximately 15 percent per year for frontline, hourly paid employees and 6 percent for salaried employees (i.e., managers and assistant managers). Ben and Elise are concerned because store number seventy-five has lost four assistant managers in less than two years. Hourly employees are turning over at a rate of 37 percent per year. This is an indication that something is not going well. It also means this store is less profitable than the others in the chain. Elise's system for tracking costs charges each store for the costs of hiring and training new employees. These costs come off the store's bottom line so that managers have incentives to try to keep their employees whenever possible. Oddly enough, absenteeism is relatively low at the store, which is surprising given the level of turnover and low customer satisfaction.

The root causes of the high turnover are negatively affecting the store's ability to deliver high-quality service to its customers: unhappy employees lead to unhappy customers. Ben needs to analyze the situation, interview former employees, and come up with an intervention plan.

Dissatisfied employees are a sign of a dysfunctional workplace. Whether the root cause is a counterproductive workplace culture, one or more bullies at work, or other systemic factors, it is clear that employee satisfaction is closely tied to profitability and achievement of the organizational mission. Even in a period of high unemployment figures when applicants are plentiful, the process of hiring and training new employees is extremely expensive. Research studies repeatedly show a clear link between employee satisfaction and customer satisfaction (Engaging employees through social responsibility, 2007). Perhaps most important, as a manager you want to go to work every day at a place that feels warm, supportive, and thriving. Life is too short to remain in a dysfunctional workplace. This chapter will help you understand the root causes, costs, and cures for low employee morale and high turnover. The good news is that there are many things you can do to change the dynamics in your organization or unit and make it become the kind of workplace where employees want to stay.

How satisfied or dissatisfied are employees in general? Recent studies show that male employees are more satisfied than female employees and that white collar employees are more satisfied than blue collar employees, even though they are under more stress because of longer work hours and greater responsibilities. For all categories of workers, employee satisfaction and loyalty have declined as downsizing and efficiency efforts have resulted in heavier workloads and stagnant pay (Duxbury & Higgins, 2003). Workers are putting in longer hours than in the past, and these longer hours are resulting in greater stresses on health and family life:

> Comparisons done using the 1991 and 2001 samples suggest that time in work has increased over the decade. Whereas one in ten respondents in 1991 worked 50 or more hours per week, one in four does so now; during this same time period, the proportion of employees working between 35 and 39 hours per week declined from 48% of the sample to 27%. This increase in time in work was observed for all job groups and all sectors. (Duxbury & Higgins, 2003)

If employers are asking more from employees and stress has increased, you can bet that workplace conflict has increased as well.

Overall, employee satisfaction is influenced by how employees are treated on the job. "The data also indicate that employees in the private sector feel more positively about their employer and their jobs than their counterparts in the public and NFP sectors" (Duxbury & Higgins, 2003). More research needs to be done as to why this is the case but anecdotal evidence indicates that some public sector and not-for profit (nonprofit) employees are dissatisfied with their pay and working conditions yet they remain with their organizations out of a commitment to the organization's mission or a preference to avoid the higher risks of layoffs or termination that historically come with private sector employment.

THE COSTS OF EMPLOYEE TURNOVER AND LOW MORALE

The costs of poor employee morale are seen in a variety of ways: absenteeism, "presenteeism," reduced productivity, sabotage, litigation, and the costs of hiring and training new employees. **Employee turnover** refers to the rate at which employees leave the organization and should be broken down by rank and location to better isolate the potential root causes. Average rates of employee turnover vary by industry and within organizations.

Although technical abilities or knowledge may help get managers into their positions, it is their ability to manage people that separates mediocre managers from successful ones. "Employees who rate their managers as sensitive miss an estimated 3.7 days of work per year, whereas employees whose managers are rated as non-sensitive miss approximately 6.2 days of work" (MacBriade-King & Bachmann, 1999, p. 3). Absenteeism is costly to organizations, especially when it occurs in positions demanding significant training, because it is nearly impossible to have someone seamlessly step into that employee's shoes during his or her absence. "Employees who report the following sources of stress are more likely than others to be absent for six or more days...interpersonal relations; job control; and management practices" (Health Canada, 1998, p. 3).

In some ways, absenteeism may be preferable to **presenteeism**, which occurs when an employee wishes to leave the organization but hasn't done so yet. Although remaining in the job, the employee is less committed to the organization, its customers, and its other employees. "Many such employees 'retire on the job' (i.e., do not do their share of the work), which causes workload problems for others in their area" (Duxbury & Higgins, 2003). Rates for presenteeism are estimated to be approximately three times higher than for absenteeism, especially in a sluggish economy when employees feel unable to find work elsewhere (WarrenShepel, 2005). Approximately 52 percent of employees claim to have lost work time being preoccupied about how they were being treated, and 22 percent claimed to have slowed down their work in response to "rude or insensitive" behaviors of their supervisors (Gault, 2011). These employees also report higher levels of work-related stress, greater use of alcohol and drugs, have higher medical costs, and more frequently seek the services of mental health counselors or use employee assistance programs. They are more likely to file a claim for disability or worker's compensation. In a weak labor market, when changing jobs is relatively harder, disgruntled employees may remain with their employer longer, all the while sowing seeds of discontent among other employees and operating at reduced levels of productivity. The key to avoid presenteeism is to address signs of employee alienation rather than ignore them by using the techniques discussed in this chapter.

The Society for Human Resource Management (SHRM) recently reported that HR managers claim "employee engagement" as a higher concern than employee turnover (SHRM, 2011), and 71 percent of companies with five hundred or more employees stated they track that engagement through the use of employment exit interviews or surveys. An **exit interview (exit survey)** is used to gather information about the reasons why employees are leaving the organization, their perspectives about how the organization could improve as an employer and in the accomplishment of its mission, and various other points of information deemed vital to constant improvement. Employees who have made the choice to leave the organization may be in a position to be more honest about their observations than ongoing employees who may fear reprisals or retribution for speaking out.

"The starting point of this was that our best managers have teams that perform better, are retained better, are happier — they do everything better" (Bryant, 2011, p. 3). "Providing first-class service often depends on employees who are willing to go the extra mile. And that often depends on how they're treated" (Tierney, 2011).

Employees who feel unappreciated, overworked, and mistreated are more likely to engage in sabotage, embezzlement, and theft at work. "Studies reveal a direct correlation between prevalence of employee conflict and the amount of damage, theft of inventory and equipment. And, covert sabotage of work processes and of management's efforts usually occurs when employees are angry at their employer" (Dana, 2001). It takes an average of eighteen months of ongoing theft before a thieving employee is caught — usually by a tip from another employee. For small businesses and nonprofits, one employee's embezzlement or theft can be enough to bankrupt the organization because the median loss for small business embezzlement is $100,000 (Association of Certified Fraud Examiners, 2004). Experts in the field often refer to **the 10–80–10 percent rule**. This means that 10 percent of employees won't steal under any circumstances. Another 10 percent are dishonest and nothing can be done to change their desire to steal, so good accounting measures and other measures need to be in place to catch them. The other 80 percent will be influenced by the workplace climate and the thoughts of their peers on the matter. If the workplace culture indicates it is alright to bring home office supplies or small items, but not large ones, then that is what will be the norm. In some workplaces, the norm is "just don't get caught," but everyone steals at least a little. So the key to avoiding theft, embezzlement, and sabotage is to create a positive workplace climate and a culture in which employees and managers agree that these behaviors are truly unacceptable and uncalled for.

Employee turnover refers to the rate at which employees leave the organization and should be broken down by rank and location to better isolate the potential root causes. Average rates of employee turnover vary by industry and within organizations. High employee turnover, by definition, means increased litigation costs. Some percentage of employees will claim they felt forced to quit or were terminated due to discrimination or other inappropriate actions on the part of the company and its managers. If yours is a unionized environment, most terminated employees will file a grievance and use that process to seek reinstatement, possibly with back pay. Employment lawsuits can easily take two to four years to resolve through either the EEOC process or through court litigation, with legal fees easily climbing to more than $100,000. In addition to the rising costs of litigation, the number of employment suits has drastically increased since about 2000. "The number of employees seeking help for harassment has almost tripled from 1999 to 2001" (WarrenShepel, 2005). The good news is that organizations that proactively manage conflict have less litigation and less turnover. "Corporations that have developed collaborative conflict management systems report significant litigation cost savings: Brown and Root reported an 80% reduction in outside litigation costs, Motorola reported a 75% reduction over a period of six years, NCR reported a 50% reduction and a drop of pending lawsuits from 263 in 1984 to 28 in 1993" (Ford, 2000).

Let's do the math for a disgruntled employee earning $75,000 per year:

Fourteen sick days: $4,200

Six months working below full capacity: $12,499

Managerial time spent listening to disgruntled employee and others: $10,000

Hiring and replacement costs: $75,000 to $150,00

Lost productivity while the position is unfilled: $23,000

Total cost: $124,699 to $199,699

Hiring and retraining new employees is costly, with costs rising with the level of education and specialized training needed by the employee. Studies routinely estimate the cost of hiring and training an employee to be approximately 75 to 150 percent of the employee's annual salary (Phillips, 1990). Even in a down economy, the costs involved in hiring and training new employees vastly outweighs the cost of additional training, professional development, and support for the employees you already have. Proactive conflict management and interventions to stop inappropriate workplace behaviors have benefits beyond reducing turnover, as we have seen.

WHY EMPLOYEES LEAVE OR STAY

Mike Pitcher, CEO of LeasePlan USA, says, "Everything we do has contributed to our very low turnover rate last year, which was about 8 percent. We have a firm belief that if employees are happy, they will stay with the company and continue to help ensure happy clients. And that belief is a reality for us. In our most recent client satisfaction survey, our client loyalty rating increased significantly and was much higher than the company's global average. In addition, the percentage of 'delighted' clients increased" (Tierney, 2011).

"We are fortunate to enjoy almost a negative turnover in our professional staff, which significantly reduces our training time and tremendously helps our advisers do a better job for their clients" says Bob Mathis of Peachtree Planning Corporation (Tierney, 2011).

According to Adam Bryant (2011), employees leave a company for three main reasons. First, bad bosses drive people away faster than any other variable. Therefore, it is crucial for organizations to regularly measure employee satisfaction with their supervisors or managers and to take corrective action to help managers improve (or leave, if necessary). Second, people need to feel a sense of belonging and camaraderie with their coworkers. Eight or more hours per day is too much time to spend with people you do not like or who do not like you. Great managers foster social interaction among employees and structure incentives in ways that build teams rather than set individuals against one another.

Let's pause here to note that the first two drivers of employee turnover are closely related to relationship building and conflict management, which we have previously discussed. Bryant (2011) goes on to state that the third largest driver of high turnover occurs when employees don't feel a connection to the organization's mission or feel their work is unimportant. Rohlander (1999) finds the best solution to this problem is to clarify a mission, goals, and objectives to help connect daily work to that mission. Remind the team members often about the ways in which their work contributes to the organizational mission as well as the importance of that mission. People want to see the results of their labors and know their efforts are important to the organization and, more broadly, to the world. According to a study in *Leader to Leader* (Engaging employees through social responsibility, 2007), when employees view their organization as socially responsible (attentive to issues of pollution reduction, charitable work within the community, committed to diversity, and so on), they tend to have higher morale and job satisfaction. People want to know their work makes a difference in the world. Employment exit interviews or surveys can be crucial in learning more about why employees leave. Although many managers assume that employees leave for better-paying positions, this is not accurate for the majority of employees.

Bob Mathis, CEO of Peachtree Planning, notes, "We remind everyone in our firm of the importance of the work we do. We make a difference in the financial lives of our clients" (Tierney, 2011). A sense of purpose can be cultivated in every type of workplace, from fast-food delivery to hospice care. Remind employees that the work they do helps others and is important.

HIRING GREAT EMPLOYEES

Maintaining low employee turnover rates and high morale starts with having an effective hiring process. If there is disconnect between an employee's work style or personality and the culture of the organization or the work team, then there are likely to be problems down the road (Lencioni, 2002). According to Mike Pitcher, "The most important thing for us is whether or not they possess the behaviors that exhibit our core values and whether or not they will be a good fit with our culture. We are fortunate to find quality candidates through two main methods—internal candidates transitioning to new roles and our employee referral program" (Tierney, 2011).

Studies show that managers tend to want to hire employees who are the most like themselves (Bryant, 2011). This tendency can lead to an organization lacking many types of diversity: intellectual, educational, experiential, personality style, racial or ethnic, gender, and so on. To overcome this, consider implementing a committee process for hiring decisions in which all have an equal vote. Screen candidates not only for technical capabilities but also for their collaborative style, preferred work schedule, ability to work in teams and independently, and so on. Think analytically about the personal and professional characteristics of the workplace culture you are creating and screen based on those goals (see Chapter Six for more on team building and retention).

DEALING WITH DIFFICULT EMPLOYEES

Let's face it, although employee turnover is expensive, occasionally there are employees you are willing or even happy to see go. The most difficult employee is someone with poor communication or people skills, a negative attitude, a shirker, a bully, or one who cannot control his or her emotional states very well. An employee who struggles to meet performance goals but is open to feedback and coaching is likely to grow and eventually succeed as an employee. Although it may not be easy to admit, not all employees fit in with the organizational culture, work well with others, or help the organization achieve its mission. Private companies generally have an easier time firing or laying off an employee for poor performance than do public sector employers or corporations with heavily unionized workforces. For these and other reasons, it may be advisable to see what can be done to help this employee improve his or her performance before making any final decision about termination.

The first step in addressing problem employees is to make sure you are doing all you can to hire, train, and acculturate employees to succeed in your organization as just discussed. Once you check to ensure that is happening, there are a number of additional factors that will help turn around an underperforming employee. Rafenstein (2000) offers some ideas to help reduce problems with employees, including strategies such as trying to understand the employee's perspective, helping the employee develop the skills necessary to give and receive feedback constructively, and making sure expectations are clearly understood by all parties as part of the annual review as well as ongoing communications. Many problems with underperforming employees can be attributed to a lack of agreement between the employee and manager with regard to goals, prioritizing resources including employee time, and difficulty in making corrections or changes when problems arise.

Everyone has had the experience of working with an "Eeyore," meaning someone who sees only clouds but never silver linings. They may be suspicious of others, whether due to an underlying problem with depression, past negative experiences, or because inadequate attempts have been made to build trust and rapport with them. Godt (2005) suggests using an educational leadership role to deal with these employees. She explains that skeptics and cynics can be used to reexamine current plans and find possible holes that were previously overlooked. This natural tendency is their strength. Although it is important for these employees to feel heard and have their opinions valued, it may be a good idea for the manager to decide how much time should be allotted, for this should happen in meetings with the whole team versus in private meetings with the manager. Preston (2005) states that difficult people are often "detail oriented" (p. 368). Use this quality to your advantage when assigning work duties. By getting to know difficult employees well, and by gaining their trust, you may be able to turn their annoying habits into strengths for the team. You may also be better at understanding what type of work best suits them. By getting to know and understand the employee it is more likely the manager will be able to communicate effectively and understand the employee's needs. It will increase the chances she will listen to managerial feedback and make needed changes. Westwood (2010) notes that rather than labeling employees as difficult, even if only in your head, managers should instead make notes of those behaviors that are helpful or unhelpful in the work environment (see Table 5.1). When providing feedback to employees, ask them to work on minimizing the unhelpful behaviors and maximizing the helpful ones. Managers should lead by example and reward

Table 5.1
Helpful and Unhelpful Behaviors in the Work Environment

Helpful Behaviors	Description
Listens actively	Eye contact, use of questions, summarizes what has been heard, refrains from interrupting
Supports	Encourages others' suggestions, recognizes others for ideas and attempts at problem solving, refrains from shooting down others' ideas prematurely
Clarifies	Asks clarifying questions to clear up confusion
Offers ideas	Shares suggestions, ideas, solutions, and proposals; does not make complaints without offering solutions
Includes others	Asks quiet members for their opinions, making sure no one is left out
Harmonizes	Reconciles opposing points of view, links together similar ideas, points out similarities
Manages conflict	Listens to the views of all, clarifies issues and key points made by opponents, seeks solutions together, nonadversarial attitude

Unhelpful Behaviors	Description
"Yeah, but . . ."	Discredits the ideas of others
Blocks	Insists on getting one's way, doesn't compromise, stands in the way of the team's progress
Grandstands	Draws attention to one's personal skills, boasts
Goes off topic	Draws attention to other topics, poor time management
Dominates	Tries to run the group through dictating, bullying
Withdraws	Doesn't participate or offer help or support to others
Plays devil's advocate	Takes pride in being contrary
Uses personal slurs	Hurls insults at others and is disrespectful
Dictates	Tries to control the agenda, negates others' priorities and concerns

Source: Based on an earlier version of a chart found in Bens (2005), p. 80.

positive behaviors and improvements. These behavioral changes can be included as categories in reviews, with incentives for improvements.

In addition to getting to know these employees well, playing to their strengths, and clarifying expectations, O'Donovan (2007) suggests various communication strategies for dealing with difficult people: listen, understand their perspective, find common ground whenever possible, problem solve, and follow through with solutions. Pelusi (2006) lists five pieces of advice for dealing effectively with difficult people: (1) uncover their interests, (2) attempt to correct overgeneralizations or perceptual distortions, (3) acknowledge a mistake but do not accept personal labels—that is, separate the people from the problem, (4) summarize what you have heard them say, and (5) use questions instead of statements to get to the bottom of what they want. Tiffan (2009) points out that many managers procrastinate in dealing with difficult employees out of fear of "escalating the situation," uncertainty about how to handle the problem, and "discomfort with conflict" (p. 86). As a result, the problem grows and becomes more unmanageable.

This advice sounds much like that given to negotiators in Chapter Three, and with good reason. Even though managers are in charge, dealing with employees is always a negotiation on some level. The employees' alternatives to an agreement with the manager include leaving the company, filing a complaint, saying negative things about the boss behind her back, calling in sick when not sick, and shirking. The goal is to avoid behaviors that indicate employee alienation by addressing difficult employees proactively.

Be aware that fellow employees may grow weary of "one-note Charlies" who seem consistently disgruntled or negative. Managerial intervention may be needed to limit the negative impact of one employee's behavior on other employees' productivity. In healthy organizational cultures, the vast majority of employees will be happy. The group norms will not allow significantly disruptive or antisocial behaviors before the Eeyore will be confronted by those who find the behaviors unacceptable. Faced with a clear consensus that labels these behaviors unacceptable, the Eeyore will usually either leave on his or her own or change the unacceptable behaviors. If that person seems willing or unable to change, then it is the task of management to make difficult decisions regarding firing, demotion, or finding a task that requires minimal interaction between the difficult employee and others. In the most dysfunctional workplaces, where terminating an employee is difficult to accomplish, managers sometimes suggest their most difficult employees for promotion elsewhere in the organization, thereby solving their own problem and passing it off to someone else.

One last thought on dealing with problem employees bears mentioning. Large and conflict avoidant workplaces tend to react to inappropriate employee behavior through the use of what I like to call, *elementary school disciplinary action* (also referenced in Chapter Two). By that I mean that when one or two people break the rules and act badly, the leadership decides to create new rules that end up punishing the entire group due to the poor behavior of these few people. Don't allow the bad behavior of one employee to lead to the promulgation of rules or policies designed to help avoid the very rare occasions when someone will break an obvious rule or norm. Instead, be proactive in addressing the transgression with that specific employee. Clearly identify the behaviors that were inappropriate, set boundaries, identify sanctions that will be invoked, and then support him or her in the effort to choose more appropriate behaviors in the future. If that doesn't work, don't be afraid to dismiss an employee for inappropriate behavior. Workplace morale will surge rather than decline as long as you have followed the steps outlined in this section.

IDENTIFYING AND ERADICATING WORKPLACE BULLYING AND VIOLENCE

"**Bullying** can be considered as a form of coercive interpersonal influence. It involves deliberately inflicting injury or discomfort on another person repeatedly through physical contact, verbal abuse, exclusion, or other negative actions" (Forsyth, 2006, p. 206). The key to this definition is that the behavior must be intentional, repeated over time, and have a negative impact on the target. Some definitions focus on the negative health effects experienced by victims. Bullying behaviors include verbal abuse; offensive conduct and behaviors that can be verbal or nonverbal; attempts to threaten, intimidate, or humiliate; and attempts to prevent the victim from accomplishing required tasks at work with the goal of negatively affecting the victim's career (Lutgen-Sandvik, Tracy, & Alberts, 2007). Bullies wear down their victims, also known as targets, usually for more than a year in workplace settings (Einarsen & Skogstad, 1996). If actions are not taken to stop these negative behaviors they generally escalate until a crisis is reached, commonly resulting in the target quitting his or her job, the bully getting fired, or violent action of an offensive or defensive nature by one or both parties.

It should be noted here that some forms of bullying constitute harassment or discrimination and others simply constitute rude, inappropriate, or intimidating behaviors. If a victim was singled out for worse treatment due in part to his or her status as a member of a protected class under US (or another country's) civil rights laws, then the bullying may result in a greater legal liability for the organization. For example, if the bully includes name-calling or disrespectful treatment based on race, national origin, sex, religion, age, or other protected status then the employee may have stronger grounds for a lawsuit or to file a complaint with the EEOC.

Although estimates of the prevalence of workplace bullying vary, some of the best research indicates that about 13 percent of employees are bullied in an average year, with 30 percent having experienced bullying at some point in their careers (Lutgen-Sandvik, Tracy, & Alberts, 2007). Corporate bullying in federal businesses cost $180 million in lost time and productivity (Farrell, 2002). "Bullied employees take, on average, seven days per year more sick leave than others" (Knight, 2004). In addition to missed work days, bullies and their victims are more likely to be involved in episodes of workplace violence. Victims of workplace bullying frequently display symptoms of posttraumatic stress disorder (Knight, 2004), leaving them with long-term health and psychological challenges. The most difficult employees will bully others, verbally and physically. Predictably, researchers found that "employees subjected to workplace aggression are less satisfied with work, experience symptoms of burnout, and their general health is poorer" (Merecz, Drabek, & Mościcka, 2009, p. 254). Even the witnesses to workplace bullying report negative psychological and health effects (Knight, 2004). Bullying in the workplace leads to increased absenteeism, stress-related illness, filing of formal workplace complaints, turnover, and an infectious negativity that can reduce the organization's ability to accomplish its mission.

Various studies indicate between 3 and 6 percent of employees fit the definition of "bullies" (Einarsen, Hoel, Zapf, & Cooper, 2003; Matthiesen & Einersen, 2007). Studies show that about 12 percent of employees have quit a job due to rude treatment and 75 percent of those who claim to have been bullied report quitting their job or transferring to get away from the bully (Namie & Namie, 2003). Rarely do victims file complaints — they are more likely to quit. This choice makes sense because being attacked triggers the fight or flight response. Once they are gone the bully will find a new target. Chronic, unresolved bullying or repeated mistreatment of an employee is cited as a factor in at least 50 percent of exit surveys as a reason employees leave their jobs (Namie & Namie, 2003).

Who are the targets of bullying at work? Men and women are equally likely to fall prey to bullies, and the lower one is on the organizational hierarchy the greater the chance of being bullied (Lutgen-Sandvik, Tracy, & Alberts, 2007). Some research has found that meek individuals with poor social skills are more likely to be targets and other researchers have found that particularly talented employees who stand out from the crowd are also likely targets. The inconsistencies of the findings of bullying research studies lead to the conclusion that nearly anyone can become a target, with those in low-power positions being the most common targets.

Most research, but not all, indicates bullies are more likely to be male and in supervisory or managerial roles, due in part to the need for bullies to be in positions of power in order to successfully intimidate their victims (Zapf & Einarsen, 2003). When bullies are female, they tend to use psychological warfare tactics such as spreading false rumors, excluding victims from important meetings and information networks, and ostracism (Crothers, 2009). Perpetrators of bullying tend to exhibit higher than average levels of aggression, whereas victims tend to exhibit low levels of self-esteem. Victims *and* perpetrators have weak social skills. "Social competency is closely linked with empathy, the capacity to share the emotional state of another, and is also associated with altruistic behavior . . . Deficits in social competency, specifically those aspects relevant to close relationships, are clearly linked to engaging in offending or humiliating behavior against others" (Matthiesen & Einarsen, 2007, p. 740). Bullies tend to seek external validation, meaning their ego needs the approval of others to thrive. Bullies who turn to violence at work tend to exhibit an inability to empathize, lack of self-control, type A personalities (on a Myers-Briggs personality assessment), unrealistically high self-esteem, and a history of depression (Lutgen-Sandvik, Tracy, & Alberts, 2007).

For the targets of bullies, low levels of social skills make it difficult for them to identify the behavior as bullying and make it difficult for them to reach out to powerful individuals who might help them. Their most common reaction to bullying is withdrawal. Ironically, a subset of victims is also composed of bullies themselves, meaning those who have been bullied are somewhat more likely to be perpetrators in the future (Palmer & Thakordas, 2005).

Bullies and targets have another key factor in common: they both report elevated workplace stress due to conflicting or unclear demands and expectations related to their daily work (Matthiesen & Einersen, 2007). Bullying behavior occurs more frequently in workplaces where lines of authority are unclear and where there is internal rivalry or competitive workplace cultures (Neuberger, 1989).

The best prevention against workplace bullying is the creation and maintenance of a positive, collaborative workplace culture that fosters strong social ties among team members and creates clarity about expectations and roles. If bullying does occur in this type of organization, it is likely to be caught sooner and dealt with more swiftly. Highly competitive organizational cultures may have greater difficulty recognizing this behavior as unacceptable because their cultural norms may actually encourage "survival of the fittest" among employees. During the employment applicant-screening process, employers may wish to use scales that measure empathy and other measures of emotional intelligence so as to screen out those who will be more apt to bully or work poorly in teams.

In addition to creating an organizational culture that disallows bullying and promotes hiring employees with good social skills and emotional intelligence, occasionally a manager or employee will need to intervene to stop workplace bullying. Workplace policies need to define bullying as well as the potential consequences of such behaviors. Victims need to know where to go for help and that their concerns will be proactively addressed. Even if a manager feels the behaviors do not fully meet the definition of bullying, the fact that an employee has raised these concerns is a sign that some intervention in the relationship between accuser and accused is necessary. Remember, only a small percentage of victims will ever file a lawsuit over a formal complaint, about 3 percent, but they may quit or be unable to fully fulfill their job duties when the target of such behavior (Wiedmer, 2011).

The first step to a successful intervention is to recognize bullying behavior using the definition shared previously. Second, the manager should speak privately with the bully to let him or her know which specific behaviors constitute bullying and the consequences for continuing those behaviors. Because bullies often act out of sense of threat to self, it is important to clarify their roles, set appropriate boundaries, and work with them to develop better coping skills and behaviors, including asking them to engage in perspective taking, which is to empathize with the target and see how this might have a negative impact on the target and the broader organization. Consider having employees attend counseling through an employee assistance program or other venues to work on improving their social and empathy skills. In the end, it will be important to set clear expectations about the behaviors that must stop and any reparations or apologies due to the victim.

Written records of this meeting and any resulting expectations should be kept in case litigation from either party arises later. Managers should meet with the target to assure him or her that the problem will stop immediately and to clarify that such behaviors will not be tolerated. Although it is important not to blame the victim, there may be similar resources made available to the victim to help reduce the chances of future victimization by this or any other bully.

GIVING AND RECEIVING FEEDBACK

Throughout the year, as well as during performance reviews, the ability to give and receive constructive feedback is a crucial skill for career and organizational success. Often managers withhold constructive feedback out of a fear that employees will be offended or angered by observations that improvements to their performance are needed. Yet, without this feedback the chances of improvement are diminished. Giving and receiving feedback can be made easier with the reliance on some specific communication and conflict management tools.

When Giving Feedback

The first step to giving feedback is to do a self-check to determine the purposes behind your desire to offer feedback. Are you angry and wanting to lash out? Would it feel really good to give them a "piece of your mind"? If your gut instinct says, "yes!" then the best advice is to wait until your anger subsides and you are able to give feedback solely to help improve employee performance.

Once you have determined that your goal is to help, then follow the EPM (empathize, pinpoint problems, move forward) formula. Let's use an example to illustrate how this works. Imagine you have an employee who consistently misses deadlines. Your first statement should show your empathy for their situation and establish a positive, collaborative tone for the discussion. For example, "I understand you are working under tight deadlines." Your next statement should specifically pinpoint the problem, being careful to avoid framings that seem to imply fault or blame. "The report due on the fifteenth did not arrive until the twentieth." Then suggest a way to move forward and invite the feedback recipient to help generate ideas to solve the problem. You might ask, "What can be done to ensure the reports arrive on time in the future?" As a supervisor or manager, you have veto power over any unacceptable suggestions but your willingness to seek out information and ideas from the employee will increase their buy-in to any solutions chosen.

Steps for Giving Feedback

1. Self-check: what is the purpose of the feedback?
2. Empathize
3. Pinpoint problems
4. Move forward

Source: Lebedun and Kantola (1996).

Framing refers to the ways in which facts or perceptions are defined, constructed, or labeled. "Framing is a process whereby communicators, consciously or unconsciously, act to construct a point of view that encourages the facts of a given situation to be interpreted by others in a particular manner. Frames operate in four key ways: they define problems, diagnose causes, make moral judgments, and suggest remedies. Frames are often found within a narrative account of an issue or event, and are generally the central organizing idea" (Kuypers, 2006, p. 7).

Framing can make all the difference in terms of having an engaging, problem-solving discussion versus inciting defensive, angry, conflict escalation. When people feel attacked, they tend to have a fight or flight response. On the conflict style inventory scale used in Chapter One, those who scored high on the accommodating or avoiding conflict styles would be likely to have a flight response to a statement that was framed in a hostile manner. Alternatively, if the score was high on the competitive style, then the response is likely to be fight. Either way, the chances of having a productive discussion or negotiation are strongly diminished by poor framings. When framing your comments to the other party, avoid statements that cast fault or blame as well as those that are too general to provide specific feedback. For example, "You're always turning in reports late! You know that is unacceptable." This framing is simply less effective at encouraging cooperation from the employee than the framing shown in the previous paragraph.

"I" statements can be used to constructively frame your feedback in ways that are less likely to trigger the fight or flight response. For example, when you feel an employee is shirking or not doing his or her share of the work, a destructive framing might be to say, "You aren't carrying your weight around here. It's time for you to do your share of the work." Alternatively, you could say the same thing using "I" statements, such as, "I feel stressed out because the workload is not being equally distributed." This formula follows the format of "I feel _____ because of _____ ." Using the EPM formula, the feedback may look something like, "I understand you have been very busy lately [E]. I feel frustrated because I have more work to do than I can handle and I believe the workload could be more evenly distributed [P]. What ideas do you have for ensuring that each team member is called on to complete an equal amount of work [M]?"

When Receiving Feedback

Feedback only works if the person on the receiving end is open to hearing it. The first step is knowing that everyone's performance can improve, even high performers, and one's performance improves with the feedback of others. The best managers refrain from becoming defensive when feedback (also known as *criticism*) is offered. In fact, they invite feedback frequently. The next step is to listen to understand rather than listening to respond, as covered in Chapter Four. By truly listening to the person providing feedback, we can hear not only what he or she says, but also listen deeply enough to understand the meaning that lies behind the words or what is unsaid. Be sure to summarize back what you've heard so as to ensure your filters have not interfered with your ability to fully listen and understand. Occasionally, people offer general rather than specific feedback, such as "I don't like the way you talk to me." For the feedback to be helpful we need to get as specific as possible. Ask for specifics and examples. Make it clear that you are not being argumentative and that your real objective is to fully understand the criticism. Finally, we take what we have heard and analyze it. What can we take from it to improve our performance or our relationship with the other party? Sometimes we can learn from others' feedback, even when it is not stated in particularly constructive terms.

Steps for Receiving Feedback

1. Keep an open mind: anticipate feedback opportunities.
2. Listen to understand, not to respond.
3. Ask questions to get specific feedback.
4. Analyze the feedback for useful information.

Fight the need to respond right away. Take some time to think through their comments. Have you received similar feedback from others? What are you willing to do to address their concern or observation? In the end, you may decide no changes are needed but you will have at least listened thoroughly and understood their concerns before reaching this decision.

PERFORMANCE REVIEWS AND EMPLOYEE RECOGNITION

Ask any organizational ombudsman or human resource manager: more complaints are filed after performance reviews than at any other time of the year. Rather than dreading giving and receiving performance reviews, these can be times to look forward to. Performance reviews provide an opportunity to sit down with employees one-on-one in order to get to know them better. You get to check in with them to see how things are going from their perspective. You can ask about their future plans for advancement in the organization, if any. It is a time when individualized plans for professional development can be discussed and developed. Managers can gain feedback from employees about their own performance during this time as well. If all participants think of this as an opportunity to share information, make improvements, and recognize accomplishments over the past year, then it will become a positive rather than dreaded experience.

For performance reviews to be fair and objective all employees and teams need to have clear goals and performance indicators against which their performance can be judged. Second, the organization needs to gather data related to individual and group performance. For example, you may ask customers and clients to complete feedback surveys related to their experiences. In manufacturing settings you can look at output or other readily quantifiable measures. All employees can be rated on their punctuality, adherence to schedules and deadlines, and so on. Be sure to include indicators of employees' collegiality and problem-solving and workplace behaviors.

Ideally, performance reviews should have a 360-degree-feedback mechanism whenever possible. A 360-degree review takes in feedback from all people you work with: peers, subordinates, supervisors, and managers to provide anonymous feedback. This system works best in large organizations but can be done in small organizations, though with less anonymity. Over 65 percent of poor performance problems can be traced to strained interpersonal relationships and communications at work (Dana, 2001), so do not forget to include measurements of collaboration, communication, and conflict management in your feedback and performance measurement tools. Employees should rate their satisfaction with their supervisors' and managers' abilities to resolve problems efficiently and collaboratively. Ask employees at all levels whether they would recommend your organization to others in their fields who are looking for work. This helps you learn more about organization or departmentwide problems that may exist with the organizational culture. In the same survey, be sure to gather their ideas about how to improve workplace morale, efficiency, and mission fulfillment.

Annual performance reviews are fairly standard in corporations and government agencies but are done haphazardly in many small organizations. Even in a two-person operation, performance reviews provide helpful opportunities to check on each employee's professional goals, skill-set development, and productivity. These can be opportunities to build and enhance relationships up and down the chain of command, and whenever possible, the employee being reviewed should also be allowed to provide feedback on the performance of his or her direct supervisor to ensure a two-way exchange takes place. Rather than limiting feedback opportunities to an annual review, consider scheduling these reviews more frequently. More frequent reviews allow increased opportunity to track growth and change, to provide specific suggestions and advice, and to address changing circumstances within the workplace. If an employee or manager is asked to work on one to two specific skills or goals, then a check-in should be scheduled in no more than one month. If the employee's efforts for improvement are offtrack, he or she should not need to wait a whole year to learn about it.

During performance reviews, some organizations create something akin to a work plan or contract that lays out the primary tasks, timelines, and expectations of the employee during the forthcoming review period. By meeting periodically throughout the year, these can be amended as circumstances change, thereby ensuring that the expectations on both sides are clear and the document remains up to date.

Performance reviews are often tied to bonuses, raises, or other rewards or sanctions. In collectivist cultures, such as Japan and China, rewards tend to be solely done on the group level, but the opposite is true in the individualistic cultures of the United States and other Western countries. Pearsall, Christian, and Ellis (2010) examined the relative benefits of rewarding individual versus group performance in US work teams. Their study found that organizations seeking to encourage team work and group projects were more likely to have group-based rewards. Yet, with group-based rewards, there can be squabbling and dissension related to the division of labor—someone tends to be the work horse and another is the shirker, or "social-loafer" (p. 188). The researchers therefore recommended that rewards or sanctions come from a combination of individual and group efforts and achievements.

A 2011 survey by SHRM found that 80 percent of companies with five hundred or more employees have an employee recognition program in place. Of those, 58 percent recognized employees for their years of service, 48 percent recognized employees who went above and beyond their regular work duties or surpassed expectations, and 37 percent recognized employees whose exemplary behavior was closely aligned with the organization's values (SHRM, 2011). Interestingly, 11 percent of the companies stated they tracked employee social media activity to view positive and negative employee comments about the organization as indicators of employee engagement.

What if you have an employee who is a poor performer? The key is to correctly diagnose the source of the poor performance. Remember, many poor-performing employees feel alienated or disgruntled, believe they lack clear communication about goals and expectations from their supervisors, or otherwise trace the root of the poor performance to poor conflict management within the workplace. If this is not a matter of poor communication or conflict management, there are a few pertinent questions to address:

Do the employee's assignments match up well with his skill sets and training?

If not, is it possible to provide additional training or support to better align the employee's tasks and skills?

Is the employee supportive of the organization's mission and how her work ties into that mission?

In a friendly way, quiz employees to determine whether they understand the mission and their role in it.

Are the performance goals and objectives clear, objectively measured, and set at reasonable levels?

Gather data on these points together and make any needed revisions.

What ideas does the employee have about the sources of poor performance and ideas for improvement?

By gaining input from employees and allowing them to have a voice in this process (remember the concepts of procedural justice), they will be more likely to support the outcome of the evaluation and any subsequent employment decisions.

Before we leave the topic of performance reviews we should note large employers require their managers to follow a specific format for providing feedback during performance reviews. These formats generally include a host of behaviors and competencies used to judge the employee's performance. However, managers will benefit from attention to the framing of suggestions, and from making this a two-way conversation in order to learn more about the employee's goals and concerns and to negotiate action plans that receive buy-in from the employee.

WHAT MAKES A "GREAT MANAGER"?

Luckily this is not merely a philosophical question, as it may seem at first glance. Thousands of studies have been conducted that help us identify effective managers and ineffective managers. A brief examination of the findings of these studies will help us as we strive to identify the characteristics and behaviors of great managers and strive to continually improve our own managerial skills.

F. Stuart Gulley, president of Woodward Academy, says the difference between a leader and a manager is that "a leader helps create a shared vision and inspires others to live in that preferred future, while a manager tends to tactical details to get the job done. Actually, a good leader does both" (Tierney, 2011). Mr. Gulley's organization was listed as one of the best places to work in Atlanta for 2011. When asked what makes him an effective company leader, he said, "I would say that it relates to my commitment to be open, transparent and accessible. I listen. I try to affirm and encourage others on the team while directing our efforts toward our mission and vision" (Tierney, 2011). On the same question, Bob Mathis from Peachtree Planning says, "I am the keeper of the culture and, based on our retention of both advisers and professional support staff, I believe that my partners and I have been effective leaders in keeping our culture and mission alive and vibrant" (Tierney, 2011).

All relationships involve some level of give-and-take or reciprocity in order to be mutually beneficial. Managers can't accomplish anything without their subordinates who do the bulk of the frontline work of any organization. Employees expect their managers to help them solve problems, communicate clearly, and remove obstacles to their ability to get their work done. This reciprocal relationship is transactional in nature, meaning there is an inherent transaction taking place between the manager and employee—each exchanging something the other needs. This makes the relationship mutually beneficial. Transformational leaders go beyond mere transactions to inspire employees to reach new heights, develop new skills, and break previously unquestioned barriers to their performance. Like parents or coaches, transformational leaders see the intrinsic value in each employee and seek to help employees maximize their performance, not mainly because it helps the manager but because it is good for the individual employee and for the organization as a whole (Bass & Avolio, 1994). The best managers focus on transforming their employees and workplaces rather than merely on improving the transactional nature of their relationships.

Organizational leaders set the tone for the organization. They create and re-create their organizational cultures by building effective teams, communicating their vision, and getting all team members on board with that vision. As we will see in Chapter Six, effective organizational leadership is central to laying the foundation for managers and employees to succeed. Once that foundation is in place and consistently communicated, organizational leaders keep the channels of communication open, clear obstacles from the paths of others, and empower those working under them to succeed. So how can mid-level managers and supervisors become great?

You can rely on your own experiences to help you identify those characteristics of good bosses. Which bosses empowered, inspired, and supported you? Which bosses made you want to call in sick every Monday? Abbasi, Hollman, and Hayes (2008) note that good managers demonstrate a high level of integrity, remove fear from the workplace, fight for employees, and help employees save face and overcome a lack of trust. A study by Bass and Bass (2009) examined multiple leadership studies for similarities and found these qualities as being key to leadership success: adaptability, adjustment, assertiveness, emotional balance and control, enthusiasm, nonconformity, originality, creativity, ethical conduct, self-confidence, resourcefulness, and tolerance of stress.

In early 2009 Google began "Project Oxygen," an internal study aimed at identifying the characteristics of the company's most successful managers. Luckily, what they found applies not only to Google managers, but also to management generally. They mined performance reviews, employee feedback surveys, and nominations for top-manager awards to find out what makes the best managers (Bryant, 2011). The Project Oxygen team asked employees to rank the qualities that made for the best managers. The research team predicted that technical expertise would be high on the list of attributes found among the best managers—after all, when employees get stumped on a technical matter they are supposed to turn to their managers for assistance. Yet technical abilities ranked last out of eight attributes of great managers. "What employees valued the most were even-keeled bosses who made time for one-on-one meetings, who helped people puzzle through problems by asking questions, not dictating answers, and who took an interest in employees' lives and careers" (Bryant, 2011, p. 2). Making a connection to employees and being accessible were key qualities of great managers. A study by Watson and Hoffman (1996) found that the most successful and powerful managers engaged in cooperative behaviors with their colleagues and employees whereas lower-power managers attempted to make gains by resorting to authoritarian and competitive practices.

More specifically, see Table 5.2 for a description of the characteristics of effective managers found during the Google study. When reading this table, you may wonder how these habits relate to conflict management. These habits are closely tied to organizational conflict management for a few reasons. Clearly, effective managers enact these habits and ineffective managers neglect them.

Inadequate managers communicate poorly or infrequently (the opposite of habit five for effective managers). Deficient managers are not open to giving or receiving feedback from their employees when it relates to the vision or goals for the work unit or for the continued improvement and growth of the manager's own skill set. Poor managers are so focused on the end goals of productivity, service delivery, or profit that they fail to recognize the means by which those ends are likely to be accomplished, for example, building positive relationships and good communication within their teams.

A body of management theory known as **leader-member exchange theory** has become popular since the 1980s. This research examines the types of relationships that form between leaders and organizational members as well as the benefits that accrue to leaders and members as a result of these relationships. This approach posits that the best managers develop positive relationships with organizational members based on "trust, respect, loyalty, liking, intimacy, support, openness and honesty" (Wilson, Sin, & Conlon, 2010, p. 358). Leaders provide members with goods such as access to information, assignment to interesting projects, and recommendations to higher managers, whereas members supply commitment, engagement, and loyalty. Both accrue benefits from the nurturing of close, effective relationships that include recognition of their interdependence.

Table 5.2
Eight Habits of Effective Managers

Habit	Description
1. Be a good coach.	Provide specific, constructive feedback with regular one-on-one meetings.
2. Empower your team. Don't micromanage.	Balance employee freedom and give advice. Allow employees to grow skills with new challenges.
3. Express interest in employee success and well-being.	Get to know employees as people outside of work. Ease transitions for new employees with warm welcomes.
4. Be productive and results oriented.	Help prioritize work. Remove roadblocks. Focus on goal setting.
5. Be a good communicator; listen to your team.	Two-way communication is key: listen and share, encourage open dialogue, hold regular meetings for all team members.
6. Help employees with career development.	Learn about employees' career goals and ways you can empower them to achieve those goals.
7. Have a clear vision and strategy for the team.	Involve the team in drafting and updating its vision and goals.
8. Have key technical skills.	Work beside employees when needed. Understand the specific challenges of each team member's job.

Source: Adapted from Blodget (2011).

In addition to yielding these eight habits of successful managers, the Google study also found three pitfalls common to their worst managers (see Table 5.3). The first pitfall is that great workers do not always make great managers. A hardworking frontline employee may or may not have the knowledge and skills necessary to successfully transition into the management role. Organizations can ameliorate these deficits through training programs designed to help employees transition successfully to managerial roles or through tests of these skills as part of the promotion process. When organizations choose to hire managers from outside rather than promoting from within, it is crucial that new hires

Table 5.3
Pitfalls of Poor Managers

Pitfall	Description
1. Trouble transitioning to team leader	A great individual performer; lacks knowledge and preparation for management role or is an outside hire who doesn't understand organization's culture or processes
2. Lacks consistent approach to performance management and career development	Not proactive—waits for employees to come to him or her; does not coach employees for their development; fails to communicate what the organization needs or wants to employees
3. Spends too little time managing and communicating	Doesn't hold regular group and one-on-one meetings; doesn't listen well or invite feedback or ideas

Source: Adapted from Blodget (2011).

take the time to learn the organization's processes, policies, and culture during their transition phase. The second and third pitfalls deal with managers who do not communicate consistently, proactively, and effectively. Ineffective managers hold meetings only when a crisis emerges. They don't follow up to ensure their employees' career development needs are being met, and they don't listen well.

Do the characteristics of good managers vary from the private sector to that of the nonprofit or public sectors? The ability to surface rather than suppress differences is seen as an act of leadership aimed at moving the organization forward yet it is a recurrent theme most prevalent in the literature on public sector leadership. Bryson and Crosby (2006) recommend that manager leaders use conflicts to purposefully structure a political environment that highlights constructive dissonance, thereby allowing for more informed decision making. Jeffery Luke offers a framework for leaders who manage public issues in a collaborative manner in his 1998 book entitled *Catalytic Leadership*. In it, Luke defines a person of integrity as "someone who acts in accord with her or his principles or commitments when facing pressure or enticement of various sorts to do otherwise" (p. 229). In some ways public managers are under more scrutiny and are expected to exhibit higher degrees of integrity. Rightly or wrongly, they are expected to behave with integrity because they are entrusted with public resources and the protection of vulnerable populations. It is important for public managers to display ethical leadership without seeming haughty or self-righteous. Humility is more often expected from an agency director than from a CEO, even though their qualifications and leadership methods may be similar in other respects.

BECOMING A GREAT MANAGER

If you read every book about golf you can find, will you become a great golfer? Although reading about managing provides the foundation of knowledge necessary to improve your managerial techniques, the key is to set specific goals related to your skill development, measure progress toward those goals, and practice new skills and behaviors frequently. Your habits took a long time to develop and they won't change overnight. When you find yourself sliding back into old habits, spend your energy refocusing your efforts rather than beating yourself up. Be explicit with your employee team about these efforts; tell them you are working on growing and developing as a manager and that you will be trying new techniques to see what works and what doesn't. Invite their feedback in this process. They will most likely appreciate your openness and desire to make positive changes. You will be modeling the behaviors you expect from them. Even the best managers strive for continual improvement and professional development.

The good news is that your managerial skills are only partly a function of your natural endowments, meaning your personality or temperament. In Google's study, they were able to see measureable improvements in 75 percent of their worst managers (Bryant, 2011). In addition to measuring managerial quality and providing performance reviews on a quarterly basis, Google provides one-on-one coaching to help improve managerial performance. Consider using the services of an executive coach in your organization or for your own development. You may also wish to seek out a mentor within your organization — someone whose management skills and style you would like to learn from. If your organization does not have a mentoring program, ask the HR department to help get one started. Setting clear goals and seeking specific feedback will help as you grow in your career and continually improve.

But remember, sometimes managers are called on to make difficult decisions. Although you cannot please all the people all of the time, creating a fair process for decision making, gathering input, listening before acting, fostering positive organizational culture, and acting swiftly to address problems will help garner support when difficult decisions need to be made.

CONCLUSION

Satisfied customers and successful organizations are built on the foundation of satisfied employees, who are treated and compensated fairly. High employee turnover results in preventable costs that limit the ability of organizations to achieve their missions and remain competitive in the marketplace. Productive workplaces require thoughtful hiring, training, coaching, feedback, and incentives that align individual incentives with group goals. When problems arise, such as bullying, collaborative managers intervene to create and maintain a positive workplace culture in which all team members can thrive. Whether you manage two employees or two thousand, reducing employee turnover will be crucial to the success of your unit and your organization.

HIGH EMPLOYEE TURNOVER AT MAIN STREET BAKERIES

Using the company's employment records, Ben contacted the last three assistant managers and three former frontline employees. He met personally with some of these individuals and over the phone with others. He explained that his goal is to help store number seventy-five improve the workplace climate and make it a place where employees feel valued, satisfied, and empowered to do their jobs well. All were pleased to talk to him—in fact, they talked his ear off! He got a consistent story from everyone: the current manager of store number seventy-five, Jane, is a bully. She pressures hourly employees to work off the clock if they are unable to complete their tasks during their regular eight-hour shifts. She accuses staff of being "lazy," "stupid," or not being willing to "take one for the team." If employees ask for time off for a doctor's appointment or a family commitment, they are punished by being taken off the schedule for a week without pay. She turns employees against one another and promotes only her pet employees who act like sycophants. She rarely holds staff meetings and then gets angry when employees fail to correctly implement new policies or procedures. She works seventy-five hours per week and cannot understand why others are not willing to show similar levels of commitment.

So, what did Ben do? Ben sat down with the manager and had a very frank discussion. He told her that her own pay and bonuses would now be tied to employee workplace climate surveys, customer satisfaction surveys, and linked to a reduction in employee turnover. Every employee that leaves store number seventy-five during the next six months will take part in an exit interview by phone with Ben so he can get more feedback about how to improve the store and its management. He arranged for an executive coach to work with Jane on her people skills and told her she was required to meet with this coach for at least two hours per week for the next six weeks, and then at least one hour per month for twelve months. He made it clear that his goal was to help her reach her potential as a manager. He explained that her own job will be easier once she feels confident in her abilities to delegate to her assistant managers—her own stress level will go down, and her job satisfaction will increase.

The manager signed a ninety-day probationary contract agreeing to abide by these conditions. She met twice with her coach and then abruptly resigned. In her exit interview she said she did not feel she was a good match for the Main Street Bakeries' approach to management. She said she wanted to be fully in charge and hire and fire as she saw fit.

Ben contacted MaryAnn, one of the previous assistant managers he had interviewed on his trip. He asked MaryAnn to sign the same ninety-day probationary contract with all the same provisions he had required of Jane. Exit interviews, executive coaching, and employee and customer satisfaction surveys would still be used and incentives for reducing turnover were tied to MaryAnn's pay. Within three months, turnover was significantly reduced, customer satisfaction was up, and MaryAnn called Ben to thank him personally for supplying the executive coach—whom she came to deeply appreciate and value as a resource for ongoing professional development. Ben and Elise can now turn their attention to other matters because store number seventy-five is clearly back on track.

KEY TERMS

Bullying

Employee turnover

Exit interview (exit survey)

Leader-member exchange theory

Presenteeism

The 10–80–10 percent rule

SUGGESTED SUPPLEMENTAL READING

Elangovan, A. R. (1999). Managerial intervention in organizational disputes: Testing a prescriptive model of strategy selection. *International Journal of Conflict Management*, 9(4), 301–335.

Lutgen-Sandvik. P., Namie, G., & Namie, R. (2009). Workplace bullying: Causes, consequences and corrections. In P. Lutgen-Sandvik & B. D. Sypher (Eds.), *Destructive organizational communication: Processes, consequences and constructive ways of organizing*. New York: Routledge.

Perry, J. L., Mesch, D., & Paarlberg, L. (2006). Motivating employees in a new governance era: The performance paradigm revisited. *Public Administration Review*, 66(4), 505–514.

Rhodes, C., Pullen, A., Vickers, M. H., Clegg, S. R., & Pitsis, A. (2010). Violence and workplace bullying. *Administrative Theory & Praxis*, 32(1), 96–115.

DISCUSSION QUESTIONS

1. Think back to the best boss or manager you have had. List the behaviors, attitudes, or characteristics that led this person to be successful. How does he or she match up against the material covered in this chapter? How has this person's example shaped your own management style? Analyze and discuss.

2. What does your organization do to minimize employee turnover? What improvements could be made at a reasonable cost?

3. In a recessionary period, when the labor market is saturated with job seekers, why should organizations still pay attention to employee turnover?

EXERCISES

1. Are great managers born or made? What can you do to become a great manager, starting this week? Make a list of experimental changes you will try

this week. Come back one week from now and evaluate the success of those efforts through a discussion with your classmates or in your work team.

2. Imagine you are about to hire a new worker or workers for your organization. Based on the information in this chapter, what screening questions would you include on a preemployment questionnaire? What questions would you ask during the reference-check phase of the hiring process?

3. Create a survey that will be used to gain feedback on workplace morale within individual work units at your organization. What questions would you include? How would you integrate this survey into the annual bonus or merit raise structure of your organization?

4. Think of some common feedback scenarios within the workplace. Come up with some feedback framings that use the EPM formula as well as "I" statements.

GOAL SETTING

Look at Tables 5.1 and 5.2. Rate yourself (or your manager) on each of these habits and pitfalls on a scale of one to five, where one equals "never does this" and five equals "does this consistently." Select one or more of these habits for improvement during the next week. What specific behaviors will you change in order to see improvement? Check back one week from now and see if the scores have changed.

chapter SIX

Building Successful Teams and Organizations

Learning Objectives

- Describe the main elements in successful team building.

- Identify and determine how to proactively manage those who do not work well in teams.

- Demonstrate an understanding of the unique conflicts that are likely to occur during mergers and acquisitions as well as how to navigate them successfully.

- Describe how to manage in difficult economic circumstances.

JOHN AT THE BUREAU OF RECLAMATION

When John Smith took over as the head of his agency, the first thing he did was meet individually with each member of his inherited team. He wanted to get to know them better, build rapport, and understand their strengths and career goals. He asked each manager about the dynamics within their own work teams: about morale, employee turnover, and perceptions about any obstacles to the fullest achievement of the organization's mission.

What he learned did not surprise him. John has five managers, each heading departments of ten to twenty-five employees. Although resources seem perennially short, some of the teams exhibit camaraderie, low turnover, and success in the accomplishment of their missions. Two of the five departments seem plagued with poor productivity, high turnover, and even occasional litigation.

John's first step is to work with his managers on the skills and practices found in Chapter Five. Visible improvements were seen in all departments after each one implemented processes to track employee satisfaction and morale, began using exit surveys to learn from mistakes, strengthened their employee recognition program (the previous one was solely built on years of service), and to provide developmental feedback to all employees. Turnover is down and productivity is up. In fact, some of his seasoned employees have decided to stay on after having reached the years of service needed for full retirement—this was unheard of in the past. Yet those two departments continue to perform at lower levels than the others in the organization. John now believes the root cause of this problem lies in the nature of their teamwork or lack thereof. He is looking for ideas to improve team functioning within these two departments but some of what he learns will be helpful for the other departments as well.

At its core, managing means the ability to create and sustain productive teams. Whether you control who plays on your team or not, there are actions you can take to improve the functioning of your team(s) in order to enhance morale, improve productivity, build trust, and reduce unproductive conflict, even during difficult transitions such as mergers and acquisitions.

DO WE STILL NEED TEAMWORK?

It is clear that young entrants into the workforce are at least as comfortable communicating through technological interfaces as with face-to-face discussions, maybe even more so. Families are smaller, so many people under thirty were raised as only children, often geographically distant from extended families. This increasing tendency toward individualism has important consequences for the workplace and for teamwork. Yet research clearly indicates that collaboration nearly always yields superior outcomes compared to individual efforts (DeCusatis, 2008; Deutsch & Coleman, 2000). Many people have a love-hate relationship with teamwork—they know it is necessary but feel they would rather work alone.

Board Dysfunction and Corporate Profitability

In 1999, Coca-Cola Co.'s CEO, Douglas Ivester, was surprised in a Chicago airport by two members of the flagging company's board of directors. According to the directors, Ivester's hard-handed tactics with local bottlers and European regulators had alienated business partners and shareholders, leaving him with a reputation for not listening to the board. Mistakenly believing that the two directors spoke for the entire board, Ivester abruptly resigned. Shares of Coke fell 12 percent in two days as the board and investors struggled to make sense of what had happened. The incident would affect the company for years, and Coca-Cola would have three CEOs from 1997 to 2004. Certainly conflict is inevitable in any organization, but, with the right approach in place, boards can greatly increase the opportunity to resolve disagreements before they get a chance to get out of control. (Hasson, 2006, p. 77)

Teamwork and clear communication are indispensable in modern, global organizations. The work products of teams typically surpass those created through individual effort. This is particularly true when one's customers, vendors, and the audience are highly diverse. Diverse work teams are more able than homogenous teams to generate creative ideas and proposals. In this case, **diversity** refers to all the ways in which individuals may differ: gender, race, ethnicity, age, technical abilities and backgrounds, sexual orientation, religiosity and religious affiliation, social class, work style, worldview, and so on.

BEST PRACTICES FOR TEAM BUILDING

Rajagopal and Rajagopal (2006) state that well-developed teams "include clear identification of goals, clarity of roles, common feeling, motivation, commitment and collaborative attitude" (p. 5). Do these words describe your team?

If not, this chapter will help you learn how to bring needed change to your group's functioning. Experts on team building usually focus on several key areas, including methods for creating and building a team, how teams think and communicate, the role of trust building and repair in teams, team conflict, and dysfunction.

Consider the Team's Purpose

When creating teams, consider their primary purpose. Teams tasked with creative duties will need to have maximum diversity, including diverse demographic characteristics as well as educational backgrounds and life experiences. Teams tasked with implementing policies or changes will need good communication, flexibility, empathy, and social-emotional skills. In some teams, you may want people who are as similar as possible to work together but in others you may want the opposite. A team's composition should be well matched to its purpose. As mentioned Chapter Five, Rohlander (1999) suggests that it helps to explicitly define the team's goals and to remind the team of its goals often. Managers should consider the team's purpose when deciding who should be chosen for that team (DeCusatis, 2008).

Teams need a little shaking up now and then. For example, a study by Skilton and Dooley (2010) provided evidence that teams who have worked together on previous projects may find it difficult to match their success on subsequent projects. The researchers suggest that a possible solution for this is to integrate a new person into the team on projects in which the production of highly creative ideas is important.

Team-Building Assessment Tools

There are a plethora of assessment tools that may be of help when hiring and creating teams. They can also be helpful to assess the underlying causes of an underperforming team. Such tools include the traditional Myers-Briggs personality assessment, the conflict styles inventory covered in Chapter One, the Hogan Development Survey, and many more. Your HR department may be able to assist you in choosing the best tools for your particular purposes depending on the internal expertise. When selecting assessment tools, remember to keep in mind the group's purpose. Different tools will highlight different aspects of the team and of individual team members.

TEAM TYPOLOGIES

So what is a good place to start when it comes to team building? A wide variety of advice is available in the management literature. A good first step is to decide which kind of team you need to build (or need to reshape from your current team). As the purpose of the team changes, it may be important to exchange team members with other teams in the organization, hire new team members, or retrain existing team members.

In a 2008 study, DeCusatis lists the following types of teams: genius teams, improv teams, virtual teams, and FourSight teams. **Genius teams** are small teams of brilliant employees who benefit from lots of close contact while working with each other. **Improv teams** are highly adaptable and adjust well to rapidly changing circumstances. Team members are interchangeable and can tag team as necessary. **Virtual teams** are Internet based and therefore may come from anywhere on the globe but can never or infrequently meet in person. Finally, **FourSight teams** are those that take a specific four-step approach to decision making that is somewhat similar to the four steps of the negotiation process covered in Chapter Three: they define the problem, brainstorm solutions, sift out the best solution, and carry out their plan. Of course, teams may shift from one type to another as their deadlines, needs, or focus change.

Although managers may not always be able to build teams from scratch for each project, it will be helpful for managers and team members to take the time to learn how each member communicates best and how the team prefers to work. This metacommunication will help teams gain shared understandings of one another's personality types and how their communication styles affect the team and its members (Gevers & Peeters, 2009). **Metacommunication** occurs when people communicate about how they communicate. This information can avoid misunderstandings and attribution biases that often occur when one communicates with someone whose preferred patterns or methods of communication differ from his or her own. Personality and communication assessment tools can be helpful in this effort: which team member is an auditory learner and which is more visual? Knowing how your team members scored on the conflict styles inventory (see Chapter One) will help you to know how best to approach them when a problem arises. It also provides an opportunity to discuss the division of tasks, shared expectations related to performance, and how problems will be addressed when they inevitably arise because they nearly always do. Learning each other's modalities and expectations will help minimize miscommunication and maximize synergy, and metacommunication will help speed up this learning curve.

WHAT IF I CAN'T CHOOSE MY TEAM?

Many, if not most, managers do not have the luxury of building a team from scratch or changing teams each time a new project comes along. Yet the information covered in the chapter thus far still can be helpful as you seek to assign tasks to team members based on their individual strengths and personalities, engage in team-building metacommunication and activities to enhance rapport and improve teamwork, and thoughtfully negotiate team tasks and timelines.

When employees seem to lack the skills or knowledge needed to accomplish shared tasks, then it falls to the manager to engage them in a problem-solving negotiation to determine whether one or more members should pursue additional training or professional development or if a new team member should be hired. Managers may wish to share some information about teamwork and team types and then engage employees in a discussion about the type of team they seek to be and how these goals line up with the tasks and mission of the organization.

HOW TEAMS THINK AND COMMUNICATE

How does your team think and communicate? According to Cooke, Gorman, Duran, and Taylor (2007), one of the most important factors in team functioning is the ability to think like a team, which is called *team cognition*. In their metastudy of the literature on team cognition, DeChurch and Mesmer-Magnus (2010) state that "team cognition has strong positive relationships to team behavioral process, motivational states, and team performance . . . team cognition explains significant incremental variance in team performance after the effects of behavioral and motivational dynamics have been controlled" (p. 32). The ability to think as a group may in fact be a prerequisite to the team's ability to act as a group.

There are two key concepts relating to team cognition: **team mental models (TMMs)** and **transactive memory systems (TMSs)** (Kozlowski & Ilgen, 2006). According to Austin (2003), a TMM is a set of jointly held information within a group and the TMS is like a mental map disseminating the information held by individual members. Those aspects of knowledge known by each team member are collectively known as the *shared mental model (SMM)* (Kozlowski & Ilgen, 2006).

So the TMM is a broad construct representing a wide variety of what the team knows collectively, the SMM is a construct representing the knowledge that all the team members share, and the TMS is an intricate web of who knows what in the team (Kozlowski & Ilgen, 2006). This information helps us understand what has long been called *institutional memory* as well as the role of individually held knowledge within teams. According to Beng-Chong and Klein (2006), the overall key to having a team mental model likely to increase performance is to focus on team members having similar, shared, and accurate concepts of who knows what in the team.

Good, clear, planned communication is the key to having institutionally and individually held information or expertise. Gillespie, Chaboyer, and Murray (2010) writes that "in surgery, up to 70% of adverse events are attributable to failures in communication" (p. 642). Most organizations do not measure the impact of poor communication as well as the health care industry but we can assume that poor communication is to blame for many lost customers, contract disputes, and general inefficiencies. "Disagreements thrive from ambiguity: around the boundaries of job roles or functional teams, the relative importance of organizational priorities, or the ownership of resources" (Haynes, 2009, p. 10).

Research by Langan-Fox (2004) shows that teams with well-developed and functional TMM share information more quickly and efficiently as well as synchronize their efforts more effectively. The improved efficiency is due to being in sync rather than spending lots of time debating the assignment of tasks out of a lack of knowledge of each other's strengths. This can only happen when team members know each other well. This finding echoes those of Patrick Lencioni (2002). In *The Five Dysfunctions of a Team* he writes that well-functioning groups have five common characteristics: they trust one another, they engage in unfiltered positive conflict about ideas and strategic directions, they commit to decisions and action plans even if some members disagree with them, they hold one another accountable for delivering their commitments, and they focus on the achievement of collective results (i.e., they are team players). Under Lencioni's model, it is the primary duty of organizational leaders to hire individuals who will fit in well with the organization's cultural norms, support its mission, and engage in these five practices. Leaders need not engage in the day-to-day work of the organization. In fact, this becomes nearly impossible in large organizations. Instead, they maintain a role in screening, hiring, promoting, and maintaining a constructive culture and make strategic decisions after extensive consultations with others in the organization.

Ensuring that your work group thinks and communicates like a team is a crucial task for managers and supervisors at every level.

CULTURAL PREFERENCES FOR TIME MANAGEMENT

Be careful about pairing monochronic and polychronic team members unless they are able to work relatively autonomously. Each cultural group develops unique understandings about how time works and how one should think about time. For example, if I invite you to a cocktail party at my house at 7:00 PM, what time would you arrive? If you come from Kansas, you might arrive any time between 7:15 PM and 7:45 PM. If you are in Korea, you would know to come at 6:50 PM as a sign of respect. In Haiti you might come at 9:00 PM or later. Cultural knowledge about time is learned through observation and most of us reach the incorrect assumption that our way of viewing time is universally shared.

A **monochronic time orientation** indicates that one prefers to adhere to strict schedules and deadlines. Time is viewed as something tangible that can be saved, spent, or wasted and the inherent assumption is that individuals control when they get work done. This orientation toward time is most common in countries such as Great Britain, Germany, Switzerland, the United States, Australia, and other cultures of Western European origin. People with this orientation may be somewhat less flexible and more driven by deadlines. They may also prefer to get right down to the task at hand rather than spend time building relationships. They tend to believe there is a right time for specific activities (e.g., arrive at work by 8:30 AM, take no more than a one-hour lunch, and so on). A **polychronic time orientation** means one believes there are many right times to do different activities (e.g., arrive at work anytime between 8:30 AM and 10:00 AM, take a flexible lunch break, etc.). Those with polychromic orientations tend to build personal relationships before attempting to accomplish tasks as a group. They tend to view time as beyond their control, a force of nature. When speaking of the future they tend not to plan six months or more in advance because to do so would be to tempt fate (e.g., "We make plans and God laughs").

Polychronic time orientations tend to develop in cultures nearer the equator, where seasonal differences are smaller (e.g., many Latino and Island cultures). Monochronic time orientations developed in cultures with four clear seasons. In these societies, if one did not engage in specific activities at specific times, such as sowing in spring and harvesting in the fall, then winter could be very long and hungry. By contrast, more equatorial countries did not need to attend so carefully to time, and as a result they have developed more flexible orientations toward time. Additionally, in countries with chaotic political and economic histories, cultures tend to develop polychronic time orientations. When buses don't run on time or when people must queue for hours to buy necessities, they develop flexible attitudes toward time because its management is in fact often beyond their control.

People with different time orientations may be able to work well together but it will be helpful for them to discuss their preferred work styles so as to be respectful of differences. Developing shared norms related to the definition of on time and the negotiability or flexibility of deadlines is also important. When corporations from monochronic cultures open branches in countries with polychronic cultures, challenges relating to conflicting norms of time management are to be expected and should be addressed proactively. Each culture believes their orientation toward time is the correct one. This reveals a form of **ethnocentrism**, which is the belief that one's cultural practices are inherently superior to those from other cultures. Recognizing this tendency will be helpful for a constructive dialogue between those of different time orientations.

PHASES OF TEAMWORK

It is helpful to understand the natural phases that most groups experience as they form, get to know one another, and seek to accomplish shared tasks. These phases have been termed: *forming, storming, norming,* and *performing* (Tuchman & Jensen, 1977). In the first phase, forming, the group comes together either spontaneously or by design. The group members hardly know one another and are in the honeymoon phase of the relationship. Individually, they strive to hide any flaws and behave more formally until they slowly get to know one another. In this phase, there is little structure to group interactions and the group is not working at maximum efficiency, if at all. Next, the group goes through a storming phase. In this phase hostility arises between members and subgroups often form. Lack of clarity among roles, differences in communication structure, as well as personality conflicts can worsen this difficult period. This phase is characterized by negativity, aggression, and rivalry. Some members may leave the group if this phase lasts too long. The third phase, norming, occurs as the group develops shared behavioral norms and expectations. They exhibit higher levels of trust and affection than in the previous two stages and the group membership stabilizes. During the fourth stage, performing, the group reaches its peak performance levels. Group members are clear about their roles, shared expectations exist, and group members collaborate effectively. Because they know one another well, they are able to communicate effectively, distribute tasks based on team member strengths, and solve problems proactively. Eventually, most groups go through a fifth stage, adjourning. In this stage, the task has been finished or the group disbands for other reasons. This phase can be quick, with all the members disbanding at once, or they can leave slowly, one at a time. This phase is often accompanied with some form of grieving, either collectively or separately, depending on the way the group disbanded. Remember, if one or more new members join the team, they may get temporarily thrown back into an earlier phase as they strive to incorporate this member into their midst.

As a manager, your goal is to help the group get to the performing stage and stay there. This can be accomplished in a number of ways. First, be sure to structure time for relationship building into the team's initial interactions. Let them get to know one another as people, share their interests, their preferred communication styles, and their strengths and weaknesses (to the extent they wish to share these). Ask them to develop group norms together—how would they like to structure their time together? What behavioral expectations can they agree on? Revisit these norms periodically as the group settles in together. Are they working or do they need to be changed? Help the group to clarify roles and responsibilities. Check in periodically to see if these need to be changed to reflect the deeper understandings that will develop concerning individual strengths and preferences. When problems erupt between team members or between subgroups, do not pretend you don't notice. Speak to individuals one-on-one, keeping a friendly and helpful tone. Ask them what is happening and how you can help. Use the coaching skills covered in Chapter Four to assist each employee as he or she develops plans to address the problems. If necessary, mediate agreements between individuals or groups and check to ensure these agreements are being followed. When problems arise in teams, proactive action can prevent small problems from becoming large ones. Remember, conflict is an opportunity to improve a relationship.

ROLES AND DUTIES WITHIN TEAMS

When creating or changing teams, managers may wish to consider the specific roles or duties of each team member. Some employees may be good at part but not all of the group's tasks, so it is useful to know their strengths and ensure that all the needed skills and knowledge for a task can be found among the team members collectively. For example, law firms have long divided the roles held by employees into four common categories: finders, minders, binders, and grinders (Lee, 2010). Although these terms were developed to explain the division of roles within law firms, they can apply to many other types of private and nonprofit organizations. Finders are the rainmakers who find new work and bring in contracts and customers. Minders are those who look after the relationships with existing clients in order to keep them happy and with the firm. Binders are the administrative and support staff who keep the team working well together. Grinders are the lawyers who actually do the bulk of the legal work of the firm. Each of these tasks requires different skill sets. For example, one must be a competent lawyer to be a grinder but it may not be necessary to have large networks of professional contacts and highly developed social skills, as it is for the finders. Some grinders may rise to the tasks of minding or finding and others never will. For the team to be successful, all of these roles must be covered. So, too, it is with most teams: each player brings his or her own skill set but collectively their skills must be enough to get the job done. Balancing the skills sets and experience levels of team members is important for any manager.

TEAMS AND TRUST

Teams do not function well in the absence of trust. Building and maintaining an atmosphere of trust are important functions for managers and supervisors. The work of Klimoski and Karol (1976) provided early evidence that teams displaying higher trust perform better than teams that are lower in trust. Although many researchers have shown that trust has important implications for teamwork and organizational groups, it is helpful to get more specific in terms of understanding the links between trust and teamwork as well as methods for building trust in teams (Friedlander, 1970; Hempel, Zhang, & Tjosvold, 2009; Lencioni, 2002).

Individual characteristics can play an important role in determining whether one individual trusts another or whether one team trusts another team. Dirks (1999) found that "perceptions of risk and vulnerability" cause trust to vary (p. 449). When an individual or team feels vulnerable, then feelings of caution are likely to lead to either less trusting behaviors or trust that grows only slowly. According to Dirks, "liking, cohesion, familiarity, and reciprocating behaviors" are all co-present with trust, so it is sometimes difficult to discern a difference between one of these variables and trust itself (p. 450). Although this makes research difficult, it helps us better understand that by working on these factors we also increase trust. In his study of trust in teams, Dirks found that decreased trust on the part of team members reduced individual members' motivation, and this is why groups with low levels of trust see reduced productivity.

Trust leads to specific behaviors that improve group outcomes. Moye and Langfred (2004) investigated the role that information sharing has in group conflict and team efficiency. The authors indicate that information sharing leads to better group outcomes, but more specifically, they predicted that information sharing in existing groups will prevent two kinds of conflict: "task conflict and relationship conflict" (p. 384). Similarly, Lencioni (2002) lists trust building as a precursor to successful team functioning. Teams without trust do not fully share their ideas, feedback, and criticisms with one another. Due to the presence of attribution bias (Chapter Two) they misinterpret one another's intentions and are more likely to take adversarial rather than collaborative positions when problems arise. To avoid this pitfall it is helpful to invest time up front, when the team comes together for the first time. Be sure to build in opportunities for group members to get to know one another as people before launching into the task at hand. Throughout the collaboration, which may be permanent in many cases, build in team-building activities and events. Sharing meals, social events attended by family members, and shared group experiences (e.g., fieldtrips, movies, games) can build rapport and enhance the ability of teams to function successfully. Managers can play a key role in building trust and repairing damaged trust within and between teams. For more on trust building and repair, see Chapter Three.

CONFLICT VERSUS DYSFUNCTION IN TEAMS

Conflicting viewpoints are inevitably present in teams. Conflict itself need not result in reduced trust or decreased group efficiency. Instead, it is the way conflict is handled rather than its mere existence that determines the impact on trust and team outputs (Hempel, Zhang, & Tjosvold, 2009). A study by Farh, Lee, and Farh (2010) found that moderate levels of conflict within teams are correlated with maximum levels of team creativity.

It seems almost a cliché that in groups you frequently see an unequal division of labor that can result in feelings of resentment by some team members against others and, eventually, against those managers who allow this to go on too long. One way to address this problem is through the use of rewards for individual and group productivity. When organizations wish to encourage more teamwork they often switch to team-based incentives and reward programs. Yet, this can lead to social loafing, also known as **shirking** or presenteeism, as mentioned in Chapter Five. Social loafing occurs when an employee chooses not to do his share of the collective workload. As a result, other members of the team have to work harder to make up for the employee(s) who is not doing his fair share. Shirkers lead others in the organization to feel disgruntled, overworked, and taken advantage of. In their study of teams and work-load distribution, Pearsall, Christian, and Ellis (2010) note the importance of rewarding individual and group achievement in order to reduce the incidence of this problem. Building in a 360-degree-evaluation tool will also help in this regard.

Tjosvold (2008) argues that positive conflict is important for the health of teams and organizations. **Positive conflict**, also called *cooperative conflict*, is the healthy sharing of differences of opinion and negotiation necessary to make tough decisions. In conflict-positive organizations, team members do not hold back their ideas or concerns out of a worry that to share them will cause conflict or disharmony. Team members will frequently debate and discuss different solutions, approaches, or ways forward for the organization, without fearing this will be taken personally or harm relationships. Through this discussion and debate, either a consensus will emerge or it will become clear that the team members see pros and cons to the multiple options under discussion. In these situations, it will be necessary for the organizational or unit leader to make an executive decision and ask all members to stand behind that decision. Lencioni (2002) calls this strategy *disagree and commit*.

Tjosvold (2008) and Lencioni (2002) speak to the positive changes produced as a result of cooperative interactions: when individuals of an organization engage one another, understand issues, and find solutions, a better relationship is formed, which results in better decision making and collaboration (Tjosvold, 2008). According to Tjosvold, conflict management is a necessary ingredient for performance improvement. Tjosvold's research points out that regular team interaction and communication are necessary for increasing collaboration and efficacy. Building rapport and getting to know each team member as a colleague helps group members have the confidence to engage in difficult decisions and come out of them without hostility and resentment.

Although positive conflict is crucial to optimal team performance, conflict avoidance can result in costly failures. When team members find problems or have ideas they aren't sure will work, they will keep them to themselves. By doing so, opportunities for positive change may be missed as well as the chance to solve problems early before they grow to threaten the bottom line or endanger the organization's brand (Tjosvold, 2008). A study by DeChurch and Marks (2001) found that groups who actively used conflict management techniques to manage conflict had more positive outcomes than those who passively managed conflict. With this in mind, it seems worthwhile to spend some time at the beginning of a group endeavor to normalize conflict (due to the fact that conflict will occur in any group project) and share tools for positive conflict management.

How do managers and teams encourage a conflict-positive environment? First, they ensure team members have time and space to build strong interpersonal relationships through shared experiences and social interactions. Second, managers and team members should explicitly create norms or ground rules to address conflict positively. The following box provides some examples of ground rules to consider. Although it may be tempting to adopt this list, it is always better to get the group to brainstorm their own ground rules so they will have better buy-in and adherence to the rules than if the manager imposes them (*hint*: remember the tenets of procedural justice). Occasionally revisit the norms, if necessary, to see how they are working or if changes need to be made.

Sample Ground Rules for Positive Conflict in Teams

- If you won't be able to meet an agreed-on deadline, communicate this with as much notice as possible.
- Avoid e-mail when complicated concepts or issues need to be discussed.
- Problems will arise. When they do, we will adopt a problem-solving approach.
- We will share our ideas and concerns openly, respecting all input.
- Once an idea has been thoroughly discussed, we will commit to the decision reached.

There are two primary sources of conflict in work teams: relationship conflict and task conflict. **Relationship conflict** occurs when two or more people experience nonstructural conflict stemming from a lack of rapport or personality conflicts between team members. Relationship conflict is associated with negative effects on the team's ability to accomplish its tasks (Farh, Lee, & Farh, 2010). **Task conflict** occurs when the group disagrees about the best ways to accomplish its tasks. Moderate levels of task conflict are associated with greater creativity and better outcomes, and relationship conflicts are associated with reduced productivity and morale. (Interestingly, teams with high levels of gender and ethnic diversity exhibit more conflict but the effect of that conflict can be good or bad depending on the way those conflicts are managed (King, Hebl, & Beal, 2009).)

Some authors convincingly argue that task integration should only begin once relationship integration has been well addressed; otherwise, the tasks will not be done well and damage may result to the organization's brand or customer relationships (Birkinshaw, Bresman, & Hakanson, 2000). (This is the cultural norm in much of the non-Western world. These findings indicate that managers should be quicker to intervene in relationship conflicts by seeking to mediate solutions between the parties and by taking affirmative steps to improve rapport among team members (Jehn, Greer, Levine, & Szulanski, 2008).)

How do you know when conflict has become dysfunctional for the group? Cole, Walter, and Bruch (2008) state that conflict becomes dysfunctional when team dysfunction is pervasive and disrupts the work environment.

The most important implications about team dysfunction are that a single disruptive member can ultimately cause a downward spiral of overall team dysfunction. This happens because the behavior of team members can be negatively influenced by observing dysfunctional behaviors of one or more members (Bandura, 1973; Cole, Walter, & Bruch, 2008). When Bandura's (1973) social learning theory is applied to team settings it is sometimes termed *the spillover effect* (Cole, Walter, & Bruch, 2008; Keyton, 1999). Hardworking, productive employees who observe others shirking without any negative consequences may reach the obvious conclusion that their hard work is not only unrecognized, but also that they would fare equally well by shirking, too. The impact on morale and productivity can be catastrophic when it grows to the point of negatively affecting organizational culture.

CONFLICT AND TEAMS DURING MERGERS AND ACQUISITIONS

Building and sustaining successful teams can be challenging tasks for managers in the best of times. During mergers and acquisitions it becomes much more complicated. A **merger** is a process through which two or more companies come together, with one retaining its corporate existence and the others losing theirs. The remaining company acquires all the assets and debts of the company it has acquired. An **acquisition** occurs when a large company acquires a much smaller company, although the terms *merger* and *acquisition* are often used in imprecise ways. From a conflict management perspective, mergers and acquisitions present myriad challenges related to organizational culture, change management, and communication that require proactive behaviors on the part of organizational leaders in order to achieve success. Whether it is a merger or acquisition (technical legal terms that do not much affect the conflict management side of things), the result is a conflict minefield that can explode the chances for success if poorly managed. The success of a merger or acquisition can be measured in terms of increased profitability, higher share prices, access to new markets or technologies that will yield greater profits down the road, and so on. During the merger and acquisition (M&A) process, leaders of the purchasing company, meaning the one that will remain after the merger or acquisition, set out specific goals by which the success of the M&A process will be judged. According to Maden (2011), when the human side of M&As is ignored, the financial side nearly always fails to meet expectations as well. "Negative behavioral outcomes associated with these events, such as high voluntary attrition rates, absenteeism, employee stress, and unprecedented acts of sabotage are proposed to affect M&As' performance negatively and subsequently deteriorate 'bottom line' figures" (p. 188). The success rate for corporate mergers is poor: 75 percent of corporate mergers fail yet their popularity has not declined (Marks & Mirvis, 2010). Why not? Because decisions about M&As are made on paper, by looking at assets, synergies, and the potential financial gains to be made via joining forces. Yet many mergers are doomed before they start due to vast differences in corporate cultures, the clash of different management styles, and poorly communicated changes that defeat many of these promising unions (Meyer & Altenborg, 2008). Often, merger implementation results in severe cultural conflict "characterized by a high level of management turnover, market-share shrinkage, and difficulty in achieving or even failure to achieve the desired operational synergy and strategic objective sought after" (Haynes, 2009, p. 7). In a study of CEOs of *Fortune* 500 companies, the ability or competence to manage human integration was rated as a more important factor to success than financial or strategic factors (Schweiger & Goulet, 2000). Organizational leaders are beginning to tune in to the deep yet manageable challenges that accompany mergers and acquisitions.

During M&A processes some of the best employees will leave the organization because of uncertainty related to their future with the organization and their ability to find a more stable environment elsewhere (Maden, 2011). Those employees who stay may engage in behaviors focused on their survival within the organization but these behaviors can be counterproductive to a positive team environment, including making political allies who can protect them in the event of likely layoffs; increased task orientation to the detriment of relationships among team members; calling attention to their power, prestige, and accomplishments to show how they excel beyond their peers (Cartwright & Cooper, 1994); and otherwise creating a competitive rather than cooperative dynamic among team members. Individual survival becomes more important than the accomplishment of the organizational mission.

Although a variety of factors surely affect the success or failure of any M&A, nearly all scholarly articles and postmortem analyses cite frequent problems with the integration of corporate culture and HR. M&As fail because of a perfect storm of factors. Interestingly, four out of six of these deal specifically with corporate culture challenges or problems with conflict management:

1. The business and/or deal were complicated. Complexity alone is not enough to predict a failure but it does provide a necessary precondition.

2. Flexibility was at a minimum. Problems in one part of the business system would radiate to other parts; trouble travels. Leveraging the firm can create incentives for management to run a tight ship, but it can also asphyxiate the company.

3. Deliberately or inadvertently management made some choices that elevated the risk exposure of the new firm. In the failed mergers studied, decisions were made that worsened the probability of success instead of improving it.

4. The thinking of decision makers was biased by recent successes, sunk costs, pride, and so forth. Due to cognitive biases, management and employees often disregard or deny risks and the crisis. Most of the failed deals started with over-optimism.

5. Business was not as usual. Something in the business environment departed from expectation. The turbulence in the business environment caused errors or problems.

6. The operation team broke down. Cultural differences between the buyer and target, unresolved political issues, and generally overwhelming stress prevented the team from responding appropriately to the unfolding crisis. (Haynes, 2009, p. 5)

Although change can be difficult and cause anxiety, employees are more challenged by the poor communication and conflict management that often surround the changes experienced during mergers and acquisitions than the changes themselves (Fedor & Herold, 2008). Employees are told, "Just do your job and don't worry about the merger," instead of receiving adequate information about what to expect or the reasons behind policy changes. Information becomes a valued commodity during M&A processes, with leaders doling it out on a need-to-know basis. This lack of transparency and fear of an uncertain future leads some talented employees to flee the organization unnecessarily. This increases the costs of the merger and reduces the strength of the resulting organization. Without frequent, clear communication about the expected changes, rumors and fear mongering will rule the day, thereby stacking the deck against successful integration of the organizations.

In addition to sharing information with employees and managers throughout the M&A process, it is important to purposefully engage in knowledge transfers between groups and work units on both sides of the merger. This knowledge transfer helps reduce miscommunications, build understandings of organizational capabilities, and create positive rapport between new team members. When employees lack knowledge of the work and capabilities of the other company, they often fall prey to attribution biases (Chapter Two) and assume the worst about the motivations of those on the other side.

Another factor in the success of M&As is the acquisition of a group identity and mission that all employees, old and new, can adopt as part of their reformed corporate identity (Ullrich & Van Dick, 2007). Subunits within the merged organization may have their own mission and objectives, which feed into the broader organizational mission and vision. Yet everyone in the reformed organization needs to understand and buy in to the broad mission, vision, and identity of the organization so as to know where they fit within that mission.

It is only natural for employees to be more loyal to their original company and to doubt the qualifications, abilities, and motives of those coming from the other side of the merger or acquisition. It takes time, diplomacy, and strong attention to relationship building before this will change. For long-time employees, part of their social identity was bound up in their association with their company. When this association changes there can be a period of grieving, as occurs in other kinds of losses such as death or divorce. It may take time before employees move from denial to acceptance—with bargaining, depression, and anger steps often occurring on the way. "The prospect of a merger intensifies many negative human emotions throughout both companies: These emotions include anxiety, loss of attachments, loss of identity, cultural conflicts, and hypersensitivity to issues of fairness" (Cox, 2010, p. 9).

Managers should not take these concerns and related behaviors personally or behave defensively—these are normal reactions to an environment perceived as uncertain and potentially threatening. The best way to combat these fears is with frequent, proactive communication that addresses concerns. Consider using a question or suggestion drop box, online bulletin board, and town hall meetings where employees can ask questions and all employees can view or hear the responses. Set a trustworthy, transparent, positive tone that builds trust in the new organization. Rarely do employees feel they were given enough information during an M&A process. Even when downsizing is likely to occur, transparency and frequent communication can make a difficult time less difficult. Some corporations have turned to hiring integration managers who are charged with managing the human side of M&As. These are specialists in organizational conflict management who assist with team building, information sharing, cultural reformation, and the integration of policies and procedures to smooth the process of change. These positions represent a relatively new and potentially lucrative specialty within the field of conflict management.

BUILDING AND REBUILDING CORPORATE CULTURE: BEFORE, DURING, AND AFTER MERGERS

In an organizational setting, culture tells us which norms, behaviors, and attitudes are expected from in-group and out-group members. Organizational culture is developed over time and often enforced informally. For example, when one talks too loudly in the boardroom or lunchroom, the speaker may realize she has transgressed against cultural expectations through the looks she receives from others. Organizational culture is at the root of unwritten policies, which are known by all or nearly all long-time employees, so they need not be written down as official policy. For example, an employee receives three weeks of vacation per year but the organization's cultural norms indicate one should not take all three weeks in a row. Similarly, an organization may not have a written dress code but new employees reach a basic understanding about how they should dress based on their observations of the dress of other employees. Individuals learn cultural expectations primarily through observation over time, usually without conscious thought. When someone violates a cultural norm, the most common response is anger and the feeling that "everyone knows you shouldn't do that." Attribution bias leads to assumptions that transgressors are selfish, rude, oblivious, and so forth. Because most organizational cultural norms are unwritten, they are likely to cause consternation when two or more organizations merge, with each having different cultural expectations about everything from dress codes, break times, and how formally or informally employees at different levels within the hierarchy communicate with one another.

It is important to remember that organizations will have subcultures as well, within departments, units, or offices that are geographically separated from one another. Managers may need to interact differently in various subcultural groups and take the time to learn the culture of each unit she or he manages. Managers should be thoughtful about which managerial and communication techniques they use in different cultural settings because one size does not fit all. Similarly, different cultures tend to occur within different types of organizations. For example, organizations seeking to maximize creativity and intellectual freedom (such as high tech companies) tend to have less hierarchical structure and value informality and autonomy in their work. Manufacturing organizations tend to have more rigid hierarchies and less personal freedom in terms of control over break times or other policies.

The concept of relatedness is important in predicting success in M&As. When an organization merges with a similar organization in a similar industry, then they have a high degree of relatedness and the end product of the M&A process may require a high degree of integration of the two (or more) organizations. However, sometimes an organization merges or acquires an organization in an unrelated industry, in which case they may decide that less integration is necessary.

Four conflict styles of acculturation are described by Nahavavandi and Malekzadeh (1988): integration, assimilation, separation, and deculturation. Using these definitions, **integration** occurs when neither group involved in the merger or acquisition dominates the other. Although both cultures change because of their interactions, the resulting cultures are not dominated by either organization and both retain some distinct cultural aspects. **Assimilation** occurs when the culture of one organization dominates and replaces the original culture of the other organization. Larger or more powerful organizations are more likely to try to force assimilation on smaller, less powerful organizations. **Separation** occurs when little or no culture change comes to either organization, with each having little interaction with the other and no significant cultural changes resulting from the M&A process. An argument can be made for any of these three forms of cultural impact, depending on the type of M&A process, the relative size or function of the premerger organizations, and the nature of organizational culture prior to the merger. This cannot be said for the fourth type of culture change. **Deculturation** occurs when employees in one of the organizations or within some subunit of an organization reject the culture of the acquiring company but realize their old cultural behaviors and beliefs no longer work well in the new organizational environment. They are literally stuck between worlds. Berry (1983) suggested that deculturation "is accompanied by a great deal of collective and individual confusion . . . and by feelings of alienation, loss of identity, and what has been termed *acculturative stress*" (p. 69).

When cultural issues are ignored, differences in organizational cultures can lead to competition between groups and hostile us-them attitudes (Pikula, 1999). These differences can lead to sabotage between groups, biased decision making as to whom to retain during downsizing, and other negative behaviors.

It is often assumed that the objectives of the acquiring company in an M&A process are those that deserve attention but it is clear by the active resistance mounted by some employees in the acquired organization that some attention needs to be paid to their needs as well. Depending on the functionality of the preexisting organizational cultures, the acquired and acquiring organizations will likely have specific preferences as to which kind of acculturation should occur (see the following box). **Acculturative stress** occurs when culture change causes confusion and frustration, accidental transgressions, and then disharmony between workers. Acculturative stress is likely to be highest in new employees as they learn the cultural norms of the organization or during the process of mergers and acquisitions because cultural norms and expectations are in flux.

Propositions Concerning Acculturation in Mergers and Acquisitions

Preferred Style of Acculturation for the Acquired Company

- When members of an acquired organization value their culture and organizational practices and want to preserve them, and they perceive an acquirer as attractive, integration will be their preferred style of acculturation.

- When members of an acquired organization do not value their culture and practices and do not want to preserve them, and they perceive an acquirer as attractive, assimilation will be their preferred style of acculturation.

- When members of an acquired organization value their culture and practices and want to preserve them, and they do not perceive an acquirer as attractive, separation will be their preferred style of acculturation.

- When members of the acquired organization do not value their culture and practices and do not want to preserve them, and they do not perceive an acquirer as attractive, deculturation will be their preferred style of acculturation.

Preferred Style of Acculturation for the Acquirer

- When an acquirer is multicultural and the merger is with a related company, integration will be the most likely style of acculturation.

- When an acquirer is unicultural and the merger is with a related company, assimilation will be the most likely style of acculturation.

- When an acquirer is multicultural and the merger is with an unrelated company, separation will be the most likely style of acculturation.

- When an acquirer is unicultural and the merger is with an unrelated company, deculturation will be the most likely style of acculturation.

Congruence and Successful Implementation

- If there is congruence between the two companies regarding the preferred style of acculturation, minimal acculturative stress will result and the style of acculturation triggered by the contact between the two companies will facilitate the implementation of the merger.

- If there is incongruence between the two companies regarding the preferred style of acculturation, a high degree of acculturative stress will result and the style of acculturation triggered by the contact between the two companies will hinder the implementation of the merger.

When dealing with culture change, managers need to be thoughtful about assessing the current culture and mapping proposed or needed changes. Culture change needs to come from the top down but must receive buy-in from employees at all levels in order to be truly successful. Organizational leaders might consider the use of employee focus groups to discuss the ways in which the current cultural practices and norms help or hinder the organization's mission and then discuss changes that would bring needed change. Alternatively, leaders should clearly and repeatedly communicate the reasons for any change in direction and seek feedback from employees at all levels about any potential obstacles or concerns regarding the implementation of those changes. It is difficult to communicate too much in regards to these changes, especially during M&As.

As this discussion has shown, for M&As to be successful, the organizations do not need to become "cultural clones" (Marks & Mirvis, 2010). Leaders in the merged organization must determine the cultural values they wish to see throughout their reformed organization. In most cases, there are positive cultural aspects at work in each individual company. Leaders need to ascertain how much change is needed in each part of the new organization and create an action plan to bring about the planned cultural changes. The larger the organization, the slower its culture will likely be to change. It is certainly possible to turn a highly dysfunctional organizational culture around—but it must come from the top and the employees must see the reasons behind the desired change. If these culture change efforts seems like the fad of the year, then employees will be jaded and resistant to change. The change must be sincere, backed up by incentives, measured by objective indicators, and backsliding must be caught quickly. The vast majority of employees will likely be supportive of changes they see as positive, empowering, and those that enhance their ability to fulfill the organizational mission.

There may be some, let's hope a small number, of employees who simply remain hostile to culture change within the organization. If this seems to be a relatively large number of employees rather than an isolated case, then it is best to engage in active listening through one-on-one interviews or small focus groups to determine the source of resistance. This is a great way to gather information about the source of the problems and learn where the obstacles to implementation lie. By addressing these concerns whenever possible, the organizational culture will be positively affected by the airing of these concerns. If the problem lies with one or just a few employees who seem to be resistant to change but are unwilling to offer constructive suggestions or specific reasons why the changes will be counterproductive, then it is possible that some employees simply will not fit in well in the new organizational structure. Firing employees should remain a last resort, not a first one. Especially during an M&A process, employee terminations can have an adverse effort on attempts at culture change if they are not supported by the remaining employees.

Differences in national cultures make mergers harder (Kim, 2011). It is easy enough for two people from the same culture to have a miscommunication or misunderstanding, adding different cultural backgrounds to the challenges of human relationships creates an additional layer of complexity for organizations (Brannen, Gómez, Peterson, Romani, Sagiv, & Wu, 2004). When companies from starkly different national cultures go through M&As their leaders need to be attuned to the cultural values held in the home countries of their employees. For example, Confucian values are highly important to understand when operating in East Asia. Without this cultural knowledge, non-Asian corporate partners may transgress against group norms and make collaboration extremely difficult.

To proactively manage the human aspect and organizational cultural needs during an M&A process, consider the use of an **integration manager** (Ashkenas & Francis, 2000). The authors argue that integration managers help the M&A process in four ways: they speed it up, create a structure for it, forge social connections between the two organizations, and engineer short-term successes. This person must be able to adapt to complex environments quickly, relate well with employees at all levels of an organization, and bridge gaps in culture and perception. In addition, this leader must understand the technical side of the organization's work in order to garner the respect of the organization's members and to understand the problems that arise during the M&A process. This person must be calm and levelheaded even when working with employees who may be highly emotional. In some ways, this person can be thought of as an M&A ombudsman—managing conflicts and problems that arise during the M&A process and proactively working to minimize those conflicts.

DOWNSIZING, RIGHTSIZING, AND CONFLICT MANAGEMENT

Economic downturns, mechanization, and overall industry trends can lead to the need to restructure operations, including a reduction in the number of people employed. It is nearly impossible to go through these periods conflict free but even these difficult situations can be handled better with some foresight and proactive management strategies. Downsizing should never be done without a thorough analysis to indicate those changes most likely to strengthen rather than weaken the organization. "Strengthening the organization and creating an environment that acknowledges conflict can be productive during periods of downsizing of a corporation. Conflicts arise when people are downsized from a crisis" (Haynes, 2009, p. 9).

The most common mistake made during organizational downsizing occurs when leaders settle on a predetermined head count targeted for payoffs. Instead, organizational leaders should consider asking themselves, "How can we restructure in ways that will maximize efficiency and the accomplishment of our mission?" Employees and managers at all levels of the organization should provide suggestions and input in order to answer this question. In nearly all cases, a simple elimination of positions will not achieve the positive change leaders seek. Instead, a deeper restructuring of job duties, processes, and policies will more likely result in productivity and profitability gains.

Poorly managed restructuring leads to increased litigation, claims of unfair or discriminatory treatment, high levels of resentment, and anxiety in those employees who remain. Hickok (1998) discusses the importance of reviewing how the process is announced, of ensuring the lines of communication are open and truthful, and of understanding the full consequences to the employees.

Although a great deal is heard about organizations being lean and mean, the importance of fair treatment cannot be overemphasized as a means of gaining employee commitment (Fedor & Herold, 2008). If restructuring will indeed result in job losses, organizational leaders need to determine what kind of services, if any, will be provided to employees including résumé preparation, severance, career coaching sessions, assistance with job placement, and so forth. Employees who have been consulted during the restructuring phase and are treated humanely during their exit phase leave with less ill will and those employees who remain will not suffer as much damage to their loyalty and commitment.

The following box summarizes some of the lessons for managers contained within this chapter.

Team-Building Lessons for Managers

- Attack the problem, not the person (Fisher & Ury, 1981). Remember, we all work toward the same mission, even if we disagree about the best way to get there.
- Focus on relationship building prior to working on shared tasks.
- Define roles and responsibilities clearly.
- Be sure the team members collectively have the skills to get the job done.
- Metacommunicate. Share information among team members about how to communicate. Develop norms.
- Reward individual and team efforts.
- "Disagree and commit" (Lencioni, 2002). Sometimes difficult decisions need to be made. When the team cannot agree on the best path forward, management will make an executive decision and all will agree to its implementation.
- Managers should facilitate early resolution of intrateam conflicts, especially when they are relationship-based conflicts.
- During mergers and acquisitions pay attention to organizational culture and repeatedly share information about expected changes. Communicate frequently with employees to minimize anxiety levels.

WHEN ONE PERSON WON'T PLAY ON THE TEAM

As a manager, what do you do when one employee refuses to "play well" with others on the team? Chapter Five discussed techniques for dealing with difficult employees and those lessons apply when you have an employee who is not a good team player. Your first strategy should be to work with that employee, one-on-one, to diagnose the source of the problem and collectively develop a plan for improvement. Develop benchmarks or some objective criteria that can be used to track progress toward goals. For example, the number of complaints from employees will go down or the group morale will increase as measured by a survey and so forth. Multiple measures are best. Consider bringing in an executive coach to help this employee set goals, track progress, and spur change. Alternatively, if coaching is not in the budget, assign a mentor from within the company, preferably a manager who is universally considered accomplished and effective.

And if that doesn't work? One truly terrible employee can drive away ten fabulous employees. An employee or manager who shows little regard for the company or work team, who lacks adequate people skills, or who is not committed to the mission will poison the well, thereby making the whole team dysfunctional. When this happens, organizational leaders need to find ways to help this person realize that his or her best career path lies outside of the current organization — either through dismissal or, preferably, through the employee's decision to voluntarily leave the organization.

In addition to the obvious reasons why some employees or managers don't play well with others, be on the lookout for "snakes in suits" (Babiak & Hare, 2006). According to research shared by Babiak and Hare, about 1 to 2 percent of people match the profile of a psychopath. Although psychopaths are commonly portrayed in the media as murderers, and indeed some are, most are able to function at some level in society and in the workplace, at least for a while. In the workplace, this type of personality can wreak serious havoc, turning high-functioning teams into disasters. The following box lists some of the characteristics common to psychopaths. Babiak and Hare caution that although only a specially trained psychologist or psychiatrist can accurately diagnose psychopathy, it remains instructive to know the warning signs. Whether the employee meets the full definition or not, these behaviors and traits signal trouble in the workplace. It should be noted here that the terms *psychopath* and *sociopath* are frequently used interchangeably and there is some debate as to their specific meanings in the psychiatric community. In general, it is believed that psychopaths are born with psychiatric anomalies that prevent them from empathizing with others, so they do not feel guilt for behaviors others would find deplorable. Sociopaths are more likely to have been exposed to environmental factors, such as abusive parents, that account for their behaviors. Both groups pursue their own goals at the expense of others and cannot maintain socially appropriate behaviors indefinitely.

Characteristics of Psychopaths

Interpersonal Characteristics
- Is superficial
- Is grandiose
- Is deceitful

Affective
- Lacks remorse
- Lacks empathy
- Doesn't accept responsibility

Lifestyle
- Is impulsive
- Lacks goals
- Is irresponsible

Antisocial
- Has poor behavioral controls
- Displays adolescent antisocial behavior
- Displays adult antisocial behavior

Source: Adapted from Babiak and Hare (2006, p. 27).

Any person may exhibit a few of these traits to a mild degree. The cause for concern arises when an individual exhibits most of them to a strong degree.

In addition to these traits, how can you spot a psychopath at work? The best chance of doing so is during the application stage. If you see a résumé that is almost too good to believe, then you need to do a deep verification check to ensure that the degrees and experiences listed are true rather than fictitious or highly inflated. Psychopaths tend to brag about their accomplishments from the past as well as overpromise about what they can accomplish on the job. Verify, verify, verify. Psychopaths may be quite friendly initially, great salespeople, and smooth talkers. They might ingratiate themselves with the organizational leaders from the outset by feigning knowledge and interest in the hobbies and passions of their superiors. Once hired, they may continue this behavior with superiors and then act mercilessly autocratic with their subordinates. They claim credit for the work of others and may claim accomplishments that don't exist. If a psychopath has control over or sole access to financial records, he may actually engage in fraud in order to skim for himself or to create the appearance of gains for the organization that do not exist. Psychopaths tend to work in one place for two to four years at the most and then move on to the next employer once they wear out their welcome. When it comes to snakes in suits, it is better to screen them out or identify them early before they drive away good employees or ruin the good name of the organization.

CONCLUSION

Managers are often expected to create, change, and inspire teams to reach their full potential. Even in difficult economic times or during M&As, a thoughtful approach to team management can enhance productivity and reduce destructive conflict. By attending to individual differences, aligning team members with team tasks, and screening out the worst team players (e.g., psychopaths), managers can reap gains for their organizations and also reduce the time they are called on to intervene in dysfunctional teams.

JOHN AT THE BUREAU OF RECLAMATION

John asked employees in the underfunctioning teams to complete a team assessment questionnaire (see online resources). This questionnaire asked about levels of trust, collegiality, rapport, and willingness to collaborate. From this questionnaire he realized that these team members spent little time outside (or inside) of work getting to know one another and building rapport. There was little trust between them. Team members exhibited a desire to claim accomplishments as individual accomplishments rather than as the result of team efforts, partially because of the existing reward structures that failed to acknowledge the team rather than individual accomplishments. Some members of the team felt their contribution to the work of the team was unrecognized and that they were doing more than their share of the work. Some tasks weren't getting addressed at all.

Based on this information, John decided to work on rebuilding these teams. He assessed each person's technical and social strengths and preferred conflict styles of communication. He used two full workdays to hold mini-retreats, which included activities designed to help the employees get to know one another as people, share their strengths and preferred communication conflict styles, and analyze ways to make the team function more smoothly. The groups crafted a list of expected norms and behaviors. They agreed to meet more frequently and set measurable goals for their projects and deliverables. They clarified over-lapping job duties and responsibilities so there were fewer turf battles. They agreed that when problems arose, they would try to work them out through direct, problem-solving discussions. If these discussions failed, they agreed to seek John's help to facilitate a fair resolution to these problems. They talked about the kind of workplace culture they wanted to create in their units and how to go about achieving it. John created institutional rewards that recognized teamwork and team accomplish-ments. This latter change required collaboration with union leaders, who feared that individual employees might suffer harm if their individual performance reviews were unfairly influenced by the poor work of other team members. He also had to persuade his own bosses that time spent in team building would yield cost savings down the line rather than be viewed as a waste of taxpayer money.

During the next two months, John checked in to see how these agree-ments were being implemented. He offered some coaching to a couple of employees who were struggling with their ability to frame concerns constructively and address them proactively. The number of formal com-plaints decreased 80 percent and productivity improved significantly. Morale has increased and these departments are now on par with the others in his bureau.

KEY TERMS

Acculturative stress

Acquisition

Assimilation

Deculturation

Diversity

Ethnocentrism

FourSight teams

Genius teams

Improv teams

Integration

Integration manager

Merger

Metacommunication

Monochronic time orientation

Polychronic time orientation

Positive conflict

Relationship conflict

Separation

Shared mental model (SMM)

Shirking

Task conflict

Team cognition

Team mental models (TMMs)

Transactive memory systems (TMSs)

Virtual teams

SUGGESTED SUPPLEMENTAL READING

Cohen, C. F., Birkin, S. J., Cohen, M. E., Garfield, M. J., & Webb, H. W. (2006). Managing conflict during an organizational acquisition. *Conflict Resolution Quarterly, 23,* 317–331.

Miles, S. A., & Bennett, N. (2008). 6 steps to (re)building a top management team. *MIT Sloan Management Review, 50*(1), 60–64.

Mohammed, S., & Angell, L. C. (2004). Surface- and deep-level diversity in workgroups: Examining the moderating effects of team orientation and team process on relationship conflict. *Journal of Organizational Behavior, 25*(8), 1015–1039.

Mohammed, S., & Dumville, B. C. (2001). Team mental models in a team knowledge framework: Expanding theory and measurement across disciplinary boundaries. *Journal of Organizational Behavior, 22*(2), 89–106.

Tzeng, J.-Y. (2006). Developing and sharing team mental models in a profession-driven and value-laden organization: A case study. *Performance Improvement Quarterly, 19*(2), 155–172.

DISCUSSION QUESTIONS

1. Think back to the most successful team of which you have been a member. This can be a sports team, a work team, or a team in your civic life. Why was

that team so successful and enjoyable? Which factors from this chapter can explain its success? Now do the opposite: think of a dysfunctional team. What was it lacking? Why was it unsuccessful? How does this analysis match up to the material covered in this chapter?

2. Using your current organization or one from a previous job, think about how the teams are built and maintained. What kind of planning, if any, goes into the creation and maintenance of teams there? Is teamwork rewarded or recognized? What can be done to make the teams more successful? What can you do as a manager in your current organization to strengthen your team(s)?

EXERCISES

1. Work in teams or singly to create a list of interview questions you might use to help ascertain how well an applicant will fit into your ideal work team. What traits or behaviors are you looking for and how would you measure them? What questions would you ask of their references?

2. Use the following assessment tool to get a picture of how well teams are functioning in your work environment.

Team Assessment

Instructions: Use the following scale to indicate how each statement applies to your team. It is important to evaluate the statements honestly and without overthinking your answers.

3 = Usually   2 = Sometimes   1 = Rarely

____ Team members are passionate and unguarded in their discussion of issues.

____ Team members call out one another's deficiencies or unproductive behaviors.

____ Team members know what their peers are working on and how they contribute to the collective good of the team.

____ Team members quickly and genuinely apologize to one another when they say or do something inappropriate or possibly damaging to the team.

_____ Team members willingly make sacrifices (such as budget, turf, head count) in their departments or areas of expertise for the good of the team.

_____ Team members openly admit their weaknesses and mistakes.

_____ Team meetings are compelling and not boring.

_____ Team members leave meetings confident that their peers are completely committed to the decisions that were agreed on, even if there was initial disagreement.

_____ Morale is significantly affected by the failure to achieve team goals.

_____ During team meetings, the most important and difficult issues are put on the table to be resolved.

_____ Team members are deeply concerned about the prospect of letting down their peers.

_____ Team members know about one another's personal lives and are comfortable discussing them.

_____ Team members end discussions with clear and specific resolutions and calls to action.

_____ Team members challenge one another about their plans and approaches.

_____ Team members are slow to seek credit for their own contributions but quick to point out those of others.

GOAL SETTING

Use the assessment above to select at least one team behavior you will work to improve during the next two weeks. Then come back, answer the assessment questions again, and see if scores have increased.

chapter SEVEN

Conflict Management in Unionized Environments

Learning Objectives

- Describe the history of labor-management relations and collective bargaining in North America.

- Describe the evolution of ADR in unionized settings.

- Demonstrate an understanding of the impact of workplace culture on labor-management conflicts.

- Analyze and describe the differences between conflict management processes in unionized versus nonunionized environments.

- Explain the common steps of a union grievance process.

- Demonstrate an understanding of conflict management trends in unionized environments.

JOHN AT THE BUREAU OF RECLAMATION

John inherited a highly unionized workforce with a history of animosity and poor working relationships between unionized employees and management. A number of sources of friction exist that are related to the unionized nature of the working environment:

- There are tensions and conflicts between those employees who pay union dues and join the union and those employees who choose not to do so. The pay rates negotiated by the union apply to nonunionized employees, too, so some employees choose to be **free riders**, meaning they enjoy the benefit of a public good without paying their share for it. A public good is something that, by its nature, is either supplied to all people or to none, regardless of whether or not each individual has paid a fair share for the enjoyment of that good. For example, national defense, clean air, public roads, and public libraries are all public goods; if they exist for anyone, then they exist for everyone.

• There is a history of adversarial relationships between union leaders and managers stemming from two main sources: (1) both groups have historically assumed their interests were mutually exclusive and any negotiations would therefore result in zero-sum outcomes; (2) past contract negotiations have led to labor strikes, **sick-outs** in which employees staged massive work stoppages by calling in sick for work to show their solidarity and bargaining strength; and (3) there have been allegations of bad-faith negotiations surrounding the union contract renewals.

• The number of alleged contract violations under the bureau's previous director was quite high, leaving union leaders and employees to feel that managers at the bureau didn't respect or adhere to the contractual obligations as they should.

What a mess! These conflicts are reducing the agency's ability to efficiently carry out its mission and reifies the public's assumptions about the demanding nature of public employees. John knows he needs to improve relations with the unions and reduce the number of grievances being filed—but how? To make matters worse, in four months the union contract comes up for renegotiation. John is looking forward to that like a root canal.

Unionized environments hold the potential for two distinct types of conflict and collaboration. First, unionized organizations have the same types of conflicts seen elsewhere: claims of wrongful termination, unfair treatment, harassment, workplace safety concerns, discrimination, intrateam disputes, personality conflicts, and so forth. Second, unionized workplaces include organized and highly ritualized forms of negotiations between labor unions and company leaders, called *collective bargaining*, which is a process of negotiation between employers and the employees' representatives aimed at reaching agreements that regulate working conditions and pay. A **collective bargaining agreement** is the agreement reached between an employees' union and the company outlining the terms of employment. This agreement covers the initial contract between a group of employees and company leaders as well as periodic renegotiation of that contract. In each of these separate arenas, various forms of ADR have been used successfully to reduce antagonism and improve collaborative outcomes. As we examine the history of unionization in the United States and current trends in unionization, we will present and define terms used commonly in unionized workplaces. These terms will then be used throughout this and subsequent chapters.

LABOR-MANAGEMENT CONFLICT IN THE UNITED STATES

In the early twentieth century, the US economy was transitioning from a heavy reliance on agriculture to a greater reliance on industrial productivity. This meant large population shifts from rural to urban areas, a trend that echoes still today. During the Great Depression, the slowing US economy generated a surplus of skilled and unskilled labor. Until 1938 the United States had no federal minimum wage law or laws governing the use of child labor. As public sentiments shifted in favor of such laws in the northern and New England states, factories moved into the southern United States, where historically higher unemployment led to less political opposition to low wages and child labor (University of Iowa, 2011).

Unions began forming in the United States as early as the 1830s but became stronger during the Great Depression of the 1930s. In the United States the National Labor Relations Act of 1935 was passed by Congress, covering most private nonagricultural employees and employers engaged in interstate commerce. The act made it illegal for companies to spy on, harass, or retaliate against employees who attempt to form unions for collective bargaining. Companies cannot refuse to negotiate with the representative appointed by union members nor can unions require employees to join as a condition of employment.

In 1947, in response to labor unrest and repeated strikes, Congress moved the mediation function from the Department of Labor to the Federal Mediation and Conciliation Service (FMCS) (Barrett, 2007). The FMCS provides mediation services to industry and government organizations, including mediation services to end the 2011 strike in the National Football League.

Unions began in sectors such as mining and manufacturing, where they remain the strongest even today. Unions have traditionally represented blue collar workers. Employees who are **blue collar** work at jobs that are based on hourly pay and usually include manual labor. They may be considered skilled laborers or unskilled laborers. **Skilled labor** is used in jobs that require special training, knowledge, and often an apprenticeship, such as plumbers, electricians, or carpenters. **Unskilled labor** is used in those jobs that require little training and education, making workers easily replaced at a lower cost to employers. Traditionally, the labor market has had a larger surplus of unskilled rather than skilled laborers, making the former more vulnerable to poverty and at a bargaining disadvantage in terms of their ability to press employers for higher wages or better working conditions.

White collar is a term used to describe skilled workers who do not usually wear uniforms, undertake intellectual rather than physical work, and usually have pursued education beyond secondary school (meaning they have attended college or university). These employees generally include supervisors and managers. The labels of white versus blue collar are loosely defined, with many jobs meeting one or more of these conditions but not all. For example, teachers and others who work for local, state, and federal government entities are often part of unions regardless of their specific job duties. Nurses wear uniforms and sometimes have physically demanding work yet are considered white collar due to the level of education and commensurate salaries associated with their jobs. White collar workers have historically been the slowest to unionize for various reasons: they have been harder to train and replace, thereby increasing their capacity to bargain individually for higher wages and better working conditions, and they often see their interests as more aligned with organizational managers and fear that alienation of those leaders will stifle their ability to move up within the organization.

Unions are commonplace for workers employed by the US federal government. In fact, multiple unions often compete for members among the same pool of government workers, thereby reducing the power of these workers to bargain as a collective.

Unions have performed a critical role in the democratization of the workplace. They have provided a voice for the needs and interests of workers within specific organizations as well as within the broader society and political system. Unions have played an important role in reforming laws concerning child labor, workplace safety, minimum wages, and antidiscrimination laws. Yet, the evolution of labor-management relations as well as the supporting legislation has codified and institutionalized a relationship characterized as adversarial.

"Yet, collective bargaining and union-management relations are as important today as ever to a healthy economy and a strong democracy. The need to achieve more competitive workplaces together with an increasing standard of living merely increases the importance of innovative, cooperative labor-management relations and effective conflict resolution. Collective bargaining, therefore, needs to be adapted and improved, not abandoned" (Chaykowski, Cutcher-Gershenfeld, Kochan, & Sickles Merchant, 2001, p. 10).

TRENDS IN UNIONIZATION

Unionization has gone through various phases of formation and reformation in the United States and Canada. Current trends indicate we are entering a difficult time for unions. Union membership is at its lowest point since the Great Depression, with about 9 percent of US employees currently covered by collective bargaining contracts (The incredibly shrinking U.S. middle class, 2011). Public employees' unions have taken a hit as the **Great Recession** has induced cuts to government budgets, resulting in stagnating salaries, reductions in force, and the resulting increased workloads for remaining employees. (The Great Recession refers to the period of negative and slow economic growth and high unemployment and underemployment that began in approximately 2007 and continues at the time of this writing [December 2011].) Technology has reduced the demand for clerical workers, travel agents, professional proofreaders and copy editors, as well as broadcast news analysts and journalists as content has moved online (Goudreau, 2011). The shrinking middle class has led to a labor surplus with unemployment and underemployment at historic levels, making this a tough time for union organizers to argue for higher wages or improvements in working conditions. Employees are hesitant to report employer violations of labor regulations or to agitate for change in other ways because they see the plight of their unemployed friends and neighbors. As the number and percentage of Americans in poverty rises, and those considered middle class continues to shrink, it is possible there will be a resurgence of unions, but this isn't likely until the problem reaches crisis proportions, if history is our guide.

In the United States, state laws regarding unions vary, with barriers to union formation and maintenance higher in some states than in others. Some states, such as Georgia, are considered right-to-work states, meaning that union membership cannot be required in order to obtain or maintain a job. This increases the incidence of the free-rider problem and creates a somewhat challenging political environment for unions. Similarly, the steps employers may take to discourage unionization efforts vary somewhat by state, resulting in vastly different rates of unionization among states, largely because of the political and legal cultures toward unions.

The changing nature of work may also bode poorly for the future of unionization efforts. As more people work from home or remotely, they are physically isolated from their coworkers, which makes collaborative efforts to unionize more difficult.

In spite of these trends, some white collar professions are seeing movement toward unionization (Stafford, 2011). For example, nurses are joining unionization efforts at a faster pace than many other workers because of frustration with heavier workloads, increased hours, and a desire to address power inequalities within hospital hierarchies that result in unpleasant working conditions. Currently, about 10 percent of nurses in the United States are part of a collective bargaining agreement but recent attempts to expand nurses' unions into nonunionized hospitals have succeeded in 80 percent of cases.

Unionization efforts are most common in dysfunctional organizational environments, where employees are disgruntled and their concerns have not spurred corrective action by organizational leaders. At the University of Missouri-Kansas City's Institute for Labor Studies, director Judy Ancel argues that efforts to unionize and the success of those efforts is proportional to the strength and efficacy of hospital management: "There's the old saying that bad managers get unions. The desire to unionize is directly related to working conditions" (Stafford, 2011).

Shelly Freeman, an employment law attorney and consultant at HROI (Human Resources Return on Investment) in Kansas City, sees a trend in the unionization of the nursing profession. She says this trend is "one based on working conditions, uncertainty about health care reform, and hospital budgets squeezed by reimbursement cutbacks from the government." She advises employers to listen to their employees. "Organizations that don't get unions are good at communicating directly with their employees and not through intermediaries" (Stafford, 2011). Unions arise when employees perceive their working conditions, including pay, to be unfair and sense that the organization's leaders are unwilling to listen, collaborate, and bring positive change.

Although unionization has been relatively slow to catch on with white collar employees, one emerging trend is for these employees to join a hybrid professional association union. These organizations can give employees greater influence on workplace policies and governance without actually negotiating collective contracts (Overman, 2011). In these hybrid organizations employees can join and pay dues if they wish and the organization takes up whatever agenda items its members deem appropriate—without negotiating collective contracts for members. For example, these organizations can be a conduit to share employee concerns, desires, or ideas regarding benefits, working conditions, and workplace policies. They can also lobby for governmental laws or policies that favor their industry, from an employees' viewpoint rather than the shareholders' or CEO's perspective. Verizon employees went on strike in August 2011, and the result of that strike appears to be movement toward a hybrid professional union organization that will work to voice concerns from employees in a more coherent and powerful fashion (Overman, 2011).

Unionization efforts in the airline industry have been highly active, with most major US airlines pilots and flight attendants covered by collective bargaining agreements. Although airline employees can bring their company's work to a halt through the use of strikes, they must use this power with restraint because the financial viability of many struggling companies could not withstand a long strike (Hirsch, 2006). Since deregulation of this industry in 1978, employees' pay and benefits have gone up and down with the economic fortunes of their employers. In good times, pay and benefits increase, and in lean times they have decreased (Hirsch, 2006). Research on the airline industry wages and unionization shows that unionized airlines have retained more of the pay and benefits for their workers during hard economic times than nonunionized airlines. What's more, pay goes up faster for unionized employees when economic booms hit the industry. This is likely due to their ability to more quickly channel the employees' voice and demands to company leaders than those airlines without unions (Hirsch, 2006).

The airline industry, particularly US airlines, has suffered a string of financial setbacks starting with the attacks of September 11, 2001. These attacks prompted a host of new security regulations that brought added costs to airlines just as consumer fears reduced demand for seats on flights. As the industry was beginning to recover from these setbacks, the Great Recession caused a reduction in demand for business and leisure travel. The airlines reacted, in part, by seeking pay and benefit cuts for existing and retired employees. Adversarial relationships between unions and management worsened in nearly all major companies. Rather than working together to get through hard times, each group seemed to assume their survival would come at the other's expense. Traditional bargaining methods and zero-sum thinking have prevailed (Gittel, Von Nordenflycht, & Kochan, 2003). This has led to increased problems with customer service complaints, decreased passenger satisfaction, and further reduced profitability.

In opposition to this trend, Southwest Airlines has used a people-first philosophy. They have not laid off employees during the recession and have made cuts elsewhere. The CEO has argued that once companies start downsizing, the impact on morale and customer service can have devastating effects. He believes that employees should be treated as members of the family. In difficult times, family members find ways to work together to get by rather than seeking individual survival at the cost of other family members. As a result, the employees at Southwest are highly loyal and have high job satisfaction and low turnover. Customers notice the difference and Southwest has been able to maintain and even expand its market share during difficult economic times. Southwest employees have not sought to unionize. It seems they feel their concerns are heard and met by the company without the added transaction costs of a union to represent them collectively.

Increasingly, companies are fighting unions without resorting to underhanded strong-arm tactics, but using collaborative initiatives designed to increase trust and meet their shared interest in a happy, stable, productive workforce that feels fairly rewarded for its contribution. This may be the biggest trend in unionization during the next generation, but it is too early to reach conclusions based on empirical evidence. As Gittel and colleagues (2003) note in their research, "We conclude that efforts to recover from the current crisis in the airline industry that depend primarily on reductions in wages or union power will at best bring only short-term relief from immediate financial pressures. Sustained improvement in service quality and financial performance will require more fundamental improvements in the quality of labor relations" (p. 3).

The future of labor relations in North America depends in part on the future of manufacturing. As the manufacturing sector's share of the economy declines in the United States and Canada, the economy has transitioned to jobs in the knowledge sector. That means jobs in education, service, technology development, research, and other skilled areas have grown. Most of these jobs involve white collar workers who have not traditionally been union members. Unions are seeking to expand their presence in this sector but have not had a high degree of success. This trend, combined with the long-term weakness in the economy, has not boded well for union expansion. Simultaneously, many employers have realized the many benefits that come from proactively addressing the needs of their workers and sought to create or maintain more collaborative rather than adversarial relationships. They have noted the impact that positive employee relations has on their public image and brand as well as its impact on profitability. These two trends appear to mean that we will continue to see the gradual decline of union power within North America, with some anecdotal exceptions, particularly in those sectors or companies in which employees have been poorly treated for long periods of time, such as the hotel and fast-food industries.

In the present and the foreseeable future, the large public and private sector employers with current unionized workers will continue to exist and relations between management and labor will continue to evolve. In some of these organizations (e.g., car manufacturing) we are seeing a shift in world-view with the heightened recognition of shared interests between workers and employers—without a competitive company, no one has a job. With this as a central focus of labor-management negotiations, unions are mindful of the need to keep their demands reasonable and organizational leaders are mindful of the benefits of creating a positive workplace culture that values the individual and collective contribution of their workers as well as harvesting their ideas for improvements in products and services. Those organizations that retain adversarial relations between labor and management are likely to become less competitive over time, with predictable reductions in profitability and longevity. In fact, the only organizations able to remain this dysfunctional in the long term are likely to be those that have a monopoly on specific types of services, such as public agencies, or cartels, such as the airline industry or nationwide health care providers.

COMMON STEPS IN THE UNION GRIEVANCE PROCESS

The earliest ADR systems in the United States evolved in highly unionized workplace settings. Collective bargaining agreements between employers and unions frequently include an arbitration clause or a broader dispute resolution clause. These clauses lay out the steps that each side will go through when either one believes a breach of the contract has occurred. Generally, allegations of contract breaches are made against the company by the employee, represented by a union delegate. It is not impossible for the company to argue that the union has not upheld its commitments as laid out in the collective bargaining agreement but it is much less common. A **union grievance** is any alleged violation of the "contract, past practice, employer rules, previous grievance or arbitration settlements [which set precedence for the contract's interpretation], or any violation of laws such as Occupational Health and Safety, Americans with Disabilities Act, Family Medical Leave Act, or EEOC regulations on race, age or sex discrimination" (UE Information for Workers, 2011).

For example, provisions for overtime pay are commonly addressed in collective bargaining agreements such that optional overtime is offered to the employee with the highest seniority first. If that employee chooses to decline the opportunity for overtime, then the opportunity would go to the next most senior employee until a worker is found who agrees to accept the added hours or additional shift(s). Supervisors may find this onerous for a few reasons: perhaps the employee with the right skills is not the one with the most seniority, the most senior employee historically has turned down opportunities for overtime yet the offer must be made to him or her before the offer can be made to a less senior employee, or the supervisor may simply believe that another worker is more enjoyable to work with or works harder than the most senior employee. If supervisors do not follow the terms of the contract in offering optional overtime work and pay to the most senior employee, then they may be seen as playing favorites, bypassing senior employees to instead benefit their friends or preferred employees. If the supervisor offers the overtime to someone other than the most senior employee, then she has breached the terms of the collective bargaining agreement and the senior employee who was bypassed can pursue a claim through the union grievance process.

The collective bargaining agreement lays out each step in the grievance process and requires all parties to use each step in order, without skipping or bypassing a step unless both sides agree to do so. There are some variations among the grievance process steps in many collective bargaining agreements but it is common to expect the employee to first engage in some form of direct negotiation before taking the first formal step in the grievance process. This means the employee should speak directly with his or her supervisor or manager, share information related to the complaint—which must be an allegation that the collective bargaining agreement has been violated in some manner. Most organizations have something akin to an open-door policy, meaning that employees can go to any supervisor or member of management to share their concerns and seek redress or assistance with problem solving. In reality, most organizations prefer for employees to use the chain of command, starting first with their frontline supervisor and moving up the chain as necessary to solve the problem. The National Labor Relations Board (in the United States) gives employees the right to talk with their supervisor with or without the union representative's presence. Employees who are covered under a collective bargaining agreement cannot craft agreements affecting wages, benefits, or working conditions without the approval of the union. This means that if a supervisor and employee strike a bargain to solve a problem, they will need to seek the blessing of the union's representatives before the agreement is finalized.

Once a union member decides she or he needs the help of the union to resolve a problem, there are specific steps to be taken. If the employee decides to get their union involved, this will trigger step one in the grievance process. A **union steward** is the first point of contact for each rank-and-file union member when a grievance arises. The union steward is usually a position elected by the union members, someone who is generally liked and trusted by the employees. The steward can advise the union member as to whether the complaint is an actual violation of the union contract as well as offer information about the available dispute resolution options. A union representative may also accompany employees to any grievance process such as mediation or arbitration and represent them in that process. The steward can provide information about the contents of the collective bargaining agreement and those issues that may or may not fall under its terms. For example, employees may be disgruntled at the general way in which their supervisor treats them or communicates with them but these are not issues that are covered under the collective bargaining agreement. Working hours, safety conditions, overtime pay, breaks and vacation days, benefits, the process of promotion and merit pay raises, and nonretaliation for the filing of grievances are the types of issues typically covered in the collective bargaining agreement.

Step One

The first real step in the grievance process may be the most important. This is the step in which the employee contacts the union steward to share his or her concern. The steward or other union representative will attempt to understand who was involved, what was said or done by the parties involved, when it happened, where it happened, and what the underlying cause of the problem was. This person will also try to find out if there were any witnesses who can support the employee's statements of fact. Then the steward must decide if this problem is covered under the collective bargaining agreement. At this step, the steward may discuss the matter with the chief steward to better understand past practice on the issue and whether any similar grievances have been filed and resolved that set a precedent that the company and the union would need to follow. The steward may develop a list of information requested from the company, which would provide their answers to these questions (what, when, where, how, who, and why). Once this information has been received the steward will usually set up a meeting with the organization's representative, such as the employee's supervisor, to speak to him or her about why the problem occurred and to get his or her perspective. Any act of discipline against an employee would follow this process. It is the supervisor's duty to tell the steward why the action was taken.

At this point, the steward would tell the company what happened from the employee's perspective, state which part of the contract was violated, state which specific action or remedy the union is seeking, and request any further information needed by the union. In the overtime case, the union would want to know which employee received the overtime, his or her seniority status, and reasons why the company chose to overlook the most senior employee (assuming the contract awarded overtime on the basis of seniority). The most commonly requested remedy would be for the senior employee to receive pay for these hours that were not worked as a result of being overlooked. The supervisor may agree with the union that a contract violation occurred, whether it was accidental or not. She may agree to grant the union's requested remedy. At this point, the agreement should be put into writing and any necessary department or division, in this case payroll, should be notified so the agreement can be implemented. Most violations of the union contract are resolved at this level. Step one often seems informal, from the employees' vantage points, meaning they may not even know this is called *step one*. They may instead think of more formal steps such as arbitration when they think of grievance steps.

Step Two

If the steward and boss are unable to resolve the issue in step one, then the steward puts the complaint into writing and it becomes a formal grievance. If the union believes the employee was in the wrong or if the union's leaders believe the complaint is not covered in the union contract, the union may decide not to proceed with the complaint and to drop it at the end of step one. Each union contract spells out the time limits for the union to file a written grievance on behalf of the employee. If these time limits are missed, the grievance is dead. The steward's written grievance report will include a statement of the problem at the heart of the alleged contract violation, which part of the contract was violated, and a requested remedy. At this point, some unions will attempt to show the employer that the other workers are supportive of their coworker against whom the violation has occurred. They may do this by wearing buttons or stickers, signing petitions, and holding meetings to keep the membership informed of the progress of the dispute. At this point the upper management of the organization gets involved and may grant the requested remedy or see the dispute progress to step three.

Step Three

The third step will vary among organizations. In some, the third step is mediation. Grievance mediation tends to be "faster, cheaper, and unused" according to Camille Monahan's (2008) research (see also Bingham, 2004). For those organizations who have implemented either mandatory or voluntary mediation, union members and managers have found it more satisfying than arbitration. Yet arbitration has been the default dispute resolution process used in collective bargaining agreements for so long that many contracts are simply renewed without much thought as to updating these procedures based on newer trends. In grievance mediation, the parties come together with the assistance of a jointly chosen mediator. They talk about the issues in dispute and see if there is a solution that they both feel is preferable to going to arbitration, where they could win it all or lose it all. If the union seeks to create a precedent for future similar disputes, then they will not want to use mediation. However, they may use mediation for exactly that reason—because they do not want one particular case to determine future outcomes. In mediation the union and management could agree to hold negotiations to amend the contract in order to accomplish the same goals as an arbitral settlement but with both sides having more control over the language and specifics of that amendment than would occur through an arbitrator's decision. In grievance mediation, if the parties are unable to reach an agreement, they could still proceed to arbitration. Because arbitration is an adversarial rather than a collaborative process, it can further erode working relationships between employees and supervisors with ongoing relationships and between the union and the organization.

If mediation has failed or if the organization does not have a mediation option, then the next step of the process will likely be grievance arbitration. Union contracts carefully detail the process by which arbitrators are chosen, with each side having some power to veto or recommend one or more arbitrators. In some cases a single arbitrator is the norm and in others the contract calls for a panel of three arbitrators. Arbitrators conduct a hearing that is similar in many ways to the format of a public hearing or trial. Witnesses may be called or asked to submit written statements. The rules of evidence and procedure will either be written out explicitly in the union contract or the standard procedures of the organization supplying the arbitrator will be used, such as the American Arbitration Association. Arbitration is generally binding for both the union and the company or agency. If the ruling covers an issue that was vague or unclear in the union contract, then the arbitrator's ruling will set a precedent for all future similar cases between the union and the organization. Some unions have developed encyclopedic rulings that continue to grow as the contract is interpreted and reinterpreted, much like the constitution and common law, forming dozens of printed volumes going back decades.

EXAMPLES OF CONFLICT MANAGEMENT IN UNIONIZED SETTINGS

In addition to the common steps in a union grievance process, employees in unionized workplaces may also have the same resolution options open to those in nonunionized workplaces. Whether unionized or not, many employers adopt some variation of the open-door policy; they may have mediation programs, hotlines to report harassment or abusive behaviors, and the right to litigate certain types of conflicts on the job. In addition to, or sometimes instead of, the dispute resolution processes open to nonunionized workers, those who are represented by a collective bargaining agreement have a union grievance process that likely includes arbitration but may also include mediation, peer review panels, the use of an ombudsman, and so forth.

It should be noted that training can itself be a way to prevent and address disputes in a unionized workplace. Employees who are aware of workplace policies and feel those policies reflect their best interests and were created through fair and transparent measures are more likely to follow them. Training in communication and leadership skills can help managers and supervisors to address problems proactively.

THE EVOLUTION OF COLLABORATION IN LABOR-MANAGEMENT RELATIONS

The concept of evolving labor-management relations was introduced in the earlier section on trends in unionization. This section will focus more specifically on the methods necessary to spur the evolution of collaborative relationships between labor and management in North American organizations. The findings noted in this section may also apply in Europe and other Western cultural regions but the shorter history of labor-management relations in the United States and Canada may lead to more rapid change than in some other regions.

On both sides of the labor-management divide, it is clear that teamwork and positive, collaborative relationships are conducive to long-term organizational health as well as to fostering high levels of workplace morale. When labor and management work against one another, they both lose. This is likely to be increasingly true in the fast-paced globalized marketplace in which a work stoppage creates an opening for one's competitors to move in and usurp market share. For labor-management relations to become more collaborative, both sides must understand the benefits of this change, build trust through reciprocity, and work creatively together to solve problems that arise, keeping the focus on shared interests. Companies have made these changes in multiple ways: "Various names have been given to these innovations, including mutual gains, bargaining, principled negotiations, employee-centered management, employee involvement, quality of working life, innovative work practices, the high-performance workplace and learning organizations" (Alexander, 1999, p. 1). Transitioning to collaborative relationships will bring the tangible benefits of reduced sick time and turnover as well as employee engagement, which brings forward innovative ideas and high morale.

To build trust, organizations should consider sharing information on profits and losses, benchmark the wages and benefits offered by competing firms, and engage in open discussions with union leadership about changes that can make both groups better off. Sharing information, listening to one another, and displaying a sincere willingness to work together toward mutual goals is the way to help transition from historically adversarial relationships to more collaborative ones. "It isn't the changes you do, it is the transitions. Change is not the same as transition. Change is situational: the new site, the new boss, the new team roles, the new policy. Transition is the psychological process people go through to come to terms with the new situation" (Bridges, 1991, p. 3). Without trust, the "corporate community is reduced to a group of resentful wage slaves and defensive, if not ambitious, managers. People will do their jobs but they will not offer their ideas, their enthusiasm, or their souls . . . The corporation becomes not a community, but a brutish state of nature, a way of all against all in which employment becomes nasty, brutish and short" (Solomon & Flores, 2001, p. 5).

The willingness to transition from adversarial to collaborative relationships needs to be led by the organization (Kotter, 1996). Leaders within the organization must make some visible changes to the way they treat employees so that it is clearly more than lip service. An easy first step is to create reward structures for employee ideas that are shared upward and adopted for the improvement of customer service or product quality or efficiency. The next step could be a formal invitation to employees to participate in focus groups, surveys, or other information-gathering methods that take the temperature to gauge morale as well as the points of opportunity for positive change. Work with union leaders and all levels of supervisors and managers from across the organization to create some overarching goals for change as well as specific actions and timelines necessary to enact those goals. This sounds like strategic planning, and it certainly can be a full-fledged strategic planning initiative designed to redefine labor-management relations. Or it can be smaller, more focused on specific changes to the organizational culture and top-down policies.

Leaders within the organization can decide to proceed with the status quo or to make a change. Big change usually comes during a period of crisis and the accompanying realization that current methods simply are not working. Many employers are unwilling to lead this change, even as they complain about the cost of adversarial relationships. "Employers have a tendency to govern by contractual rights using their position and power as a threat; unwilling to involve unions in the decision-making process, while protecting their turf, and perpetuating conflict" (Blackard, 2000, p. 49). This behavior reflects an unwillingness to share power, with the belief that the success of the enterprise rests on the unilateral control of power by the organization's leaders, perhaps addressed to some extent by the countervailing strength of the collective bargaining units. This mind-set is becoming increasingly antiquated—it reflects a rigidity that makes organizations less able to adapt to change and compete globally. For public organizations, it reifies negative public stereotypes of these agencies as inefficient, bloated, and rule bound. In 2004, the Conference Board of Canada stated that the Canadian labor relations system is based on assumptions of adversarial relationships. An us-versus-them mentality permeates the relationship. "Work stoppages, whether lockouts or strikes, illustrate this confrontational reality" (Colvin, 2004, p. 695).

When senior management pursues significant changes to policies without seeking the advice or consent of the union or the input of nonunionized workers, then it is clear that the mental switch to a collaborative style has not yet occurred. This behavior sends the signal that workers' ideas and concerns are not important to the successful accomplishment of the organization's mission and it is generally wrong. Not only could nearly all organizations benefit from the input of their internal stakeholders, but they will also need their buy-in in order to successfully implement any significant changes. Especially in large organizations, employees know they can drag their feet to torpedo any changes they deem unappealing; eventually top leadership will either give up on the changes that are not bringing the desired results quickly enough or they will be replaced through normal turnover processes. Upper leadership generally turns over more quickly than mid-level managers, and many employees use this to their advantage.

BECOMING A COLLABORATIVE LEADER IN A NONCOLLABORATIVE ENVIRONMENT

What if the senior leaders in your organization are unwilling to make the deep cultural and policy changes necessary to reverse the ingrained habits of distrust and opposition between themselves and their unionized employees? Then you as a manager at any level within your organization can likely make changes within your work unit that seek to create a microculture of collaboration and mutual respect. Change in an organization's culture or patterns of behavior must come from the executive level to have the most impact but absent that will, managers and supervisors at all levels can affect the outlook and behaviors of those in their units. Be transparent about what you are doing and why you are doing it. Let employees know that you value their ideas and want everyone to be as happy as possible in their working lives. Get to know them as individuals—an important step toward building the trust necessary for reciprocal relationships and mutual support. Work with them to create benchmarks or goals to work toward within your unit and discuss any rewards or recognition that you or the group will provide for realization of those goals. Be clear about what is within your control and what is not. Communicate to the union steward or other union officials that you see them as partners in change and success rather than as obstacles. In fact, the union's structure and close communication with its members can serve as a conduit for information and ideas upward in the organization as well as communicating problems early on. Linden (2003) describes collaborative leadership as the "art of pulling people together from different units or organizations to accomplish a task that none of them could accomplish—at all or as well—individually" (p. 42).

The characteristics of a collaborative leader include the willingness to take risks, accept responsibility, adapt to change, maintain a future orientation—meaning you do not allow past problems to define the present or the future and you have a good sense of timing and good interpersonal skills, especially listening and framing skills (Linden, 2003). It takes courage for leaders to initiate this change when maintaining the status quo might buy enough time to meet one's own financial needs. True leaders are willing to pursue deep change, which means they will be "purpose-centered, internally driven, other-focused, and externally open (Quinn, 2004, p. 21). Collaborative leaders build trust through open communication, listening, and responding with empathy. It is important to keep commitments, and if doing so becomes impossible, leaders must communicate why this is the case and seek help with overcoming obstacles. Managers seeking to change the culture and adversarial nature of relationships between themselves and unionized workers must model the trust, transparency, empathy, and respect with which they hope to be treated. When faced with a dysfunctional history of labor-management relations, supervisors and managers at all levels should view this as an opportunity to bring effective change rather than continuing to complain about the ways in which the unions create obstacles to organizational success.

ADR IN THE CREATION OF COLLECTIVE BARGAINING AGREEMENTS

For more than one hundred years, arbitration has been used to settle disputes over wages, working conditions, and benefits between collective bargaining employees and their employers. The Erdman Act of 1898 is only one such example. It arose after the volatile labor unrest between railroad workers and required arbitration to settle disputes regarding the terms of labor-management contracts when bargaining and negotiation failed to result in an agreement. As opposed to the arbitration of union grievances, also called *rights arbitration*, the arbitration of the terms of the actual union contract has come to be known as interest arbitration. Historically, when unions and management cannot reach agreements about wages and working conditions, they have resorted to a contest of power to see who will prevail through the use of strikes and lockouts. Whichever group can last the longest, wins. Yet both groups also lose, and this has been repeatedly demonstrated throughout labor-management history. This fact has been acknowledged most explicitly in the public sector, in which the general public suffers when police, firefighters, and other public employees strike.

In 1962, Executive Order 10988 made it illegal for many types of public sector employees' unions to resort to the strike option. In fact, employees may risk jail for striking in spite of this order. Disgruntled public employees have found many ways to display their dissatisfaction with proposed contract terms that work around this ban on the use of strikes, such as the blue flu or massive sick-outs, in which employees call in sick or do the minimum amount of work necessary to avoid the penalties of officially violating the order. In 1981, US president Ronald Reagan fired ten thousand air traffic controllers for striking after being warned that a strike would not be met with a compromise from the Federal Aviation Administration. In an effort to avoid these negative outcomes, interest arbitration has been used either by mandate or by mutual agreement between labor and management.

There are various forms of interest arbitration. For example, "last, best offer" arbitration is famously used by professional baseball players but it is also used by many public employees as well. In this kind of arbitration, the arbitrator examines the last offer made by each side to determine which was the most fair and the most generous. Then, the arbitrator chooses the best offer in its entirety without picking and choosing the best elements of each proposal or deciding to compromise between the two offers. The goal of last, best offer arbitration is actually to avoid arbitration. Both sides have incentives to be as generous as possible or risk having to accept the other side's proposal.

In 2010, the US Congress rejected the Employee Free Choice Act yet some of its provisions may be adopted voluntarily by unions and organizations, especially those seeking to create their first contract on the creation of a new employee union. Under this proposal, the union would have only ninety days to negotiate a first-time collective bargaining agreement. If no agreement is reached, either side can demand mediation. After thirty days, if no agreement is reached through mediation, then a contract will be imposed on the company and the union by a third-party arbitrator.

So how do contracts created by arbitrators compare to those reached through mutual negotiation? "Interest arbitration tracked the downward path in wage growth; there is no evidence that interest arbitration 'pulls up' or 'pushes down' wages. We do find that wage settlement patterns through arbitration have less variation as compared with bargained settlements" (Zullo, 2011, p. 1). On the whole, there appears to be relatively few differences in the outcome of arbitrated versus negotiated agreements, except that agreements reached through negotiation allow union and company negotiators to claim more agency in the outcome as well as use the negotiations as a forum to share information and build better relationships.

Although some union contracts for the private sector include resorting to binding interest arbitration, others retain the right to strike when the two sides cannot find mutually agreeable terms for contract renewal. During the Great Recession, historically high labor surpluses have worked to depress wages and reduce the profitability of many companies. In these hard times, a strike by collective bargaining employees is highly risky, and some employers may choose to replace striking workers rather than continue to compromise on issues of wages or benefits. However, the cash reserves of most corporations are also lower than in the past and few companies seek to harm their brand name or relationships with customers by engaging in a highly visible labor dispute. These economic circumstances mean labor and management need each other more than ever and could view this as an opportunity to build more collaborative relationships for mutual survival during rough times.

EXAMPLES OF COLLABORATION IN LABOR-MANAGEMENT RELATIONS

Increasingly, there are many examples of positive evolution in the relationships between labor and management. These changes reflect increased realization that neither group is served by maintaining an adversarial mind-set and working to undermine the other side only makes one's own group weaker in the end.

In 1980, the United Steelworkers of America (USWA) was in the middle of a labor crisis. The US steel industry was faced with cheap competition from countries with few environmental and worker safety laws as well as miserably low wages. These factors led to pressures for cuts in the workforce and wage reductions, with workers angry at the union and their employers. Faced with this situation, the union decided that collaboration between labor and management was the best method to promote "genuine worker involvement while tapping into the talents of our members . . . We [USWA] took a very proactive and positive approach to labor-management participation teams (LMPT's) which, in turn, made a very significant contribution to improvement in quality and productivity in many plants" (Kaufman, 2001, p. 159).

In their 2005 book, Linda Kaboulian and Paul Sutherland examined innovative collaborations between teachers' unions and school districts. For example, the Cities of Rochester and Boston agreed to create various forms of autonomy so the schools have more discretion over curriculum, budgeting, and personnel to shape an approach that best serves their students. In Toledo, union members and teachers agreed to play an active role in evaluating teacher performance as a peer function designed to not only affect merit pay but also to help struggling teachers improve their performance so that students can succeed. Rather than allowing administrators to evaluate teachers, in spite of the fact that some of these administrators had been out of the classroom for years, the teachers' union worked with district leadership to craft a system that was not only more fair and transparent but that also had a better chance of improving classroom outcomes. Kaboulian and Sutherland say that the most important factors for creating collaboration between unions and district leaders is to have regular, no-surprises communication between the two groups. Bring in mediators or facilitators as needed to help address difficult problems together. In those school districts where collaboration between the union and school district has failed, it can nearly always be traced to a lack of frequent, open communication.

The contracts between the unions and school districts are all about relationships between adults rather than focusing on the relationships between adults and students or the needs of students. Both sides can benefit from seeing their relationships differently and that the core common interest they share is a desire to educate students and improve student achievement. They need to work together to create a better product: education. Rather than seeing labor-management relations as a negotiation that occurs every four to five years when the contract comes up for renewal, both sides see their relationship as one that requires ongoing negotiation, discussion, and problem solving as issues and opportunities arise.

The executive branch of the US federal government has recently acknowledged that the negative relationships between employee unions and management has been an impediment to mission accomplishment and is in need of change. Toward this end, President Barack Obama signed Executive Order 13522 (December 2009), which established the National Council on Federal Labor-Management Relations (Kohli, 2010). This council will establish forums to discuss and promote closer collaboration, transparency, and joint efforts related to improved service delivery and mission accomplishment within federal government agencies in the executive branch, training of executive branch employees in dispute resolution techniques, and increased employee engagement in mission accomplishment and problem solving. This order requires forty-seven agencies to submit plans for the improvement of labor-management relations, including the development of metrics used to evaluate progress toward this goal. One sample plan from the Department of Health and Human Services (HHS) includes a plan to improve the quality of workforce life as well as enhance its service delivery. The plan includes methods for addressing workplace disputes quickly and in a nonadversarial way, focusing on the use of ADR processes such as mediation. This agency, like many others, has a long way to go. A recent study revealed that only 48 percent of HHS staff said the organization is able to recruit staff with the right skills, only 40 percent felt that promotions were truly based on merit rather than favoritism, and less than one-third believed that adequate steps are taken to address a poor performer who cannot or will not improve (Kohli, 2010). Addressing these problems will require better collaboration between unions and organizational leaders than has occurred in the past. But doing so is crucial, especially when we consider the size and scope of the federal workforce. "A 1 percent productivity gain across the federal workforce is worth $1.5 billion a year. But more important than increased efficiency is the potential change in how Americans view government. It's not hard to imagine that citizens would perceive the government more favorably if every interaction they have is one where the federal employees are committed to going the extra mile to make a difference" (Kohli, 2010).

There is a clear trend toward greater labor-management collaboration and a rethinking of this important relationship. Clearly, changing the adversarial nature of these relationships brings risks for unions and the organizations in which their members work. Employers and managers often fear giving up coercive control in favor of having power over employees. Unions may fear that these efforts are backdoor attempts to lead workers to feel the unions are no longer necessary. Instead of envisioning these changes as threatening, there is more to be gained from viewing them as an opportunity for mutual gains. The existing union structures can be used to funnel workers' ideas and concerns to management as well as to mobilize workers to adopt changes to work processes and policies that will have mutual benefit.

Interest-Based Negotiation in San Francisco Hotels

The San Francisco Hotels Partnership Project was created in 1994, involving twelve unionized first-class hotels and two of the city's largest union locals. The project's primary goals included increased market share for participating hotels, retention and improvement of pay and job security, and new programs for employee involvement, training, and career development. Labor and management agreed that they had a common interest in raising the quality of service in the hotels through joint problem solving, increased on-the-job training, and the creation of opportunities for advancement within and across participating hotels. A joint steering committee controls funds from state training agencies and employer contributions. Problem-solving groups have been created in each hotel, composed of two-thirds workers and one-third managers, with facilitation by a neutral third party. The teams deal with issues of job design, workload training, job security, and hotel operations. A training program for 1,600 workers in ten hotels has provided a common foundation in communications skills, critical thinking, problem solving, and teamwork. A recent pilot effort trained 160 workers, many of whom work in non-food service positions, for certification as basic banquet servers. These workers are available through the union's hiring hall to any of the participating hotels to help alleviate the heavy workload demands during the end-of-year holidays. Future study teams will explore additional ways to increase job stability through referrals of part-time workers across participating hotels, increased training and promotion opportunities, and work redesign to accommodate older

(continued)

(continued)

workers. These innovations were the product of an IBN following training and with the facilitation of the Federal Mediation and Conciliation Service.

Source: Chaykowski, Cutcher-Gershenfeld, Kochan, and Sickles Merchant (2001, p. 21). Reprinted with permission of the Association for Conflict Resolution.

CONCLUSION

Nothing in this chapter should be interpreted as an attack on the importance of unions. In fact, unions have an important role to play in enhancing employee engagement and collaborative workplaces and ensuring fair wages and safe working conditions. Union workers tend to earn more than nonunionized workers in the same profession. Union workers also have fewer wage differences based on gender or race. These are important accomplishments that should not be overlooked.

Both unions and management need to acknowledge they have shared interests in maintaining positive working relationships, an efficient and economically competitive organization, high morale, and low employee turnover. When employers and employees fully recognize their shared interests in the success of the organization and adopt a worldview that sees the other's success as key to their own, then unions can fulfill the role of being a communications conduit and organizing structure to realize jointly planned initiatives. As the saying goes, "We all succeed together."

For those organizations and leaders stuck in the adversarial patterns that have tended to characterize labor-management relationships in large public and private organizations, it is time to rethink and restructure this relationship. In their research into the challenges facing the US airline industry, Kochan, Von Nordenflycht, McKersie, and Gittell (2003) found that "efforts to recover from the current crisis in the airline industry that depend primarily on reductions in wages or union power will at best bring only short-term relief from immediate financial pressures. Sustained improvement in service quality and financial performance will require more fundamental improvements in the quality of labor relations." As Robert Quinn (2004) explains in his text on leaders and change, "To refuse to change while the universe changes around us, is ultimately to choose a slow death" (p. 21).

JOHN AT THE BUREAU OF RECLAMATION

John knows that changing the nature of the relationship between the union and management at the bureau will be critical to his success as an organizational leader. The union grievance process takes employees and managers away from their important work and the adversarial relationships of the past no longer serve either side well. In the end, if the bureau does not accomplish its mission or gets a negative public reputation, it hurts unionized and nonunionized employees at all levels. What can John do to improve the working relationship with unions and union members in his bureau?

John began by having an informal lunch meeting with union leaders and shop stewards. He told them that he valued the union as an important vehicle for sharing employee concerns and ideas for organizational improvement with management. He told them he believed the union has great, mostly untapped potential as one of the drivers of organizational success. He hoped that they would join him in a day-long workshop with union stewards and managers in which the two sides will talk about ways they can work together to make the bureau a great place to work and one of the most admired and efficient state government units. John argued the organization's success would benefit management and labor; therefore, they should put their heads together to find ways to work with one another rather than against one another. The first step was to get to know each other as people through informal dialogue efforts before any formal negotiations occur down the road.

During the workshop, union-management teams used an open-space technology format (see Chapter Twelve) to set the day's agenda: (1) how to reduce the number of contract violations and grievance filings, (2) methods for funneling employee ideas for better service delivery to management, and (3) win-win proposals that should be considered in the upcoming contract renewal negotiations.

These workgroups developed concrete ideas, many of which were implemented successfully. For example, some of the grievances were occurring because frontline supervisors had different interpretations of some provisions within the union contract. A jointly led training was developed and delivered to ensure that all supervisors had the same understanding of the contract's provisions and the best way to implement them. This resulted in a rapid reduction in grievance filings.

Although this relationship will require ongoing efforts at trust building and negotiation, John now feels confident that the union will serve as a pillar of strength for his organization rather than as a continued source of unproductive conflict.

KEY TERMS

Blue collar

Collective bargaining

Collective bargaining agreement

Free riders

Great Recession

Sick-outs

Skilled labor

Union grievance

Union steward

Unskilled labor

White collar

SUGGESTED SUPPLEMENTAL READING

Lipsky, D. B., & Avgar, A. C. (2004). Commentary: Research on employment dispute resolution: Toward a new paradigm. *Conflict Resolution Quarterly*, *22*(1/2), 175–189.

Mayer, G. (2004). *Union membership trends in the United States*. Federal Publications. Paper 174. Retrieved from http://digitalcommons.ilr.cornell.edu /key_workplace/174

Monahan, C. (2008). Faster, cheaper, and unused: The paradox of grievance mediation in unionized environments. *Conflict Resolution Quarterly*, *25*(4), 479–496.

DISCUSSION QUESTIONS

1. For employees, what are the costs and benefits of working in a unionized environment? What are the costs and benefits for managers and organizational leaders?

2. What are some common differences in disputing processes between unionized and nonunionized environments?

3. What can you, as a manager or organizational leader, do to reduce the animosity that may exist between workers and managers (whether you work in a unionized environment or not)?

EXERCISES

1. Research and discuss the trends in unionization in your state, region, or industry. How do you anticipate that unionization will affect your work as a manager?

2. Consider this scenario: it is time to negotiate the renewal of the union contract. The union leadership has asked for an increase of $2.00 an hour of wages and three more days of vacation for employees. Company leadership is arguing against any changes to the current contract in order to maintain competitiveness. The company has a hard-nosed positional bargainer. You represent the union and seek to engage in an interest-based negotiation. What techniques would you use to get the other side to engage in interest-based negotiations? What are the positions, interests, and BATNAs of each side?

GOAL SETTING

Think of one change you can make in the next week to improve the relationship between different stakeholder groups within your organizations (e.g., managers and employees). Enact one small change and see what happens. It could be as simple as meeting for coffee to improve communication.

chapter EIGHT

Designing Disputing Systems for Organizations

Learning Objectives

- Demonstrate an understanding of the methods for conducting a needs assessment.

- Demonstrate an understanding of the role of internal and external stakeholders during DSD processes.

- Demonstrate an understanding of the role of power, rights, and interests in DSD.

- List and describe various process options to consider when creating dispute systems.

- Demonstrate an understanding of the costs and benefits of systematizing processes for dispute management.

- List and describe the best practices for engaging in DSD.

- Demonstrate an understanding of the different trends in DSD for private corporations, public sector agencies, and nonprofit organizations.

ELISE AT MAIN STREET BAKERIES

Elise does everything she can to keep her employees happy and minimize turnover. In spite of her efforts, her company occasionally encounters a disgruntled employee or someone claiming to have suffered from sexual harassment or discrimination. This is nearly unavoidable in a company with thousands of employees. Elise's goal is to constantly improve her company as a place to work and shop. Therefore, she has hired a consulting firm to conduct a needs assessment and make recommendations to further reduce the costs of unproductive conflict within her organization.

The term *dispute systems design (DSD)* refers to the strategic arrangement of dispute resolution processes within an organization (Costantino & Merchant, 1996). Disputing systems are commonly defined for internal employment disputes or disputes with external stakeholders such as clients, customers, or regulators (e.g., EEOC complaints within a federal agency or environmental enforcement cases with polluters). The goal of DSD processes is to track and reduce the occurrence and costs of disputes that can reasonably be predicted to occur within an organization and between the organization and external audiences such as customers, vendors, and regulators. Instead of treating each dispute as a unique, one-time event, a DSD approach seeks to identify the sources of recurring disputes, take preventative steps to avoid such disputes when possible, and take a problem-solving approach to efficiently resolve those disputes that cannot be avoided. All organizations have dispute systems, either by design or by accident (Nabatchi & Bingham, 2010). By working to prevent and efficiently resolve disputes, organizations can enhance their reputations, improve their products and services, and reduce the costs of conflict.

DSD is key for reducing, predicting, and addressing internal workplace conflicts as well as external disputes with clients, customers, and regulators. This chapter will primarily focus on internal workplace applications but will lay the conceptual framework for the discussion of dispute systems for external stakeholders in Chapter Nine.

PROCEDURAL JUSTICE AND REDUCING COSTS OF CONFLICT

When considering the creation of systems, policies, and procedures for managing conflict it is crucial to focus on procedural justice issues. As these systems are being forged, transparency and stakeholder participation will be key to their later success. If employees or other stakeholders feel these changes are forced on them from above or perceive the disputing system to be biased, unfair, or confusing, it will serve to increase rather than reduce unproductive conflicts.

It is not uncommon for employees to be skeptical of new dispute resolution procedures. They may wonder why the organization would assist them with the pursuit of a complaint or they may doubt that it will be done impartially. Workplace ADR programs live or die by their reputation. If employees feel coerced into settlements or mistreated at any phase of the process, word will spread like wildfire. Unfortunately, bad news seems to spread faster than good news but a solid dispute resolution program will grow a positive reputation that results in appropriate levels of use over time.

POWER, RIGHTS, AND INTERESTS

Disputes can be resolved in three basic ways: through a resort to power, rights, and interests (Ury, Brett, & Goldberg, 1988). Power is the ability to assert one's preferred outcome onto others. In workplace settings power is used to resolve disputes through mechanisms such as strikes—in which the organization and the union seek to show they are more powerful than the other. Workplace violence or the threat of violence is also a way that individuals in dispute try to assert and display their power over others. Rights are established through law, union contracts, or official policies. Contests over rights are often played out in the courts, the EEOC, or through union grievance arbitration. Interests, as mentioned throughout this book (see Chapter Three), are the needs and desires of individuals and groups. They are addressed through negotiation, mediation, and other processes in which all parties seek to reach agreements that meet each other's needs without resorting to the coercion of power-based approaches or the use of an external decision maker with rights-based approaches. In terms of costs, power-based approaches tend to be the most expensive, then rights-based approaches, and finally, interest-based approaches. Interest-based approaches also hold the possibility of addressing the underlying causes of the dispute more thoroughly than the other two approaches (Costantino & Merchant, 1996; Ury, Brett, & Goldberg, 1988).

Unfortunately, hierarchical organizations tend to use power and rights-based approaches to solve problems. They do so out of the perception that it is more efficient for a boss to enforce his or her decisions on subordinates than it is to learn about the needs and interests of each person and design more tailored solutions. This approach works in many cases but some will generally fall through the cracks and receive a solution or decision that just doesn't fit or is inappropriate given the specific circumstances. Research has shown that interest-based approaches are more cost effective, satisfying, long lasting, and sustainable for recurring problems in ongoing relationships, such as those in workplace settings (Colquitt, Conlon, Wesson, Porter, & Ng, 2001).

VALUES UNDERLIE THE DESIGN

What motivates you or your organization to consider redesigning its systems for disputing? Well-established organizations tend to invest in DSD in the face of a crisis. They come to realize their current system is inefficient due to expensive litigation, high turnover, loss of business or reputation, and new efforts by the employees to unionize. Sometimes a lawsuit changes the way organizations handle disputes, as was the case with the Coca-Cola Enterprises. If the organization's leaders are sincere about making changes that prevent and efficiently process disputes to fair resolutions, then there is a good chance that long-lasting improvements can be made. However, sometimes organizational leaders bring in DSD experts in order to appear willing to make changes rather than having a sincere desire to change (Greenberg, 1990). This lip service usually comes back to haunt organizations because the existing problems were enough to make leaders believe they needed to calm down the employees or external stakeholders — and usually they are right.

Stakeholders are those who are directly or indirectly affected by a proposed change — they have a stake in the outcome. Within organizations **internal stakeholders** include employees at all levels and the legal and HR departments. **External stakeholders** could include customers, vendors, shareholders, patients or the affected public, and regulators. For public policy facilitation, **primary stakeholders** are those most immediately affected by the policy outcomes. **Secondary stakeholders** are individuals or groups who are indirectly affected by decisions or actions of an organization. For example, when the US Environmental Protection Agency (EPA) creates a new regulation regarding fuel efficiency in cars, the primary stakeholders are the members of the automobile industry and the secondary stakeholders are all people who drive cars and breath air . . . literally everyone is affected at some level by these policies. Some secondary stakeholders will be affected more than others, such as children suffering from asthma versus those who have no special health needs.

For efforts at DSD to be taken seriously, the organization's leaders must be sincere in their desire to bring positive cultural and procedural changes to the organization. They must convey their support for these efforts to management and employees at all levels. They must walk the talk and avoid meddling in dispute processes that are piloted, such as mediation programs or an ombuds office. They must be open to criticism, feedback, and change in company policies and procedures, as long as those changes are designed to improve the way problems are resolved. Efforts to change conflict management across whole organizations will not succeed without the support of organizational leaders, the implementation of managers at all levels, and the buy-in from rank-and-file employees.

What values are at the heart of efficient versus inefficient disputing systems? Inefficient systems are not equally accessible to all comers. They do not allow all parties to feel heard. They are slow, expensive, and do not fully address all of the issues in dispute. Nabatchi and Bingham (2010) note that

> better dispute systems foster and reinforce norms of reciprocity, which aids in creating shared confidence and trust among disputants, and increases the prospects for cooperation. The extent to which dispute systems achieve reciprocity, confidence, trust, and cooperation determines, in part, the likelihood of reaching satisfying and sustainable solutions to conflicts. Moreover, the better the dispute system is at resolving conflicts in terms of satisfaction and sustainability, the greater the likelihood of employee retention and the possibilities for future cooperation, as opposed to more conflict. (p. 215)

The values that underlie the creation of a disputing system should be tied to the purposeful evolution of the organization's culture. If leaders seek to nurture a spirit of cooperation, self-determination, understanding, and fairness, where people feel valued, then they will craft a dispute system that mirrors and upholds those values. Perhaps they will choose to emphasize mediation and an ombuds office to maximize the opportunities for parties to share their perspectives about problems and craft their own solutions in a confidential atmosphere. If they see employees as somewhat disposable, then the values underlying their DSD model may instead focus on quick resolutions through the use of binding arbitration and an arbitration clause in their employment contracts. Whether the leadership team explicitly imbues their system with values or does this accidentally, the disputing systems within organizations point to the values that are representative of the organizational culture.

When hiring or promoting individuals into managerial positions, it is important to consider their ability to articulate clear values and lead their teams and the organization in pursuit of positive values. They must be able to embody positive, ethical, effective handling of problems that arise. According to a study by Van den

Steen (2001), "Managers with strong beliefs about the right course of action will attract, through sorting in the labor market, employees with similar beliefs. This alignment of beliefs gives direction to the firm and has important implications for incentives and coordination . . . it may be optimal to hire managers with such strong beliefs. Vision will be most important when uncertainty is high and actions are difficult to contract on." In other words, it is crucial to hire managers with a clear vision and strong values. These characteristics are particularly important during times of change such as mergers and acquisitions or the creation of new systems for managing conflict within an organization. These abilities are generally found to be more important than technical knowledge within the literature and are especially crucial when considering the design and implementation of disputing systems. Managers who do not believe in the importance or utility of the disputing system become obstacles to positive change.

GENERAL DSD CONCEPTS AND PRACTICES

In their seminal work, Costantino and Merchant (1996) discuss six key principles of dispute system design. These principles are helpful as you consider best practices for DSD.

Focus on Interests

As already discussed, resolving disputes through a focus on interests tends to be less costly, faster, and less damaging to continuing relationships. Although it may be possible to get a final, relatively quick decision through arbitration, the use of adversarial processes such as arbitration make it difficult for the parties to continue working productively together. Each side presents their arguments to the decision maker to convince him or her that the other person is wrong and has misbehaved or violated law or policy. It is difficult to attack the other party in an adjudicatory forum and then work next to him or her on the workroom floor in a collaborative manner. Additionally, many disputes deal with interpersonal differences or differences in communication styles. These are not able to be resolved through adjudication, although they may indeed lead individuals to file claims of discrimination or inappropriate treatment. When employees feel mistreated or sense that "the manager just doesn't like me," they may feel subject to unequal treatment. Often, there is no litigation or internal recourse mechanism to deal with true personality conflicts — only illegal behaviors such as discrimination are grounds for formal action. When employees feel they are being mistreated or can't get along with a supervisor, their only recourse may be to make a formal claim of discrimination, harassment, and so on. Therefore, it is crucial to create informal mechanisms through which these day-to-day problems can be resolved early and efficiently before they become formal complaints.

By way of example, one employee interviewed for this book stated that he and his coworkers repeatedly filed union grievances and EEOC complaints against his supervisor in order to ensure the supervisor would spend more time off the factory floor. Because of these complaints, the supervisor was required to spend a great deal of time meeting with the legal and HR departments as well as union officials. The employees did not honestly believe that any contract violations or discrimination had occurred. They simply wanted to avoid working with an obnoxious boss. In a case like this, interest-based processes and services such as speaking to an ombudsman, executive coach, or mediator would be much less expensive and likely more effective at addressing the root causes of the conflict than the traditional union grievance and EEOC processes. Unfortunately, this organization had no such interest-based mechanisms.

Interest-based processes such as negotiation, mediation, facilitation, and so on may be best able to address the root causes of many workplace conflicts, whether those conflict are occurring up or down the hierarchy or between coworkers as peers.

Provide Low-Cost Processes to Secure Rights

If interest-based processes fail to resolve the dispute and an authoritative decision is needed, such an option should be provided for within the DSD. Whether this process is peer review, arbitration, or some other process, parties in dispute should have a quicker, less costly, and more final route for reaching a decision than going to civil courts or the EEOC. Individuals who believe their rights have been infringed should have a forum where they can feel heard, seek restitution, and bring change to the company. Creating an internal rights-based option will achieve savings and shorten the pain of such a process and preserve the organization's external reputation.

In general, it is best to recommend or require resorting to an interest-based process such as an ombudsman's services or mediation prior to the use of a rights-based process such as arbitration. Processes that are used to determine who is right and to secure rights for individuals and groups are inherently adversarial processes. These processes such as arbitration, case evaluation, or peer review require parties to argue to the neutral(s) as to why their position is correct and the other parties' position is incorrect. This can create ongoing strife and tension in the work environment before, during, and after the proceedings occur. Although rights-based processes are necessary, it is best to consider less adversarial and less formal means of dispute resolution first.

Provide Loop-Backs to Interest-Based Procedures

If the parties initially try to negotiate a resolution to their problem and this effort fails, then they may choose to move to another process such as a nonbinding peer review. If employees are dissatisfied with the outcome of that process, then they should be able to loop back to an earlier process to try negotiation or mediation again. Sometimes a case takes time to ripen. Employees may not be willing to settle at first, but after trying one or more settlement processes, they may be inclined to reopen the settlement negotiations. Providing loop-backs means that disputes need not always move toward ever-more costly dispute resolution processes.

Learn from Each Dispute

It is important to gather feedback from the parties in dispute so that future similar disputes can be avoided, not only by these parties but by others facing similar circumstances. This can be done through an ombudsman's office, through an ADR administrator, or other mechanisms. The goal is to gain specific feedback about the perceived causes of the conflict as well as satisfaction with the dispute resolution processes available for handling the dispute. Parties who take part in processes such as mediation, arbitration, peer review, coaching, and so on should be asked to provide formative feedback about their satisfaction with the process, the neutral person involved, and the outcome. That feedback should be used to improve the options available to disputants, to refine or change the constitution of rosters of neutrals, and to put into place preventative measures to reduce future conflicts whenever practical. Disputes create learning opportunities for organizations to enhance their services, change training methods for managers or employees, and address needed policy or procedural changes. Companies that treat each dispute as a unique event lose the opportunity to constantly improve the efficiency with which disputes are prevented and managed.

Try Low-Cost Processes First

The process options should be arranged in a stepwise fashion with the lowest cost options tried first and the highest cost options reserved for a time when other options have failed to settle the dispute. This means interest-based options will come first and then rights-based options (see Figure 8.1). When, if ever, should the lower-cost options be skipped? Most DSD experts agree that there is little to be lost in attempting direct negotiation or mediation before going to peer review, arbitration, or other rights-based processes. Many parties are skeptical and feel that their dispute is too complex or the parties are too entrenched for an interest-based process such as mediation to work. Sometimes parties are conflict avoiders and are uncomfortable discussing their concerns face-to-face. Yet workplace mediation programs in the United States commonly have full settlement rates of between 60 and 85 percent. Therefore, there is little harm done in trying these processes first. It should be noted that the intervention of an ombudsman can occur at any point along this continuum in order to serve as a

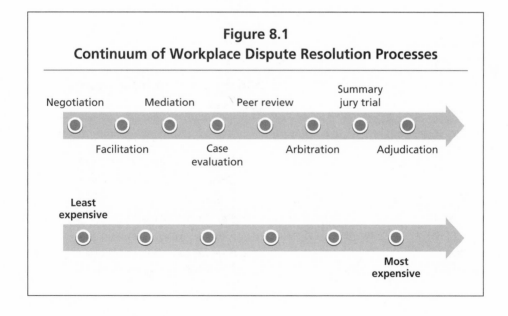

Figure 8.1
Continuum of Workplace Dispute Resolution Processes

go-between or other informal dispute resolver. The ombudsman can coach the parties about the ways they may be able to solve the dispute themselves, provide information on process options, conduct shuttle diplomacy between the parties, or even mediate if they ask him or her to do so.

What if a disputant wants to skip a step? Each organization designs their program rules somewhat differently. For example, case evaluation or peer review may not be standard in all systems. Some organizations create a stepwise system and do not allow any step to be bypassed. Others see their system as more of an ADR menu from which the parties choose the process that best suits their needs. These decisions will be determined during the needs evaluation process. It is a good idea to pilot the system for a specific period of time, commonly twelve to twenty-four months, and then assess whether tweaks or changes to it are needed.

Additionally, each organization will need to decide what kinds of cases can or cannot use the internal ADR process. Table 8.1 lists complaints that are often included in or excluded from internal ADR processes.

In addition to ADR processes that may be created during the design phase, other interventions may be recommended for the organization, such as training in communication or conflict management skills, meeting facilitations, changes in the frequency or methods for communications, and so on.

Table 8.1
Disputes Commonly Included in or Excluded from Internal ADR Processes

Included Complaints and Disputes	Excluded Complaints and Disputes
Wrongful termination	Worker's compensation claims
Favoritism	Social Security benefits claims
Discrimination in promotion, raises, or treatment based on race, religion, sex, age, national origin, physical disability, accessibility complaints, and so on	Individual complaints regarding health, dental, vision benefits
	Unemployment compensation
Interpersonal disputes, for example, "My boss and I don't get along"	Severance packages that have already been accepted by the employee
Sexual harassment	
Bullying complaints	

Ensure Organizational Members Have the Skills, Knowledge, and Resources Necessary to Make the System Work

If you build it, will they come? Nothing is as frustrating as a brand-new disputing system that no one knows about or wants to use. If you create a complaint hotline and no one calls, does that mean there are no complaints or that employees are too afraid of retaliation to make a call? Once a system is in place, a significant effort to educate employees needs to be made. The system needs to be advertised to employees so they know it exists, why it exists, and under what conditions they may wish to use it. This means employees need to know where to go when they have a complaint. Whether the administration is handled through an ombudsman's office, an ADR office, or someone otherwise entitled, employees need to know where to go. Once there, the staff can educate the employee about the differences among the various process options. Some organizations include a disputing provision within their employment contracts that requires employees to exhaust internal mechanisms for resolution before resorting to the courts. These mandatory ADR clauses have been upheld by the US Supreme Court and lower courts as long as the processes and any chosen neutrals are free from any pro-company bias.

In order to build employee confidence in the fairness of the internal disputing system, some companies make the offer to pay employees' lawyers for a set amount of consultation. This consultation may help employees to choose the best ADR options, help prepare them to successfully participate in one or more of these processes, and give employees an unbiased view about the strength of their case. We know from materials presented in Chapter Four that fewer than 6 percent of EEOC cases are decided in favor of the complainant. More often than not, when employees receive a legal opinion from an employment attorney, they learn their case will be much harder to win in court than they anticipated. We will discuss these provisions of legal services more in depth when we benchmark the DSD landscapes in the private, public, and nonprofit sectors at the end of this chapter.

FOUR STAGES OF DSD

The DSD process occurs in four stages: (1) organizational diagnosis, (2) system design, (3) implementation, and (4) exit, evaluation, and diffusion (Costantino & Merchant, 1996).

Organizational Diagnosis Stage

A **needs assessment** (also known as an *organizational assessment*) is an evaluation of the conflict, issue, or organization to understand the history, identify the stakeholders, and calculate the costs related to the status quo in order to determine the likely success of changes, including the use of a collaborative process(es) to address dispute(s). During the assessment of current disputing systems, the design team examines the history of disputing at the organization. What are the sources of recurring disputes? How much has been and is being spent on the current system of disputing, including lost time and productivity for those employees involved and any damage to the brand or reputation? How many disputes are there? Who handles them and how? What is working well? What isn't? What role does the organization's culture play in the management of disputing within the organization or with external disputants? The analysis needs to examine the "goals, processes, structure, stakeholders, resources, success, and accountability of the dispute system . . . For example, it is important to know whether the disputes involve factual, technical, legal, procedural, or interpersonal issues" (Nabatchi & Bingham, 2010, pp. 216–217). Begin with a macro focus, looking at issues of culture, communication methods, organizational structure, and decision-making methods across the organization. Map the flow of current conflicts through existing processes to get a clear understanding of the baseline. Decide whether to focus on internal or external disputes. These systems should be designed separately because the conflicts are likely to be distinct. Then examine the micro level by analyzing the number, source, and costs of complaints. Be sure to benchmark the company's current DSD compared to its competitors or peer organizations. How do they manage disputing? What costs or benefits have they realized?

The individual or team that conducts the assessment should interview and survey individuals from across the spectrum of the organization to gather all possible perspectives on these questions, perhaps even including former employees and customers. Key stakeholders should not be overlooked, such as the leaders in the legal and HR departments, union leaders, as well as managers and employees from different parts of the company. These interviews provide an opportunity for the designer(s) to build rapport and gain the trust of the organization's stakeholders. You will need their buy-in not only for the needs assessment to be accurate, but also for any eventual changes in the system to work. During the needs assessment you will be asking tough questions about what is working and what is not. Particularly in the legal and HR departments, there may be some fear that the assessment will cast their work in a negative light or that the proposed changes may encroach on their turf. For these reasons, it is important to communicate the values that underlie this effort and the ways in which this effort is supportive of the organization's overall mission. The needs assessment should share aggregate information only — avoid revealing the names of the participants if possible and do not identify problem employees by name in the report. Tell participants there will be no retaliation for their participation after first securing this promise from upper- and mid-level managers. Will employees have access to read the report? These are issues to be negotiated with the company during the contracting stage. Again, the purpose of this endeavor is constructive rather than destructive. The end result should make the organization a better place to work for all. If the designer communicates these values and takes the time to build rapport and trust with key stakeholders, it is usually possible to gain access to needed information as well as build buy-in for the DSD process as a whole.

Who is the best person to conduct the needs assessment? Although existing employees know the organization, its culture, and key players, they may be viewed with skepticism by colleagues. If one or more existing employees are chosen for this role, they should have positive reputations within the organization, with widespread approval at their selection. Although small organizations may find success with a small internal team of designers, medium to large organizations will usually need to obtain external expertise from a paid consultant. This designer will create a **design team (DT)** composed of employees from different parts and levels of the organization who will assist in the development, implementation, and evaluation of the DSD. The DT will need to be trained in the basic concepts and practices of DSD. This training can last one day or up to a week, depending on the size of the task at hand. The DT is critical in ensuring that the outcome of this process will be workable and will not encounter unanticipated obstacles during the implementation phase. The DT will discuss various design options and help the designer better understand how they might fit within the organization's culture. Most important, the DT will become internal supporters of the eventual design and promote its use and acceptance among the rest of the employee population. For these reasons, it is important to be sure this is a representative group using a transparent process.

If there are union representatives or members of the legal or HR team who seem highly skeptical of the DSD effort, be sure to include them on the DT. As they see the process unfold and learn more about how and why it will benefit the organization and its employees, their hesitance will nearly always decrease. These individuals will be helpful in pointing out the obstacles to the creation and implementation of a new disputing system. Winning over these individuals can be key to successful implementation and uptake of the new system.

During the needs assessment phase, the organization's leadership should clarify the goals of the potential DSD process. Common goals include reducing litigation costs, reducing employee turnover, improving the company's public image, improving morale, preserving relationships, and so on. During the evaluation phase, it will be necessary to find methods to evaluate progress toward these goals. With that information, organizational leaders can decide whether the new system is worth maintaining or expanding.

At the end of the needs assessment phase, a written report is issued to the organization's leadership. If the organization already has a positive culture and system for disputing, the assessment may indicate that only small changes are needed. In cases like these the leaders may decide to create a stand-alone process such as mediation to add to their existing disputing system. Or the assessment may indicate a need for the implementation of broader changes designed to revamp current practices and create an integrated conflict management system with multiple steps to address many types of disputes. This report will include an analysis of the costs and benefits of the current system, potential gains from a new system, resources needed to implement a new system (including time), and benchmarking information on the best practices in DSD used by similar organizations. Then, the leadership team will discuss whether, when, and how to move on to the next phase.

System Design Phase

An analysis of multiple dispute system design efforts reveals a pattern of about fifteen different decisions that must be made during the design phase (Bingham, 2008, pp. 12–15):

- The sector or setting for the program (public, private, or nonprofit)
- The overall dispute system design (integrated conflict management system, stand-alone program, ombuds program, outside contractor)
- The subject matter of the conflicts, disputes, or cases over which the system has jurisdiction

- The participants eligible or required to use the system

- The timing of the intervention (before the complaint is filed, immediately thereafter, after discovery or information gathering is complete, and on the eve of an administrative hearing or trial)

- Whether the intervention is voluntary, opt out, or mandatory

- The nature of the intervention (training, facilitation, consensus building, negotiated rule making, mediation, early neutral assessment or evaluation, summary jury trial, nonbinding arbitration, binding arbitration) and its possible outcomes

- The sequence of interventions, if more than one

- Within intervention, the model of practice (if mediation, evaluative, facilitative, or transformative; if arbitration, binding or nonbinding, etc.)

- Who pays for the neutrals and the nature of their financial or professional incentive structure

- Who pays for the costs of administration, filing fees, hearing fees, hearing space

- The nature of any due process protections (right to counsel, discovery, location of process, availability of class actions, availability of written opinion or decision)

- Structural support and institutionalization with respect to conflict management programs or efforts to implement

- Level of self-determination or control that disputants have as to process, outcome, and dispute system design; qualifications of neutrals and stakeholder input therein

Source: Reprinted by permission of the *Ohio Journal on Dispute Resolution*.

Additionally, or perhaps more explicitly, it is important to think about how this DSD will fit in with other services offered to employees through the EAP, HR, unions, or other resources within the organization. Consider creating some sample decision trees that walk employees through the various choice points of a problem-solving or dispute process so they can better understand which venue or process is best for different kinds of problems.

Decisions made at the design stage are influenced by the information gathered during the needs assessment. "For example, an organization with a flat structure, a cooperative culture, and disputes that center on factual or technical matters may likely want or need a system different than that of an organization with a hierarchical structure, a competitive culture, and disputes about interpersonal or relational issues" (Nabatchi & Bingham, 2010, p. 218).

Ideally, these decisions should be made by a DT composed of representatives from across the organization, with the facilitation of an outside consultant expert. In order to get as much buy-in as possible from the potential users of the system, it is important to maximize self-determination at the systems level and at the case level. This means that employees have input into the decisions made during the system design process. Consider using focus group discussions, suggestion boxes, online boards, or other mechanisms through which all employees are invited to share their concerns, ideas, and questions during the design phase. Make this a completely transparent and participatory process to maximize its perceived legitimacy among future users.

During this phase it is necessary to deal with the administrative questions that arise during implementation: who will administer these programs or processes? Will it be an ombudsman or some other type of administrator? How big should this staff be and to whom will they answer within the organizational structure? What kind of budget will be required? There are no right or wrong answers to these questions because all will depend on the context of the organization.

Implementation Phase

In some ways, the first two phases are the most difficult and they are the most determinative of success. If the planning is done thoughtfully, then it makes the implementation much easier and provides a blueprint for those tasks with implementation. The challenge during this phase is to stay true to the values agreed on during the earlier phases and to maintain enough flexibility to deal with unexpected obstacles as they arise. Those tasked with implementation need to be excellent communicators, even diplomats. They will be called on to explain repeatedly why the system was created, how it works, and why parties should use it.

The new dispute system will need staff to administer it. In small organizations, this can be existing staff who have other duties but who receive some reduction in duties in order to assist with the administration of the dispute resolution system. In small organizations, these individuals will usually be called on only intermittently to assist with the processing of disputes through the system as well as any annual evaluation reports, and so on. In larger organizations, where a higher volume of complaints are to be expected, it is better to hire either internally or externally for one or more full-time positions. The DT may be included in some of these hiring decisions, when appropriate. The DT should also be called on to help educate and acculturate these employees into their new role. Who better to explain the system than those who had a hand in creating it?

Once the decisions identified in the design phase have been made and the system is ready to launch, it will be crucial to undertake an employee awareness campaign. Large organizations often do this through intranet postings, e-mails, and inclusions in organizational newsletters, looping videos on break-room televisions, regular staff meeting updates, brochures, flyers, and so on. In some organizations, participation in the internal system will be mandatory for disputes as part of an employment contract. In these cases, there needs to be a mechanism created that will steer employees to the process administrator, who will then assist them with using the process steps.

Do not be surprised if it initially appears that the number of disputes is on the increase since the creation of the ADR system. If there was pent-up demand for a dispute resolution mechanism, and if these processes are deemed relatively low cost to try, then we would expect an initial surge in the number of complaints. This is actually positive—it means that previously unaddressed problems are now surfacing and being managed proactively.

Before we leave the design phase, it is useful to draw your attention to the work of Craig McEwen on the use of ADR in corporations. In this work, McEwen persuasively argues that the creation of mediation, arbitration, and other ADR processes can certainly be useful and result in cost savings in organizations. However, the biggest cost savings and improvements are to be found when organizations imbue their corporate cultures and organizations with positive problem-solving methods rather than merely creating some new programs. He argues that the costs of disputing need to be measured and tracked over time. Employees at all levels within the organization need to have incentives for proactively managing problems with customers as well as with fellow employees. Conflict management skills need to be taught and performance reviews need to include measures of these behaviors and rewards for improvement and for high performance.

McEwen gives the example of managers within an anonymous company that we will call company A. When managers at company A have complaints or disputes, they simply hand them over to the legal department. That way any cost of resolution comes out of the legal department's budget and the manager's time is freed up for other tasks. As a result of the handoff, the legal department must fulfill its due-diligence requirements, investigating each claim fully before determining how to proceed or respond. This process often involves costly discovery of evidence, including depositions and thumbing through records, and so on. Eventually, the case may end up in mediation, arbitration, or court. This method of resolution does *not* encourage early resolution at the lowest possible levels within the organization. Compare this to company B, which gives managers some authority to settle complaints directly, within specified limits. Company B tracks the number of complaints as well as the time to settlement, time spent by in-house attorneys on each case, and the cost of eventual settlements. In company B, all of the costs of disputing are billed to the department from which the dispute originated, and managers are rewarded for their efficient handling of disputes. In the end, organizations that weave ADR principles throughout the incentive structures and work flows will see the greatest benefits.

Exit, Evaluation, and Diffusion Phases

Evaluation is often the last thing on the minds of organizational leaders as they implement new programs and policies—it gets too little attention and resources and is often forgotten until its absence begins to cause problems. Even when training is given to employees, for example, the most evaluation typically done is an exit survey that indicates whether they liked the trainer rather than an evaluation of the impact of that training on employee performance or customer satisfaction. Without thoughtful evaluation, how will you know if a new system is superior to what came before it? How will you know if the lofty goals of the ADR system were achieved partially, fully, or not at all? How will you argue to the organizational leaders that money spent on these preventative measures will result in less money spent on litigation, less employee turnover, a better reputation, and so on? A thorough evaluation is truly useful yet it is often neglected and underappreciated.

It is sometimes a struggle to implement a disputing system in a manner that remains true to the initial values and goals of its creators. During the implementation phase, shortages of time, money, or administrative staff may result in some drift away from the initial concept proposed in the design phase. Basically, the ideal and the real collide. One way to minimize this drift is to think about evaluation early, during the design phase. For each value established and goal that is set, ask yourselves, "How will we measure attainment of this value or this goal?" If you create your evaluation framework early in the design phase, well before implementation begins, you will be able to use that framework as objective criteria to determine whether changes to the initial design are justifiable and not overly injurious to the likely outcome of the evaluation. Another benefit of planning ahead for evaluation is that it allows for the gathering of baseline data (pre- and post-implementation comparisons). This leads us to the number one rule of evaluation: start early, not late.

As the examples at the end of the chapter will demonstrate, organizations go into DSD with many goals in mind. The most obvious goals are also the easiest to measure: reduced employee turnover, higher morale, reduced litigation costs, fewer EEOC case filings, and so on. Satisfaction with the process, the neutral, and the outcome need to be measured and evaluated. Additionally, designers may seek to see culture change within the organization. They may seek to improve labor-management relations and see improvements in the workplace climate.

Some DSD evaluation experts argue that greater focus should be placed on measuring changes in perceptions of organizational justice, which in turn affects behavior within organizations. **Organizational justice**, according to Moorman (1991) is composed of four components: distributive justice (whether outcomes and payouts are fairly distributed); procedural justice (fairness in processes); **informational justice** (the quality of explanations about issues, outcomes, and procedures for decision making); and **interpersonal justice** (whether one is treated with dignity, respect, kindness, honesty, and so on). Perceptions of organizational justice are important because they are related to a host of behaviors within organizations that are crucial to mission achievement, including employee turnover, sabotage or embezzlement by employees, shirking, absenteeism, presenteeism (see Chapter Five), and the commitment to caring for customers and clients. Measures of organizational justice may be closely tied to the values chosen early on in the needs assessment and design phase. For example, self-determination is closely related to procedural justice and therefore positively relates to perceptions of organizational justice. It turns out that caring for employees is good business.

Make sure your evaluation process does not overlook the deeper change in culture and organizational justice that may have long-term effects on organizational health but be slightly harder to measure. Culture change and perceptions of organizational justice can be measured via the use of surveys or interviews, as long as participants come from a randomly selected group of employees from all parts of the organization and enough surveys are taken to make generalizations about changes throughout the organization.

Diffusion occurs when the pilot program is expanded to the rest of the organization or grows to handle a broader array of disputes. Growth and diffusion of the program requires training employees who will take part in its administration, maintain quality control as the program grows, and engage in periodic evaluation to check for continual improvement, high levels of user satisfaction, and broader effects throughout the company.

Different organizations will create disputing systems that match their own needs, cultures, and missions. By examining disputing systems in corporate, government, and nonprofit environments we can learn from the work of pioneers in the design of disputing systems.

SAMPLE PRIVATE SECTOR DSD

Private sector businesses, whether large or small, may find their dispute resolution needs to be somewhat different than organizations in the public and nonprofit sector. Private sector companies may pursue DSD out of a desire to reduce turnover, prevent and settle lawsuits early, or improve the bottom line through the maintenance of a collegial and productive workplace. Some companies seek to address employee concerns proactively rather than face unionization efforts. Whatever the reason, many corporations have experienced the benefits of a well-designed and executed conflict management system.

The "Solutions Program" at Coca-Cola

In 2000, the Coca-Cola Company, which is headquartered in Atlanta, Georgia, settled a class action lawsuit alleging widespread racial discrimination for $156 million with an additional $36 million to fund organizational changes (Winter, 2000). The terms of the settlement included substantial changes to personnel policies and procedures, eventually including the creation of an ombuds office to deal more effectively with complaints of discrimination and other workplace challenges. The market for Coca-Cola products is global, and company officials acknowledged the need to build and maintain a positive corporate image through greater attention to issues of respect and diversity in the workplace.

A few years later, in March 2005, the "Solutions Program" started. This program provides mediation, arbitration, training, and ombuds services to nonunionized employees throughout the North American offices of the organization. Mediators and arbitrators can be internal employees of the organization or external neutrals may be hired. The process options are not arranged in a stepwise fashion but can be used in any order.

An interesting aspect of Coke's ADR system is that it includes one-way binding arbitration (Malveaux, 2009). This is a process in which the employee and company submit their dispute to arbitration but the arbitrator's decision is binding only on the company. The employee can accept or reject the arbitrator's decision. This is a sign of the company's desire to resolve disputes and build employee trust in the disputing system. Employees will be more willing to use arbitration with the knowledge that it is nonbinding should they believe the outcome to be unfair or less than they may be able to receive in an alternative forum.

As another way to build trust in the disputing systems at Coca-Cola, employees are provided with a legal services plan. This means that any employee who wishes to seek the consultation or representation of an outside attorney in regards to a workplace complaint will be provided with reimbursement of up to $1,000 per year, minus a $50.00 deductible and a 10 percent co-pay. As discussed in Chapter Four, employment attorneys are quite careful about the cases they take on because they are generally paid on a contingency basis and relatively few employment law cases are decided in favor of the plaintiff. Therefore, employees who feel they have been mistreated at Coca-Cola can receive legal advice from the attorney of their choice, with the cost of that advice subsidized by the company itself. This is not only a way of demonstrating good faith in their dealings with employees but it also reduces the number of cases filed in court because employees learn more about the likely difficulties associated with pursuing a claim all the way to trial.

There were many goals for the Solutions Program: improve company culture (building trust, respect, job satisfaction, and so on); effectively address conflict; contribute to profitability and shareholder value (reducing litigation costs, reducing employee time spent in conflict, reducing absenteeism); and limit negative publicity (Lewis, 2007).

The conflict resolution and prevention programs at Coke are administered through the office of the ombudsman. The Coca-Cola ombuds handle a wide variety of complaints, including those surrounding the following issues: termination, unfair treatment, discrimination, compensation, interpersonal conflicts, team conflicts, performance appraisals, safety concerns, discipline, fear of retaliation, violation of the law, ethical concerns, working conditions, and harassment (Coca-Cola Enterprises, 2011). As with all true ombudsmen, visits to the office are confidential and the neutrals working in this office are pledged to remain neutral when assisting employees as they try to solve problems.

Since its creation, the Solutions Program has won acclaim from many observers, including the Harvard Program on Negotiation in 2008. Satisfaction rates are high and disputes are being resolved earlier and with less expense for all parties. Currently, the company is undergoing a merger between the bottling side of the company and the syrup manufacturing side, which split into two companies almost a century ago. During this transition, the fate of the Solutions Program is unclear because it may be expanded, contracted, or changed to accommodate the needs of the newly formed organization.

Johnson & Johnson Inc.

With more than one hundred thousand employees in fifty-one countries, Johnson & Johnson Inc. supplies products such as Tylenol, Band-Aids, and biotech products to homes and hospitals worldwide. Interestingly, it remains largely family owned. Employees at all levels of the company are bound by its "credo," which is a document spelling out the company's values, the bond between employees, and the philosophy that its employees are the company's most valuable asset. In part, the credo states that

> we are responsible to our employees, the men and women who work with us around the world. Everyone must be considered as an individual. We must respect their dignity and recognize their merit. They must have a sense of security in their jobs. Employees must feel free to make suggestions and complaints . . . there must be equal opportunity for employment, development and advancement for those qualified . . . (Malin, 2004, p. 237)

Similar to all US organizations, the 1980s and 1990s saw an increase in litigation, with resulting costs and disruption to the workplace. Johnson & Johnson began implementing employment ADR programs in 1998. They trained their HR professionals in the skills and techniques of mediation. They also used videos to train HR employees companywide as they began to roll out their program called "COMMON GROUND." They advertised their workplace mediation program through company newsletters, e-mails, letters from the president of the company, and so on. The local HR leaders at each office took charge of rolling out the program in their areas. The overall message was that this is a "great way to get issues out on the table, and to address them early, quickly, quietly, and effectively.

We did not want to create the impression that this was a 'take away' program" designed to limit their options (Malin, 2004, p. 237).

Step One: Open Door   This step already existed and was incorporated into the new COMMON GROUND program, with increased trainings and a bigger role for HR. Many problems are resolved at this level but no inventory of disputes is taken here due to the highly informal nature of this step.

Step Two: Facilitation   This step is somewhat loosely defined in order to allow for an approach that can be unique to every problem. In general, the facilitator ensures the open-door step has been used and any manager that needs to be in the loop for problem solving gets into the communication cycle. Facilitation is a confidential process, if the employee wishes it to be so. Facilitators can be reached via e-mail, phone, or in writing. The facilitator could serve as a go-between or share information that may help to resolve the problem. The facilitator does not act as a judge or tell parties what to do. In the pilot project, about half of the disputes were resolved at this stage. In the first two-and-a-half years of this program, eighty-three disputes reached this step with about a 60 percent resolution rate (Malin, 2004).

Step Three: Mediation   Mediation is seen as an opportunity to seek resolution by all parties without resorting to costly and hostile litigation. Expert neutral mediators are used to engage the parties in a negotiation with the goal of finding a resolution that is agreeable to all parties. In the first two-and-a-half years of the program, approximately fifty cases went to mediation, some of which had been in litigation prior to the program's creation and the parties agreed to put litigation on hold to give mediation a try. Nearly all resolved at the mediation step.

During this two-and-a-half year period, only one employee filed suit after going through the COMMON GROUND program. The resulting savings to the company were significant, with a reduction of more than $200,000 in outside legal fees during the first year of the pilot alone (Malin, 2004). Equally or more important, employees have voiced acceptance and appreciation of the program as a way to solve problems without resorting to the courts.

Darden Restaurants Inc.

Darden Restaurants Inc. is a $6.7 billion dollar company that includes well-known restaurants such as Red Lobster, Olive Garden, Longhorn Steakhouse, Smokey

Bones, Bahama Breeze, Seasons 52, The Capitol Grille, and more. Their motto is "to nourish and delight everyone we serve." The company's founder, William H. Darden, writes that "I am convinced that the only edge we have on our competitors is the quality of our employees as reflected each day in the job they do" (Darden Restaurants, 2011).

Their dispute resolution program is widely held up as a model for the restaurant industry and is composed of four main steps.

Step One: Open-Door Policy This open-door policy includes a toll free number to their employee relations department in Florida. If employees feel they cannot speak to any of their supervisors or managers then they can contact employee relations directly to seek assistance.

Step Two: Peer Review Panel If employees disagree with a decision taken by management and the problem was not successfully resolved at step one, then they can request access to the peer review process. The peer review panel is composed of coworkers and managers who investigate the complaint and then make a decision. A facilitator helps set up the process, trains the panel members, and assists the employee to prepare for the process. The process is confidential and the decision is advisory. Employees are informed of their rights to take their complaint to the EEOC or the National Labor Relations Board as well at this time. If employees feel the peer review panel was not adequate to solve the problem, then they can take the dispute to either mediation or arbitration.

Step Three: Mediation Mediation has been covered at length but it should be mentioned that Darden Restaurants uses only outside neutrals jointly chosen by both sides. The company pays the mediation fees so the process is available at no cost to the employee.

Step 4: Binding Arbitration Darden Restaurants and the employee may jointly choose an arbitrator from a list supplied by the American Arbitration Association. Employees are welcome to bring an attorney, but if they refrain from doing so, the company will not bring one either. The outcome is binding on employees and the company. The company's promotional material claims that the entire arbitration process generally takes less than six months, and similar cases going through the litigation process typically drag on for years.

The materials available to employees via Darden Restaurants' websites and YouTube videos indicate the company values its employees, offers opportunities for professional development and advancement, and seeks to remind employees they are the bedrock of the organization's success. The company's positive culture helps to reduce the incidence of destructive employment conflicts by fostering a collegial, transparent atmosphere in which supervisors and managers are empowered to solve problems as early as possible.

SAMPLE PUBLIC SECTOR DSD

Public sector employers generally have some common characteristics that will influence the type of disputing system they select. Government agencies tend to have lower employee turnover than the private sector so a DSD must take into account the need to nurture and sustain relationships over long periods of time. In some public sector organizations it is difficult to terminate employees who are underperforming or who create strife within their work teams. Therefore, a system that includes skills coaching and relationship building may be more useful than one in which a neutral renders decisions about particular disputes. Due to the public nature of these organizations, there may be some limits on confidentiality that are less likely to be present within the private sector. For example, public sector ombudsmen or mediators may be required to report fraud or waste, whereas their counterparts in the private sector have more leeway. The heads of many government agencies change with each election. As a result, employees have grown weary of fads in leadership or new initiatives that last only as long as the organization's director remains in favor with his or her party leader. As a result, agency employees tend to find ways to resist change, with the knowledge that the impetus for the change itself may be gone if they can hold out long enough. For these reasons, DSD in public sector organizations needs not only buy-in from the highest leaders, but also from individuals and groups agencywide. In all, the characteristics of public sector employers lead to a unique culture and political environment in which DSD is necessary and challenging.

The United States Postal Service REDRESS Mediation Program

Few government organizations have reputations for being as dysfunctional as the United States Postal Service (USPS). During the early 1990s an outbreak of workplace violence involving postal workers led to the coining of the phrase *going postal* to indicate that one is so frustrated, the resort to violence may be imminent. In 1997, the postmaster general was called to testify before the US Congress to share any plans he had for addressing the problem. Coincidentally, some members of the USPS legal staff had recently returned from mediation training and urged him to adopt a workplace mediation program. The timing was perfect: postmaster Runyon assured Congress that he was taking steps to resolve employee disputes and disgruntlement more proactively, and their employment mediation program called REDRESS was born.

REDRESS stands for "redress employment disputes, reach equitable solutions swiftly." It is an example of a stand-alone ADR process rather than an integrated conflict management system. It is used exclusively for the resolution of claims of discrimination that have been filed as EEOC complaints or in which an employee is threatening to file such a claim. As such, this program addresses claims of discrimination but does not address other disputes, including those in which employees feel they have been treated unfairly but cannot trace that treatment to a protected status such as race, national origin, sex, religion, age, and so on. Although this sounds like a relatively small category of disputes, the USPS generates a disproportionate number of EEOC claims each year, with the average claim taking nearly two years to be investigated at a cost of over $50,000 per claim. By1996, there were nearly ninety thousand union grievances filed by USPS employees at a cost of over $200 million dollars per year. Nearly thirty thousand EEOC claims were filed annually in the mid-1990s, making up nearly 40 percent of all such claims from federal workers (US General Accounting Office, 1997). With over eight hundred thousand employees, REDRESS quickly became the world's largest mediation program.

The disproportionate number of complaints and disputes occurring in the USPS can be traced back to its organizational culture. The USPS was modeled along military lines, with a clear hierarchy, strict discipline, and a leader who is given the title of *postmaster general.* Job applicants must take the US Civil Service exam, which gives extra points to those who have served in the military. Managers are nearly always promoted from within, and although they know the technical side of the job, they have little in the way of management skills training. Supervisors and managers often use techniques that can be commonly found in the military: with superiors barking orders at the rank-and-file employees, even occasionally using name-calling or other intimidation tactics to clarify the pecking order and urgency of the tasks at hand. This may work in the military but the USPS is also populated by civilians, who are unaccustomed to being treated so roughly. The workplace culture showed little concern for face-saving and inter-personal rapport. In 1997, the US General Accounting Office castigated the USPS, citing "autocratic management styles . . . adversarial relationships between postal management and union leadership . . . and an inappropriate and inadequate per-formance management system" as evidence of "the persistent labor-management problems in the Postal Service" (pp. 1–4).

The work itself is similar to a factory setting, with increased mechanization and reduced mail volume resulting in frequent downsizing efforts. In this highly unionized setting, there are clear us-them divisions among rank-and-file employ-ees, supervisors, and managers. Everything from the distribution of overtime to the number of bathroom breaks is governed by highly detailed labor-management contracts. The union grievance process is used to address alleged violations of the contract but that doesn't address the overall hostility, heated verbal exchanges, and bullying that can be seen in some postal facilities on a daily basis.

With great insight, the developers of the REDRESS program sought not only to solve EEOC cases quickly but also to address the underlying causes of complaints among workers, supervisors, and managers. Supervisors and managers had almost no incentive to use the mediation process: EEOC complaints could take as long as ten years to work their way through to a hearing before an administrative law judge, and nearly 95 percent of complaints are either dropped by the complainant or they lose at the hearing stage (Bingham & Novac, 2001). In order to get supervisors and managers to the mediation table, the USPS leadership decided to make mediation optional for employees but mandatory for supervisors and managers. But why should the organization mediate when it will win 95 percent of the time? Because these claims cost tens of thousands of dollars to investigate and the parties involved often remain hostile and ripe for further conflict as they work together for years during the investigation and litigation of these claims.

The underlying goals of the REDRESS program are not only to settle cases but also to improve working relationships between managers and employees. The program seeks to empower both sides by improving their communication and dispute resolution skills so they can resolve the current disputes as well as future problems more productively. For this reason, the USPS chose the transformative model of mediation (see Chapter Three), which focuses on relationship building rather than merely settlement. USPS mediators are trained to empower the parties to find their own settlement to the dispute and to maximize recognition between the parties. Recognition occurs when parties "voluntarily choose to become more open, attentive, sympathetic, and responsive to the situation of the other party, thereby expanding their perspective to include an appreciation for another's situation" (Bush & Folger, 1994, p. 89).

Additionally, the program guaranteed that mediation would be offered to the complainant within four weeks of its request, and outside mediators were employed. Employees and supervisors could jointly select a mediator from a roster of outside expert mediators at no cost to the employee. Research indicates that early mediation results in higher satisfaction levels with the dispute resolution process and fewer costs for all parties (Charkoudian & Wilson, 2006). Mediations are scheduled during work hours and the parties can bring any support person they desire: an attorney, a union representative, or a friend and spouse, and so on. Interestingly, parties are happiest when they come without any support person, probably because they can tell their story themselves (Bingham, Kim, & Raines, 2002).

The REDRESS program was piloted in three Florida cities in 1994. It was so popular that it was expanded to the rest of the country within five years. The evaluation effort was highly detailed and included mediation exit surveys to gauge satisfaction with the mediator, the outcome, and the administration of the process. Interviews were conducted with about two hundred randomly selected employees at all levels in order to better understand the workplace climate before and after the rollout of the REDRESS program.

How well has it worked? There are many criteria on which to judge success. One way to judge success is the percentage of complainants opting to use the mediation process. By 2004, 88.1 percent of those offered mediation agreed to use it (Bingham, Nabatchi, Senger, & Jackman, 2009). This indicates that employees are aware of the mediation option and trust it enough to give it a try. Nearly all (92 percent) of the parties to these mediations agreed or strongly agree that the process is fair: 96.5 percent are satisfied or strongly satisfied with the mediators and 64 percent of complainants and 70 percent of respondents (i.e., supervisors) said they were satisfied with the outcome of mediation (Bingham, 2002). Although settlement is not the key indicator of success, 54.4 percent of complaints are resolved at the mediation table. Another 15 to 25 percent of complaints are dropped by the complainant within thirty days of the mediation (Hallberlin, 2001). This means a total case closure rate of 70 to 80 percent saving millions of dollars per year and shortening the life cycle of disputes.

There is also evidence of a broader positive impact on the workplace climate and a reduction of the overall number of disputes being filed. An interview study of USPS employees before and after the rollout of REDRESS indicates the presence of more open doors from managers and less use of yelling, arguing, disciplining, and intimidating by supervisors and managers (Bingham, Hedeen, Napoli, & Raines, 2003). In fact, one supervisor stated that "since I'm going to have to listen to their problems in mediation anyway, I just go ahead and listen to it when they come to me so we can get it resolved without any need for a complaint." Discrimination complaints have lowered by 30 percent since their height before the USPS implemented REDRESS, and complaints are now coming from 40 percent fewer people (Bingham, Nabatchi, Senger, & Jackman, 2009).

The REDRESS program is widely viewed as a success by internal and external observers: it saves money, reduces the life cycle of most disputes, and is viewed as fair and efficient by the vast majority of its users. In addition, there is evidence of some positive spillover effects on the broader workplace climate and labor-management relations. Workplace climate studies at USPS indicate incremental improvements in the relationships between supervisors and employees, including increased positive communication and reduced use of authoritarian management practices. In addition to the creation of the REDRESS program, concurrent efforts to provide managerial training and to reward managers for positive conflict management have been instituted, although there remains work to be done in these areas.

DISPUTING SYSTEMS IN THE NONPROFIT SECTOR

Nonprofits generally attract employees who deeply share a belief in the organization's mission and are committed to its work. Yet they may disagree about how best to accomplish that mission. DSD within nonprofits should include a focus on the disputes common to other organizations but they may also wish to consider conflict management techniques for creating or changing its mission, goals, and objectives. These can be highly stressful environments in which to work, with resources stretched thinly and difficult choices about the allocation of resources. Additionally, some nonprofits have missions that require employees to be in high-stress environments (e.g., humanitarian or disaster relief, homelessness assistance) with limited time frames for action or service provision. Many of these organizations operate in a near constant state of crisis, which takes a physical and emotional toll on employees, leading to increased conflicts. The often precarious state of revenues in nonprofits can mean that employment seems constantly tenuous. In these environments, one often hears "there is no time to focus on fire prevention because we're too busy putting out fires." The nature of nonprofits creates a unique employment environment as well as a unique need for DSD experts with an understanding of the challenges facing managers and employees in nonprofits.

The World Bank

The World Bank (WB) was established in 1944 to aid in the reconstruction of Europe after WWII. Its current mission is to fight poverty through the funding of development projects worldwide but particularly in poorer countries. The WB is headquartered in Washington, DC, but has offices worldwide with a total of more than ten thousand employees. The bank brings employees together from 160 countries, with the predictable culture clashes and interpersonal conflicts.

The WB offers a host of conflict resolution services, starting with the ombuds office. Communication with the ombuds is confidential, with the exception of "imminent harm" to the employee or others. The role of the World Bank ombudsman is to help staff and managers resolve problems in the workplace, inform management about trends and potential problems that require changes to enhance the working environment, and to administer the "Respectful Workplace Advisors (RWA) Program" (World Bank, 2011). The following box describes the functions of the ombuds at the World Bank.

Services of the World Bank Ombuds

- Hold confidential discussions to listen to concerns or inquiries
- Analyze the facts of a given situation
- Complete an impartial review of the matter
- Help identify and evaluate options
- Help decide which option makes the most sense

- Coach on how to deal with the problem directly
- Facilitate resolutions to disputes
- Assist in achieving outcomes consistent with fairness and respectful treatment
- If requested by staff, may become actively involved in trying to resolve problems and may speak with anyone in the organization in order to do so
- Provide information on policies and procedures
- Help raise issues people are reluctant to raise within regular channels
- Explain other available resources and refer people to other units in the bank that may help provide information and advice about the bank group's formal grievance system
- Alert management to systemic trends and issues
- Make recommendations for a change in policy or practice

In addition to the ombuds office, the World Bank's dispute system offers a plethora of options tailored to various types of concerns. These services include respectful workplace advisors (RWA), mediation services, peer review, administrative tribunals, and a vice president for integrity.

The RWA program is overseen by the ombuds office and consists of trained volunteer peer advisors stationed throughout the World Bank offices globally. These volunteers are nominated by their peers and serve four-year terms. The RWAs listen and provide guidance to employees facing harassment or inappropriate treatment at work. The RWAs do not get directly involved in the conflict. Instead, they serve as a sounding board for employee concerns, advise their peers as to the services available through the WB system, and report trends to their managers or the ombuds office. Like the ombuds office, RWAs provide informal and informational services rather than a formal dispute resolution process.

Mediation services are available to WB staff and managers faced with a workplace conflict. Internal and external mediators are available at no cost to the employee. Mediation satisfaction rates are about 95 percent, with settlement rates of 80 percent (World Bank, 2011). Mediation at the WB is seen as a method for improving communication and enhancing relationships as well as settling particular disputes.

The peer review service (PRS) is available to employees who believe a WB decision, action, or inaction was inconsistent with their terms or conditions of employment (World Bank, 2011). This is important because many employees are hired under temporary or fixed-term contracts or as consultants. Contracts spell out expected work duties and the rubrics by which performance reviews will be evaluated. An employee can request a peer review at any time, even after termination. The panel can refer the case to the vice president for HR if they feel the bank's decision was inappropriate. Alternatively, the panel can dismiss the case or suspend it for a specific period of time. The results of this process as well as the evidence presented are confidential. No one outside of the peer reviewers, PRS chief (administrator), and the HR department will be aware of the proceedings. Before the PRS is used, informal methods such as mediation should be attempted. WB employees may request a PRS process within 120 days of the event giving rise to the complaint. The PRS process is considered a formal process.

The administrative tribunal process hears similar complaints to the PRS process but is heard by a seven-member judicial panel and its outcome is binding. Each of the judges comes from a different nation and must be of "high moral character." Judges are chosen by the bank's executive directors from a list drawn up by the bank's president. Complaints come from employees "alleging non-observance of their contracts of employment or terms of appointment. Depending on the nature of the case, recourse to the appeals committee, the pension benefits administration committee or the workers' compensation administrative review panel is a requirement before you submit your application to the Tribunal. As an exception, the parties may agree that the application be submitted directly to the Tribunal" (World Bank, 2012). Judgments and orders are available on the WB tribunal website and can serve as guidance for future similar cases. The tribunal is the most formal of all employment dispute resolution processes at the World Bank.

The vice president for integrity is tasked with preventing and punishing fraud and corruption within World Bank–financed projects. This office trains employees about how to spot fraud, operates a fraud-reporting hotline, and investigates fraud. Companies found guilty of fraud or corruption can be banned from all future work with the WB, but the WB also encourages national governments to disbar these companies from any other government contracts. This office is included within the scope of an employee conflict resolution system because it works at the preventative level and it has the power to sanction and terminate employees accused of misconduct.

Finally, the office of ethics and business conduct trains employees on ethics rules and appropriate business conduct in the hope of minimizing problems with fraud, corruption, coercive practices, and so on. This group has many duties beyond those related to employee issues but it is involved in investigations of certain types of staff misconduct, specifically those that violate the WB's ethics rules. This office also reports trends and concerns related to ethics practices in the workplace to the senior management.

A large, multicultural organization such as the WB demonstrates that a robust ADR system will have multiple points of entry, including formal and informal dispute resolution processes. This menu of ADR services makes sense for a large organization, but what about smaller organizations that can ill afford so many options? Are dispute systems only made for large organizations?

DSD IN SMALL ORGANIZATIONS

The examples given so far come from organizations with tens or even hundreds of thousands of employees. What about designing disputing systems for small and mid-sized organizations? There is a clear economy of scale with any kind of system design. That means the costs associated with creating a disputing system are relatively less when there is a high number of disputes to process each year. In organizations with fewer than fifteen to thirty employees, a formal dispute design endeavor may be overkill.

If your organization is so small that disputes are relatively rare events, then it may make more sense to focus on creating and sustaining a positive organizational culture with warm interpersonal relationships and problem-solving attitudes. This will go a long way to preventing unnecessary disputes and resolving those disputes that cannot be avoided. Additionally, it is helpful to create a dispute resolution menu in preparation for any serious disputes that arise. This menu should include a description of all of the processes the company would like to encourage, the cost to the employee (if any) for using these services, and whether or not there is a binding ADR clause in the employment agreement that requires employees to use these processes before they can turn to the courts. It doesn't cost much to train supervisors and managers in the skills necessary to make an open-door policy meaningful, and organizations of all sizes could benefit from this type of training. Finally, some entrepreneurial ombudsmen are available to assist small businesses to access their services on an hourly basis rather than asking small companies to hire a permanent ombuds who may not be fully used in small organizations.

As companies grow in size, they might find it useful to send a trusted employee for ombuds training. This employee could be the go-to person for coaching and problem-solving assistance in addition to holding other duties within the organization. This is not uncommon in mid-sized organizations and even in universities and colleges. If your organization generates some reasonably predictable, recurring disputes that are costing time, money, energy, and damage to the organization's reputation, then it is worthwhile to engage in a needs assessment. The needs assessment will indicate whether a full-blown DSD effort is in order or if smaller tweaks to existing systems will do the job.

DSD GONE WRONG: HOOTERS OF AMERICA, INC.

The previous examples have examined dispute system designs that have reaped substantial benefits for employees, managers, and for mission accomplishment. However, it is also instructive to examine the ways in which disputing systems can be used against employees to limit their options and craft unfair outcomes to disputes. These systems arise when leadership looks for shortcuts to settlement, when concern for employees and a just workplace are low.

The courts at nearly all levels have been supportive of mandatory arbitration clauses or other ADR provisions in employee and customer contracts (see Legal Information Institute, 2012). As long as the arbitration process is unbiased, the courts have asserted that arbitration does not revoke an individual's right to adjudication; it merely changes the venue for that process. In 2000, the Fourth Circuit Court of Appeals ruled that the mandatory arbitration process created by Hooters was so patently biased and unfair that, in essence, it denied employees the right to a fair hearing in their case, thereby making the promise of arbitration "illusory," "unconscionable," and "egregiously unfair" (*Garland's Digest*, 2012).

Here are the basic outlines of Hooters's arbitration program: plaintiffs are required to supply the company with notice of their claim as well as the specific nature and legal basis for the claim; the company is not required to respond or provide notice of its defenses. Hooters creates a list of arbitrators from which it chooses one, the employee chooses one, and these two jointly choose a third. Again, all arbitrators on the list were initially chosen by Hooters and can be removed from the list at Hooters's discretion. This means that if the neutrals want repeat business from Hooters, they had better not issue any large judgments against the company. These arbitrators can include company shareholders or anyone selected by Hooters, irrespective of an apparent conflict of interest. Hooters has the right to expand the scope of the arbitration to any issue involving the employee, whether it is directly related to the claim under review or not, but the employee cannot do the same. Hooters can move for summary dismissal of the claim in advance of the hearing if it believes the claim to be unfounded but the employee cannot move for summary judgment. Summary judgments are granted when a claim is so clearly true that one need not hold a hearing. Hooters is allowed to audio- or videotape the proceedings and produce transcripts but the employee cannot. Hooters has the right to bring suit in court to vacate (overturn) the ruling but the employee cannot. Hooters has the right to cancel the agreement to arbitrate with thirty days' notice but the employee has no similar right. And the grand finale: Hooters reserves the right to change or modify the arbitration rules either in whole or in part. Not only were the rules clearly unfair, but Hooters also did not do a very good job of camouflaging the unfairness behind a cloak of respectability. As a result, the American Arbitration Association, the largest supplier of arbitrators in the United States, refused to supply arbitrators for Hooters cases. It is likely that some employees were dissuaded from pursuing a claim at the outset due to the incredibly biased arbitration process rules.

In the end in *Hooters of America* v. *Phillips*, the plaintiff was allowed to proceed with her case in court and was not required to submit it to arbitration. Hooters has become the widespread example of a company that tried to cheat its employees out of a fair dispute resolution process—a reputation that may take years to overcome. Clearly, the underlying motives behind the drive to create or re-create disputing systems needs to be legitimate, the process transparent, and the outcome fully evaluated to ensure it is working in a way that helps the organization by helping the employees. Organizations that are committed to treating employees fairly have nothing to fear from this endeavor.

CONCLUSION

All organizations have dispute management systems but they may not know it. Problems that arise related to employment or customer complaints get addressed one way or another: perhaps through informal discussions with managers, perhaps with litigation, or perhaps with complaints to the Better Business Bureau. Organizations of every size stand to benefit from taking stock of the types of recurring complaints or problems encountered, the existing methods for dealing with those complaints, the direct and indirect costs of the current methods, and an analysis of the costs and benefits stemming from designing new dispute management systems. Existing employees may be trained to engage in this endeavor or an outside consultant may be brought in to help. Either way, it is important to engage all stakeholder groups in a collaborative effort to understand and improve disputing within the organization. Whether this is a first effort or a periodic tune-up, it is helpful to take stock of the costs and benefits of the current methods for dispute resolution.

For dispute system designers this work brings with it a host of ethical considerations to be addressed explicitly: why is DSD being considered now? Who benefits from the status quo and will they object to changes to the disputing system? Will all voices be heard in this process? If written recommendations are issued as a result of a needs assessment, who will have access to that document? What, if any, risks of retaliation are there to employees who share their disputing experiences or problems during this process? Will the outcome of this process increase or decrease the efficiency and fairness of dispute resolution for all involved?

Throughout the phases of dispute system design, it is critical to ensure transparency and procedural justice if the system is to be trusted and used by those facing conflicts in the workplace. Well-designed disputing systems will save resources, improve the organization's image internally and externally, and assist in creating a positive culture in which the company and its stakeholders work together for mutual success.

By thinking critically and speaking explicitly about the disputing methods within your organization, you can reduce the incidence and expenses of negative conflicts at work and create a culture of respect and collaborative problem solving.

Collaboration Consultants Inc. (CCI) conducted a thorough needs assessment. They analyzed data from the legal department to determine the average number and type of employee complaints as well as the costs associated with those complaints. To calculate costs they included not only settlements but also money spent on legal and court fees, managerial time away from work, and damage to the brand. CCI spoke with former employees as well as current employees at all levels to learn more about the potential sources of complaints. Once the needs assessment was complete, CCI made the following recommendations:

- *Open-door policy and related trainings*: Managers at all levels will be trained in open-door skills, meaning they will learn listening, framing, and problem-solving skills. Elise will attend this training too and communicate her expectation that any employee can come to any manager for help in solving problems. If any manager feels unsure about the appropriate methods for dispute resolution with an employee, then he or she can contact Ben in HR for assistance.

- *ADR programs*: Main Street Bakeries will create in internal ADR program that includes mediation using outside neutrals for all claims of harassment or discrimination, a peer-review process for disputes arising from disciplinary actions, and binding arbitration for any complaints that did not get resolved through either of these processes or as the preferred process for those employees who seek a quicker and binding resolution.

- *Data gathering*: HR will implement a quarterly employee satisfaction survey that will query randomly sampled employees on a host of questions regarding morale, perceptions of organizational justice, satisfaction levels in regards to supervisors' conflict management skills, and their ideas for improving the company.

- *Ombuds*: At this time, the relatively low volume of complaints may not warrant the creation of an ombuds office. CCI and Elise have decided to pilot the recommended changes and revisit the issue in six months.

KEY TERMS

Design team (DT)	Needs assessment
External stakeholders	Organizational justice
Informational justice	Primary stakeholders
Internal stakeholders	Secondary stakeholders
Interpersonal justice	Stakeholders

SUGGESTED SUPPLEMENTAL READING

Alter, K. J. (2003). Resolving or exacerbating disputes? The WTO's new dispute resolution system. *International Affairs, 79*, 783–800.

McEwen, C. A. (1998). Managing corporate disputing: Overcoming barriers to the effective use of mediation for reducing the cost and time of litigation. *The Ohio State Journal on Dispute Resolution, 14*, 1–27.

Nabatchi, T., Bingham, L. B., & Moon, Y. (2010). Evaluating transformative practice in the U.S. postal service REDRESS program. *Conflict Resolution Quarterly, 27*(3), 257–289.

DISCUSSION QUESTIONS

1. Discuss the current system of disputing in your organization. Every organization has methods of resolving disputes, either directly or indirectly. In that system, what is working well and what isn't? What are the costs, benefits, and consequences of the current disputing system? Who are the stakeholders in that system?

2. What are the values that your organization's current dispute system embodies? What does the current system say about your organization's culture or your leaders' vision for the organization? Pair up with a colleague or classmate and discuss the role of organizational culture and values in your organization's disputing system in the past, present, and future. Share your key insights with the class or your colleagues.

3. Have you used the formal or informal dispute resolution mechanisms in your organization or in a previous workplace setting? Was the dispute resolved to your satisfaction? Did the process leave you feeling better, worse, respected, ignored, and so on?

EXERCISES

1. Benchmark the disputing systems of organizations like yours. How are your competitors or peers addressing employment disputes? Which organizations are the leaders or innovators and how can your organization learn from them?

2. Make a list of interview questions that you would include as part of a needs assessment for an organization with which you are familiar. Whom would you interview or survey for your needs assessment? Would there be any obstacles to conducting a needs assessment in your organization? How might those be overcome?

GOAL SETTING

This week, learn more about the formal mechanisms to resolve disputes in your organization. What is your role in that structure? Your position in the hierarchy will determine which goals you can realistically set in regards to the design of disputing systems:

- If you are near the top of your organization's structures, consider asking for a review of the current system of disputing so you can decide if it is serving the organization's needs and resolving disputes efficiently and constructively.

- If you are in the middle of your organizational hierarchy, consider how you might communicate to your employees that your door is open so if a problem arises they feel comfortable bringing it to you early in its evolution rather than waiting until a formal complaint arises. If you believe the current method of disputing is dysfunctional, consider sharing your concerns with a key organizational player at a higher rank. Focus on the gains to be made by DSD changes.

- If you are near the bottom of your organizational hierarchy, be sure you are familiar with your disputing system and your options for dispute resolution. If you believe changes should be made to that system, consider speaking to your union representative or supervisor. Focus on the gains to be made by DSD changes. Use the CSI from Chapter One to analyze the costs and benefits of raising this issue to your superiors.

Preventing and Resolving External Conflicts

Part Three builds on all of the knowledge and skills covered thus far. There is a reason why we address customer and vendor disputes after those of the workplace. A harmonious, collaborative, and productive workplace is a prerequisite for satisfied, happy customers and clients. Chapter Nine takes the ADR processes and concepts covered in earlier chapters and applies them to the assessment, prevention, and resolution of disputes with external parties such as customers and vendors. Next, Chapter Ten shares examples of innovative systems for the delivery of exceptional customer service from leading organizations in the public, private, and nonprofit sectors. Additionally, Chapter Ten presents some customer service worst-case examples that are also instructive.

chapter NINE

Prevention and Resolution of Conflicts with Clients, Customers, and Vendors

Learning Objectives

- Demonstrate an understanding of the root causes of common customer service complaints.

- Demonstrate an understanding of the linkages between satisfied employees and satisfied customers.

- Compare and explain the relative benefits of seeking out new customers versus increasing customer satisfaction with existing ones.

- Develop monitoring tools to gather data on customer and client satisfaction and use that information to make improvements to products and services.

- Explain methods for creating employee incentives for superior customer service.

- Describe the benefits of a relationship management approach to reducing and managing conflicts with repeat customers and vendors.

ELISE AT MAIN STREET BAKERIES

In spite of a sluggish economy, Main Street Bakeries is doing alright. The trend toward locally grown and organic foods has helped the company grow quickly and establish a stable niche in the marketplace. But for the last twelve months, growth and profits have flattened out. Additionally,

Elise can't help but wonder if she is reaching her full market potential; her customers are generally upper middle class, educated urbanites and suburbanites. She believes that healthy, local, organic foods should be available and attainable for everyone but she is not sure how to reach out to new customers while keeping her existing ones.

Whether you work in the private, public, or nonprofit sector, you must pay attention to the needs of the end users of your products or services. You may call them *clients, customers, patients, guests, constituents, the community,* or *the public.* For the purposes of simplicity, in this chapter we will call the end users of our services *customers.* "**Customer satisfaction** is defined as a measure of how a firm's product or service performs compared to the customer's expectation" (Zondiros, Konstantopoulos, & Tomaras, 2007, p. 1086). Consulting firm Bain & Company surveyed managers across US industries to find that 80 percent of managers believe their organizations provide excellent customer service but only 8 percent of their customers agree. "Horror stories abound. Callers get trapped in seemingly endless interactive voice response (IVR) loops; they can't find phone numbers at web sites; no one responds to their e-mail messages; and, if they manage to get through to a representative, they cannot get the problem resolved promptly" (Greengard, 2003, p. 32). These horror stories are not isolated events—we've all experienced frustrating customer service, whether in restaurants or as citizens seeking services from public agencies.

Duarte and Davies (2003) studied the relationship between conflict and efficiency in business relationships, finding that "when efficiency or performance drop drastically, conflict seems to rise drastically in response" (p. 96). Preventing disputes with customers and efficiently addressing those disputes that cannot be prevented are critical to attracting and retaining customers. "During a recession, with consumer confidence at a low ebb, keeping your customers satisfied and retaining them is vital for survival. Retailers need to understand how they satisfy their shoppers in order to enhance their appeal and increase customer loyalty. Moreover, an insight into what drives customer satisfaction at competitors is essential to win customers from them" (Datamonitor, 2010). Ensuring a pleasant transactional experience will make your organization a more positive place to work as well as enhance your competitiveness. Few private or nonprofit organizations can survive for long if they alienate their clientele or disregard their feedback. In the public sector, public complaints about poor service or inefficiencies will likely lead to ousted leadership or reform from above. When it happens, the managers and leaders may suffer significant damage to their careers that could have been prevented.

This chapter will examine the best practices for preventing, tracking, and reducing disputes with customers. The following box introduces some key rules for delivering superb customer service. Each will be further elaborated.

Rules for Stellar Customer Service

Rule one: A house divided will not stand.

Rule two: Be sure you deliver what you promise (quality products and services).

Rule three: Improvements require monitoring.

Rule four: Create incentives for desired behaviors.

Rule five: Empower employees to resolve disputes at the lowest level possible.

Rule six: Avoid a myopic focus on new customers over existing ones.

Rule seven: Devise, evaluate, and revise systems.

RULE ONE: A HOUSE DIVIDED WILL NOT STAND

Proactive conflict managers strive to create a culture in which employees at all levels feel valued, they buy in to the organizational mission, and they treat each other and customers with respect and appreciation. Happy employees are foundational to satisfied customers. Dysfunctional workplaces simply do not result in consistently high levels of client satisfaction. According to Zondiros, Konstantopoulos, and Tomaras (2007), "Employee satisfaction is one of the most important factors leading to customer satisfaction, the others being expectations and disconfirmation of expectations" (p. 1086). In other words, customer expectations are important for satisfaction—if your marketing efforts set up unrealistic expectations and those expectations are disappointed, then satisfaction will decline. Although these factors are important for predicting customer satisfaction, employee satisfaction actually tracks customer satisfaction more closely than either of these factors. Creating a positive workplace culture and rewarding those who strive to give great customer service is critical to creating a positive experience for customers and clients.

Increasingly, disgruntled employees are the cause of bad press because they use blogs, Twitter, Facebook, and other social networking mechanisms to communicate their disgruntlement. Employees who have been mistreated, just like customers who have bad experiences, are likely to share their stories with literally a dozen or more others, further damaging the organization's reputation and brand. In the worst cases, employers accused of discrimination or blatant disregard for their employees' welfare have been on the receiving end of customer boycotts — remember the accusations of sweatshop conditions against Nike, Walmart, and others?

Some organizations have figured out the link between employee satisfaction and customer satisfaction. Southwest Airlines explicitly states its unique operating style: "Employees come first and customers come second." Southwest has earned a profit even in years where every other US airline lost money and as a result has grown faster than any other US airline. Even during the Great Recession, when most other airlines have reduced staffing levels, Southwest has refused to lay off workers. Customers rave about Southwest's fun, informal, and enthusiastic staff members. Southwest's employees are "hired for attitude and trained for skill" (Garrison & Keller, 2008, p. 13). Managers at Southwest are trained in a leadership style that gets them to "coach and encourage" rather than pursuing a style of "supervising and enforcing rules" (p. 14). The employee turnover rate is the lowest in the industry and 80 to 90 percent of managerial jobs are filled internally.

So, rule one is to get your internal house in order (see Chapter Five). Treat your employees well so that they have the energy and the will to pass on that same treatment to your customers.

RULE TWO: BE SURE YOU DELIVER WHAT YOU PROMISE (QUALITY PRODUCTS AND SERVICES)

The best customer service in the world cannot make up for defective or underperforming products. Be sure your products are meeting the needs of your current customers and are innovative enough to attract new ones. For many organizations, their product is a service. For example, universities offer educational services; marketing firms, law firms, and health care practitioners all offer a service as their product. For these industries, the quality of the service and the service experience will be central to building a reputation that keeps and attracts clients.

Whether you make widgets or conduct market research, "if the quality of your products is great and your service is mediocre, a customer might return, but you won't gain any repeat customers if you have subpar products, even if your service is outstanding" (McGown, 2009, p. 66). There is no substitute for doing your homework. What do your competitors charge for the same products or services and how does their quality compare to yours? If your products are equivalent to others on the market then you have only two routes to success: (1) find ways to improve your products or pricing to gain a competitive advantage or (2) beat them by offering a superior service experience.

Be sure to avoid a common pitfall—overpromising. Sometimes an organization's marketers are better than their engineers. If your marketing efforts create unrealistic expectations among consumers and your products and services do not fulfill those expectations, then costly conflict is likely to result.

There are many books that deal with methods for creating a can't-miss product. Much of this information will be industry specific or confined to the type of good or service being offered. Rather than helping you think up the next consumer fad, this chapter is focused on methods for ensuring you minimize unproductive conflicts with customers and provide the best dispute resolution options possible for those problems that cannot be reasonably avoided. Creating, marketing, and sustaining high-quality products (or services) is foundational to this effort. Rolex makes great quality watches and Harvard trains great lawyers. The quality of their products and services does not substitute for good customer service but they could not have built solid reputations spanning generations without building and maintaining high-quality control standards that have become synonymous with their brands.

RULE THREE: IMPROVEMENTS REQUIRE MONITORING

As this book has indicated repeatedly, feedback is the lifeblood of a successful collaborative manager. This is equally true for the organization as a whole: feedback on the product itself, feedback on the sales experience, feedback on the payment and delivery processes, feedback about the organization's

Internet or telephonic resources, feedback on the cleanliness or attractiveness of the facilities, feedback on any dispute resolution processes used, feedback about ways to improve the customer's experience, and overall feedback as to whether the customer would recommend the organization's products or services to a friend. This information forms a vast reservoir of ideas for constant improvement.

There are myriad ways to gather feedback. Think about the customer service satisfaction processes you have taken part in as a consumer or end user. Your restaurant has included a telephone number or Internet site you use to take a survey and receive a free appetizer on your next visit, your car dealership asks you about your customer service experience, your physician or hospital asks you to rate your wait time and overall experience. These are attempts to gain detailed information about the customer's experience on an ongoing basis to ensure consistently high levels of performance and to catch problems early on. Data should be gathered on the quality of the goods or services themselves as well as the customer's experience during and after the transaction. Look for repeat customers who stop coming back. "Businesses need to monitor defection triggers and identify customer problems through customer activity. Often, that means monitoring" (Bland, 2004, p. 20).

In order for these instruments to be useful and worth the time and money it takes to administer them, the organizational leaders must be open to whatever results they may find. "Customer satisfaction surveys frequently create a skewed picture. Many companies use self-serving questions—or fail to address key issues such as whether the resolution process was handled efficiently. So, while the rep may have performed admirably and received the highest rating, the caller may remain frustrated by the length of time or effort it took to reach a rep or because the incident wasn't resolved in a satisfactory way" (Greengard, 2003, p. 35). Asking the right questions is clearly important in order to get the detailed feedback necessary to pinpoint problems and address them quickly. Customers' perceptions are just that—their perceptions. It makes no sense to argue about why customers should not have felt the way they did; their perception of their experience is inherently valid. Although the occasional curmudgeon may be impossible to please, trends in the data cannot be ignored. And a small warning is in order: although you are likely to aggregate this data to look for trends or repeated sources of problems, be sure you do not leave your customers with the impression they are just a number or case. Anything you can do to personalize the customer's experience and meet their individualized preferences is likely to serve you well (Rigge, 1997).

A corporate manager interviewed for this book stated that her company gathers feedback about every aspect of a transaction—from the contact with the sales staff, the signing of the contracts, to the delivery company that brings the item. When the feedback reveals anything less than a completely positive experience, the relevant manager conducts a root cause analysis to determine what went wrong. Then an action plan is developed to make it right with the specific customer as well as to ensure that the problem does not recur. Also, this information is also used for quarterly departmental and individual performance reviews. Raises and promotions are tied to the number of problems that are flagged through the monitoring system, but more emphasis is put on the ways in which managers and employees responded to those problems. All are expected to respond without defensiveness or excuses. Managers who use this information to make constant improvements in their team's performance more consistently reach their sales and service goals, have fewer conflicts within their work teams, and move up through the ranks faster.

Costs of Disgruntled Customers: What Not to Do

A New Zealand family was holidaying at a resort island in Fiji. During the stay, the mother suffered food poisoning. Her worried husband asked for help for his wife and their five-month-old baby because his wife was breastfeeding. The resort promised to bring a nurse with access to medical supplies across from a nearby island. Several hours passed. When the anxious husband asked what was happening, the resort manager explained he hadn't sent for the nurse because the boat would cost $40 and the resort wouldn't cover the cost. The husband exploded and paid the $40 on the spot. Three hours later the boat arrived—without the nurse. Instead, the boat driver handed the husband a small packet of unmarked pills, which

(continued)

(*continued*)

he gave to his wife in desperation. Strong tranquilizers, the pills knocked his wife out and compounded her medical problems and the well-being of their baby. Upon their return to New Zealand, and after spending $4,500 on a disastrous holiday, the husband set about revenge. He spent hours on the Internet campaigning hard for travelers to avoid that Fiji island resort. He posted messages to Internet bulletin boards, put warnings in travel chat rooms, e-mailed business and personal colleagues, and told everyone he could think of. He later said these actions were the only thing that assuaged his fury.

Source: Bland (2004, p. 19). Reprinted with permission.

RULE FOUR: CREATE INCENTIVES FOR DESIRED BEHAVIORS

People respond to incentives. Want to see customer service improve? Tie raises and promotions to consistent improvements and high levels of customer satisfaction at the individual and team-unit levels. For example, when a car dealership from company *x* performs well on measures of customer service in the sales and mechanical service departments, they qualify to receive in-demand new models and parts faster than those with lower ratings. So, if Main Street Motors wants to stock the newest hybrid vehicle that is all the rage, they had better keep their customers satisfied. Otherwise, they get put on a waiting list behind those with better service records. Or when merit raises are handed out each year, Bob from accounting may get passed up because the internal managers and employees he supports have said he consistently does not meet his deadlines. The information gained from monitoring performance must be tied to employee incentives; otherwise, there is a missing link between knowledge and action. Incentives can include merit raises, promotions, public recognition (such as "employee of the month"), preferred parking, and preferred job duties or other benefits.

It is important to create challenging yet attainable goals and objectives for customer service. If deadlines or goals are repeatedly missed, regardless of the personnel tasked with meeting them, then they are clearly too high. Unrealistically high goals lead to cynicism and apathy on the part of employees: "Why should

I even try? I'll never be able to reach that goal." If you are unsure about how to set realistic goals, make the first few months or quarters a pilot phase that allows you to experiment with an offer of carrots (positive incentives) rather than sticks (negative sanctions for missing the mark). Consider offering financial incentives, recognition, and rewards for employees who come up with improvements to products, processes, or services. Frontline employees are likely to know the products and customers better than those at higher levels.

RULE FIVE: EMPOWER EMPLOYEES TO RESOLVE DISPUTES AT THE LOWEST LEVEL POSSIBLE

Nothing is more frustrating than explaining your complaint to the sales clerk at the store or the representative on the phone only to be transferred to someone else, requiring you to start over from the beginning. Once this has happened three or more times, what might have been a relatively small complaint has now become a big one. Many frontline employees have zero authority to address customer complaints. This frustrates the employee and the customer and results in wasted time for supervisors and managers.

Instead, consider the following plan: use the data gathered from rule three to determine the most common types of customer complaints. After taking steps to reduce or eliminate the root causes of as many of these complaints as possible, organizational leaders should determine which complaints warrant the attention of supervisors and managers versus those that can be handled by the frontline employees. If your leaders decide none of the recurring complaints can be handled by employees, it may be the case that (1) your leaders are uncomfortable with delegation as a managerial skill (if so, see Chapter One); (2) you have not properly hired, trained, and acculturated your employees so as to entrust them with these tasks (see Chapters Five and Six); or (3) your organization has so few complaints that each one needs to be handled as a unique event by middle to upper management. If explanation three is the case, yours is indeed rare among organizations and you may wish to reconsider one and two as possible options.

Employees need to be trained to handle complaints efficiently, fairly, and in a way that makes the customer more rather than less likely to return. Nearly all frontline employees can benefit from training in listening, framing, and problem-solving skills. This training will help them convey empathy to customers, deeply listen in order to understand the customers' needs, and work with customers to find a solution that meets their needs. Scott (2008) advises individuals in conflict situations to avoid the tendency to vent anger or frustration, understand the reasons behind the conflict, and then use intuition to solve the problem. However, employees should also be prepared to deal with customers who do indeed voice their anger or disappointment in hostile ways. The trick is to remind employees not to take it personally — any employee could have answered that call or waited on that customer. By remaining calm, reassuring the customer that the issue will be fairly and efficiently rectified, the organization can seize an opportunity to improve a relationship with a client. Remember, it is not conflict that harms relationships; instead, it is the way in which conflict is handled. In fact, good customer service in response to a complaint is one way to solidify a customer's loyalty.

Each employee should know where her settlement authority begins and ends. For example, when a customer is unhappy with our product, the employee can offer a full refund or an exchange (in addition to a sincere apology, when warranted). But be wary of template solutions that do not allow employees to use their own judgment to come up with more creative solutions in order to meet the occasional customer whose complaint or needs are unusual. This flexibility respects the employee's intelligence and ensures the customer is not passed around like a hot potato, seeking someone who can be of assistance. Frontline employees and each layer of management above them need to be clear about their settlement authority as well as be required to provide feedback upward about what is working well and what is not.

Sometimes a customer will be satisfied with a sincere apology and an effort to fix the problem through a refund or replacement of the item or service. A study by Robbennolt (2003) indicated that recipients of full apologies are more likely to accept a settlement, whereas recipients of settlement offers with no apologies are less likely to accept a settlement. The results for partial apologies were mixed. The "I'm sorry for your harm" type of apologies did not result in settlement rates as high as full apologies (Robbennolt, 2003). Other research has found that approximately 8 percent of the disputes stemming from eBay transactions involved a request or demand for an apology as a condition of settlement (Raines, 2005). In fact, a significant percentage of disputants rejected monetary offers of equal or greater amounts than the value of their purchase if no apology was forthcoming. Giving your employees the permission to offer a sincere apology and to work to fix the problem can go a long way to reducing the number of disputes that escalate and become formal complaints or litigation.

Another customer service pitfall is to create a punitive policy based on the bad behavior of a small number of customers who try to game the system. "What pains many organizations . . . is that they apply a general template to all customers or penalize 99 percent of their customer base because of the bad behavior of 1 percent" (Greengard, 2003, p. 35). For example, when a customer buys an airplane ticket online with Delta Airlines, using their self-service portal, it is predictable that an occasional user error will occur. For example, "I accidentally booked the ticket for March 5 but I meant to select April 5." As long as the customer calls soon after the sale, and this is not a repeated problem for this customer, then the Delta Airlines employee can assist the customer to change the ticket without paying a change fee. Another example comes from retail stores: some require a store receipt for a return and only allow the return within a specified period after the purchase (thirty days, for example). They may do this to avoid customers who buy clothes for a special occasion only to wear them and return them. Other retailers convey they trust their customers but track returns to be able to spot those customers who abuse the organization's policies.

What makes for a fair and efficient resolution process? Gilly and Gelb (1982) conducted research into customer complaints and found that customers sought swift resolution for nonmonetary complaints (defective products, poor service) but were willing to wait longer when the complaint involved a monetary resolution. Similarly, Ito, Toshihiko, and Fujimura (2010) found that a quick response was linked to customer satisfaction with disputes over quality matters. If you are unsure of the best methods for addressing customer complaints, consider tapping the collective wisdom of your employees as well as asking for feedback from complaining customers. Use this information to pilot various approaches and tweak the system until the desired results are achieved.

Costs of Disgruntled Customers: What Not to Do

If only it were as easy to keep customers as it is to lose them. At the height of summer an energy provider received a phone call from a distraught customer saying she lived in a rural area and

(continued)

(*continued*)

her power had been cut off, leaving her and her children without water. The energy provider was barely polite; until the customer had paid her bill, power would not be restored. The recently relocated customer became apologetic; she explained she had called the energy provider with her change of address but had not received a bill and had been too busy to notice. The provider replied such notification had not been received and inferred the customer was lying. After a significant amount of upset, the provider told the customer they would do her a "favor" in allowing her to pay her bill over the phone by credit card. The minute the power was restored the furious customer changed energy providers and lobbied local newspapers to write a story saying her previous energy provider left women and children in the countryside without water.

Source: Bland (2004, p. 19). Reprinted with permission.

RULE SIX: AVOID A MYOPIC FOCUS ON NEW CUSTOMERS OVER EXISTING ONES

This rule is the perennial downfall of credit card companies and cable television services across the United States. These companies often attract new customers by offering extremely low prices or interest rates for the first six or twelve months only to have them jump up thereafter. This reflects a strategy designed to attract new customers and disregard current ones. It is likely that the internal incentive structures in these companies also reward the acquisition of new clients over the retention of existing ones.

Why are existing customers more important (or at least as important) as new ones?

The first reason is that some customers who have had a particularly bad customer experience may make it their mission in life to destroy the reputation of a business. A second, more obvious, reason for customer retention is that customers cost money to win in the first place. To survive, businesses must attract return business—ongoing revenue not offset by the cost of acquiring a new customer for every sale. At first glance, customer retention is a simple concept—happy customers who feel important and are regularly communicated with in the right way will keep coming back. (Bland, 2004, p. 16)

An increasing refrain heard in the literature on business management is the need to view **customers as business partners**. This means organizations should evolve their mind-set from a worldview that sees each transaction as a one-time event to instead seeing each transaction as a chance to build a long-term, mutually beneficial relationship (Witschger, 2011). The business literature often refers to the specific techniques used to court and retain valued customers and partners over a long period of time as **relationship management**. This can be as benign as assigning one consistent employee to large customers or business partners with the goal of ensuring smooth communications and institutional memory so that these partners' needs are consistently met. In other cases it can include rather obvious or obnoxious attempts to bribe organizational leaders by providing free theater tickets and rounds of golf. When done right, relationship management allows two individuals (or a small team) from one organization to develop strong relationships with their business partners or repeat customers in the service of an ongoing, mutually beneficial business relationship.

In some ways, this is where small and mid-size companies have a comparative advantage. In small businesses, the owner or manager often has more direct contact with the customers or clients. This access provides the venue for a customized, personable, responsive experience that large corporations or the federal government cannot as easily provide. Yet regardless the size of the business, customer retention and attention to existing customers should never be ignored to give higher priority to the courting of new clients.

Similarly, citizens have more access and influence in local government matters. It is easier to meet their locally elected leaders, attend public meetings, and converse with decision makers. Managers and leaders in local and state government can benefit from purposefully gathering input and feedback from the end users of government services as well as from local taxpayers.

Coleman (1992) provides advice about how business partners can build healthy relationships. He gives nine dimensions of business relationships that should be explored during the formation of **business-to-business (B2B)** partnerships: autonomy, goals, compensation, decision making, cost sharing, entrance and exit of partners, equity, firm management, and type of partnership. He recommends that partners rank these items from most to least important and share their rankings to make sure they are in agreement about the prioritization of each element in their business relationship. The same is true for a valued and repeat customer—if any one customer is critical to the life of your business or organization, then it behooves you to sit down face-to-face to better understand that customer's needs, share yours, and develop methods for working together.

What about **customer loyalty programs** that encourage customers to come back again rather than merely seeking out the best price or most convenient vendor? For example, many hotel chains, airlines, and even coffee shops offer something akin to a baker's dozen reward system. This is a method for rewarding return customers by giving them, for example, their thirteenth night free or a free domestic airline ticket once they accumulate fifty thousand frequent flyer miles, and so on. These programs may help lure customers back to your business when there are others offering basically the same products and services at similar prices. However, "they provide a discount because points are easily converted to dollars. But you cannot buy loyalty" (Greengard, 2003, p. 35). These incentives will not be enough to overcome persistently bad service experiences. Increasingly, as nearly all airlines and hotel chains offer similar customer loyalty programs, they are becoming less valuable as a way to retain customers or differentiate your company from others.

What about public sector or nonprofit organizations who do not seek repeat customers? If you work for Child Protective Services, a drug rehabilitation center, or the unemployment office, you are not seeking out repeat customers. In fact, one indicator of a job well done is that these customers or clients do not come back at all. In these cases there are two critical questions: (1) who are my organization's customers? and (2) how should my organization (or my unit within the broader organization) define and measure customer and client service?

For public and nonprofit sector organizations, customers may include the public as a whole or a narrower segment of the public (such as children in state custody, addicts and their families, unemployed people and potential employers). Regulatory agencies have at least two sets of customers: the businesses they regulate, which seek an efficient and fair regulatory process, and the public. One could argue that regulatory agencies must also be responsive to informational requests posed by the legislature and to demands from the leader of the executive branch of government.

In order to achieve the organization's mission, public and nonprofit sector organizations should follow all the same recommendations listed thus far, including gathering feedback about the quality and efficiency of their services. From the length of the wait times at the Department of Motor Vehicles to the rate of tax collection for the IRS, every organization can come up with metrics by which to gauge service delivery and mission accomplishment.

RULE SEVEN: DEVISE, EVALUATE, AND REVISE SYSTEMS

Your internal house is in order. Your product and services are competitive and attractive to customers. You are monitoring, incentivizing positive employee conduct, and empowering employees to resolve problems at the lowest level. You are focusing on retaining current customers and attracting new ones. Now that your system is designed and in place, be sure to analyze the data, take stock, and make any needed changes to processes, products, or personnel to maximize the achievement of your organizational mission and maintain a positive workplace environment. Reassess and make needed changes periodically to ensure consistent improvements. For some organizations, this will be every quarter; for others it will be every six months or annually. The key is to make sure you are mining the data necessary to make appropriate management decisions.

Technology and Customer Service

Advances in technology are resulting in the increased automation of interactions between organizations and their customers: robocalls confirm doctors' appointments, Internet surveys are used to gain customer feedback, and web platforms are used to log complaints. There is no doubt that technology can save money for organizations seeking to reduce personnel expenses associated with customer services. Yet there are costs to automating customer service functions, especially customer complaints. When a customer is upset or disappointed with a product or service, an automated system cannot listen, show empathy, or look for creative solutions to the problem. Although automation may indeed be a good idea in some circumstances, be wary of the rush to technology purely as a cost-saving mechanism. In the long run, it may be more costly than anticipated.

ADR for External Stakeholder Disputes

What happens when conflict prevention and early resolution have failed? What if the customer threatens litigation, goes to the media to complain, or files a complaint with the Better Business Bureau or a similar organization? Once a dispute takes a turn toward a formal and public path to resolution, the stakes are higher. At this point, you and your organization may wish to consider the menu of ADR options covered in Chapter Four. If direct negotiation with the customer has failed to resolve the matter, then perhaps mediation should be tried. The parties can jointly select a mediator and seek his or her assistance in the resolution of the complaint. What happens in mediation and in many mediated agreements are covered by confidentiality provisions, thereby making this a good process for the protection of your organization's public image and reputation. Mediation settlement rates for most types of commercial cases range between 55 and 90 percent. Remember, mediation is a nonadversarial process in which both parties seek to explore the possibility of reaching an agreement that leaves them better off than going to court. Because parties work together to find a resolution in mediation, this process is advisable if there is any desire to maintain an ongoing business relationship between the parties. This may apply more often in B2B disputes.

Citing statistics gathered from a survey of one thousand US corporations, Mallick (2007) argues for the use of mediation as an effective means for disputes with consumers. The author shares results from ADR programs used by many US corporations (Toro; Wells Fargo; US Postal Service; Air Products and Chemicals, Inc.; American Express). Even though Toro had successfully litigated cases in the past, the implementation of a mediation program actually saved the company money overall and enabled it to reduce costs spent on legal fees. Wells Fargo implemented a multistep process for consumers with disputes of $25,000 or more, believing that this alternative to litigation would create a less negative experience for customers and improve its reputation. American Express took an interest-based approach, employing experienced mediators as their attorneys with a focus on settlement.

If mediation fails to resolve the matter or if you instead prefer to receive a binding decision from a third-party expert, you can enlist the services of an arbitrator. The benefit of arbitration is that it guarantees a binding, generally unappealable outcome that is private rather than public knowledge. When swift closure is necessary and both sides are willing to abide by the arbitrator's ruling, this may be the best choice. Arbitration is most common when there is a disagreement over the meaning of contract terms, allegations of breach of contract, or other failure to perform as expected. Chapter Four goes into additional processes and greater detail on their relative costs and benefits.

ADR Clauses in Customer Agreements

Increasingly, businesses are using mandatory ADR clauses in their customer and user agreements. The best known type of mandatory ADR clause is the **mandatory arbitration clause**, which is a binding predispute contract committing both parties to use arbitration for dispute settlement in the event of a future dispute. By signing a mandatory arbitration clause both parties give up their right to resort to resolution through the court systems. In January 2012, in *CompuCredit* v. *Greenwood*, the US Supreme Court upheld the use of mandatory arbitration clauses in employment and consumer contracts over the outcry of many consumer groups that claim these processes deny citizens their due process rights.

Arbitration was first recognized in the Federal Arbitration Act of 1925, a statute that legitimizes the use of private arbitration as an alternative venue to the courts for the purposes of dispute resolution. As long as both parties agree to the arbitration, either pre- or postdispute, then the US courts generally uphold the outcomes reached in arbitration as long as no conflict of interest or clear ethical breach was enacted by the arbitrator. Although arbitration is the most common form of binding ADR clause, there is an uptick in the use of mediation as a settlement tool as well. If mediation fails to reach agreement, then arbitration tends to become the default process in these binding clauses.

These clauses have proliferated and are generally unavoidable if you want to rent a car, open a bank account, use a credit card, rent a DVD, carry health insurance or insurance of nearly any kind, and they are even a condition of admission to many movie theaters and theme parks. Arbitration clauses usually run only a sentence or two, such as this one from the International Court of Arbitration (nd): "All disputes arising out of or in connection with the present contract shall be finally settled under the Rules of Arbitration of the International Chamber of Commerce by one or more arbitrators appointed in accordance with the said Rules."

These contracts often require the plaintiff (usually the consumer) to pay a steep filing fee as well as to split the arbitrator's hourly fees. Therefore, the cost of arbitration may be hundreds or even thousands of dollars to each party when the case's value is itself much smaller (such as the cost of a mistaken charge by a car rental company or a movie rental). Although small claims court fees might be reasonable given the value of the case, arbitration fees may put justice out of reach for many consumers and provide the advantage to businesses with deeper pockets.

It is for this reason that the Arbitration Fairness Act of 2009 was introduced in the House of Representatives and if passed into law will make it illegal for companies to force binding arbitration on consumers. Thus far, attempts to turn this bill into a law have met with opposition from powerful business groups, with consumer and employment groups lined up on the other side. At this point in time, it does not appear that the act is likely to become law. What does this mean for the resolution of consumer disputes? When combined with the 2012 US Supreme Court's decision in *CompuCredit* v. *Greenwood*, it is likely that arbitration will remain the most frequently used method of dispute resolution in consumer and employment disputes. Yet arbitration remains an adversarial process that bodes poorly for continuing the relationship between the parties after the arbitrator's decision is made.

In their work on mandatory arbitration clauses, Devasagayam and DeMars (2004) advise that ADR processes will be the most pleasing choice to consumers only when they perceive these methods as fairer and as less risky than litigation. However, they also argue that the use of ADR processes will likely increase as consumers become increasingly familiar with these options, thereby becoming more comfortable and less distrustful of them. When the procedures are viewed as affordable and fair and are seen as having advantages over litigation, then consumer support for ADR will grow. Unfortunately, these clauses have sometimes been used in ways contrary to a desire to foster genuinely fair dispute resolution mechanisms. For example, Drahozal and Ware (2010) reviewed multiple studies regarding business contracts and the use of arbitration clauses. They conclude that some businesses use arbitration clauses in order to avoid class action lawsuits. On the whole, ADR clauses have the potential to be beneficial to consumers and businesses — it is all in the way the programs are designed and funded, which goes to the underlying motivations of the businesses using these clauses. These are merely tools that can be used for good or ill, depending on how they are wielded.

When engaging in B2B contracts internationally, mandatory arbitration becomes much more attractive for both parties than litigation. When it comes to international business, questions of jurisdiction may complicate resolution through the courts as well as provide added difficulty to collecting on a court settlement that might have originated in a different country than the one in which the defendant resides. The costs of international travel to attend court proceedings make resolution for relatively small matters unaffordable. Most companies that conduct business internationally have developed a level of comfort with the use of binding arbitration or mediation than arbitration for dispute resolution. In some cases, these processes may be conducted virtually using video or teleconferencing services to further reduce the time and expense associated with resolution.

In keeping with the tenor of this book, companies should weigh the costs and benefits of mandatory arbitration clauses before requiring them, for a number of reasons. First, enactment of a mandatory arbitration clause may send the wrong signal to your customers. However, there is less harm in requiring either mandatory mediation or arbitration as long as the company is willing to pay the associated fees so they do not become a barrier to dispute resolution for customers and clients. Second, some customers will balk and refuse to engage in business if a mandatory arbitration clause is required. The decision to include a mandatory ADR clause will need to be made by each organization as it seeks to find the most efficient and customer-friendly methods for dispute resolution. However, be careful not to miss the opportunities to gain information and craft creative responses to problems that may come with these clauses. Resort to an adversarial process is helpful only in those cases in which no continuing relationship is likely to exist and when it is the choice of the lesser of two evils, so to speak.

Cultural Differences in Expectations for Customer Service and International Client Conflicts

In our increasingly globalized world, dispute prevention and resolution requires an understanding of intercultural communication differences. I am not referring to the mere challenge posed by differences in language but to deeper differences in meaning and the prioritization of values that varies across cultures. Expectations and norms about appropriate methods for dispute resolution are indeed influenced by national and subnational cultures. Understanding the root causes of some of these differences can help you and your team to avoid common mistakes made when individuals and organizations seek to work together across cultures.

As discussed in earlier chapters, when conferring on overall patterns of difference in communication styles between cultures, generalization becomes necessary but should not be used to make assumptions about individual preferences or habits. A great deal of variation exists within cultures as well as between them, as any New Yorker and Georgian will tell you.

Let's start with two cultures that have commonalities and differences: US Americans and Canadians. Both of these national cultures are derived from Western Europe and evolved unique qualities based on their political affiliations and geographies. Yet work by Abramson (2005) indicates that, in general, Canadian and US American customers prefer somewhat different approaches. In buyer-seller relationships, his research found that Canadians tended to respond more to price flexibility and to value formal introductions and relationship building more than their US counterparts. Canadians are more attuned to equality and fairness in buyer-seller relationships. However, US Americans responded more to marketing and promotional efforts than price flexibility and desired less time spent in trust building during business negotiations.

Other scholars have echoed Abramson's core finding that customer satisfaction in commercial transactions is indeed affected by cultural differences between buyers and sellers. Vaaland (2006) noted that the further the cultural distance, the more likely communications differences were to arise. Some national cultures, such as the cultures of Japan or Afghanistan, prefer indirect communication styles in which efforts are made to save face with all parties by avoiding any direct disagreement or through the use of intermediaries to communicate difficult information or bad news. In contractor-client disputes studied by Vaaland, transactions between indirect and direct communication cultures were found to yield less satisfying results.

In related work, Vaaland, Haugland, and Purchase (2004) found that the greater the cultural distance between two business partners, the greater their chances for a breakup. Although many facets of cultural difference can lead to challenges between business partners or between organizations and their customers, this study emphasizes the importance of risk tolerance and its variation between cultures. Aversion to risk, or lack thereof, is associated with nearly every short- and long-term decision businesses need to make. Managers from national cultures with an aversion to risk may have difficulty reaching consensual decisions with managers coming from cultures with higher tolerance for ambiguity and risk. The United States generally has had a risk-tolerant culture and bankruptcy laws that support risk taking and short-term decision making. When working with organizations or individuals whose national culture and decision-making preferences are different, managers will need to take on a metacommunicative style in which they make clear their assumptions, the reasons behind them, and seek out similar information from the other side.

It should be noted that cultural differences will significantly affect preferred processes for dispute resolution as well. For example, Darowski (2009) found that US Americans conducting business in China should be aware of a cultural preference for mediation over litigation. Mediation has been practiced for many centuries in China and is seen as a reasonable way for business partners to fairly resolve disputes without a significant loss of face that would come from a public airing of grievances in court. Darowski (2009) argues that to litigate a case with a Chinese business is to end all chance of having a future business relationship. Although an American company may see it as "just business," many other cultures are less litigious and prefer dispute resolution mechanisms that rely on collaborative methods over adversarial ones.

CONCLUSION

As successful managers know, great service does not imply that mistakes are never made. It implies that employees at all levels of an organization are committed to proactively addressing problems that arise, without defensiveness, and with an eye toward problem solving and consistent improvement. Proactive customer dispute prevention and early resolution involves planning. It requires monitoring customer feedback for nuggets of knowledge that hold the key to improved goods and services. Yet some organizations fail to gather input from their customers or clients or they gather it but disregard its implications. Gathering feedback during the design of dispute management systems will be important to ensure perceptions that the system is fair and designed with an eye toward fairness rather than simply for the convenience of the institution in the more powerful position (Bingham, 2008).

The ostrich approach to conflict management serves as an invitation to one's competitors. By resolving problems at the lowest levels and using well-trained and empowered employees, organizations can maximize the accomplishment of their missions and make their workplaces more harmonious and profitable.

ELISE AT MAIN STREET BAKERIES

On the advice of her marketing team, Elise and her team decided to hold focus group discussions with a diverse group of her existing customers as well as inviting some noncustomers. All participants were paid for their time, given a tour of a store, and they sampled various products during the introductory period and breaks. The team asked the participants to describe Main Street Bakeries in three words, to discuss why they did or did not shop there, and to share ideas about ways in which the company could appeal to a broader clientele without alienating its current base. In addition to these focus groups, customers were asked to take a survey via a link printed on their receipts in exchange for discounts on products at their next visit.

The information received identified some important areas of improvement for the company. People with household incomes of less than $75,000 per year perceived Main Street Bakeries as being a luxury food boutique in which specialty items were found rather than as their routine grocery store. Even existing customers voiced a desire to see more everyday items at the store in addition to a greater variety of sales or bargains. To address this perception, Main Street Bakeries initiated a marketing campaign using the slogan "seasonal means reasonable" through which they promoted a rotation of seasonal vegetables and food items at low prices while stocking a wider price range of items such as pasta, dairy, and canned goods.

The feedback they received from existing customers was used to identify what customers liked the best about the store (things such as the cleanliness, friendliness, and free cooking lessons) as well as the things they liked the least (shortages of fresh baked goods during afternoon hours and long checkout lines). Each individual store used the data collected to develop goals for improvement, with guidance from upper management. Different survey questions were designed to ensure data would be available to assess progress toward goals. Employees at all levels of the organization received feedback about their customer service performance and incentives were developed to encourage superior efforts on the part of employees.

As a result, satisfaction among existing customers started to rise and new customers started coming in. The stores seemed reinvigorated.

KEY TERMS

Business-to-business (B2B)

Customer loyalty programs

Customer satisfaction

Customers as business partners

Mandatory arbitration clause

Relationship management

SUGGESTED SUPPLEMENTAL READING

Cheng, L.-Y., Yang, C.-C., & Teng, H.-M. (2012). An integrated model for customer relationship management: An analysis and empirical study. *Human Factors and Ergonomics in Manufacturing & Service Industries*. doi: 10.1002/hfm.20343.

Drahozal, C. R., & Rutledge, P. B. (2012). Arbitration clauses in credit card agreements: An empirical study. *Journal of Empirical Legal Studies, 9*, 536–566.

Friedman, R., Olekalns, M., & Oh, S. (2011). Cross-cultural difference in reactions to facework during service failures. *Negotiation and Conflict Management Research, 4*, 352–380.

DISCUSSION QUESTIONS

1. Think, pair, share: What type of customer service information does your organization gather and analyze? How could that data gathering and analysis be improved?

2. What customer loyalty programs do you participate in? Are they effective tools for attracting or retaining your business? Why or why not?

3. Describe your best and worst customer service experiences. What differentiated the approach of these two organizations or their employees that made the difference?

EXERCISES

1. Make a list of the most common complaints from your customers, clients, patients, or stakeholders. How does your organization catalog, study, prevent, and resolve these disputes? What do the measures of client satisfaction tell you about how these are working?

2. If your organization is not gathering the information needed to fully answer question one, create one or more questionnaires you would use to gather this information.

3. Does your organization use a mandatory arbitration clause in its employment or consumer contracts? How is this perceived? What are the costs and benefits implicit in your organization's decision to use or not to use such clauses?

GOAL SETTING

Use the information in this chapter to devise one or more improvements to your current customer satisfaction system. If you are on the front lines of customer service delivery, incorporate one change to your current methods and the measures necessary to gauge how well it works.

Case Studies of Organizational Success Through Exemplary Customer Conflict Management

Learning Objectives

- Demonstrate an understanding of how to maximize customer satisfaction through appropriate resolution methods.

- Examine and describe best practices for complaint response systems and customer recovery methods.

- Demonstrate an understanding of the cultural and training requirements necessary for successful complaint management systems.

- Demonstrate an understanding of the role of employees and customers in the improvement of products, services, and complaint management systems.

- Explain the techniques and tools used by exemplary organizations to achieve high levels of customer satisfaction and complaint resolution.

JOHN AND CUSTOMER SERVICE AT THE BUREAU OF RECLAMATION

For many people, the word *bureaucracy* has negative connotations. Yet the rules and procedures the bureau must follow were put there for a reason: to ensure compliance with the law and to avoid any appearance of favoritism toward or against any one individual or company seeking services from the bureau. In order for a coal mining company to receive or renew its license through the bureau, many different employees must review it—a geologist, an accountant, and a hydrologist, just to name a few. Each of these staff members is supposed to hand off the application to the next person on the list when he or she completes the review. From start to finish, a new license application should take ninety days to process and a renewal should take thirty days. In truth, new licenses are taking between six and nine months and renewals are taking four to six months. John has been receiving angry calls from mining executives who are sure this is a sign of the bureau's "green bias" and an underlying desire to reduce the number of mines in the state. In John's mind, nothing could be further from the case . . . but he can see that it doesn't look good.

Why does a book on conflict management for managers include a section on customer service? Customer satisfaction is directly linked to the methods used to manage conflicts when they arise. High-quality customer service, by necessity, includes the use of efficient and satisfying conflict management systems. Customers understand that problems will arise from time to time. The way in which those problems are handled makes the difference between losing a customer (and all the friends they tell) versus building a long-lasting customer relationship.

In the field of business, there are literally thousands of books that offer information about how to improve customer service satisfaction, often at an industry-specific level. This chapter does not seek to mimic information available there but instead will show examples of those organizations that have developed exemplary methods for preventing and managing complaints from customers.

CUSTOMER SATISFACTION IN A SALES EXPERIENCE

Salespeople need to hit or exceed their sales targets and also ensure that customers have a positive experience during the transaction. A pushy salesperson may indeed make sales but those customers won't return and they may spread the word of their bad experience to others. When hiring, training, and rewarding a sales or customer service team it is crucial to track the customer's experience rather than solely relying on sales numbers, length of interaction, and so on. American Express provides a good example of putting these concepts into practice.

AMERICAN EXPRESS: RELATIONSHIP CARE

American Express (Amex) offers credit card, travel, and financial services worldwide and is well known in its industry as an innovative leader in customer service. In fact, its approach to service, and therefore complaint avoidance and handling, is the envy of companies inside and outside of the finance industry. Amex is a single, globally integrated business unit with over twenty thousand employees involved in customer service in fifteen languages in twenty-two locations worldwide, serving sixty-three million customers.

In most companies, customer service is seen as a cost rather than as an investment. Therefore, when it is time to cut costs to update technology or make other necessary business expenditures, customer service is often the first place to get cut. In 2007, Jim Bush (executive vice president of world service) began a transformational approach to customer service that has led to astounding gains in customer satisfaction. His company's approach is trademarked and called *Relationship Care*. Before any changes were made, Amex gathered information from their customers to learn more about how they defined excellent service and what kinds of behaviors would be perceived as providing excellent service. Equally important, Amex asked their customer care professionals (CCPs) what would help them to do their job better: what kinds of technology, what kinds of philosophy, what incentives or support would they need? This information led them to institute a novel approach to service and complaint management, including a few characteristics of interest for managers everywhere, some of which may seem counterintuitive or at least counter to the decisions typically made by corporations in regards to customer service.

First, Amex changed its metrics in important ways. Rather than measuring the time spent on phone calls, the number of customers served in a given time period, and asking staff to follow scripts, Amex asks its CCPs to instead focus on allowing the customer's voice to be heard. Customers can make the call as long or short as they need it to be. CCPs have access to information on each customer that helps them to build on previous conversations with the customer. CCPs are encouraged to allow their own personalities to come through and to make a personal connection in the service of building a relationship with each client they serve. By learning more about each client, the CCPs can figure out how best to meet their needs. Amex asks its CCPs to ensure the customer's needs and communication styles drive the way the communication occurs and the issues raised are addressed.

> We recognize that great service is not about what the company thinks about its performance internally; it's all about what the customer thinks. So we stopped measuring our performance through "internal quality monitoring" and moved to [our current] model. After every service interaction, we ask customers whether they would recommend American Express to a friend based on their service experience. At its core, this program is about caring for customers in ways that deepen our relationship with them over time. Instead of just fixing customer problems, our people are empowered to go the extra step and offer tailored information about how the customers can get more value out of their relationship with American Express. (Bough, 2011)

So what metrics do they use when each call is a customized experience? Customers are asked only two questions: (1) would you refer us to a friend (RTF)? and (2) how would you rate your customer service experience? On the second point, "excellent" is the standard to which each CCP is held. By eliminating a more cumbersome and less useful internal monitoring system they were able to save significant time and costs used for the review and see gains in customer satisfaction (Manning, 2011). The old system was demoralizing to staff members who felt it didn't allow them the freedom to give great service and then measured them on metrics unrelated to actual customer satisfaction (e.g., length of call, etc.). In a related article, an expert on call center service explains, "Numbers surrounding talk time, productivity and customer-service satisfaction seem to tell the story of how adequately customer service representatives conform to a set of rules and *not* how well they engage, charm, understand and enjoy serving the customer" (Rains, 2011). Excellent customer service should be pleasing to the customer and convey a desire to sustain and nourish an ongoing, mutually beneficial relationship. In place of the old system, Amex now seeks to "enable, engage and empower employees" (Manning).

Second, Amex selects its CCPs carefully. As we have seen from Southwest Airlines, Amex believes they need to select employees with the right people skills and attitude. They can be trained to use the necessary technology or to learn about Amex's products and services but their crucial feature is their ability to build relationships with customers and focus on providing excellent service.

Rather than hiring employees with call center experience, they have instead focused on those with an aptitude and experience in customer service, whether that experience came from retail or another seemingly unrelated field. According to Jim Bush, the Amex vice president in charge of this revolutionary change in approach,

> We looked at what distinguished our best performers. We determined that they truly "get" our brand, love to build relationships, are able to empathize and connect with customers over the phone, and have a passion for delivering exceptional service. We decided to focus on these abilities, which hadn't always been taken into account during the hiring process. We decided not to worry so much about candidates' previous call-center experience. We took our cue from that old basketball philosophy that "You can't teach 7 feet." One challenge we faced is that the intangibles we are looking for don't always show up on résumés. To attract the right candidates, we changed the job descriptions to make clear that relationship skills are more important than the positions' purely transactional elements. (Bush, 2011)

Amex looked to the fields of hospitality, cruise ship personnel, and other areas famous for having warm, friendly people. So although training remains important, what's more important is selecting employees who have a passion to serve and wonderful people skills.

Once selected, Amex treats its people well. Their careers website sums up the American Express employment culture: "We strive to create an environment where people are respected, feel personally and professionally fulfilled, and look forward to coming to work. We empower our people to do the best job possible, while creating a life that's truly extraordinary . . . Every employee has a development plan, which gives them the opportunity to map out what they want to achieve, how they want to get there and importantly, what support they need to do it."

Third, CCPs are fully engaged in the service of building relationships with their customers and are rewarded for doing so. CCPs have performance targets based on the two metrics (RTF and excellence). "What gets measured, gets done" (Manning, 2011). They receive monthly financial incentives for meeting or exceeding those goals. "Employees can earn an incremental 25%–35% of their base pay if customers are satisfied" (Bush, 2011). Instead of spending 75 to 80 percent of their training dollars on technical training, Amex decided to spend 75 to 80 percent of its training funds on helping employees hone their listening and relationship-building skills (Manning, 2011).

The data are used to understand which employees are struggling with the skills of Relationship Care and offer them coaching for improvement, often from those whose scores indicate greater skills in these areas. This has worked so well that RTF scores have doubled in five years and put them among the elite in the field of customer service. How do the employees like these changes? Between 2006 and 2009, employee attrition was cut in half (Bush, 2011). So not only do happy customers make happy employees, it works the other way around.

Reena Panikar is the vice president of American Express's customer service center in Fort Lauderdale, Florida. She described changes the company made in six areas using input from call center employees: "professional recognition, workplace convenience, flexibility, compensation, career development, and policies and procedures. Other companies can learn from American Express's experience by adding a closed-loop voice of the employee (VoE) program to existing voice of the customer (VoC) efforts" (Burns, 2010). By tapping into the experiences, creativity, and hands-on knowledge of customer service personnel, American Express has been able to improve its customer service systems in ways that would have been impossible using only the knowledge and insights of upper management.

So how is it working? What's the bottom line? They have turned their customers into their biggest promoters. "Our promoters spend 20% to 25% more on the American Express card, and their attrition rate is six times lower" (Bough, 2011). American Express is "winning the hearts, minds and wallets of our customers by delivering extraordinary customer care, . . . [through] extraordinary people delivering extraordinary service at the right margins" (Manning, 2011).

CUSTOMER RECOVERY SYSTEMS

Customer recovery refers to the policies and practices put into place to address a disgruntled customer with the goal of winning back the customer's loyalty and business. A customer recovery program is built on the foundation of a successful customer satisfaction and complaint tracking system. Customers need to have opportunities to share their experiences with management, either through a face-to-face interaction (e.g., in a restaurant setting) or via web surveys, online complaint lodging systems, and through telephonic systems. Organizations need to make it as easy as possible for customers to voice their dissatisfaction so that the problem can be rectified as early as possible before the customers feel the need to spread the word about the bad experiences or, in the worst case scenario, file a lawsuit.

However the complaint is received, once received organizations need to have a system in place to respond quickly, efficiently, and appropriately to complaints. As mentioned in other chapters, it is helpful to give frontline staff the authority to resolve low-level grievances quickly, efficiently, and creatively to meet the customer's needs. This makes sense when a full or partial refund or a replacement is in order. These employees can also apologize for the problem and convey their desire to meet and exceed the customer's expectations. For more serious complaints such as product liability concerns, potential class actions, or when the complaint indicates a systemic problem with the product or service, it makes sense to have specially trained employees who can handle each matter individually. A good example of this comes from Toro, the lawn equipment company.

TORO: TURNING LIABILITY INTO ABILITY

When you make and sell lawnmowers, it is inevitable that some customers will be injured during their use. Although it is in the company's interest to create products that are as easy and safe to use as possible, the nature of the product makes it likely that injuries will occasionally occur, despite the company's best efforts. When injuries happen, customers often resort to the courts, claiming the product was defective or that the injury could have been avoided through changes to the product's design. They typically seek damages for injuries or their families seek damages for wrongful death — settlements out of court or judgments received in a trial can potentially be in the millions of dollars. The bad press that results from these cases can result in untold damages to the brand name and product reputation, resulting in reduced sales. These suits have the potential to be a lose-lose for both sides and injured customers endure years of litigation in the process of seeking restitution.

Toro, based in Bloomington, Michigan, manufactures and sells more than $1.3 billion a year worth of outdoor maintenance equipment (Aronson, 2011). More than a decade ago, Toro's Drew Byers created a program to deal with injury claims. The program uses ADR practices and precepts and is based on safety and prevention as well as the early investigation of accidents (Trevarthen, 2011). Rather than see product liability suits as an inevitable cost of doing business, Toro has taken the position that each claim is an opportunity to provide compassionate customer service and gain information necessary to improve its product line in the hopes of consistently reducing the number and severity of accidents stemming from the use of its products.

When customers call Toro to notify them of an injury or when a suit is filed, the company has a nonattorney "product integrity specialist" contact the customers or their surviving relatives and express the company's condolences. Then Toro enlists their help to investigate the accident immediately. The product integrity specialist has authority to offer a settlement to the parties. If an agreement about settlement is not reached through the product integrity specialist, then the parties are offered mediation. In the last two years, only one case has failed to settle using these two steps. "Although most sophisticated companies today participate in some type of mediation to resolve some of their products' liability, commercial and employee disputes . . . Toro was the first to establish a two-step national mediation program, which it did in 1991. It was also the first company to hire a full time outside mediation counsel, they say. The . . . program is still held up as a national model" (Aronson, 2011).

The use of ADR processes and techniques at Toro began in 1990 with the hiring of James J. Seifert, now the general counsel for The Tennant Company, a manufacturer of street sweepers and floor scrubbers. Prior to Seifert's hiring, Toro had pursued an aggressive litigation policy in the hopes of discouraging these claims and keeping settlements down. The result of this strategy was annual double-digit increases in litigation costs and the organization's insurance premiums. With the leadership of Drew Byers and James Seifert, Toro changed its orientation toward these claimants from litigation adversaries to unhappy customers (Trevarthen, 2011). This orientation allowed a problem-solving approach that sees each incident as an opportunity to address a customer's needs and improve the product line to avoid future similar incidents. The company sees about seventy liability complaints each year. Two-thirds of these are settled by the product liability specialists with nearly all of the remaining cases settling in mediation. The product liability specialists are trained as paralegals and tasked with meeting with the customers or their attorneys, face-to-face when possible, investigating the incident, interviewing witnesses, and examining the machine used in the incident. They bring along an engineer who is familiar with the equipment in question.

Jim Bruckner represented two burn victims who recently settled a case with Toro. He says he has not seen a company act as responsibly as Toro in his forty-four years of practicing law.

His two clients suffered second- and third-degree burns over about 20% of their bodies when the lawn mower being operated by one of them ignited on refueling. The accident took place in August 2001 and was settled in April. Toro had a huge legal incentive to settle the case because there had been a recall of 34,000 mowers for the refueling problem. Nonetheless, Bruckner says, "To settle a case like this in eight months from the time it happened, is extremely unique. . . I think it is the most rational thing they can do, particularly from the standpoint of their shareholders." (Aronson, 2011)

One key factor in explaining Toro's success in early settlement is the innovative way it pays its outside counsel. **Outside counsel** refers to attorneys hired from outside the organization to which legal matters are referred for settlement or litigation. Historically, these attorneys have less incentive to settle cases early because they are paid by the hour and early settlement reduces billable hours per case. **Inside counsel** refers to attorneys who are employees of an organization and are salaried. As a salaried employee, incentives for settlement may differ from outside counsel. To encourage early settlement, Toro pays its outside counsel a set fee annually, regardless of how many cases arise or how long each case takes to settle. Although the more customary hourly contracts incentivize prolonged litigation, this payment structure incentivizes early settlement (CPR Institute for Dispute Resolution, 2002). Lawrence McIntyre, Toro's outside counsel representative, stated that the attorneys have "no incentive to have the case drag on one day longer than necessary" (CPR Institute for Dispute Resolution, 2002, p. 14). As a result, the attorneys share information with the plaintiffs regarding the accident investigation, model specifications, and any other information needed for both sides to assess or make offers of settlement. "How am I going to expect the plaintiff who is making a $700,000 demand to settle for $25,000 if I do not share the 'smoking gun' with him?" says one attorney for Toro (CPR Institute for Dispute Resolution, 2002, p. 15). Additionally, each mediation begins with a statement of apology to the plaintiff. This communicates the company's sincere sympathy for the loss or injury and conveys a willingness to work together to make the situation better for everyone involved. Prior to the creation of the ADR program, Toro won 82 percent of the cases it took all the way through litigation but the average litigation cost per case was in the six-figure range (CPR Institute for Dispute Resolution, 2002). Not only was this inefficient, it did nothing to help repair the company image in customers' minds.

The use of ADR to enhance customer service, reduce liability, and improve products has been a great success in terms of dollars spent and increases in customer loyalty and satisfaction. According to statistics for 1992 to 2000 on more than 900 products liability claims that referred to the program, Toro says it has cut its legal costs per claim (attorney fees and litigation expenses) by 78% — from an average of $47, 252 to $10,420. Toro also says its average resolution amount for the period was reduced by 70%, from $68,368 for settlements and verdicts to $20,248 (Aronson, 2011).

In the first six years of its program, Toro estimates it saved $50 million dollars with most claims settled within four months (CPR Institute for Dispute Resolution, 2002). In a 2002 interview, Byers of Toro claimed, "We decided that we wanted to regain control of our money, of our documents, of our reputation and of our time. . . We haven't had a single corporate officer deposed in 11 years, since we started this program" (CPR Institute for Dispute Resolution, 2002, p. 13). Another benefit was a drop in the company's insurance premiums of $1.9 million in each of the program's first three years (CPR Institute for Dispute Resolution, 2002).

Equally or more important, those who have suffered a loss appreciate this approach to dispute resolution. For example, Ms. Soles-Smith's seventeen-year-old son was killed when the mower he was riding tipped over on an embankment. Her attorney states, "I told [Toro] from the start that I think it made a difference to my client that you came down and expressed condolences and took the matter seriously and seemed genuinely concerned"(Aronson, 2011). The case settled in mediation for $500,000 although the plaintiff originally asked for more than three times that amount. Through their negotiations, the plaintiff and company were able to work together to discuss ways to make the product safer, including the creation of a safety advisory council. This held great value for the mother: "It appears they are willing to work with us in what I feel I need to do in Cory's memory and that is to prevent anyone else from having to go through this" (Aronson, 2011, p. 1).

RITZ-CARLTON: EMPLOYEE EMPOWERMENT FOR "DELIGHTED" CUSTOMERS

The Ritz-Carlton hotel chain seeks to "delight" its customers. This means they seek to exceed customer expectations every time, not just meet them. Recall from Chapter Nine that customer satisfaction is "a measure of how a firm's product or service performs compared to customers' expectations" (Zondiros, Konstantopoulos, & Tomaras, 2007, p. 1086). So part of the goal is not to overinflate customer expectations by overpromising. The second part of the equation is to overdeliver. By exceeding customer expectations, organizations are likely to win new customers and gain market share or improve their organization's reputation.

At the Ritz-Carlton Hotels, all personnel in direct contact with customers are empowered to drop what they are doing to help a customer or take actions to exceed their expectations. This means the front-desk staff, the concierge, housekeepers, food servers, everyone can tap into their own creativity and kindness to help out a customer who has had a bad day by sending them flowers or running an errand for them. In fact, a budget is set aside for these activities. If a customer is feeling sick, the staff might send them flowers or bring a special treat from the kitchen; whatever it takes to show they want the customer's experience to be memorable and unique. The Ritz-Carlton has realized that by empowering the staff to make the customers happy, they have made the employees happier, too. It turns out that random acts of kindness equate to stellar customer service, repeat business, and low employee turnover.

PUBLIC AND NONPROFIT SECTOR SERVICE DELIVERY

The previous examples have used private sector organizations to illustrate the benefits of superior customer service systems and early compliant resolution methods as two sides of the same coin. But how can public sector organizations or nonprofits take these lessons and implement them for the benefit of their clients, customers, or patients? The same principles apply but it is occasionally harder to identify the customer. For some public agencies, nearly every person in the country is the customer or recipient of services. For example, the Department of Defense, the US Postal Service, and the US Environmental Protection Agency provide public goods that are supplied to all citizens and residents, whether or not they paid for them through taxes or user fees. In addition to the public, each of these agencies has more specific customers as well: Congress oversees their operations and can hold them accountable, they all have vendors and suppliers with whom relationships must be maintained, and they all have large numbers of employees on whom they can call for feedback to improve their operational efficiency. Although customers and clients for public sector managers may be different in some ways from the private sector, the methods for designing and improving service delivery are remarkably similar. Monitoring service delivery and customer satisfaction is critical, as is gathering data from high-performing employees, hiring selectively, and rewarding those who perform well. "Today's citizen-customer expects the same instant communication and instant government response that she gets every day from the business community. And customer service strategies, developed in the private sector, have refined these expectations. Customer experience strategy is not a competitive business tactic exclusive to the private sector anymore. It lies at the very heart of successful policy design and execution" (Deloitte, 2012).

PATIENT CARE ADVOCATES: REDUCING FORMAL COMPLAINTS IN HOSPITAL SETTINGS

Hospitals are unique among organizations in that they can be private sector, for-profit endeavors or they can be run as nonprofit organizations. Either way, addressing patient complaints early is crucial to providing high-quality health care and avoiding future litigation. Toward those ends, many hospitals have created positions for conflict management experts who are on staff to intervene as soon as a conflict comes to light. These individuals are most commonly called *patient care advocates*, but they can hold other titles depending on whether they work under the auspices of the risk management or patient care departments.

A **patient care advocate (PCA)** works either in the emergency department or in the other parts of the hospital and is on call to manage patient complaints, to deescalate conflict when it arises, and to solve problems whenever possible. A few scenarios are illustrative:

- A patient in the emergency room becomes irate because he feels he is waiting longer than is fair and that other patients who arrived later than he did have already been seen. He is getting increasingly agitated and begins yelling at the staff. The PCA intervenes, takes him aside or to a private space for conversation. She listens to him and assures him that his needs will be met. She seeks out information from the other staff members to share with him regarding his expected wait time and the reasons for the delay. She seeks to calm him down through listening and tells him she will be his point of contact in case other problems arise during his stay.

- In the maternity ward, a nurse is seen to be stumbling as she walks and could not walk without holding on to the rail on the wall for support. When a new mother asked that the nurse refrain from carrying her baby, the nurse exclaimed, "I haven't dropped him yet! Let me do my job." An argument ensued between the nurse (who was suffering from the flu but still reported to work) and the baby's parents. The parents took a video of the nurse stumbling down the hall and threatened to post it on YouTube for the whole community to see. The PCA intervened, assured the parents that another nurse would be assigned to them instead, and contacted the nurse in charge to see that the sick nurse clocked out and went home until she was well enough to return to work.

- At a teaching hospital, a patient was recovering from surgery and under the influence of pain medication. The patient was about to receive a blood transfusion from a nursing student when she became panicked and yelled to the staff that her blood type was O positive rather than AB negative, as the label on the bag indicated. The nurse assured her that her blood had been drawn and the type had been checked twice. The nurse told her she was "woozy" from pain medication and she needed to trust the staff to do their jobs right. The patient picked up the phone and dialed 911. She verbally withdrew her consent for care and told them to stop treating her immediately. The nurse called the PCA advocate who arrived at the same time as the police. The PCA offered to have the patient's blood type checked one more time to reassure the patient. She convinced the nurses this was a small price to pay to calm the patient and get on with her care. The patient said, "I'm forty-two years old and I donate blood every three months. I know what my blood type is, but go ahead and check it!" As it turned out, the patient was right, and the protocols for administering a blood transfusion were not being correctly followed in this hospital. A potential health care disaster and a lawsuit were averted.

PCAs do not need to be a nurse or medically trained specialist. In fact, the lack of specialized knowledge helps maintain their neutrality and their ability to view the situation with an outsider's eyes, the way a potential jury might do. This lack of inside information helps them ask similar questions that patients might ask or seek a layperson's explanation of a medical procedure or diagnosis on behalf of a confused patient.

Sometimes the PCA accompanies doctors as they deliver the news of a death to family members or checks in on patients to make sure all their questions have been answered clearly. The PCA is there to ensure that all patients receive the best service possible and address complaints and problems before they become formal complaints. There is an increased use of PCAs within hospital settings, a trend that indicates recognition of the benefits of early resolution for complaint prevention and customer recovery.

PUBLIC SECTOR: WHAT NOT TO DO

The five o'clock news showed the White River bubbling like a child's bath. Huge soap bubbles frothed on both sides of the river, apparently the result of a spill of industrial waste into the stream. The reporter said, "Officials from the state's Department of Natural Resources (DNR) have traced the contamination back to the Smithville Industrial Chemical plant. Officials promise that the company will be forced to pay all the costs of cleanup from this spill. In the meantime, citizens are asked to stay away from the river and keep their pets away, too. As the contaminant continues to pour into the river, no one knows when this situation will end." In the next scene the same reporter is shown knocking on the door at the home of the owner of the Smithville Industrial Chemical plant. When the homeowner comes to the door she says, "Mr. Jones, what is your response to allegations from the DNR that your plant is spilling industrial waste into the White River?" Clearly in shock, Mr. Jones replies, "Really? I had no idea. Are you sure? Why didn't they contact me? I'll get to the plant right away and check it out!"

Clearly, the DNR was not meeting the needs of its customers—those it regulates nor the public as a whole. In their effort to build a case and find the "bad guy," they ignored the need for an immediate, problem-solving response. The first step to accomplishing the organizational mission is to maintain a problem-solving attitude!

As an aside . . . the pollution was not coming from the Smithville plant, but their failure to communicate with those they deem polluters worsened the severity of the emergency because it took a few days to locate the source of the contamination and shut it off.

CHILDREN'S HEALTH CARE OF ATLANTA: MEASURING AND REWARDING QUALITY PATIENT CARE

Children's Healthcare of Atlanta (CHOA) is a chain of hospitals and clinics providing health care services to approximately 315,000 children inside and outside of the metro Atlanta region. With more than 7,500 employees and 6,500 volunteers, CHOA is a nonprofit health care provider and a leader in research and education on issues affecting pediatric healthcare (Children's Healthcare of Atlanta [CHOA], 2011). As an organization, CHOA has worked hard to measure patient satisfaction and outcomes, link those measurements to reward structures for employees, and seek consistent improvements in patient care and satisfaction. After patient visits, parents receive a satisfaction survey that asks them about their visit: everything from the cleanliness of the rooms to the friendliness of the receptionists, technicians, nurses, and doctors. Did they get the information they needed to make decisions regarding their child's care? Was the staff attentive to their child's pain management or other needs? Was the billing procedure clear and efficient? What ideas can parents share to improve the quality of care offered by CHOA? In addition to information gained from these surveys, the hospital can track readmission and infection rates. Each department has goals for patient care and satisfaction. Progress toward those goals as well as their attainment and maintenance result in financial rewards and recognition at the departmental and individual levels.

As it has grown, CHOA has acquired hospitals and clinics around Atlanta, each with its own culture toward customer service. By using uniform measures to track patient satisfaction and care, CHOA has made improvements in customer service in acquired organizations that had previously experienced great variation in satisfaction among patients and their parents. Although work remains to be done, particularly in fostering a uniform culture of patient-centered care across facilities, the use of these tracking and rewards systems provides a baseline of information necessary to make adjustments within individual units or facilities.

In addition to tracking and rewarding customer service directly, CHOA has developed a process to improve the products and services it receives through its numerous suppliers of medical devices and equipment. Through the use of employee focus groups, the supply chain manager gathers information about the products regularly used for patient care: from the syringes and bed pans to the electronic heart monitors and surgical supplies. Nurses, doctors, janitorial staff, and others are asked to share what they like about the product, what they don't like, and ideas for product improvements. That information is then shared with the products' manufacturers and vendors and used to negotiate improvements in products. The supply chain manager is trained in negotiation, facilitation, and conflict management skills as well as systems design (see Chapter Eight). She uses these skills to gather and process information to make systemwide improvements with regard to the supplies used throughout the organization.

CHOA's efforts to measure, reward, and improve patient services have resulted in numerous awards and national recognition. *US News & World Report* has listed CHOA on its "one hundred best companies to work for" list every year since 2004, as has *Working Mother* magazine since 2006. In 2009, CHOA made the "top ten pediatric hospitals" list for *Parents* magazine. Although it strives for continual improvement, CHOA's efforts to measure, reward, and improve care have resulted in an organization with low employee turnover and high patient satisfaction.

CUSTOMER SERVICE IN THE NONPROFIT SECTOR

Helping Hands (HH) is a nonprofit that seeks to prevent homelessness as well as serve the needs of the homeless in their urban community. In order to better meet the needs of their customers (the homeless and those facing homelessness) and also meet the needs of the broader community, the director of HH secured the services of some volunteers from the local college's social work program to interview service recipients to learn more about how HH might better meet their needs. The interview included questions about what led customers to seek services from HH, had they been there before, as well as what services they might need to have a stable housing situation. The volunteers also gathered information on the customers' perceptions of the facility's cleanliness, safety, and friendliness.

Using this information, HH instituted a number of changes including the use of a new mediation program designed to prevent homelessness and restore the recently homeless into the homes of their families or friends. The survey indicated that many of the homeless clients had family members with whom they would like to live either temporarily or permanently but unresolved conflicts prevented this from happening. Sometimes the conflicts revolved around issues of money, chores, and other contributions the client could make to the household. Other times, there were differences with respect to house rules that caused conflict (e.g., curfews, use of foul language, concerns about drinking, etc.). When both sides were willing to do so, specially trained mediators would discuss these matters to see if a mutually agreeable solution could be found. If so, a behavioral contract and ground rules were drawn up that each party committed to abide by. Mediators checked in after three, seven, fourteen, and thirty days to see how the agreements were working and to conduct additional mediations as necessary. Each agreement included a list of services that HH could provide to help support the goal of keeping the client housed with family and friends as they transitioned to eventual independence. These services often included assistance with the process of applying for Social Security, unemployment, food stamps, job training, or other programs. Sometimes they included assistance with drug or alcohol rehabilitation treatment, outplacement during daytime hours, or other services.

As a result of the feedback from these endeavors, the incidence of repeated homelessness declined 32 percent in six months and improvements were made to the facility and staff training programs. The ultimate measure of customer service—levels of homelessness—dropped, indicating increased achievement of the organizational mission and putting HH in a good position with its funders.

CONCLUSION

Whether in the private, public, or nonprofit sector, leaders in customer service have a few things in common: they gather feedback about customer's experiences, they make it easy for customers to share their concerns or complaints, they empower employees to resolve problems at the lowest level possible, and they see the connection between customer service and the collaborative resolution of complaints. Similar to other types of conflict, customer complaints provide an opportunity to demonstrate the importance an organization places on maintaining a positive working relationship with each customer. As Rita Callahan, organizational conflict management specialist, notes, "Ah, conflict . . . an opportunity to enhance this relationship" (personal communication). The way in which your organization addresses conflict with its customers and constituents sends a signal to them. Be sure it is the signal you wish to send.

JOHN REDESIGNS CUSTOMER SERVICE AT THE BUREAU OF RECLAMATION

John decided to hold a meeting with each department manager to learn more about the underlying sources of delay on the permit review process. He began by explaining that his goal was not to bust heads or point the blame at any one manager or department. His goal was to gather information on the source of the delays and brainstorm ideas about how to improve the process. Once his managers understood they were not in trouble, they began to share information about the inner workings of their departments.

Similar to nearly all public agencies, the first unanimous complaint from the managers was that they were understaffed. There had been a statewide freeze on hiring for more than a year due to budget problems. As a result, when employees retired, they were not being replaced and each department manager voiced a concern about understaffing. John conveyed sympathy with their collective plight and asked the managers to work with him to ensure their personnel resources were being deployed as efficiently as possible in light of the staffing situation.

Next, John learned more about the existing system for tracking license applications from the time they were submitted until the time they were approved. It turns out there wasn't much of one. Each application was contained in a paper file and a check-off sheet was used to determine which departments had reviewed and approved the application. Once all departments had given their approval, the application was filed with other existing applications. There was no formal process for notifying the mining company that had applied for the license. "Usually they call to check on it after a while, we chase it down, and then let them know the status."

Based on this information, it was determined that some files literally would get forgotten on someone's desktop for months at a time until an inquiry was made, at which time the file would move to the top of the pile and eventually move on to the next department. John calls this the "squeaky wheel gets the grease" method of application processing. No feedback mechanisms had been created to gather customer service feedback from applicants or others involved in the licensing process.

To remedy the situation, John instituted the following:

- An online submission and tracking process for all license applications and renewals. Through this system the applicant, members of the public, and any internal employee could check on the status of the application, see which departments had issued a recommendation, which had not, and the average time the application spent in each department.

- In consultation with each department's staff, goals related to processing time were created. The online system was set to generate quarterly reports to John, showing the time each department spent in application review and whether they were meeting its goals.

- At the end of each application process, a decision was rendered that either approved or declined the license application. The point of contact for the mining company was then sent an online feedback survey that asked the following questions: "Did the bureau respond to your inquiries in a reasonable time frame? Were your questions answered completely? If your application was denied, were the reasons for the denial fully explained? What can the bureau do to improve the efficiency and quality of the application review process?"

- Because the bureau processes approximately thirty applications or renewals each year, each survey would be read by John's assistant director and feedback would be provided to departments during quarterly meetings.

- Working with the union, John designed an incentive system by which those departments and individuals who met objective targets for improved customer service would receive recognition (e.g., employee of the month and year) as well as rewards (e.g., first in line for merit raises).

Using this system, the time necessary to process applications and renewals dropped by 25 percent in the first quarter and continues to improve. John sent a memo to all existing license holders in the state to explain the new feedback and tracking system and to enlist their support in his efforts to continually improve the agency's efficiency and fairness in the allocation of the agency's personnel resources. When John gets phone calls from mining company executives, which still happens from time to time, he is able to log into the system and tell the caller the exact status of the application. He can also see where it is stuck and then communicate with that manager to learn more about the source of the delay. This allows John to allocate resources where and when they can do the most good.

This system has been so well received that John has had a few inquiries from other agency heads seeking out his advice for their own improvements. John and his agency are now seen as emerging leaders in the area of public sector customer service.

KEY WORDS

Customer recovery

Inside counsel

Outside counsel

Patient care advocate (PCA)

SUGGESTED SUPPLEMENTAL READING

Froehle, C. M. (2006). Service personnel, technology, and their interaction in influencing customer satisfaction. *Decision Sciences, 37*, 5–38.

Harris, L. C., & Ogbonna, E. (2010). Hiding customer complaints: Studying the motivations and forms of service employees' complaint concealment behaviours. *British Journal of Management, 21*, 262–279.

DISCUSSION QUESTIONS

1. Think, pair, share: Think back to the best customer service you have experienced recently. What made it so good? What can you learn from that experience to translate to your current organization?

2. Who are the external stakeholders for your organization? How would they rate the service they receive? If you could make one change to improve your customer, client, or patient's experience what would it be? What costs would be incurred by making this change and who would need to support this change internally?

3. Changes to customer service systems must be authorized from the highest tier of the organization's leadership structure. Yet good customer service is built on changes at the frontlines of the organization. What changes can you personally make in order to improve the experience of your customers and clients?

EXERCISE

1. How do the customer service techniques in this chapter compare to those of your organization? Create a list of those strategies or techniques you read about in this chapter that might be of use to your organization.

PART FOUR

Collaboration and Conflict Management Between Regulators and the Regulated

Whether you work for a government agency, a private business, or a nonprofit organization, government policies affect your daily work. Regulations cover everything from wages and working conditions to product safety, fairness in advertising, and environmental effects of the manufacturing process. Many nonprofits rely on government funds to carry out their work and as a result are open to public and governmental scrutiny as to how they spend those funds and the results achieved.

Relationships between regulators and members of regulated communities have historically been adversarial but that serves no one well. Instead, regulators and those they regulate can accomplish the best results possible for all sides by working collaboratively to craft rules and regulations that are practical, effective, and implementable. When problems arise, collaborative relationships allow regulators to reach out to business and the nonprofit community to work together to enhance compliance or fix problems of noncompliance as quickly as possible. The chapters in this part provide insights into the unique relationships that exist between regulators and those they regulate.

Chapter Eleven examines innovative processes and techniques used for collaboration among regulators, the business community, and the public at large. Through the use of transparent, participatory, and collaborative processes, public trust in government can be increased and can improve the ability of regulators to safeguard the public interest.

How often do you attend large-group meetings? All managers need the ability to effectively design and lead large-group meetings. For public sector managers these may include public meetings needed to meet rule-making requirements. For those in the private or nonprofit sectors these may include meetings of the board of director or shareholder meetings. Even regular staff meetings can be made more effective through an application of the skills and recommendations contained in Chapter Twelve.

Public Policy Decision Making and Collaboration

Learning Objectives

- Describe the common characteristics of public disputes compared to other venues for conflict (workplace, courts, and so forth).

- Describe the differences among various types of commonly used public dispute resolution processes.

- Analyze the characteristics of a public dispute or large-group decision-making process in order to match the problem with the most appropriate process for resolution.

- Demonstrate an understanding of the evolution and trends in public dispute resolution and collaborative governance.

- Demonstrate an understanding of the common steps in the process of making administrative rules and regulations.

ELISE AT MAIN STREET BAKERIES

In an effort to deal with the obesity epidemic plaguing the country, the US Food and Drug Administration (FDA) has implemented a new rule that requires restaurants and sellers of prepared food items to include nutrition information on their menus or on the packaging of the food items. This new requirement also requires all items to be labeled as to their content of gluten, nuts, dairy, and other common allergens. This rule applies to any chain restaurant or retail food supplier with more than five locations. Small mom-and-pop chains are exempt from these regulations. Elise knows that her clientele tends to be more health conscious than the average consumer, which is why her stores specialize in locally grown, organic and healthy foods. In fact, she has often wished that nutritional information were required on all baked goods because a donut or cookie from her shop is likely to be healthier than one from the large bakery chains. This requirement is a potential marketing and sales opportunity for her company yet because her chain uses locally grown and baked products, there is significant variation in stock from one region to another and from season to season. She likes the idea of including nutritional information on all prepared foods but is not quite sure how to make this work because the bread baked in Kansas is slightly different from the bread baked in Boston. To make matters worse, some of her kitchens prepare items with nuts, so all items would need to have a nut warning, even if they do not contain nuts as an ingredient. She might need to bake nut-containing items in one central location and ship them nationwide to allow local kitchens to be labeled *nut free*. It may take months for her bakeries to make the changes necessary to comply with the new regulations—closing down in the meantime would mean financial disaster for her company and for her thousands of employees nationwide.

Last year Elise called the FDA to find out more about the process for decision making. She learned that they were in the process of convening a group of stakeholders to discuss this new initiative, share information with the agency, and engage in negotiated rule making. Elise had never heard of this before but agreed to participate in a teleconference call with other potential stakeholders to hear more about this process.

Managers from public, private, and nonprofit sectors often interact in ways that indicate adversarial rather than collaborative relationships. This is not necessary to protect the public good or to keep businesses profitable. In fact, adversarial relationships between regulators and those they regulate frequently reduce the efficiency of both. There are many shared interests that can mitigate these previously hostile relationships. Corporations seek to keep their brand name clean and bright and government agencies do not want to get the reputation for stifling job creation or encouraging companies to relocate to "pollution havens" or other low-regulatory environments. Civic and nonprofit groups may accomplish more change by nurturing collaborative partnerships with regulators than by being thorns in their sides. Managers from the private, public, and nonprofit sectors are increasingly coming together through the use of collaborative processes to create or change policies in ways that further the missions of their organizations. By being proactive in these efforts, managers can enhance the ability of their organization to work successfully on these issues as well as make themselves indispensable to their organizations. The ability of regulators and regulated communities to proactively avoid problems and to jointly address any problems that cannot be avoided are core managerial skills that are central to the mission of most organizations. Poor relationships between regulators and those they regulate can be costly to both types of organizations and to the public interest. The application of ADR methods to public policy issues is referred to as *environment and public policy conflict resolution (E/PP)*.

From negotiated rule making to policy dialogues or case evaluations, this chapter will examine innovative efforts to transform regulatory relationships with the goal of creating policy that is more effective, implementable, and subject to fewer legal challenges. From zoning disputes to new health care regulations, case studies will be used to show how leaders in regulatory and regulated communities have successfully reached out to one another in order to protect and promote public and private interests. These two need not be mutually exclusive. If you work for a nonprofit or a corporation, do not jump to the false conclusion that this chapter and the one that follows do not involve you or your organization. Nothing could be further from the truth. Public disputes occur at the nexus of the private, public, and nonprofit sectors. Every regulatory dispute affects those who are regulated, not just those creating and implementing the regulations. Developing positive working relationships and collaborative processes to use for the resolution of public disputes involves managers in every sector and can result in greater mission accomplishment, an untarnished brand, and career advancement (not to mention better policy outcomes). This chapter will introduce the menu of processes related to managing public disputes as well as other stakeholder gatherings, such as shareholder meetings and other forms of large-group decision-making processes.

CHARACTERISTICS OF PUBLIC DISPUTES

The state wants to build a juvenile detention facility near a middle-class suburban neighborhood. Local residents have staged protests, moved to block the rezoning effort, and groups have lined up on both sides of the facility.

A young African American man was found guilty of murdering an off-duty police officer but he maintained his innocence up until his execution last week. Immediately after his execution riots ensued at the state capitol with hundreds of thousands of dollars of damage to vehicles, shops, and buildings. More than one hundred arrests have been made and the city's simmering racial tensions have boiled over.

The EPA has been sued by a civic group claiming it has not adequately protected the safety of America's drinking water by failing to create standards for many common forms of prescription drugs that find their way into the water supply. The judge agreed with the civic group and now the EPA is tasked with creating a host of new water-quality regulations. Local governments, the US Association of Mayors, pharmaceutical companies, and hundreds of water utilities across the country are concerned about the costs of any proposed new regulations. The EPA is entangled in its mission, a court mandate, and with stakeholders on all sides of the issue.

Each of these scenarios depicts a dispute, or more broadly, a decision-making process that involves managers of public, private, and nonprofit organizations. Increasingly, managers are called on to use their skills and the visibility of their positions to speak as representatives for their organizations at public meetings or within some type of decision-making processes that affect their products, services, or missions. By working together to find workable solutions to complex problems, both public and private interests can be protected, and prolonged, unproductive conflicts may be avoided or at least shortened.

Public disputes are different from the labor-management and employment conflicts previously discussed in this book in many ways. We must begin with a broad definition of **public disputes** as complex, multiparty, decision-making, or consensus-building processes on issues affecting the public interest or policy that involve complicated networks of interests, unequal accountability among stakeholders, strongly held values, and that are highly influenced by governmental rules and regulations.

In the EPA scenario, stakeholder groups include the FDA, state and local government representatives, local water utilities (some of which are publicly operated and some of which are privately operated), potentially dozens of pharmaceutical manufacturers, drug retailers such as CVS, civic groups representing public health or the environment, and technology manufacturers that wish to sell water-quality equipment or services involved in the purification of drinking water or the detection of impurities. Each of these stakeholder groups would want one or more representatives at the negotiating table if talks were to occur related to new regulations. These negotiations would likely occur over a long period of time, perhaps over months or even years. Each stakeholder would need to commit to keeping his or her constituency updated of the status of the negotiations and any proposals under discussion. The stakeholder representative (we'll call this person an *advocate*) will need to funnel the concerns of his constituency back to the larger group as well as serve as an intragroup negotiator to help his own constituents gain a realistic understanding about the nature of the compromises likely to be necessary to reach an agreement that is superior to litigation. Some of these advocates are bureaucrats working for governmental agencies. As such, they can be officially reprimanded or even fired as a way of holding them accountable. Sometimes elected officials take part in these efforts, and they are held accountable at election time. Still others, citizens who represent themselves or a civic group, may have no accountability at all. The same goes for corporate advocates, who are not necessarily expected to uphold the public good. These varying levels of accountability make collaborative processes more complex than the other processes discussed in this book.

To complicate matters, it is not uncommon for new groups to emerge even late in the negotiation process. Perhaps a local or national environmental nonprofit learned about the negotiations months after they began. Or once the group has crafted a specific proposal and this proposal was released to the press, a group that was not previously interested now believes their interests are threatened. Because of the nature of public meetings and public policy processes, it is usually difficult, unwise, or even impossible to exclude individuals or groups who wish to be included in these negotiations, even if they come late in the game.

In some public disputes the parties will come together for a few meetings and never see each other again, as may be the case with the juvenile detention facility vignette. More commonly, in cases such as the race riots or water-quality issues, the stakeholders will have repeated contact with each other either as neighbors or colleagues throughout their careers. Whether they come together in the future on the same issue or on other issues of mutual concern, these groups are interdependent and their paths likely will cross repeatedly over many years. Therefore, these collaborative processes represent an important opportunity for building social capital and networks that will enhance current and future communications and problem-solving abilities. By getting to know one another as people, neighbors, and colleagues, these collaborative processes can serve as springboards for other joint efforts and as mechanisms that can be called on throughout the process of decision implementation. When problems arise during the implementation phase, which they often do, parties can call on one another to again work together collaboratively in order to efficiently and fairly discuss and solve those problems. They have built relationships as people, not just as representatives of their particular interests.

Each governmental agency has developed different protocols for decision making that must be followed. In many federal government agencies this means that a draft rule or regulation is created and published in the *Federal Register*, a daily publication of the US government. Public comments are accepted for a specified period of time, after which the final rule or regulation is issued. In some cases, especially at the state and local level, public meetings must be held to gather comments or announce planned changes before they can take effect. Yet the specifics of these processes are unique to each government agency and sometimes one issue crosscuts the jurisdictional boundaries of multiple federal, state, and local governmental agencies. In the public sector, corporations have clear hierarchies through which decisions are made and implemented. Civic groups may have less hierarchical and more consensus-based or democratic decision-making processes. When a decision must be made quickly, and the decision affects government, industry, and civic groups, these varying processes for decision making can lead to delay and confusion. The complexity of these decision-making structures and the necessity of getting them to converge when necessary means that public disputes are much more complex than intraorganizational disputes. These disputes occur at the nexus between organizations rather than within them. As you will see from the variety of collaborative processes described in this chapter, most governmental agencies and corporations do not have formal guidelines for participating in collaborative processes. This means that each opportunity for collaborative decision making or problem solving is handled differently by each agency and even dispute by dispute. This is not necessarily a negative, considering that each dispute may be unique enough to justify an individualized approach. But it also means that some agencies are leaders in the use of dispute resolution processes and others are laggards who rarely entertain collaborative processes.

The public nature of these negotiations can also be a complicating factor. In 1976, in the wake of the Watergate scandal and heightened levels of public distrust of government leaders, the Government in the Sunshine Act was passed. This act requires all agencies of the federal government, except the Executive Office of the President, to conduct meetings publicly and allow citizens to testify and present concerns about past, present, and future agency actions (Harrison, Harris, & Tolchin, 2009). State and local governments have generally followed this example. The term *sunshine laws* refers to federal, state, and local laws that require regulatory meetings, decisions, and records to be open to the public. This means that the media are often present during the negotiations and mediations that occur on public issues, making frank discussions difficult. Elected or appointed leaders may be afraid to engage in creative brainstorming, knowing that any idea they suggest or anything they say may end up on YouTube or the five o'clock news. Advocates know they can often use the media to pressure fellow negotiators or to sabotage proposals before they are fully discussed. The open nature of public disputes makes them more complex and difficult to navigate. Dealing with the media, and turning them into a process ally rather than a process scuttler is a skill we will cover a bit later.

Public decision-making processes involve deeply held values tied closely to personal and community identities. The choices we make about methods to care for our sick or elderly, provide education for our children, punish or deter wrongdoing, protect our environmental resources, or regulate economic activity reveal our underlying values as people. When something appears to threaten these values, people react strongly, sometimes even violently. Discussions on these issues bring out passionate pleas to do the right thing from the advocates involved. Yet, the dilemma is that we are often faced with the need to prioritize or choose between these values and therefore different people will weigh them differently. Do we take away the right to drive from elderly people who may pose a risk to public safety? Do we save an endangered species at a cost of millions of tax dollars? The moral and often personal implications of public decisions make these negotiations quite difficult and exhausting yet terribly important to society as a whole.

Managing these complex issues increasingly calls for the skills of **collaborative public management**, "the process of facilitating and operating in multi-organizational arrangements to solve problems that cannot be solved or easily solved by single organizations. Collaborative means to co-labor, to achieve common goals, often working across boundaries and in multi-sector-actor relationships. Collaborative public management may include participatory governance: the active involvement of citizens in government decision-making" (O'Leary & Blomgren Bingham, 2011, p. 3).

THE SPIRAL OF UNMANAGED CONFLICT

In the field of conflict management, experts frequently refer to a concept called *ripeness*. A conflict is ripe for intervention once it is clear who the major players or stakeholders are, once the issue is of significant urgency to demand action but has not yet reached crisis style, and before the relationships between stakeholders are characterized by demonization and disrespect and the dispute becomes intractable. Yet intervene too early and it is difficult to sustain energetic participation by stakeholders or there may be a lack of data on which to base ideas for resolution. Although it is never too late to attempt collaboration, the odds of success are greatest if the intervention occurs when the dispute is ripe for intervention.

Carpenter and Kennedy (2001) have outlined the common phases that public disputes experience on their way to becoming intractable, what they call "the spiral of unmanaged conflict" (p. 12). Each individual dispute may go through these phases faster or slower or may skip a step only to circle back to an earlier one. Progress through the phases may be linear for some disputes and circular for others. Recall Figure 2.2, which graphically depicts these phases. In the first phase, the problem emerges. Generally, a private or public organization announces some planned change—a new building, a widened road, a new regulation, a change to products or services, and so forth. There is mild concern that grows slowly at first, starting with those most directly affected by the planned changes. Stakeholders seek to get more information about the planned changes and are often frustrated by the response they receive. Organizations do not like to share information about plans until that information is relatively finalized. This lack of information and uncertainty feeds fear among stakeholders who begin to contact their elected officials or others in power to help them get the information they need.

The apparent unwillingness or inability to share information leads to negative attributions by stakeholders, who may say things like, "they are being sneaky!" or "they are withholding information until it will be too late for us to do anything about this!" Groups of stakeholders start to form on all sides of the issue; rarely do these issues have only two sides, even though the media often find it simpler to portray issues in this manner. These groups start to get organized, gather resources to support their future activities, and make their game plans. As the sides form, the media begin to cover the issue more and more, thereby increasing the rate at which the sides form. Individuals begin to talk only about the issue with those who have similar views. They tune out the opinions of those who disagree with them and as a result, their positions harden. They may develop ideas about the dispute that favor their position as the morally right, prudent, or obvious course of action. This only serves to further alienate those who hold differing opinions on the matter at hand. As a result, communication and any attempt to negotiate between the two groups comes to a standstill. The less communication that occurs, the smaller the likelihood of a collaborative resolution to the problem.

Because it has become clear to the stakeholders that the other side(s) are unwilling to capitulate, they begin to commit resources to promote adversarial paths to resolution. They may spend money to hire lawyers and file a lawsuit or injunction. They may seek the services of a media consultant to make their case in the press and garner further support for their cause. They may hire expert witnesses or hire consultants to gather data that support their cause. Once these resources are committed, no one in the group will settle for less than what has been spent so far, including an outcome that is worthy of the time and energy they have committed to the cause.

As the conflict grows, it leaves the confines of the original parties and comes to the attention of regional, national, or international groups who may join the fray. At some point along this path, perceptions of the other get distorted as attribution biases and other forms of cognitive bias take hold. Nothing they say can be trusted, even proposals for resolution or new data that could undermine your group's position. As time passes and the problem grows unchecked, a sense of crisis emerges. Clearly something needs to be done. As the crisis grows to a fever pitch, actions that would have initially been seen as over the top are now on the table. Each side is willing to spend more than originally planned and compromise becomes unthinkable.

The goal of effective conflict management is to increase and improve communication across opposing groups, seek data jointly to avoid a battle of the experts from occurring, and bring in a facilitator or other process neutral early on, as necessary, to disrupt the cycle of escalation common in public disputes.

PUBLIC POLICY PROCESS AND BASIC CONCEPTS

Before we examine public dispute resolution processes in greater detail it is important to develop a shared understanding of the traditional process for public decision making. The first set of key concepts deals with laws, statutes, ordinances, rules, and regulations. Laws, statutes, and ordinances are passed by the legislative branches of government at the federal, state, and local levels that assign rights and responsibilities to various members and groups in society. The legislative branch creates these laws but it is up to the executive branch to see to the details of their implementation, which is accomplished via the bureaucracy through their administrative law powers. "**Administrative law** is the name given to agencies' rule making and resolution of conflicts regarding their rules" (Harrison, Harris, & Tolchin, 2009, p. 479). **Administrative rule making** is the "process by which upper-level bureaucrats use their administrative discretion and their expertise in the policy area to create rules, regulations, and standards that the bureaucracy will then enforce" (p. 480). In the United States, federal administrative law is codified as the Code of Federal Regulations. In essence, Congress passes laws and administrative agencies pass rules that allow them to put the laws into practice. For example, Congress may pass a law that requires workers to be safe from known and avoidable hazards in the workplace. But this is too vague for practical enforcement. Therefore, it would be the duty of the Occupational Safety and Health Administration (OSHA) to determine what specific actions employers would need to do (or refrain from doing) to ensure a safe workplace. For example, what safeguards need to be in place to ensure employees' safety within industrial chemical plants? Can restaurants allow smoking and create a safe environment for their food servers? OSHA would need to make specific regulations as necessary to meet the requirements of the law as set out by Congress. Additionally, agencies involved in administrative rule making have the authority to impose fines or criminal penalties on those individuals or groups who violate administrative rules. **Administrative adjudication** refers to the process by which agencies determine whether an individual or group is guilty of violating administrative rules (Harrison, Harris, & Tolchin, 2009). Citizens who believe an agency has not acted correctly in its application of the laws passed by Congress can file suit to force the agency to change its behavior and enforce its rules more or less stringently, depending on the court's ruling. For example, in 2007 several states successfully sued the EPA for its failure to fully implement the Clean Air Act.

The process for drafting new rules for executive agencies is laid out in various federal statutes, including the Administrative Procedure Act of 1946. This act requires nearly all federal agencies to publicize proposed rules in the *Federal Register*. State and local governments have generally adopted this practice as well, with more regional or local newspapers serving the same function as the *Federal Register*. This is the first official step to creating a new rule. Although variations among agencies exist, it is most common for the agency's staff to study the issue and issue a draft rule. Interested citizens, corporations, and civic groups have a specified period of time in which to respond with their comments, objections, or preferred alternatives. The agency is required to consider these comments and then issue a final rule that reflects the public interest. In general, there tends to be little change in the rule between the first issuance of the draft and the final rule. The most important time to influence the content of a rule is before the first draft is issued. Once a rule is finalized, the stakeholders who are negatively affected by the rule may seek to halt its implementation through the courts. For example, when the EPA considers regulating greenhouse gases or requiring increased fuel efficiency in cars, agency leaders know that powerful industries and civic groups on all sides of the issue are ready to challenge their action in the courts to argue they are overreaching the authority granted by Congress or they are not doing enough to protect the environment and public health. Proposed rule changes that affect the strongest interests may spend literally a decade or more in the courts, costing the parties tens or even hundreds of millions of dollars to fight. In the meantime, the public interest waits.

This expensive, slow, adversarial process of regulation is complicated by a couple of other important challenges that often work against the public interest. First, there is a revolving door between government agencies and many of the industries they regulate. The **revolving door** refers to the fact that government bureaucrats often leave their government careers behind and go to work for the agencies they used to regulate. Similarly, members of Congress often become lobbyists when they leave elected office. The powerful ties among industry, Congress, and government regulatory agencies mean that a relatively small, tight-knit group of powerful decision makers are usually involved in rule making within each agency's issue area. This reduces the number and variety of voices heard when important decisions are being made and increases the public's distrust of many decision-making processes. The revolving door can also lead to a concept called **agency capture**, which occurs when governmental regulatory agencies begin to advocate for the industries or interests they are supposed to regulate rather than objectively ensuring they adhere to all applicable laws and rules.

HISTORY OF ANTAGONISTIC RELATIONSHIPS BETWEEN REGULATORY AND REGULATED COMMUNITIES

The history of relationships between regulatory agencies and regulated communities swings wildly from periods of agency capture in which working relationships are too close and clear conflicts of interest are not publicly acknowledged to the other end of the spectrum in which there is an absence of trust and antagonistic relationships between both groups. Most commonly, members of industry view regulators warily, worried they are there to impede progress and profits by heavy-handed enforcement. Regulators are often viewed as traffic cops waiting to give fines for everyday behaviors. Civic groups representing workers, the environment, immigrants' rights, and other issues view agencies as unsympathetic and largely captured by the powerful interests they regulate. Among regulators and the regulated, there is often a cultural norm that assumes a distributive bargaining, zero-sum situation in which gains for one side can only come at the expense of the other. This mind-set is outdated and fails to adequately serve the interests of either side. Don't corporations and the EPA have a shared interest in avoiding unnecessary pollution and cleaning up any accidental spills quickly? Is it in the interest of OSHA to make US industries noncompetitive? To a large extent, regulators and those they regulate have many legitimately shared interests on which they can focus as a starting point for collaboration.

The beginning of public policy collaboration can be traced to various sources, with an interesting example coming from the Quincy Library Group. For fifteen years local environmentalists and loggers engaged in heated, often violent actions designed to thwart each other, which came to be known as the *timber wars*. When tree spiking, blockades, and other tactics led to a mutually hurting stalemate, a group of diverse stakeholders began meeting at the library in Quincy, California. The library proved to be a good place for these meetings because the parties could not raise their voices without facing ejection. In the early 1990s this group created a joint plan for logging the Lassen, Plumas, and parts of the Tahoe National Forests. Unfortunately, government officials had not been involved in the negotiations and decided not to abide by the group's agreement. In a show of unity, none of the timber companies put in bids to log the forests until the Department of Interior agreed to implement the plan created by the Quincy Library Group (Varettoni, 2005). Although the negotiations among the environmentalists, logging companies, and local and federal government agencies are an ongoing effort, with the expected ups and downs, this group is seen as one of the most notable early efforts to reach collaborative decisions that address the interests of all major stakeholders.

On a nationwide level, the EPA instituted mediation for Superfund disputes in the late 1980s. Superfund refers to cases occurring under the Comprehensive Environmental Response, Compensation, and Liability Act. Under this act, toxic and hazardous waste sites are cleaned up by the EPA and then those who contributed waste to that site are sent the bill. The EPA will usually send the bill to the company with the deepest pockets even if there are many other companies that also contributed waste to the site. Under the legal concept of joint and severable liability, the EPA can send the entire bill to any polluter as long as it can show that the polluter contributed some of the waste to the site. This led to waterfall litigation in which the company receiving the bill from EPA would, in turn, file suit against any and all additional companies potentially responsible for contributing waste to the site. In many cases, the litigation costs were equal to, double, or even triple the costs of the actual cleanup. This costly process led to the creation of a mediation program designed to negotiate settlement terms among as many of the potentially responsible parties as possible. By 1995, mediation was the most common process for dealing with these scientifically and economically complex cases (Raines & O'Leary, 2000). Successes in these tough cases led to the expansion of mediation, case evaluation, and other forms of ADR within the EPA and other federal agencies.

President Clinton passed the Administrative Dispute Resolution Act of 1996, which required each federal agency to create some sort of ADR program and track progress in the encouragement of ADR over litigation. This act allowed agencies to hire external neutrals such as mediators, arbitrators, and facilitators as well as training employees to conduct these services internally or in a shared neutrals program between agencies. Most agencies chose to implement workplace mediation programs and hire ombudsmen to deal with internal workplace disputes. The EPA created a variety of ADR programs to address disputes against potentially responsible parties (also known as *polluters*) who have been accused of violating agency regulations. A few other agencies also began experimenting with the use of ADR processes internally with employees, externally with regulated communities, or both. Once agency personnel and managers became familiar with the concepts and practices of ADR, the use of these processes slowly spread.

The state of ADR in US federal agencies continues to evolve. On November 28, 2005, Joshua Bolten, director of the Office of Management and Budget, and James Connaughton, chairman of the president's Council on Environmental Quality, issued a policy memorandum on environmental conflict resolution. "This joint policy statement directs agencies to increase the effective use of ECR and their institutional capacity for collaborative problem solving. It includes a definition of ECR and sets forth 'basic principles for agency engagement in environmental conflict resolution and collaborative problem solving'" (USIECR, nd-a). It also includes a compilation of mechanisms and strategies that may be used to achieve the stated policy objectives.

ENVIRONMENTAL AND PUBLIC POLICY CONFLICT RESOLUTION

Environmental conflict resolution (ECR) refers to people with differing views and interests working together in a systematic and organized way to find workable solutions to shared problems about environmental issues, usually with the assistance of a neutral third party. These same procedures and processes can be used for environmental and nonenvironmental cases of decision making but environmental agencies have led the way in designing, evaluating, and promoting the use of these processes so the most common term used to describe them has become *environment and public policy conflict resolution (E/PP)*. A government agency has been created to promote the use of these processes, called the US Institute for Environmental Conflict Resolution (USIECR), in Tucson, Arizona. Their website includes a host of examples for which ECR processes have been used:

- Managing public lands for people to use and enjoy in different ways, such as planning how a national forest can serve future needs for watershed protection, timber harvesting, and recreation

- Natural resources disputes, for instance, fairly allocating rights to use water, timber, or mineral resources

- Conflicts over facilities siting, such as where to locate highways, dams, power lines, or wind farms

- Protected area disagreements, for example, managing recreational uses while still protecting a sensitive natural area in a park

- Endangered species issues, for instance, how to implement protective actions that are required to prevent the extinction of a species
- Federal and tribal government relations, such as how to respect tribal sovereignty and protect sacred sites when planning or implementing projects
- Disputes related to pollution, for instance, how to best implement air, water, or soil contamination cleanup activities.

In addition to these examples from the environmental arena, similar processes have been used to draft new statewide policies: for dealing with mentally ill people who come into contact with the criminal justice system, to make decisions about the allocation of tax dollars on educational infrastructure spending, for the design and construction of megaprojects such as bridges and airports, to design a new rule related to interstate highway access management (such as where to place on- and off-ramps), and to make decisions about which schools to close because of a shrinking youth population. When decisions must be made on scientifically and economically complicated matters, having more experts at the table can increase the quality of the outcome — especially when viewpoints from the public, private, and nonprofit sectors are all represented. Decisions made through consensus and collaboration are also likely to encounter fewer snags on implementation (Raines, 2002). When problems occur during the implementation stage, which they nearly always do, the relationships built between the parties makes it easier for them to work together to solve problems rather than focusing on accusations and blame (Anderson & Polkinghorn, 2008). In fact, research has shown that parties have increased their negotiation and collaboration skills as a result of participation in these collaborative processes as well as building trust among private stakeholders, government regulators, and civic groups (Raines & Kubala, 2011).

E/PP processes are a good choice when no single stakeholder group can resolve the problem on its own, when the outcome is genuinely in doubt, when all major parties are willing and able to participate, and when the issue is considered important to all major stakeholders (www.ecr.gov). ECR processes are not likely to work when one or more parties believe they have a quicker, more surefire method for accomplishing their goals, such as a public relations campaign in the media or a court case. It also is unlikely to work if one or more of the major stakeholders will not acknowledge the existence of the problem or participate in the process. It is crucial for all major stakeholders to be represented at the negotiating table because the absence of any major group means that one or more types of interest will not be heard or considered during the discussions. For example, what if new regulations were made to address pollution and safety concerns on offshore oil rigs but only the oil companies and the EPA were present? In the absence of input from environmental groups or worker safety organizations, it might appear as if an inappropriate amount of influence had been exerted by the oil company interests. Such a decision would be more likely to be challenged in court and might not adequately reflect the needs of all the groups affected by the regulations. Getting all stakeholder groups to the table is crucial to the perception of legitimacy and the efficacy of the outcome.

Politicians are some of the most enthusiastic supporters of collaborative processes for complicated public decisions for this reason: when groups are aligned on all sides of an issue, then politicians risk alienating a significant proportion of their constituency no matter what decision they make. By delegating decision-making authority to a group of representative stakeholders, including government agencies, politicians can claim that the outcome was reached democratically, transparently, and that everyone had an equal chance to influence that outcome. In fact, decisions reached through collaborative processes nearly always produce more support from the participating stakeholders than decisions reached unilaterally by regulatory agencies, thereby being a politically safer route in many cases.

Other stakeholders, including government agencies and civic groups, typically voice more satisfaction with decisions made through collaboration as well (Raines & Kubala, 2011). Studies of more than forty-eight environmental conflict resolution efforts in the western United States found that 87 percent would recommend a collaborative process to others and only 7 percent would not, 77 percent indicated the collaborative process resulted in more effective and durable outcomes compared with a traditional decision-making process, 96 percent of participants understood the terms of the agreement reached, 100 percent felt the agreements addressed parties' interests more than the traditional process, 100 percent felt all legal requirements were addressed in the agreement, and 100 percent felt that the agreement took advantage of all available information relevant to the issues under discussion (Raines & Kubala, 2011). In a study of water collaboration efforts in metro Atlanta and north Georgia, 100 percent of participants agreed that their knowledge of the water resource was increased through the collaborative process. About 71 percent of the participants agreed that relationships between regulators and regulated organizations had improved as a result of collaboration. Beierle and Cayford (2002) examined 239 cases of environmental decision making, taking into account the five goals typically exhibited by these processes: (1) addressing public values, (2) improving decision quality, (3) incorporating conflict resolution tools, (4) building trust between institutions and groups, and (5) addressing public education on the issues under negotiation. The authors found that these five goals were better addressed through collaborative processes but that more progress could be achieved by spreading the outreach and trust building beyond the core group of participants. Getting all stakeholder groups involved is key. Even more so, it is critical to help stakeholder groups inform and educate their individual members across the community. Only then will these processes fully achieve their potential to transform public consciousness on policy matters as well as increasingly empower members of a democratic society.

Yet these processes are not universally popular. They are time consuming and occasionally frustrating. Sipe and Stiftel (1995) found that the median cost savings for mediation compared to court action for the respondents (the parties accused of polluting) was approximately $150,000 per case. Multiple studies show that collaboration may take more time up front than traditional decision-making processes. Collaborative processes require parties to listen to the ideas and opinions of those with whom they disagree, and to seek out common ground. In the study by Raines and Kubala (2011), only 12 percent of the water managers studied felt that they were not fully heard during the process. Although further study is required, initial findings indicate that those with more extreme views on either side of the issue are given less attention in collaborative processes out of a desire to find common ground and the evolution of shared norms and values that tend to emerge over time. In some ways, this is an understudied and underacknowledged benefit of these processes; they force parties to become more moderate and those who refuse to "play nice" cannot grandstand the way they can during traditional public meetings. According to the USIECR, "Sometimes there is resistance simply because of a lack of familiarity with ECR and how it works. The time and costs associated with ECR can also cause resistance. Other factors include fear of losing control over a process. For example, when one party has responsibility for a situation or issue, the party may not be willing to allow others to influence its decision making" (www.ecr.gov/Basics/FAQs.aspx). Sponsoring an ECR or other public policy collaborative process takes time and resources for the sponsoring agency. Even if these resources may be less than the regular process, they tend to be more up front and require one person to take a lead role to manage the agency's participation. When no one comes forward to take the lead on these initiatives, they often founder.

There are some important ways in which environmental and public policy conflict resolution differ from employment disputes or customer conflicts discussed already in this book. First and foremost, these processes involve more people than a typical workplace mediation or resolution process. Depending on the issue, there can be anywhere from five to literally hundreds of stakeholders who seek to participate in meetings and negotiations. Second, because of the numbers of stakeholders affected by the issue, most stakeholder groups appoint one or more representatives to attend meetings and funnel back the issues raised and generate or review proposals. In other words, the negotiators are representatives of much larger constituencies. This means negotiations are occurring on at least two levels: within each stakeholder group the individual parties must seek to reach consensus as to the positions and interests of the group itself and then the representative of that group will negotiate with the other representatives within the E/PP process itself. It is not uncommon for stakeholder groups to bicker internally or even fracture into multiple groups when they cannot reach an internal consensus. Stakeholder representatives must work hard throughout the process to keep their constituencies informed of the ongoing negotiations. They must clarify the limits of their settlement authority so as not to commit their group to a position that the membership will not support. Facilitators, mediators, or other neutral third parties may need to visit with these stakeholder groups to assist them with their intragroup negotiations before convening the broader group of stakeholders for negotiations. Because some of the participants will be volunteers, it may be a struggle to find the resources necessary to secure their full participation. The EPA has recognized this as a challenge and developed some funds to assist civic and tribal groups to participate in collaborative processes.

Third, these negotiations can literally last years. For some of these initiatives, the goal is to negotiate an agreement and then disband. For others, the mission involves permanent ongoing negotiations and decision making surrounding a shared resource, such as shared waters from a common river. A representative for a governmental agency may retire only to go to work for one of the agencies that she previously regulated or join a civic group working on the same issue. Because relationships between stakeholders may span years or entire careers, it is helpful to build in time for relationship building, recognition of individual and shared milestones, and other traditions that help to bond the group together and build camaraderie.

Fourth, unlike most types of disputes, public decisions typically involve highly complex and technical matters, yet the stakeholders vary widely in their educational backgrounds and levels of knowledge. In a meeting on climate change you might see a citizen with a high-school education sitting next to a PhD in meteorology, who sits next to someone from the Department of Defense. Each organization has its own jargon and subject-matter-specific knowledge. It is the role of the neutral to help create a shared level of knowledge in the room and ask all participants to define terms, avoid jargon, and share information.

Fifth, the diversity in stakeholder roles means that some representatives are accountable to voters directly through election (the politicians) or indirectly as employees of a government agency who can be dismissed for overstepping their authority or inadequately safeguarding the public interest. However, some stakeholders represent small civic groups or their own interests as farmers, business owners, parents, residents, and so on. Corporations send lawyers, managers, scientists, or professional negotiators to the collaborative process to further their organization's interests. Many of the advocates are experts on the issue at hand, having advanced degrees in science, policy making, or other related specialized knowledge. However, you will encounter regular citizens with no specialized expertise who participate as representatives of a neighborhood or nonprofit group. The use of jargon, acronyms, and incorrect assumptions about shared knowledge makes these meeting unwieldy. Discussions on technical matters may engage only 20 percent of the attendees and others are baffled and unable to follow the discussions. Sometimes this happens even to the facilitator! Therefore, it becomes important to consider the utility of beginning this kind of collaborative process with some sharing of basic information that will be foundational to the productivity of subsequent discussions. Some of this presentation will focus on the technical terms and issues under debate, and basic skills or concepts related to collaborative decision making may also be covered. The facilitator or lead government agencies may decide to create a list of definitions and acronyms that parties can refer to throughout the process as well as an organizational chart or other tool that clarifies the roles for each public organization represented at the table. Unequal levels of accountability raise thorny issues about the democratic nature of these processes. Some believe them to be more democratic due to the fact that citizens can participate and directly represent their interests and others find the lack of accountability counter to the goals of representative democracy. For these reasons, environmental and public policy decision-making processes are significantly different and likely more complex than the conflicts experienced by managers within their own organizations or between their organizations and customers or vendors.

PROCESS MENU OPTIONS

Since the 1980s a plethora of processes have sprung up to meet the demand for greater stakeholder participation in public policy decision making. Ideally, the process chosen should be tailored to the needs of the parties and the issue under discussion. Indeed, some governmental agencies have become adept at matching the process to the dispute. In others, one or two processes have become the default methods for managing collaboration out of a belief that these processes are well-suited to the types of decisions made by a particular agency and the desire to avoid the transaction costs inherent in designing new processes with each dispute. Reinventing the wheel is not something agencies have time for, so they rely on practices and procedures previously used by their agency or similar agencies. It is helpful to provide the general outline of some of the most commonly used processes for environmental and public policy decision making. When these processes are applied to individual cases, they are likely to vary a bit in the details of their application. In some E/PP cases, the process of collaboration is broken down into phases, with the first phase consisting of an assessment of the conflict to determine which process, if any, is best suited to the dispute as well as to better understand who the parties are, learn more about their interests, and gauge their willingness to take part in a collaborative process.

Conflict assessment helps to identify the issues in controversy in a given situation, the affected interests, and the appropriate form(s) of conflict resolution. The assessment process typically involves conferring with potentially interested persons regarding a situation involving conflict in order to assess the causes of the conflict, identify the entities and individuals who would be substantively affected by the conflict's outcome, assess those persons' interests and identify a preliminary set of issues that they believe are relevant, evaluate the feasibility of using a consensus-building or other collaborative process to address these issues, educate interested parties on consensus and collaborative processes to help them think through whether they would wish to participate, and design the structure and membership of a negotiating committee or other collaborative process (if any) to address the conflict (USIECR, nd-b).

Case evaluation and neutral evaluation is a process in which a neutral expert is hired to evaluate the strengths and weaknesses of each side's case and predict for the parties what would happen in court. If the parties are unable to reach agreement during the evaluation session, the neutral evaluator may offer an impartial nonbinding opinion as to the settlement value of the case. If both parties agree, the evaluator's opinion may become binding.

Collaborative monitoring seeks to engage interested and affected stakeholders, public agencies, and scientific and technical experts in a more direct fashion to jointly gather data and information in an ongoing manner. This helps avoid the tendency for each group to gather information on its own that supports its own preferred outcomes. Participants in collaborative monitoring may play a variety of roles: determining target outcomes, defining criteria and indicators to monitor those outcomes, determining the appropriate system for monitoring, participating in the data gathering and analysis, and interpreting the data over time. Collaborative monitoring is being implemented in a variety of program contexts and it has been conducted within many different structural settings.

Consensus building describes a number of collaborative decision-making techniques in which a facilitator or mediator is used to assist diverse or competing interest groups to reach agreement on policy matters, environmental conflicts, or other issues of controversy affecting a large number of people. Consensus building processes are typically used to foster dialogue, clarify areas of agreement and disagreement, improve the information on which a decision may be based, and resolve controversial issues in ways that all interests find acceptable. Consensus building typically involves structured (yet relatively informal), face-to-face interaction among representatives of stakeholder groups with a goal of gaining early participation from affected interests with differing viewpoints, producing sound policies with a wide range of support, and reducing the likelihood of subsequent disagreements or legal challenges.

Dispute systems design (DSD) is a process for assisting an organization to develop a structure for handling a series of similar recurring or anticipated disputes (such as environmental enforcement cases or EEOC complaints within a federal agency) more effectively. A dispute systems designer typically proceeds by interviewing representatives of interested or affected groups (including people in the agency) about their perceptions and interests; analyzing the organization's existing system for handling these conflicts; designing and implementing conflict management or dispute resolution procedures that encourage early, informal resolution of conflicts; and perhaps evaluating the impact of these new dispute resolution procedures to ensure their effectiveness.

In public policy decision-making processes, facilitation is a collaborative process in which a neutral seeks to assist a group of individuals or other parties to constructively discuss a number of complex, potentially controversial issues. The facilitator typically works with participants before and during these discussions to ensure that appropriate persons are at the table, help the parties set ground rules and agendas, enforce both, assist parties to communicate effectively, and help the participants keep on track in working toward their goals. Although facilitation bears many similarities to mediation, the neutral in a facilitation process (the facilitator) usually plays a less active role than a mediator and, unlike a mediator, often does not see resolution as a goal of his or her work. Facilitation may be used in any number of situations where parties of diverse interests or experiences participate in discussions ranging from scientific seminars, board meetings, and management meetings to public forums.

Joint fact finding is a process by which interested parties commit to building a mutual understanding of disputed scientific or technical information. Interested parties can select their own experts who presumably reflect differing interpretations of available information. Alternatively, they can also jointly decide on an unassociated third-party expert or a panel of experts. This process is similar to case evaluation yet different in that the fact finder does not make recommendations as to how the facts should be used as a settlement tool by the parties. A facilitator or mediator works to clarify and define areas of agreement, disagreement, and uncertainty. The facilitator or mediator can coach the experts to translate technical information into a form that is understandable to all interested parties. The goal is to avoid adversarial or partisan science in which competing experts magnify small differences rather than focusing on points of agreement and creating a strategy to provide for a joint conclusion.

Mediation has been defined and discussed at length previously. When applied to environmental and public policy processes, mediation refers to facilitated negotiation in which a skilled, impartial third party seeks to enhance negotiations between parties in a conflict or their representatives by improving communication, identifying interests, and exploring possibilities for a mutually agreeable resolution. The disputants remain responsible for negotiating a settlement and the mediator lacks power to impose any solution; the mediator's role is to assist the process in ways acceptable to the parties.

Negotiated rule making (also called *regulatory negotiation* or *reg-neg*) is a multiparty consensus process in which a balanced negotiating committee seeks to reach agreement on the substance of a proposed agency rule, policy, or standard. The negotiating committee is composed of representatives of those groups that will be affected by or have an interest in the rule, including the rule-making agency itself. Affected interests that are represented in the negotiations are expected to abide by any resulting agreement and implement its terms. This agreement-seeking process usually occurs only after a thorough conflict assessment has been conducted and is generally undertaken with the assistance of a skilled, neutral mediator or facilitator.

Policy dialogues are processes that bring together representatives of groups with divergent views or interests to tap the collective views of participants in the process. The goals include opening up discussion, improving communication and mutual understanding, exploring the issues of controversy to see if participants' different viewpoints can be distilled into general recommendations, and trying to reach agreement on a proposed policy standard or guidelines to be recommended by government. They are often used to address complex environmental conflicts or public policy disputes constructively. Unlike processes that explicitly seek to obtain consensus (such as negotiated rule making or mediation), policy dialogues usually do not seek to achieve a full, specific agreement that would bind all participating interests. Rather, participants in a policy dialogue may seek to assess the potential for developing a full consensus resolution at some later time or may put forward general, nonbinding recommendations or broad policy preferences for an agency (or other governmental entity) to consider in its subsequent decision making. Policy dialogues can take the form of town hall meetings or many other forms and can include relatively small groups of five to ten key stakeholders or can grow to include hundreds of participants.

Advances in technology have led to new efforts to reinvigorate public debate on complex policy issues through the use of deliberative democracy and related processes. Public deliberation is central to legitimate lawmaking in democracies. Deliberative democracy refers to a process of public decision making that uses consensus decision making as well as elements of majority rule, particularly when a full consensus cannot be achieved. Although deliberative democracy processes vary, they generally include groups of citizens coming together to learn more about a particular public policy issue or problem and to discuss or create options for addressing the problem at hand. Through the use of instant voting via iPads, laptops, and handheld devices, small discussion groups can share their ideas or votes with larger groups as they work toward consensus. AmericaSpeaks (www.americaspeaks.org) has used these techniques to hold deliberative democracy gatherings on topics ranging from what to do with Ground Zero to municipal budgetary decisions, health care reform, disaster recovery planning, and climate change.

PUBLIC-PRIVATE PARTNERING: BEST PRACTICES

Multimillion or billion dollar construction projects have historically been a cash cow for litigators. When one subcontractor makes a mistake or runs behind, it causes challenges for all the other subcontractors whose own work was dependent on the successful completion of the phase coming before their own. In 1987, the Construction Industry Institute at Texas A&M University created a task force focused on finding new ways to prevent and effectively manage construction disputes in the hope of breaking the increasing cycle of litigation and counterlitigation that was plaguing the industry and driving up the costs of construction. The process created by the task force came to be known as *partnering*, which is defined as a long-term commitment between two or more organizations for the purpose of achieving specific business objectives by maximizing the effectiveness of each participant's resources (Anderson & Polkinghorn, 2008). Partnering relationships must be based on trust, a focus on common goals, and an understanding of each party's expectations and values. The task force subsequently issued guidelines for the implementation of partnering in construction projects, which included provisions for the management of disputes. Successful partnering requires frequent communication, relationship building between individuals and organizations, a focus on problem solving rather than blame casting, and proactive collaborative processes that involve stakeholders at every step of the process, from planning to construction and evaluation. The following box lists the key leadership insights that help to ensure successful partnering projects. Nearly all of these insights apply to collaboration between large stakeholder groups outside as well as inside the construction industry.

Key Leadership Insights for Partnering

1. Establish and maintain public trust.

2. Prevent counterproductive behaviors.

3. Keep senior management informed.

4. Make decisions to increase bid competition.

5. Make friends with key stakeholders.

6. The manager is not the smartest about everything.

7. Recognize showstoppers early and take action.

8. Step outside the box.

9. There will be technical problems.

10. We all succeed together.

Source: Anderson and Polkinghorn (2008, p. 176).

These insights warrant further elaboration. Although insight one may appear obvious, it is a relatively common industry practice to lowball bids on public contracts. Once the contract is awarded, contractors may come up with a host of reasons for asking for increases in the original bid price (such as bad weather, price increases for needed commodities, and so on). They typically also provide reasons for failures to meet targeted completion dates. Therefore, to build and keep trust, partners need to create reasonable expectations and be completely honest in the original contracted promises so as to avoid later losses of trust. Transparency is key to building and maintaining trust. The lowest bid should not always be awarded the contract. Firm reputation and realism within the bid must be taken into consideration. With the public, those who will be affected by a decision need to have their concerns heard early and often. When possible, accommodations should be made to make the construction process less inconvenient to neighbors.

Insight two refers to problematic behaviors sometimes exhibited by individuals that make the team's success harder to achieve: insisting on having the last word, inability to admit mistakes and seek help, desires to settle scores or seek retaliation when another stakeholder makes a mistake, and taking things personally rather than remembering that this is business. This would be close to the principle espoused in *Getting to Yes* (Fisher & Ury, 1981), which advises parties to attack the problem, not the person. The third lesson requires that all parties be clear as to which decisions can be made at the lowest level and which require input and authority from higher up the chain of command. When peers in collaboration cannot reach agreement on a decision, then in a short period of time the decision gets elevated to the next highest level of decision making. They agree to abide by any decision made higher up the chain, with no hard feelings. When decisions are made higher up the chain, it is crucial that those decisions be communicated and explained to those lower on the chain, thereby closing the loop. Anderson and Polkinghorn's (2008) work shows that a common failure in partnering lies in the communication up and down the chain of command, with distrust resulting.

Insight four applies to nearly all government agencies and corporations that put projects out to bid. By breaking huge projects into manageable pieces, bid competition is increased as well as the ability to choose contractors with specialized abilities. When enormous, multipart projects are put out as one bid, the contracting agency loses control over who does the work because much of the work will be accomplished through the subcontracting process. By purposefully creating interdependence among successful bidders, the sponsor is able to build in collaboration, enhance creativity, and produce better outcomes. It also means more eyes on the work being done at each phase of the project in order to catch mistakes early on, when it is still possible to address them at a reduced cost.

Insight five is not as intuitive as it seems. Rather than cultivate superficial relationships through the use of cocktail parties and meet and greets, the goal is to build strong relationships between key stakeholders before any problems or crises emerge. The rapport built between parties provides a deep well of support when problems invariably arise so that parties can focus on joint problem solving rather than blame casting and seeking cover for themselves. During multiyear collaborations, as is common in the public policy arena, it is important to recognize milestones in the project and in individual careers. Celebrating retirements, project anniversaries, and other ceremonial occasions allows parties to know each other as people rather than only as functionaries; such celebrations and milestones should not be underacknowledged. When technical problems arise, as they surely will at some stage (insight nine), it is easier to normalize them and proactively work together once trust and rapport between parties has been built.

Insight six addresses a key assumption underlying this entire book: managers who seek out employees' knowledge, expertise, and ideas will be more effective, more respected, and responsive. In addition to reaping the knowledge of one's employee base, it is important to include the abilities of outside experts as needed: technical experts to give occasional advice, public relations specialists to help publicize success and gather public opinion, and coaches or mediators to help solve problems that arise. Asking for input and assistance when needed models the behaviors we seek in our employees as well and should be acknowledged. Otherwise, employees may act in the absence of correct information and make costly mistakes.

Insight seven has important implications for all large-group conflict resolution processes. "One essential characteristic of megaproject leadership is the combination of vigilance for trouble and propensity for action. Paying attention to potential problems by encouraging everyone to focus on 'surprises as opportunities to learn' is a hallmark of early warning systems that has been honed to a fine art through this project" (Anderson & Polkinghorn, 2008, p. 185). When problems arise, rather than taking defensive action to build a case against the others, the goal in partnering is to engage in creative problem solving in order to minimize the cost and disruption caused by the inevitable problems and rely on strong relationships and trust to avoid counterproductive behaviors. This is closely related to insight eight (step outside of the box). When problems arise or are anticipated, decision makers need to engage in joint brainstorming to consider all possible venues for proactive conflict resolution and problem solving. This may include going to influential community members in advance to discuss potential disruptions or hear their concerns. It may include experimenting with new methods or materials as makes sense to all involved. Many large organizations, whether public or private, get hamstrung by the idea that we have never done that before. This should never be a reason to avoid trying something new that seems to make sense. Do not be afraid to blaze new trails within your organization. The red tape involved in doing something new may seem daunting but if your organization is unable to consider new ways of doing things, it will stagnate as its competitors continue to evolve and adapt to rapid change.

The final insight involves sharing recognition for successes throughout the partnering organizations during the project rather than only at the end. It also requires an acknowledgment that one stakeholder's loss or gain affects all the other stakeholders involved in the partnering project. What if one of the contractors suffers a loss? For example, suppose the company's leader encounters health problems and is out of work for six months. Rather than allow the whole project to fall behind, with cascading effects for everyone, the other parties should jointly strive to share the workload until he returns. Or, suppose the price of steel drops, leading to significantly increased profits for one of the partners. That partner may choose to share some of that unexpected gain with others whose commodity prices increased, thereby threatening their ability to continue in the project. Through collaborating in innovative ways, partners are able to take the long view and act in ways that will keep their organization's reputation and future prospects strong.

Finally, partnering and collaboration have been shown to improve significantly the communication and conflict resolution skills of the managers involved, thereby empowering them to succeed on other future endeavors (Anderson & Polkinghorn, 2008; Raines & Kubala, 2011). "Without much fanfare, conflict intervention practice has moved into highly specialized public and private arenas as industry insiders incorporate basic conflict resolution skills into their occupational skill sets" (Anderson & Polkinghorn, 2008, p. 167). The increased use of conflict management skills and processes by managers within public and private organizations is a testament to their utility in saving time, money, and angst for those seeking to simply get their jobs done.

COMMON ERRORS IN COLLABORATION: A CAUTIONARY TALE

When done well, the techniques of environmental and public policy conflict resolution can result in superior outcomes to complex problems. However, there are some key pitfalls to avoid in order to ensure that ECR techniques result in positive rather than negative outcomes.

Mistake One: Asking for Opinions and Collaboration When Your Organization Does Not Really Want Them

One of the most frequent mistakes made by organizations occurs when they invite stakeholder input on pending decisions and then disregard that input because the answer they got was not what they anticipated. Sometimes organizational leaders want to appear open to participation from the public or affected stakeholders when they really are not. A great example of this comes from the School Board of Cobb County, Georgia. The board adopted a new school calendar called a *balanced calendar*, which included one week off in September and one week off in February, in return for a shorter summer vacation. They did this for a few reasons: parents were taking their kids out of school to take advantage of low-season rates on cruises, flights, and vacations, thereby increasing absenteeism; long summers are associated with reduced retention of learned material by students; and these breaks would allow school administrators to take their vacations when the students are out of class, making their vacation time less burdensome on the schools.

Although some parents initially found the calendar odd, after the first year of this schedule the majority of parents and school district employees seemed to like it. The board promised they would keep this schedule in place for three years and then reassess whether to make the change permanent or not. Then, an election was held and some new members were elected to the school board. These members had voiced disapproval of the new calendar during their election campaigns and promised voters they would push for a return to the traditional school calendar. Before making any final decision, the board opted to conduct an online survey of parents, teachers, and administrators in the district. Surprisingly, 71 percent voiced their preference for the balanced calendar.

Within one month, the board voted to disregard the online survey results and reinstate the traditional school calendar. This caused public outrage on the part of many parents and school staff. Groups formed for and against the balanced calendar, with many parents and teachers for it and local summertime businesses (such as the local water park and theme parks, employers of teenage summer labor) against it. Each group took their complaints to the newspapers and received local television coverage. None felt the process was fair, transparent, or met their needs. First and foremost, the majority of stakeholders felt their voices were not heard. "Why would they ask us what we think and then totally ignore it?!" Many parents and teachers had already booked fall vacations during the September break that had been promised because the balanced calendar was to be in place for three years but was actually only in place for one year. To make matters worse, members of the board were fighting among each other, with the old members supporting the balanced calendar and the new members adamantly preferring the traditional calendar. There were accusations between the old and new board members that the new members had met in secret to plan their strategy for regaining the traditional calendar, a meeting that perhaps ran afoul of the open meeting requirements for school boards in Georgia (Fowler, 2011). It did not take long before parents were complaining to the regional accreditation agency citing poor communication between the board and parents as well as a failure to follow appropriate procedures. According to the *Atlanta Journal-Constitution*, "Hundreds of parents have sent letters asking the agency [SACS, the Southern

Association of Colleges and Schools] to investigate the board's governance practices. They accused board members of making decisions with a four-person majority rather than a consensus approach" (Sarrio, 2011, para. 10). The same article explains that "SACS will review the complaints before deciding whether to launch an investigation into governance issues. An accreditation loss can impact scholarship money, federal funding, college acceptances, property values and pre-kindergarten funding." The state's attorney general has received complaints regarding alleged violations of Georgia's open meetings laws (sunshine laws), and even some of the board members are unclear as to whether secret meetings had occurred (Fowler, 2011).

The lesson here is that decision-making processes must be transparent and adhere to the principles of procedural justice. If stakeholders are asked for their opinion, the extent to which that opinion will influence the outcome of policy should be clarified in advance. If the public's opinion will be advisory only, then those in power need to clarify their intent to retain decision-making power. In the case of the Cobb County School Board, it *appears* that public input and collaboration was sought, with the assumption that it would bolster the board's preexisting preferred outcome. When it did not, the board disregarded that opinion at great cost to its own legitimacy. It is acceptable that an elected or appointed board retain full decision-making power without seeking input from stakeholders but the intent to do so should be clear.

Mistake Two: Not Allowing Enough Time, Space, and Money to Support Collaboration

When collaborative public decision making fails, it is often because the sponsors did not adequately prepare participants for the length of time and depth of participation that would be necessary to make it work. Unilateral administrative decisions are generally quicker than those achieved through collaborative processes. When stakeholders gather to share information and perspectives on a policy issue, it takes time to hear from all the affected interests, to gather the high-quality information needed for a comprehensive solution, and to engage in negotiations with the help of a facilitator or other neutral. The meetings necessary to accomplish these tasks may take weeks, months, or even years, depending on the nature of the decision at hand and whether this is a one-time decision or an ongoing collaborative decision-making process. These efforts usually kick off with much fanfare but can run out of funds to support collaboration, such as to pay the neutrals, gather and assess data, and write reports (Raines & Kubala, 2011). Collaboration fatigue can occur when parties sense that discussions are endless and decisions are few and far between. To counteract this tendency, collaboration efforts should include clear milestones within the project to recognize and assess progress toward deadlines. An open-ended process without timelines can indeed encourage lots of talk and little progress. Timelines and deliverables should be one of the first issues discussed and agreed on by the stakeholders and sponsors. Sponsors and neutrals need to be on the lookout for meetings with dwindling attendance as a sign that progress is not coming fast enough and efforts toward progress require invigoration. Otherwise, groups drop out in the middle of the process when the hardest work occurs, only to reappear near the end in order to voice disapproval for the consensus reached by those who stuck around for the hard work! Gathering and keeping stakeholders involved in an efficient and effectual process is key, as is cultivating reasonable expectations from the outset. Collaboration takes time, money, and energy from all involved.

Mistake Three: Proceeding in the Absence of Key Stakeholders

Imagine your organization is charged with the siting of a new municipal garbage dump. You know there will be strong opinions as to where the dump should or should not go. Your agency already has a place in mind. You decide to hold a stakeholder discussion forum so as to better understand the concerns of the community members and affected groups. You hold this meeting at 10:00 AM on a Wednesday at city hall and only two people turn out, both of whom work for the contractor that will be doing the work on site. How should you proceed? Issues such as this one typically bring NIMBY (not in my back yard) issues to the fore. Yet those most affected may be least likely to show up at 10:00 AM on a Wednesday. Making decisions in the absence of key stakeholders leads to accusation of bias in the decision-making process. In any collaborative process the stakeholders most likely to participate are those who can do so as part of their regular job duties—city planners, water treatment plant managers, and paid staff of civic or environmental groups. Local citizens, small business owners, and volunteers for civic groups are least likely to attend because they are forgoing income in order to take time off of work to attend. In these cases, meetings may need to occur in the evenings or on weekends. Sponsoring agencies may need to find grant money to help subsidize the participation of key stakeholders. In some cases, collaboration is simply not possible due to the absence of key groups. Continuing with a process that is clearly not representative of all major interests may be worse than having no collaboration at all. A needs assessment should be done near the beginning of the process so that these issues can be fleshed out before any decisions are made about whether to proceed with collaboration.

CONCLUSION

The good news is that the use of collaborative processes is becoming more common in the public policy arena. Traditional ADR processes such as mediation and facilitation are supplemented by policy dialogues, negotiated rule making, partnering, and many others. These processes typically bring stakeholders, including regular citizens, together to share their ideas, concerns, and knowledge in the hope of reaching sound, implementable, and sustainable decisions. Governmental and nongovernmental organizations are springing up to provide support for these efforts in the hope that our increasingly complex world will be better managed through these collaborations.

ELISE AT MAIN STREET BAKERIES

During the teleconference, Elise learned that the FDA had wanted to gather opinions as to the creation of a new rule on nutritional labeling. The sponsoring administrator at the FDA said his agency needed more information on the financial impact of any new rule on businesses of various sizes and types as well as information on timelines for implementation and the details that would be included in any new rule. The agency's goal was to give consumers better information and create the least burdensome regulations possible for businesses. In the end, the agency issued a draft rule based on the input it received from this stakeholder group but it wanted to see whether or not some consensus was possible between affected stakeholders about what the rule should include or exclude. After learning more about this process, Elise agreed to participate in meetings with other stakeholders that would be held in person for one whole day each month as well as teleconference for four hours each month for six months. Each participant agreed to study the financial impact of various different rule proposals and funnel that information back to the larger group. Professional facilitators called or met with individual stakeholders throughout the process to gather and prepare information for presentation and discussion at the monthly meetings.

At the end of the six months, the group agreed on language for the new rule as well as a twelve-month implementation timeline so that kitchens, packaging, menu, and other changes could be made by affected businesses. The group presented its recommendations to the FDA and the FDA agreed to issue these recommendations as the draft rule. Although these negotiations took Elise away from other activities, she felt less threatened by the changes and even saw them as a potential marketing advantage for her business. Of course, she was at times frustrated to listen to the views of other stakeholders whose motives were in some ways antithetical to her own, such as selling junk foods and advertising items as "food for real men" or "'pie crust with lard, just like grandma made it." In the end, customers grew to know more about the food they were consuming and Main Street Bakeries was able to comply with these changes without any significant long-term costs to the company. Elise also made some important networking contacts with other businesses and regulators. She felt more in control and less at the mercy of government dictates. If given the opportunity, she would definitely participate in this kind of process again.

KEY TERMS

Administrative adjudication

Administrative law

Administrative rule making

Agency capture

Collaborative monitoring

Collaborative public management

Conflict assessment

Consensus building

Environmental and public policy conflict resolution (E/PP)

Environmental conflict resolution (ECR)

Joint fact finding

Negotiated rule making

Partnering

Policy dialogues

Public disputes

Revolving door

Sunshine laws

SUGGESTED SUPPLEMENTAL READING

Quinn, C. (2012). Changes to licensing proposed for half-million Georgians. *Atlanta Journal-Constitution*, February 21.

INTERNET RESOURCES

AmericaSpeaks: www.americaspeaks.org

Collaborative Decision Resources: http://www.mediate.org/

Mediate.com: http://www.mediate.com/

Policy Consensus Initiative: http://www.policyconsensus.org/

US Institute for Environmental Conflict Resolution: www.ecr.gov

DISCUSSION QUESTIONS

1. Which governmental agencies regulate your company or organization? What does your organization do to work smoothly with them?

2. If you work for a regulatory agency, what steps are taken to encourage collaborative and mutually beneficial relationships with the organizations you regulate and other stakeholders?

EXERCISES

1. Scan the newspaper or Internet to find a contemporary public dispute. Who are the parties? What are their interests, positions, and BATNAs? Where does the dispute fall on the spiral of unmanaged conflict?

2. Using the story about the Cobb County School Board, explain the ways in which this conflict follows the spiral of unmanaged conflict. Analyze a local conflict in comparison with this spiral as well.

3. Attend a public meeting or other large-group decision-making process (e.g., in a religious organization, corporation, and so on). Map out the process for decision making as it was demonstrated at the meeting. Was there place for public or stakeholder participation? Were decisions made by vote, consensus, or something in between? Were all stakeholders heard or able to share their concerns? Who was the final decision maker?

GOAL SETTING

If you work for a private company or nonprofit, make a list of those regulatory agencies that have the most impact on your organization. If your organization depends on these agencies for funding, licensing, or has other repeated interactions, make a point of getting to know at least one point of contact within that (those) agencies. These connections can be useful when any problems or questions arise and will allow you to be proactive in the management of this relationship.

chapter TWELVE

Designing and Facilitating Effective Large-Group Processes

Learning Objectives

- Explain the steps necessary to successfully convene and facilitate a large-group decision-making process.

- Describe the common skills and techniques used by large-group facilitators.

- Describe the ways in which the media can be either an asset or a liability in large-group decision-making processes.

- Demonstrate an understanding of the benefits of various meeting formats and when and how to apply them.

- Describe and perform the tasks of a successful facilitator.

JOHN AT THE BUREAU OF RECLAMATION

John's agency is plagued by an antiquated system for the management of public meetings and decision-making processes, not unlike many other state and federal government agencies. When a coal mining company seeks to open a new mine or to expand an existing operation, the mining company meets secretly with property owners, slowly buying access to desired properties until all or nearly all the needed plots have been purchased. With each purchase, they require the seller to sign a nondisclosure agreement so that the company's desire to open a new mine does not become public knowledge until all the plots needed have changed hands. Then, the company applies for a mining license from the Bureau of Reclamation. As long as the company has prepared an environmental impact statement, posts the necessary bond (to guard against a company going bankrupt and leaving a mess behind), and shows it has no outstanding violations on any other mines in the state, the license will be granted. Local members of the community first learn about the mine when the bureau announces the license application in the local paper, as required by state law.

Next, the employees of the bureau have the unenviable duty of holding at least one public meeting in which they record public comments regarding the license application. To be clear, there is almost nothing the public can do to stop the granting of the license, according to state law. Once the license is granted, another public meeting is required to announce the issuance of the license. The law was written with the explicit input of the mining companies and many of the legislative members on the relevant committees have previously worked as employees of the mining committees. Once they leave office, they may go into the lucrative field of lobbying, where their ties to industry and politicians will serve them well. This is not corruption; it is perfectly legal (or imperfectly legal, depending on your perspective). Unless a citizen can show the company is in violation of state or federal rules on one of their other mines or they can show the company submitted false financial statements, it is nearly impossible to stop the issuance of a coal mining license. For this reason, John and his employees at the bureau are generally viewed by citizens as being in the pocket of the mining companies. Of course, the mining companies know that the bureau's employees will not hesitate to revoke an existing license or issue a fine for violating any relevant environmental regulations, so they view the bureau's employees as rabid environmentalists.

On the day of the required public meetings, many of John's employees mysteriously become ill. Some of them are genuinely ill due to the stress these meetings cause. He consistently has difficulty in getting bureau employees to attend the public meetings and record public comments, as required by law. Citizens come to these meetings with a desire to stop the mine and they voice many concerns: noise and shaking from blasting, lost property value as a result of living near the mine, damage to local roads from the heavy volume of truck traffic, as well as related safety concerns: the safety of ground water supplies because blasting may damage the underground aquifers, pollution from chemicals used in the mining process, and increased dust from the mining process that may make it difficult to open the windows of their homes or may worsen health conditions such as asthma. Yet, the purpose of these public meetings is to gather public comment, not supply information. Additionally, most citizens come to these meetings with the idea that their voice will matter. Sometimes they bring petitions with thousands of signatures in the hope that this will halt or delay the issuance of the mining license. It won't.

At the public meetings, the bureau's staff sit at a head table on a raised platform at the front of the building with pads of paper on which to record public comment. Citizens can step up to the microphone and share their concerns for up to five minutes per person. This leads to grandstanding by some local leaders, especially during election season. Usually the speaker makes a statement against the mine and the audience applauds vigorously, hooting their support, which takes up a lot of the speaker's time. Occasionally, someone will speak in favor of the mine. This is usually someone hoping the mine will bring needed jobs to the town. In other cases, it is an existing employee for the mining company or someone who hopes to sell their property to the mining company. They are usually heckled after the first few sentences and are unable to finish their presentations. To make matters worse, some people wait all evening to speak, but at the end of the ninety-minute meeting, some have not yet had their turn and the meeting ends on time.

John is concerned because these meetings not only leave the public with a negative view of his agency, but they can also be dangerous. At the last meeting someone slashed all four tires on his car and the local sheriff had to accompany John and his staff as they left the town hall out of fear for their safety. Clearly, something needs to change. John has been doing some reading about the management of public disputes and is nearly ready to make some radical changes to the current process—changes that do not require any modification of existing laws.

Whether you organize meetings for the corporate shareholders, a group of nonprofit volunteers, or public meetings for a government agency, facilitation skills are indispensable for managers. Large-group decision-making processes are important for every type of organization. Managers who display these skills stand out as leaders within their teams and organizations. Those who fail to master the skills necessary to lead efficient and productive meetings will encounter low attendance, low levels of attention from those in attendance, and a general sense of dread at the thought of approaching meetings. This chapter will convey methods for holding effective, efficient, useful meetings with minimal drama. Although the emphasis here is on large-group decision-making processes, most of the skills and content knowledge apply to smaller team and staff meetings as well. This chapter introduces screening tools managers can use to determine which issues are most likely to benefit from a collaborative decision-making process; outlines choices about meeting logistics; explains how to deal with the presence of the media during negotiations and public meetings; examines the skills, characteristics, and habits of effective facilitators; and presents a variety of potential meeting formats from which to choose.

When applying ADR to large-group decision making, it is important to understand key terms such as *consensus, collaboration*, and *deliberative democracy* as applied to large-group processes. **Consensus** occurs in matters of policy when "the parties have reached a meeting of the minds sufficient to make a decision and carry it out; no one who could block or obstruct the decision or its implementation will exercise that power; and everyone needed to support the decision and put it into effect will do so" (Arthur, Carlson, & Moore, 1999, p. 5). In terms of large-group processes, collaboration occurs when multiple parties come together to accomplish a common objective because of a shared need through authentic conversations in which people speak frankly and listen to one another under norms of reciprocity that require a cooperative give-and-take that enables the group to negotiate effectively (Arthur, Carlson, & Moore, 1999). **Deliberative democracy** refers to the underlying principle that for laws to have true legitimacy they must be subject to authentic deliberation prior to a majority vote. (The term *deliberative democracy* was originally coined by Joseph M. Bessette [1980].) Authentic deliberation means that decision makers engage in discussion, debate, and analysis that are free from the influence of unequal power derived from wealth, status, or other sources of inequality. The goal of deliberative democracy is to move toward consensus but decisions can be made based on majority vote once deliberations have occurred and all have had a chance to participate. Deliberative democracy is a founding principle of Western governmental systems, albeit incompletely achieved in practice.

PUBLIC AND LARGE-GROUP MEETING DISASTERS

No one comes. Everyone comes. The room is too small. The room is cavernous and there is the faint sound of crickets. Grandstanders monopolize the microphone and shout unhelpful criticisms and those on the podium alternate between disinterest and intimidation. No one speaks at the meeting that was intended to gather input from stakeholders. No clear agenda exists and the meeting seems to wander wildly off topic. A clear agenda exists yet the meeting wanders wildly off topic. One person dominates the discussion and is seemingly indifferent to the annoyance of the others present. The issues on the agenda were composed of announcements that could have been disseminated via e-mail, taking people away from other pressing tasks. Important decisions could not be made during the meeting because long debates failed to lead to a consensus among decision makers. Do any of these sound familiar? Sitting through poorly designed and executed meetings can feel like torture. Leading such a meeting is even worse. Yet with some planning and preparation, attending or leading group meetings can be invigorating and instrumental to decision making within an organization or on issues of public policy. Whether you are a wallflower who hates public speaking or are a founding member of Toastmaster's, learning the art of skillful meeting design and facilitation will serve you and your organization well. Not only can some up-front preparation make all the difference, when you find yourself in the middle of a meeting that just isn't working, you can change course midstream and be transparent about your observation by saying something like, "It seems this isn't working; let's try it another way."

Why should individual stakeholders and representatives of stakeholder groups be included in decision making? It turns out that regular people tend to have intimate knowledge about the problems affecting their lives, communities, and work. They often come up with innovative ideas for problem solving—innovations that policy makers might not think up on their own. Including stakeholders, as appropriate, into decision-making processes can simply yield better, more sustainable, implementable, politically palatable decisions that uphold the ideals of democracy. As this chapter will show, collaborative processes are most useful and have maximum legitimacy when all relevant stakeholders are engaged in the process and have a voice.

Inadequate Input Leads to Unanticipated Failures

A federal agency was organizing a review of the potential effects of shale oil development on water resources in Western Colorado. Agency officials invited federal and state officials, industry representatives, and urban environmentalists to participate. The plan was to discuss the issues, produce agreements, and then announce them to the world. No public meetings were held. The opinions of the agricultural and community water interests were not sought until after the discussions were completed. As a result, the agreements reached by the group omitted subtle but important long-term consequences to agriculture of diverting water to the shale oil industry. The report, and the work that had gone into it, were so flawed that it was never given serious consideration. (Carpenter & Kennedy, 2001, p. 177)

Expert outside neutrals may be brought in to help with these processes or inside manager leaders may be used. The term *facilitator* is most commonly used to refer to the leaders of these large-group processes but the term *mediator* is also frequently used, especially with smaller groups or when the group's task is to reach a formal agreement. In truth, the terms *mediator* and *facilitator* are often used interchangeably in the literature but for the sake of consistency, this chapter will refer to the leaders of large-group collaborative processes as facilitators. It is the role of facilitators to help "create the conditions for new understandings, solutions, agreements, deals, accords and plans to emerge" (Adler & Fisher, 2007, p. 21).

NEEDS ASSESSMENT STAGE

Before diving in headfirst for a collaborative effort or to convene a group of stakeholders to discuss a contentious issue, it is critical to conduct a thorough assessment of the issue or conflict in order to determine the likelihood of success.

A needs assessment (also called *conflict assessment*) is an evaluation of the conflict or issue to determine whether a collaborative process is appropriate. What are the goals of the potential effort? The goals will have a formative impact on the process choices: is the goal to reach a collaborative decision on an issue of policy? Is the goal to exchange information in two directions (or share information in one direction) between government and the public or between a corporation and its customers? Is the goal to build understanding and community between groups with a history of conflict in order to reduce the incidence of future conflict (such as Catholics and Protestants in Northern Ireland or African American and Korean American communities in Los Angeles)? Each of these goals would necessitate different process choices. Information about the dispute can be gathered through firsthand observation, interviews with stakeholders, reviewing documents and media reports, and so on.

The **process sponsor** is the organization that convenes and usually financially supports the large-group process of decision making or information exchange. The sponsor is usually a governmental agency but it can also be a private or nonprofit organization or the process can be jointly sponsored by more than one organization. The sponsor generally conducts an assessment of the conflict or, ideally, hires an outside consultant to conduct an unbiased assessment. The assessment will determine who the key stakeholders are; their positions, interests, BATNAs (see Chapter Three); the salience of the issue to each stakeholder; and their willingness to participate in a collaborative process (see Table 12.1). The assessment will examine the ripeness of the dispute to determine whether the timing is appropriate for a large-group effort. As discussed in Chapter Eleven, if it is too early in the life cycle of the dispute or issue, there may not be enough information available or an adequate sense of urgency to motivate stakeholder groups to participate. Alternatively, if the issue has risen to the crisis stage and an immediate decision is needed from an authoritative body such as a court or government agency, it may be too late to begin a collaborative process. The conflict assessment must include an analysis of the dispute's ripeness. Related to ripeness, the assessment should examine the timeline available for the group to meet and accomplish its goals. If the group's task is to reach a collaborative decision, then a clear deadline is necessary. Otherwise the group may talk and talk, with no definite end in sight, putting off difficult decisions because no deadline exists.

Table 12.1
Conflict Assessment Protocol

Parties	Issues	Interests	Importance of Issues (High, Medium, Low)	Source of Power and Influence	Positions and Options	Interest in Working with Other Parties	Other Comments
Party 1.							
Party 2.							

Source: Carpenter and Kennedy (2001, p. 87).

During the assessment stage, the sponsor must determine whether sufficient resources exist to support a collaborative process. If a facilitator, mediator, or other expert neutral will be hired, who will pay for those services and how will the resources be found? Will all the key stakeholders be able to send at least one representative to the meetings or will they need some financial support to participate? This is especially important for volunteers who represent civic groups. Participation may mean missed work, thereby making it a burden that is not sustainable for some groups. It may be possible to find grants or government agency funding to enable civic or nonprofit groups to send representatives to these meetings so their voices are not overshadowed by commercial and government interests.

If the process would benefit from having a facilitator (see Chapter Four for a detailed explanation of facilitation versus other types of ADR processes) or other neutral to lead the effort, should that individual come from inside the sponsoring agency, from one of the other stakeholder organizations, or should an outside neutral be hired? The question of whether to hire an outside or inside neutral is not always simple to answer. Outside neutrals will bring process knowledge, experience in handling other complex large-group processes, and an objectivity that comes from *not* being from one of the stakeholder groups. However, there may be no money to hire an outside neutral or the group may believe that the technical aspects of the issue are so complex that only someone from one of the stakeholder groups could possibly meet the groups' needs. If the groups decide to use an inside neutral, there needs to be a supermajority (as close to unanimous as possible) for that choice. It needs to be clear as to whether the neutral will give up his advocate role and act as the neutral or retain his right to share his own comments and preferences and still facilitate the group discussion. In general, the former seems to work better and with less friction than the latter option. It is also possible to combine the inside or outside neutral role in interesting ways. For example, many large government agencies have trained employees in facilitation and mediation skills. It may be possible to invite a facilitator or mediator from a government agency that is not a party to the current dispute or decision-making process. These shared neutral programs are designed to meet the demand for expert neutral facilitators and also save the expense and contracting process hurdles required when hiring an outside neutral. Stakeholders may decide they wish to hire an outside neutral for the purposes of objectivity and expertise yet pair this person up with one or more inside stakeholders who will serve as a team to make process-related decisions and ensure that the facilitator or other neutral has the subject-matter specific knowledge the group feels is necessary to fully understand the issue under discussion.

What happens if a collaborative decision-making or dialogue process is undertaken, yet one or more key stakeholders were uninvited? The legitimacy of the process becomes immediately suspect. The decision that results is likely to be seen as skewed toward the interests of those who were invited and indeed it will probably reflect the voices of those present more than those who were absent. Imagine the US president is considering new environmental and safety regulations concerning oil pipelines and all the major American oil companies are invited to participate in initial talks on the matter. But the Sierra Club and other civic groups are not invited. The result of these meetings will be viewed with cynicism by many. Those who were not invited to participate may seek to block the implementation of any resulting policy change through the courts, claiming that the agency has overstepped its mandate from Congress or has been captured by the interests it is supposed to regulate. Clearly, identifying and recruiting the participation of all key stakeholders is critical to the success of any collaborative effort.

So how do you know which groups or individuals to invite? Try using a snowball sampling method. Begin by speaking with the obvious stakeholders—organizations from the public, private, and nonprofit sectors that are clearly affected by the issue under discussion. Speak to leaders within those organizations to ascertain their interest and willingness to participate in a collaborative process. Ask them, "Who else should participate?" and "Is there anyone who should not be invited to participate?" Then go to those individuals and organizations who were mentioned by others and ask the same questions. Once you stop hearing new names, it is probable that most or all of the key stakeholders have been identified. Interestingly, the answers to both of these questions are likely to indicate other groups or individuals who need to be invited to participate. Anyone who has the power or incentive to block the implementation of the group's decision is someone who has a stake in the issue. Their voices need to be heard. Remember the advice of the famous Chinese general Sun-tzu, "Keep your friends close and your enemies closer." By inviting the most cynical or extreme groups, along with the moderate ones, you ensure that no group can later claim the process was tilted against them. More important, their views and the views of all participants will probably evolve as they take part in the group process. At a minimum, all groups should leave the process with a deeper understanding of the others' concerns and the complexity of the problem itself. These more complete understandings as well as the relationships and rapport formed between negotiators can become the basis of a future agreement and collaboration.

In spite of your best efforts to identify and invite all key stakeholders to participate in the process, it is not uncommon for an individual or organization to appear halfway through the process and insist on joining the group. This happens for three main reasons: (1) a stakeholder group was overlooked during the snowball sampling mentioned previously, (2) the group formed recently and now wants to be recognized and included, (3) a stakeholder group was invited early in the process but chose not to participate. Now that the process is under way and draft policies or decisions are being formulated, the group has decided that its interests are indeed affected by the groups' activities, thereby necessitating its late inclusion into the process. In other words, they were hanging back to see what the group was going to do and whether their participation was warranted. In any event, if the process involves issues of public policy, it is best to allow latecomers to participate and encourage the other members to welcome them into the process. This can be frustrating for those who have participated from the outset and may require the neutral to explain the benefits of including all comers, regardless of when and how they arrive.

Screening cases for the appropriateness of an ADR process is a key step in the assessment stage. Screening needs to occur on two levels. The sponsoring organization or agency needs to decide whether it is willing and able to engage in a collaborative process, as do the potential participants. The following box lists the questions commonly asked in a sponsor's assessment. As the box shows, a sponsor should consider a collaborative process when none of the parties is seeking to set a precedent through the courts, when all key stakeholders are willing and able to participate, when adequate time exists along with a reasonably firm deadline for action, when financial and personnel resources exist to support a collaborative process, when the agency is honestly willing to share decision-making power or at least take the group's decision under advisement (and be transparent from the outset what the effect of the group's decision will be), and when ongoing communication and buy-in will be necessary for the implementation of any policy changes resulting from the process. On this last point, it should be noted that when stakeholders believe a policy or rule was created arbitrarily or that it is unreflective of their operational realities, they tend to drag their feet on implementation. Creating new policies or rules is useless if they are not implemented.

Assessment Screening Questions for Process Sponsors

1. Do the issues appear to be negotiable?
   Are parties framing this as an issue of fundamental rights or moral values that cannot be negotiated?

   Are parties seeking to establish a legal precedent?

2. Are the interests clearly defined?

3. Where does this issue fall on the spiral of unmanaged conflict?
   Is this issue a priority for stakeholders?

   Is there enough time for parties to deliberate or is it an emergency?

   Is there a deadline that would help avoid endless negotiations?

4. Who are the parties and how is power balanced among them?
   Are there any parties or stakeholders who can accomplish their goals without negotiation?

(continued)

(continued)

5. Are there issues of race, class, culture, ethnicity, education, or ethnicity that will make it difficult for one or more key stakeholders to participate on equal footing? If so, is there anything that can be done to overcome these differences or enable fuller participation?

6. Will the sponsor be able to provide or locate the financial and personnel resources necessary to support this process?

7. Is the agency's leadership truly willing to engage in a good faith effort at shared decision making?

8. Will the parties, including the sponsor, continue to interact with one another in the future?
   In other words, are they interdependent?

   Will any agreement require ongoing participation, collaboration, and buy-in to be fully implemented?

When the sponsor's assessment is complete, create a written summary that identifies the key stakeholders along with their interests, positions, and willingness to negotiate; the substance of the problem itself including various ways to define the problem; the negotiability of the key issues; any ethical dilemmas or value conflicts inherent in the problem; and the various processes that may be used to constructively address the problem. The following box summarizes the elements of the conflict assessment.

Questions for the Conflict Assessment

Parties

1. Who are the main parties and their key spokespeople?

2. Who are the secondary parties and their key spokespeople?

3. Are the parties well defined?

4. Do the parties want to work toward a solution?

5. Are the parties capable of working with each other?

Substance of the Problem

6. What description is the most constructive way to define the problem?

    a. Conflict focuses on different interests.

    b. Conflict focuses on strongly held values.

    c. Conflict focuses on perceived differences that do not really exist.

7. What is the most constructive way to define the problem?

8. What are the central issues?

9. What are the secondary issues?

10. Are the issues negotiable?

11. What are the key interests of each party?

12. What interests do the parties have in common?

13. What positions have been taken?

14. What other options for resolution exist?

Procedures

15. What do parties think about using some form of conflict management? What suggestions do they have?

16. Does a consensus process service the parties' interests?

17. What constraints might affect the structures of a conflict management process (timing, legal activities, resources)?

18. What other obstacles must a process overcome?

19. Which parties are experienced in using alternative dispute resolution procedures?

20. What are the chances for success?

Source: Carpenter and Kennedy (2001, p. 91).

In addition to the sponsor's assessment, all potential stakeholders will need to determine for themselves whether their interests and resources are suited to participation in a collaborative process. What will be the effect of sitting it out when the process may go on without your organization? Are your organization's needs more likely to be met through court action? How important is it to cultivate ongoing collaborative relationships with regulatory agencies and other stakeholders on this issue? How might your brand be affected by participation or nonparticipation? Will your organization be in a better position to influence the outcome of the decision-making process through participation or nonparticipation? Will implementation of a new policy or regulation be easier as a result of participation in the formulation process? Will your organization learn more about the issue and its competitors or other stakeholders through participation? What is the overall ratio of benefits to costs for participation? Do not forget that the middle ground is always possible: participate now and decide later if participation should be ended.

CONVENING STAGE

Convening is the process of bringing stakeholders together to design the process jointly and begin the dialogue or negotiation. If the needs assessment led to the conclusion that a collaborative process is a good idea, the next phase is to convene the key stakeholders and begin discussions about the process itself. During the assessment phase key stakeholders were identified and all or most of them were interviewed to learn more about their willingness to participate, their motivation to negotiate in good faith, and any resources they might need in order to fully participate. Facilitators do not get to choose which individuals serve as delegates from the various stakeholder groups. However, if they are able to use their influence or make suggestions, "in multi-party cases, mediators must perpetually scan for participants who will imagine the big picture, enhance trust, integrate disparate interests, coordinate tasks and emerge as bridge-builders" (Adler & Fisher, 2007, p. 21).

This is the phase during which primary stakeholders work together to craft the problem statement or task description that will guide the group's time together. The sponsor may seek to suggest the problem statement and task description but in the end participants will need to concur with the framing of this statement in order to consent to participate in the process.

During the convening stage participants work with the facilitator to craft and consent to the ground rules and procedures that will guide their time together, including the length and frequency of meetings, rules about who speaks when, and decision rules.

A word about decision rules is in order at this point. Although 100 percent consensus is a wonderful goal, in a large and diverse group it can be nearly impossible to reach. For example, a local church was seeking a new pastor after their long-serving leader announced his retirement. Each Sunday the congregation would host a guest pastor or job applicant who would give the weekly sermon and then join the congregation in a potluck lunch. A few days later the congregation would meet, discuss the job applicant, and vote as to whether or not to hire him. There were approximately four hundred officially registered and voting church members, but the church's bylaws were written when the church was much smaller and required a 100 percent agreement to hire a new leader. As a result, each week there would be at least one church member who was a holdout. Getting four hundred people to agree on anything is nearly impossible. Slowly, members began leaving the church for other congregations and eventually the church completely closed. The rule of 100 percent consensus was well intentioned but unworkable. It also gave attention and power to those who seek to act as spoilers. A **spoiler** is someone who uses his power to sabotage the group's progress in order to gain attention or further his own goals. Spoilers usually hold significantly more extreme views than the majority of process participants and can use consensus processes to stall or sabotage outcomes they wish to avoid.

When leading large-group decision-making processes, consider selecting something short of a 100 percent consensus rule unless the agreement of every stakeholder is necessary for the implementation of any resulting decision. For example, a "consensus minus one" rule will make it clear to the group that if only one party does not join in on the agreement, it will go forward without their support. Other options include a vote that requires a supermajority. The percentage required to reach agreement is something that can be negotiated among group members. The key is to make decision rules at the outset of the negotiation rather than waiting until it is time to take a vote or reach a decision. At that point, those who are unhappy with the agreement will insist on 100 percent consensus and those in favor will prefer a simple majority.

The convening stage is the time to teach consensus building 101. In other words, for a group that will meet repeatedly it is important to build a baseline of knowledge regarding collaborative skills, including the difference between interests and positions, listening and framing skills, and techniques for keeping constituents informed and on board with agreements reached at the table. In fact, it can be a facilitator's duty to train participants in facilitation skills with the goal of helping them eventually take over the facilitator's role. The best facilitators are those who are able to model and train parties in these skills to empower them to create a self-managing group, especially if the group will be together permanently.

During the convening phase it is crucial to build in social and networking time so the participants can get to know each other as people. In most cases, dialogue must come before negotiation—this means the participants simply need to get to know one another, overcome any preexisting stereotypes or assumptions made in the absence of real interactions, and develop the trust necessary to have frank and open discussions.

During the convening stage it is also important to create a timeline for process milestones and for the close of the group's work. Some groups work in an ongoing manner, making decisions as necessary to manage shared resources or deal with recurring challenges rather than having a specific timeline for completion. In these processes it remains important to have timelines for decisions and milestones so as to discourage endless discussions without resulting decisions.

In order to evaluate the efficiency, efficacy, and value of the large-group process it is important to build in evaluation methods from the very beginning. For example, a pretest and posttest may be crafted in order to understand the effect of the process on the management of a resource such as water supply, forest health, hospital quality of care, and so on. The development of evaluation tools will ensure the group has clear goals and methods for evaluating progress toward the goals.

DURING THE PROCESS

Once the meetings or negotiations are under way, the facilitator plays a role in ensuring clear and consistent communication between the negotiators and the constituencies they represent. Any negotiation in which participants represent broader constituency groups is in effect a two-level game, to borrow a concept from game theory. In other words, *intra*group negotiations occur in order to arrive at unified bargaining positions or to respond to offers made. Concurrently, *inter*group negotiations occur between stakeholder groups. Although the traditional facilitation role occurs in the intergroup negotiations, facilitators may also be called on to assist with the intragroup negotiations that must successfully occur in order for a stakeholder group to effectively participate in the larger discussions. Many a negotiation has fallen apart because one or more representatives could not get their constituents to agree on a negotiating position or agree how to respond to a specific offer.

Be on the lookout for **collaboration fatigue**, which is the weariness that sets in among negotiators after talks have been ongoing for months or even years, especially if progress seems elusive or minimal. The signs of collaboration fatigue include falling meeting attendance, growing impatience or inattentiveness of representatives, and a decreased willingness to financially support the collaborative process. Through the use of ongoing evaluation tools it may be possible to gain feedback from stakeholders that will enable process changes to be made that will help avoid collaboration fatigue.

For public policy decision-making efforts, keep in mind the importance of timing — election cycles, agency leadership changes, funding cycles, and personnel changes. Few large decisions are made or endorsed by politicians just before an election. However, new dialogue or collaborative processes are often endorsed prior to elections as long as the timeline for decisions occurs comfortably after election day. Politicians and agency leaders may flock to collaborative processes not only because they produce better-quality decisions, but also because they provide political cover. A decision reached through a consensus process is likely to occur only if a supermajority of stakeholders reaches agreement. By delegating decision-making authority to a stakeholder group, politicians can give them credit and declare the outcome to be reached through a fair and democratic process. Be sure to pay attention to the timing of a collaborative process in order to maximize the chances of finding and sustaining political and leadership support. Yet a collaborative project supported by one politician or agency leader may be abandoned by the next, especially if it is viewed as the pet project of the previous administrator. Similarly, each participating organization will have a delegate in the stakeholder group. For long-term negotiations, the group will inevitably need to weather retirements, family leaves, and personnel changes for individual delegates. Recognizing these milestones can become a unifying tradition within the group. Welcoming in new members and getting them up to speed and on board can be crucial to the group's continued success, as this story illustrates:

> In one case involving proposed development in an environmentally sensitive area, leadership came primarily through the government's lead lawyer. As with

most effective negotiators, he was an avid listener who anticipated the other parties' issues, worked hard to figure out potential solutions before they raised concerns, and created a vision for the future that integrated everyone's interests. This resulted in a level of trust that enabled significant progress. Then, overnight, everything changed and his replacement, who had not been involved with the previous discussions, had different ideas and a less collaborative and more adversarial style. He did more talking than listening, the collaboration ended and the deal fell apart. (Adler & Fisher, 2007, p. 21)

Although finding and keeping the right people at the table is an ongoing struggle, it is also important to realize that the project is bigger than any individual stakeholder. Stakeholders should be encouraged to keep others from their organization in the wings and in the loop in case they need to step away from the project for any reason. Although this is not always possible, anything the manager facilitator can do to ensure the longevity of the project beyond the career changes of any one person will contribute to the collaboration's ultimate success. Be creative—Raines and Kubala (2011) detail how their collaborative effort lost its main keeper of the flame when the project manager left the US Army Corps of Engineers to go to work for a private company. His contribution was so pivotal the group found funds to hire him through his private company in order to finish the project under his stewardship.

Finally, a few words about agreements are in order. Agreements generally take one of three forms: (1) agreements in principle outline the process through which the problem will be solved, for example "a committee of delegates will select the best person for the position"; (2) each issue is negotiated separately until all issues are resolved (also known as the *building block approach*); or (3) an entire package of proposals is developed that addresses all issues in a comprehensive manner and is accepted or rejected (Carpenter & Kennedy, 2001). As discussed in Chapter Three, it may be helpful for the group to develop objective criteria against which any proposal can be examined. A plan and timeline for implementation should be part of the agreement rather than con-sidered as an afterthought. Before any final agreement can be concluded, each representative must take the draft agreement back to his or her constituents and gain their approval before a final decision can be made. Once the agreement has been finalized and any required signatures attained, the next step is implementation.

AFTER THE PROCESS

Once regular meetings cease or become less frequent, and with the expected challenges that come with the implementation of any agreement, it is not unusual for preexisting animosities to return or trust to wane. For implementation to go smoothly, some form of ongoing monitoring will likely be necessary along with a plan to deal with those who fail to fulfill their commitments. Periodic meetings may be necessary to discuss progress with regard to implementation, maintaining cooperative morale, or even renegotiating parts of the agreement when unexpected circumstances or unforeseen problems arise during the process of implementation. Evaluation of the process and its ongoing impact on the policy issue should continue in order to institutionalize and improve the success of collaborative efforts and gain feedback that may be of continued use as the project matures. Process evaluation is an important topic but beyond the scope of this book. Luckily, there are many useful guides to evaluating large-group decision-making processes from which you can borrow survey questions and ideas for data gathering (see Emerson, Orr, Keyes, & Mcknight, 2009; Orr, Emerson, & Keyes, 2008).

THE ROLE OF THE MEDIA IN PUBLIC DISPUTES

As discussed in Chapter Eleven, sunshine laws generally require that decision-making meetings held by government agencies are open to the public and therefore the media. In truth, most policy-making meetings are simply not riveting enough to attract media attention. When an agency is operating smoothly and no crisis exists, the media is notably absent. Yet when there has been a mistake or a crisis has arisen that necessitates a change in course or new policy action, then the media is more likely to be present. Unlikely as it seems, the media can be a positive asset for collaborative governance and decision making, but many leaders miss opportunities to develop a positive working relationship with the media or to use them appropriately as a venue for communicating with the public about important policy issues. Chapter Two presented Maslow's hierarchy of needs. Recall that most basic needs are for food, shelter, and physical security. Any issue of public policy that deals with these most basic needs are likely to be heated, to draw out passionate pleas on all sides of the issue, and therefore to pose the greatest likelihood of attracting media attention. These issues may be about jobs, food safety, housing demolition or creation, prices for heating oil or food staples, and so on. When people sense their basic needs are threatened, they are likely to have strong reactions. People fear losing control over these areas of their lives, hence, the pervasive distrust of many governmental institutions that have the power to affect citizens on these issues. The media may be tempted to oversimplify policy issues into hysteria-producing sound bites that attract an audience to their stories with headlines like these: "Is the meat in your refrigerator dangerous?" or "The city government has decided to demolish five homes along the banks of the East River—could yours be next?" Any hint that the government is meeting in secret or withholding information from the media will only feed these fears. The trick in working with the media is the same as it is in working with any other organization or individual—meet needs through interest-based strategies. Help them meet their need for interesting news that attracts an audience and provides the public with accurate, useful information in a timely fashion.

As many public officials and higher-level bureaucrats have learned, contact with the media can result in incomplete and even factually inaccurate stories that can embarrass managers and even end careers. One public sector manager recently conveyed how he was misquoted in the local paper: "They misspelled my name, incorrectly listed my rank as higher than it is, and got the numbers in the article all wrong. Yet the public have taken the article as 'gospel truth' and we've been inundated with angry phone calls from concerned citizens." Incidents like these can lead managers to try to avoid contact with the media, yet their very avoidance is seen as a challenge to reporters, a sign that the managers are hiding information from the public. What can be done?

First, organizational leaders, upper-level managers, and professional policy facilitators should cultivate positive relationships with media representatives in their regions. If you work for the department of education, you should know the names of the reporters who are typically tasked to cover education stories in your city and state. Be careful not to be perceived as wasting their time because they are constantly running under tight deadlines. They will only meet with people who have something of interest to tell them. When you know changes are in store for your organization, set up meetings with relevant reporters to share the news of these impending changes. Tell them about your plans to use a collaborative process that engages the public and key stakeholders. Explain to them the reasons why your organization is willing to undertake this type of process. Invite them to attend as observers. Observers to the negotiations cannot speak or ask questions unless invited to do so by the facilitators or key stakeholders. Tell them they can funnel questions to you and you will seek answers from the participants, as time allows. Ask them to refrain from popping in and out during sessions but instead to be present for the entire work session. This will help avoid their tendency to look for a sound bite to take out of context (but is no guarantee). Ask for their advice because they probably know who the key stakeholders are as well as some of the history on any contentious public issues. They often have a good feel for the political dimensions of policy issues and may be willing to point out stumbling blocks in advance. Tell them you will prepare news releases to share with them when important decisions or milestones have been met within the group process. These press releases should include the proper spelling and titles for all participants as well as some background information on the issue itself (for example, "why is clean water important to our economy?"), define technical terms in layperson's language and include a brief description of the collaborative process itself. Remember to keep all press releases brief and succinct to maximize the likelihood they will be used as written. These releases should be agreed on by all key stakeholders or a subcommittee elected by the larger group. In some contentious policy negotiations, participants may wish to agree on ground rules for dealing with the media. For example, "We agree not to speak to the media individually until the negotiations are over, but to instead craft mutually agreed-on press releases." This strategy reduces the incidence of having individual stakeholders trash talking their fellow negotiators via the media when talks get difficult. Assure the media of your intention to share information with the public rather than withhold it—especially the information they need to reach informed opinions on policy matters. In some ways, you are educating the reporter about the ways in which she can serve as a conduit for information to the public and developing a deeper level of understanding and analysis on the policy matters relevant to your organization's mission. With a little luck and some finesse, you will turn the media's presence from a liability into an asset. The following box summarizes these guidelines for working with the media.

CHARACTERISTICS OF SUCCESSFUL LARGE-GROUP FACILITATORS

Few organizations have had more experience facilitating group decision making than the United Nations (UN) member bodies. It is not surprising the UN has developed specific advice for their team members who frequently facilitate meetings composed of culturally diverse stakeholders seeking to collaborate for mutual gain. The following box paraphrases the characteristics of a successful facilitator and is based on the materials developed by the United Nations Economic and Social Council.

- Use perseverance and patience.

- Use knowledge of multiple approaches and have a willingness to change an approach that isn't working (i.e., knowledge and flexibility).

- Have the ability to monitor, assess, and summarize the outcomes and effects of the group's efforts.

Source: Adapted from http://www.unevoc.unesco.org/fileadmin/user_upload/docs/04-facilitator_guide .pdf

To add to this list, Adler and Fisher (2007) argue for facilitative leaders as able to "foster better communication, brokering concurrence, taming tough problems and managing the inevitable conflicts that occur in politically charged environments" (p. 21). They add that facilitators do everything from arranging the room and setting out the cookies to addressing the "political choreographies" that address "complex intellectual and emotional moves that are needed to bring a dialogue or negotiation to a productive fruition" (p. 21). Perhaps that is why many observers have noted that successful facilitators seem to exude humility, transparency, the ability to think on their feet, can change course when necessary, maintain healthy emotional boundaries, remain calm in the face of the storm, show empathy, remain flexible, and understand the need for structure. Facilitators are resilient, adaptive, and proactive at managing positive change and constructive communication between disparate groups and individuals. Although individuals may be born with natural endowments that make them great facilitators, these skills and techniques can also be honed through practice and purposeful application.

HABITS OF AN EFFECTIVE FACILITATOR

Whether you are leading a meeting of five or five hundred, mastering the skills of facilitation can be key to ensuring productive group performance and decision making. Being a facilitator requires responsibility and authority. If the facilitator is a neutral in regard to the decisions under discussion, she will generally be trusted to be fair, unless her actions lead some parties to believe otherwise. If the facilitator is not neutral in regard to the issues under discussion, then trust may need to be earned through a display of fairness, impartiality, and competence. The following box displays the key tasks of successful facilitators. Some of these tasks require additional elaboration.

Primary Tasks of Effective Facilitators

- Establish an agenda.
- Keep the discussion focused on the agenda.
- Clarify statements.
- Summarize statements.
- Explore ideas.
- Encourage all members to participate.
- Maintain a calm and positive tone.
- Enforce the ground rules fairly.
- Transparently describe what is happening.
- Offer process suggestions.
- Supervise record keeping.
- Test for agreements.
- Manage communications and activities between meetings.
- Verify that constituents are informed.

Source: Adapted from Carpenter and Kennedy (2001, pp. 158–168).

A mistake made by many a formal or informal facilitator is the failure to work with the parties in advance to create an agenda around which there is agreement. In advance of the meeting, send around a draft agenda or a request for agenda items. Work with the key stakeholders to ensure the agenda is of sufficient interest to draw players to the table and is manageable based on the available time frame for the meeting. Make sure the meeting's sponsor and facilitator are clear about the goals of the meeting. Is the goal to make a joint decision? To build rapport among parties? To provide a venue for communication between representatives of different work units or organizations? The goals of the meeting should be clear to all invitees. Once the meeting commences, do your best to stick to the agenda using good time management skills. The agenda should have a timeline for each item's discussion, around which there can be some limited flexibility to account for the fact that it is impossible to fully predict how much time it will take to address each agenda item in advance. Be sure that each agenda item is indeed something that requires discussion, brainstorming, or negotiation during the meeting. Announcements can be shared in advance of the meeting via memos or other venues and should not take up the bulk of the time assigned for the meeting. For each agenda item, ask yourself, "Can this be addressed outside of a group meeting? If so, how? If not, then is it appropriate fodder for group meeting time?" If a public meeting is required in order to announce a draft policy, then consider using the meeting to accomplish additional goals, such as listening to feedback from stakeholders or gaining input as to potential process choices that may improve the final decision or its implementation.

Occasionally, entirely new items will arise during the meeting that threatens to swamp the group's ability to address the preexisting agenda items. At that point, it makes sense to ask the group whether they prefer to discard the original agenda for the more-pressing issue or whether a separate meeting should be called to deal with that issue. If the group has a tendency to get easily off track, you may choose to create a parking lot, which is a list of issues that one or more of the members wish to discuss but is not on the agenda. By placing these on the parking lot list, the facilitator is putting the issue to the side, temporarily. At the end of the meeting, with whatever time remains, the facilitator will tackle those issues that have made their way to the parking lot list. If time runs out, then the parking lot list will become part of the next meeting agenda or it can be addressed through online discussion boards or other communication used in between the regular meetings. When meetings lack clear agendas, they tend to get bogged down in details or easily sidetracked into nonessential issues. Like the old adage says, "If you don't know where you are going, you probably won't get there."

Keep some flexibility as necessary to account for exigent circumstances but be careful about starting meetings late. Although cultural variations should be considered, starting late tends to lead down a slippery slope: the first meeting started five minutes late, so those who were on time come five minutes late to the next meeting. Those who were five minutes late, now come ten or more minutes late. Therefore, the second meeting starts ten minutes late. Then, each subsequent meeting gets started later and later. Do not be tempted to skip breaks or shorten the lunch breaks to account for starting late or having an overly packed agenda. These breaks not only provide the respite needed for parties to maintain their patience and stamina, but they also provide a venue for building rapport and informal discussions of important issues.

Facilitators serve their group by frequently clarifying the meaning of what group members have said. Saying "If I understand you correctly, you said . . ." serves to ensure that everyone present hears and understands the same message to the extent possible. By summarizing progress that has been made, facilitators highlight areas of consensus that have occurred and organize the group's focus on the next task at hand. Summarization helps to move the group forward from where they have been to where they are going. When working in large groups, facilitators are faced with some participants who are able to clearly articulate their thoughts and concerns and others who have more difficulty in formulating their thoughts into words. Once one individual gets embarrassed publicly, it creates a chilling effect on others who may be timid about speaking up and sharing their concerns or ideas. Facilitators often need to invite participants to further explain their concerns and engage in an exploration of those ideas so they feel their participation is welcomed, even if it requires some coaching or assistance on the part of the facilitator: "Can you tell me more about your concern? I'm not sure I understand" or "It is important that we hear from everyone and understand your needs. Could you give me an example or elaborate more about your needs?" This approach will help those quieter members feel able to participate. Likewise, there may be some who dominate the airspace in the room by sharing every thought that comes into their head or responding to every comment made by others. In these situations, it may be necessary to speak to that person during a break and invite them to help create some space for others to participate. It can help to explain that some participants might not speak up until there is a silence to fill or when they are sure that no one else is trying to get a word in. By making room for others, the participation of all parties will be possible. Discussing norms or ground rules for sharing the discussion space can be helpful prior to the commencement of the actual dialogue or negotiation in order to set the tone for a discussion in which all participate and none dominate. Enforcing the ground rules fairly helps the facilitator maintain trust and the efficiency of the process.

Large-group meetings and collaborative processes can be exhausting. Emotions may be high; listening to others for long periods can be draining. Facilitators can assist by keeping a positive tone, pointing out the progress that has been made, and normalizing the difficulty of decisions such as those under consideration. By emoting a calm, reassuring demeanor, facilitators can help to assure parties that the task ahead of them is indeed doable.

By being transparent and explaining techniques and observations, facilitators not only help to build trust with the parties but they also help to steer the process away from potential pitfalls or icebergs. For example, when the facilitator notices that parties seem to be mentally checking out, he can say, "It seems like we are getting pretty fatigued at this point. How about a quick break?" or after presiding over bickering between the parties he might say, "I'm not sure the last few minutes have helped us to reach our goal. Let's try breaking into smaller workgroups and focus on these remaining questions, okay?" By describing what he is doing and why and by offering process suggestions, facilitators can assist parties as they navigate the shoals of the dialogue or negotiation process.

Facilitators need to be transparent when they test for agreement, meaning the facilitator affirmatively asks the parties to confirm whether they agree with a particular decision or consensus the group has been working toward. Depending on the group's rules for decision making, which were discussed at the outset of the group's convening, decisions may require 100 percent consensus or something less than that. Regardless of the decision rule, facilitators need to ask the group to affirm any decisions made and entered into the minutes.

One of the most important and under-recognized tasks of facilitators is to keep meeting minutes and facilitate communications between meetings. Meeting minutes do not need to be akin to transcripts that show who said what and exactly what was said. In fact, the parties and facilitator may need to negotiate from the outset as to what goes into the minutes. If the meetings are to be frank, it may be better to refrain from identifying speakers in the minutes but instead stick to a basic summary of the discussions. The minutes should also include a detailing of any agreements reached and action items assigned to parties as a result of the meeting. The minutes should indicate when the next meeting will be held and any activities that should occur in the interim period.

During the periods between meetings, facilitators can further the success of the group by working to confirm that each stakeholder representative at the negotiations has been communicating with her constituents concerning the direction in which the negotiations are headed and any tentative agreements being made. It is truly devastating to a group process and morale to learn that a stakeholder representative at the negotiations has voiced support for a proposal, only to find out that the group she represents disagrees with that decision and withdraws their support for the decision or for the entire negotiation process. Therefore, one key ground rule for successful large-group decision-making processes is to keep your organizations informed and confirm their support before any decisions or commitments are made by the negotiators at the table.

Be sure to include an evaluation tool to gain feedback as to how to make future meetings as efficient and successful as possible. Consider using an exit survey that participants leave by the door, or for participants within an organization, send around a brief online survey to gather this information. Strive for continual improvement as a facilitator and consensus builder to encourage rather than discourage continued participation from your members.

CHOOSING AMONG MEETING FORMATS

The menu of meeting formats is as varied as the decisions undertaken by large groups. Understanding the pros and cons of each format can assist managers as they select the most appropriate process for the issue at hand. This is not an exhaustive list of process options because processes can be custom-made to meet the needs and constraints of each group or issue.

Charrette

A charrette is a method of organizing thoughts from experts and the public into a structured gathering that is conducive to creative problem solving. A charrette refers to an intensive period of workshop-style meetings that typically occur over one to three days. In a charrette, the group typically divides into smaller working groups and then reports back to the full group at the end of the work session. The findings of each subgroup may become the fodder for additional dialogue for the present or a future charrette. This format enables maximal input from a large and diverse group of participants as well as increases the opportunity for creative ideas to arise.

Town Hall Meeting

A town hall meeting is an informal gathering open to all members of a community. Typically the meeting centers on a specific theme, such as health care reform or improving public education, and local elected leaders or high-ranking bureaucrats are on hand to answer questions from the audience in a talk-show fashion. These meetings are helpful when a leader wishes to make his or her views known on a particular subject but are less suited to sharing complex information with the public and do not engage the public in deliberation or decision making. If speakers are not screened, those seeking to compete with the elected officials for the public's attention or votes can end up by grandstanding.

Twenty-First Century Town Hall Meetings

A relatively recent hybrid process combines the most important elements of deliberative democracy and the old-fashioned town hall meetings (also known as *deliberative democracy dialogues*). These gatherings occur around specific issues such as the Walter Reed reuse plan, which examined ways to redevelop and use the campus of the former Walter Reed Hospital in Washington, DC, or listening to the city, which gathered the opinions of New Yorkers concerning the fate of the Ground Zero site (see http://americaspeaks.org/). This meeting format involves hundreds of regular citizens and begins with a presentation of various ideas or options along with the pros and cons of each option. Then citizens divide into smaller groups (of up to ten), with one facilitator at each table. Participants are asked to discuss each option, generate any questions, and offer alternative options. These are shared using computers at each table and are grouped into themes by process organizers. These are presented to the whole group and the meeting proceeds in an iterative process. At the end of the meeting, each individual votes on the option they prefer. The outcomes of these gatherings are shared with governmental decision makers who take into account these findings as they make final decisions on these matters. These deliberative dialogues are becoming increasingly popular because they allow the public and relevant stakeholders to learn more about the complexity of policy problems, discuss and debate various approaches to dealing with those problems, and then communicate their preferences back up the decision-making chain. As a positive spillover, these events often increase the sense of community among citizens and build social capital.

Open-Space Technology

Open-space technology (OST) is a process somewhat similar to the charrette but with a more specific format and rules. OST is used for strategic planning within organizations as well as for community-based decision making. An OST process takes one to three days and can be used for anywhere from ten to hundreds of people. The key is that all are invited, with the knowledge that those who come have some interest or passion for the issue under discussion. The beauty of OST is that it creates a format for a group to self-organize, create an agenda for workshop activities, and end with a next-steps list of action items for group members or committees to pursue after the end of the process (Harrison, 2008). Basically, the convener creates a framing question such as "How can we reinvigorate our local economy?" or "What changes should our company make to maximize our success over the next ten years?" Participation is voluntary. At the beginning of the gathering, the framing question is posted for all to see. Participants sit in a large circle with a whiteboard or large flip chart at the ready. A "marketplace," or blank chart with times written across the vertical axis and meeting room locations across the horizontal axis, is posted so volunteers can post topics for smaller-group discussion (see Table 12.2 as an example). Anyone interested in hosting a discussion on a particular idea stakes claim to one of the boxes on the marketplace matrix, acts as facilitator for that discussion, and prepares a summary of discussions to share with the larger group at the end of the day. This is called a marketplace for a specific reason; each topic or idea posted is competing with the others to gather participants for the discussion sessions. If an idea does not appeal to others or is not viewed as important, no one will come. This is itself instructive when one or two people in a group may care passionately about an issue but come to realize they are in the minority on the issue. If two participants post similar discussion topics, no problem—more than one group can address the same issue and see if they arrive at the same or different conclusions.

Table 12.2
Marketplace Time-Space Matrix

Time	Room A	Room B	Room C	Room D
9:00–10:30				
10:45–12:15				
1:30–3:00				
Reporting session				
3:30–5:00				

The OST process has a couple of catchy ground rules, including the law of two feet; if you do not like what is happening in a session or feel you are not being heard, you simply leave and go to another session. This creates an imperative for discussion facilitators to remain on topic and facilitate a dialogue in which everyone feels heard and respected. After the reporting session, the group should prioritize its tasks and develop action items for individuals or groups to work on during and after the OST session. This can be done by simple voting or consensus building discussions. OST is not an appropriate format for issues of low salience to stakeholders or for those issues in which an authoritative decision maker is unwilling to share decision-making power with the group. Nothing would be more damaging than for a group of committed stakeholders to engage in a process such as this only to learn their recommendations were disregarded by governmental or organizational leaders.

Traditional Public Meeting Format

As the chapter's opening vignette indicates, one option is to use the old-school traditional public meeting format. In this format, notices are made to announce a public meeting on a particular topic. Agency or organizational leaders sit on a raised dais at the front of the room and record comments raised by members of the public. Anyone who wants to speak can take a turn speaking, usually by signing up on a speaker's list just before the meeting commences. The time for public comments is fixed, commonly at thirty to sixty minutes, with each speaker (typically) allowed to speak for between two and five minutes. Depending on the regulations governing the meeting, the leaders at the front of the room may simply record public comments or they may respond to questions or comments. There are a few challenges associated with this format. First, if the matter is contentious, members of the public turn out in droves, seeking to influence the decision being made, but often these meetings occur late in the decision-making process and comments are unlikely to change the outcome. Second, local politicians, members of the media, or irate citizens use their time at the microphone to voice their anger, hurl insults, or stir up the crowd's passions rather than calmly voicing concerns or asking nonrhetorical questions. Third, members of the public rarely understand the purpose of the public meeting and the mission or constraints of the managers leading the meeting. In the mining example used at the beginning of this chapter, members of the public incorrectly believed that if they turned out in large numbers, brought petitions, and had their local officials voice disapproval, then the mining license would not be issued. Because they did not understand the factors that go into the issuance of a mining license, they went to the meeting with the false belief that their opposition mattered. Once they realized their numbers and opposition were immaterial to the factors under which a license could be denied, they became outraged, with negative consequences.

So why do so many organizations stick to the traditional meeting format? It can be useful for one-way information sharing or to fulfill a statutory requirement to hold a public meeting. It may suffice on issues of low salience to stakeholders, as evidenced by traditionally low turnouts. When true input is needed, when an agency or organization needs to share complex information with the public, or when public or stakeholder opinions are strong, this format is generally insufficient and outdated.

Small-Group Public Meetings

As in the story from the Bureau of Reclamation in this chapter, sometimes it is important for government agencies or other organizations to receive information or comments from the public and also share information with them. In this case they can consider using the traditional public meeting format or they can consider various alternatives to enhance authentic information sharing between groups. If the issue is likely to evoke strong opinions or it involves complex technical issues, it may be best to consider using a format that breaks the issue and the crowd into more manageable pieces. Consider placing multiple tables around the room with a topic placard clearly visible on each table. In the bureau's example, one table would address blasting and noise, another would address water concerns, and still another might address property values. Place a staff member at each table with either a computer or a pad of paper on which to record comments and questions from each attendee. Staff members can answer questions on a one-on-one basis as they are able and promise an individual response through a follow-up call or e-mail on those issues that need further research. Staff members can share information about the agency's mission, constraints, or mandates as well as redirecting citizens to other agencies or elected officials who can address issues outside of their own organization's mandate. By splitting the crowd up into smaller groups, with no microphone, managers can avoid the grandstanding and blustering that might otherwise occur, and still ensure that information is shared between citizens and agency staff. The one-on-one conversations with staff members can better convey the agency's genuine concern and empathy for the situations faced by individual citizens and serve as a conduit for mutual education about the decision-making process and the issue under review.

Visioning Sessions

When developing or redeveloping a public space, consider using a process called *visioning*. In this process community members and leaders are invited to attend one or more visioning sessions in which they seek to create a joint vision for how a section of the neighborhood or community should look once it has been reclaimed or redeveloped. For example, a section of largely abandoned industrial lots along the riverfront in Memphis is slated to be redeveloped into public space, perhaps including a linear park with walking trails and other amenities. Local residents and businesses are invited to a gathering in which they literally draw pictures to show their ideas for what the site should look like once it is finished. A professional artist in attendance takes these individually created drawings, pulls out themes with the help of audience members, and creates a poster to show a shared vision of the space. This vision then becomes the basic plan used for the site's development, perhaps with more public input throughout the process. This hands-on involvement gets community members engaged in shaping their neighborhoods, influencing the ways in which public funds are spent, and involved in dialogue about the trade-offs among various choices between competing visions.

World Café

The world café defines itself as "a conversational process based on a set of integrated design principles that reveal a deeper living network pattern through which we co-evolve our collective future" (Brown & Isaacs, 2005, p. 2). The unique contribution of the world café process is that it encourages participants to share information about their own experiences and worldviews with the goal of building interpersonal and intergroup understandings around issues of shared interest. For example, a neighborhood could convene a world café to discuss local crime, school quality, or economic changes. Through these discussions an agenda for future collaboration may emerge but the main goal is to build relationships and understandings within and across groups. This is a useful process with groups who have been traditionally distant or at odds with one another. The focal issue of discussion engages the group in an examination of what they have in common and allows for the sharing of diverse experiences and perspectives.

CONCLUSION

Managers regularly facilitate meetings, whether those are simply staff meetings, meetings of shareholders, board of directors meetings, or public meetings. This chapter examined a number of meeting formats and skills designed to assist managers as they improve their facilitation skills. The trick about facilitating productive meetings is that they require careful planning. From agenda setting to selecting the meeting time and location to inviting all the key stakeholders, successful meetings are built on a foundation of thoughtful planning. Whether you are a public sector manager who regularly facilitates public meetings or a manager from the nonprofit or private sector who leads board meetings, skilled facilitation is an indispensable skill to develop and employ as a collaborative manager.

JOHN AT THE BUREAU OF RECLAMATION

It has been six months since the meeting in which the tires on John's car were slashed. A lot has changed. His employees no longer stage a sick-out on public meeting days. Local residents sometimes even thank them for the work they are doing rather than try to run them out of town. In order to bring about this enormous change, John made many small changes in the way his agency handles the public involvement issue. First, all of his staff underwent training on listening, framing, and facilitation skills. They use these skills to convey to citizens their sincere empathy for the situations they face and to build rapport. They will even meet concerned citizens one-on-one when possible to answer their questions and diffuse their anger before the public meeting. The bureau has developed a brochure that explains their mission, the mining law, and the extent of their authority. Although the bureau cannot lobby for changes to the mining laws, they have included the contact information for state elected officials on the relevant committees so that if citizens wish to convey their concerns to the appropriate person they can do so. The brochure also includes a list of other agencies the citizens can call with their specific concerns: concerns about trucks and roads go to the state's Department of Transportation, concerns about the safety of drinking water go to the state's EPA, and so on. At the public meeting, the format has been changed. Instead of a head table with a speaker in the middle of the room, the room is set up in round tables that seat six to ten people. At each table, a bureau employee sits ready to record public comments and answer any questions he or she can about the process of licensing, the public record of the specific mining company that seeks the license, and to refer people to the appropriate agency or individual who can answer questions about groundwater, noise, or other concerns. Instead of holding only one public meeting at the beginning of the process, the bureau has set up three meetings so that people can get information when the license application has been received, and also later in the process, as more questions or concerns arise. Bureau employees stay as long as it takes to answer questions, although this rarely exceeds the ninety minutes allotted for these meetings.

Officials from the mining company are invited to attend, meet the local residents, and share information about the ways in which they will be good neighbors, making a positive impact on the community. In fact, this is the accomplishment about which John is the most proud. He has asked a number of mining companies around the state to meet with concerned citizens' groups to negotiate voluntary actions that mining companies can do to address some of the citizens' concerns. For example, one mining company, Voltron, has agreed to hold a pancake breakfast for the whole town in which the CEO will shake hands, meet locals, and tell them why the town will be better off after the mine opens. After meeting with concerned residents, Voltron reached an agreement to do the following: no fewer than 70 percent of the mine's employees will be hired out of the local population rather than brought in from outside, thereby guaranteeing local job creation; Voltron will build a public park with a playground near the mine so that property values will increase for those living closest to the mine rather than decrease; Voltron has agreed not to blast on weeknights after 8 PM, even though state law would allow blasting until 10 PM; and Voltron has agreed to form a problem-solving task force with the mayor and a representative group of stakeholders to address ongoing problems or issues as they arise, even after the mine is up and running. These changes cost the company very little but did a lot to show their willingness to be a good neighbor. When interviewed for the local paper, the CEO was asked, "Why would you agree to these requests when you clearly didn't have to under current state laws?" He replied, "Our managers and employees will be living here, too, as neighbors in this community. We want to make this a workable partnership for everyone involved. When we open a mine in another town a few years from now, the residents will hear about our good reputation and know they have nothing to be afraid of. This is the right thing to do and it is good business." As the leader of the Bureau of Reclamation, John's job has become much more pleasant since these changes were implemented. These changes have been noticed by other agencies, who are now asking John for his advice about how to improve their public engagement processes, too. John is now seen as a leader on public engagement issues, as is Voltron's CEO.

KEY TERMS

Collaboration fatigue

Consensus

Convening

Deliberative democracy

Process sponsor

Spoiler

SUGGESTED SUPPLEMENTAL READING

Addor, M. L., Cobb, T. D., Dukes, E. F., Ellerbrock, M., & Smutko, L. S. (2005). Linking theory to practice: A theory of change model of the Natural Resources Leadership Institute. *Conflict Resolution Quarterly*, *23*, 203–223.

Pyser, S. N., & Figallo, C. (2004). The "listening to the city" online dialogues experience: The impact of a full value contract. *Conflict Resolution Quarterly*, *21*, 381–393.

Sachs, A. M. (2000). Understanding public disputes resolution in community mediation. *Conflict Resolution Quarterly*, *17*, 341–349.

DISCUSSION QUESTIONS

1. Think back to the most productive meetings you have attended. Make a list of the characteristics that described these meetings and the people leading the meetings. Now, make a list of characteristics to describe the last meeting you led or participated in as a manager. Compare the two.

Share these with a classmate or colleague and consider the changes you could do to implement positive changes.

2. Which of the qualities of a skilled facilitator do you already have and which would you like to work on?

EXERCISES

1. Go to the website of any local, state, or federal government agency to find one or more upcoming public meetings on a topic of interest. Alternatively, if you are a shareholder or manager within a corporate environment, attend a shareholder's meeting. Answer the following questions:

   - How was the meeting advertised? Was it advertised adequately so stakeholders were aware and able to attend?

   - How was the room arranged?

   - What was turnout like? If it there were too many or too few participants, was it handled appropriately?

   - Was there a clear agenda and did the facilitator stick to it? Alternatively, if it became clear that the agenda was not working, did the facilitator make reasoned changes?

   - Take the temperature of the room. What was the level of interest, anxiety, excitement, or anger?

   - Was the decision-making process or the purpose of the meeting clear to attendees? Was their role in that process clear? How was it received?

   - What mechanism was used to gather public input or share information with the public? How effective were these mechanisms?

   - How did the meeting end? Were next steps discussed with those present? Will there be minutes shared publicly? Will there be additional opportunities for input or information sharing?

   - What recommendations for process improvements would you make?

2. Select a current hot topic of debate in your community, such as the siting of new public facilities, zoning issues, plans to build or widen roads, changes to policies regarding public health or welfare, and so forth. Screen this issue using the screening tools supplied here (www.wiley.com/college/raines) to

determine whether this issue would be a good candidate for a large-group consensus and collaboration process.

3. Use an online chat or bulletin board to post discussion questions from this chapter with your classmates or colleagues. Take turns facilitating the group discussion online, seeking feedback at the end of the exercise so as to work on continual improvement of your facilitation skills.

GOAL SETTING

At your next opportunity, ask one or more trusted colleagues to observe your facilitation skills and provide feedback after the meeting. Consider videotaping yourself to review and critique yourself.

CONCLUSION

In addition to introducing basic conflict management skills and theories, *Conflict Management for Managers* has been designed to address all realms of managerial conflict: from internal employment disputes to external conflicts with customers and clients as well as conflicts between regulators and the regulated. You have read multiple examples from organizations that have grown stronger, even during difficult economic times, because they have systematically monitored and reduced the costs of unproductive conflict.

EVERY MANAGER IS A CONFLICT MANAGER

Long before you read this book, you were managing conflicts. Whether your day includes complaints from customers, in-fighting between employees, poor team work in work units, providing feedback during performance reviews, negotiating with suppliers and vendors, hiring and training new employees due to turnover, or a myriad of other managerial tasks, your day involves the management of conflict and frequent negotiations. According to Cloke and Goldsmith (2011), exceptional leader managers have a number of traits and habits that set them apart. First, they make good decisions in chaotic or challenging environments and those decisions remain true to their espoused values. They don't sacrifice their belief in treating people right just because times get tough. Second, they are able to enlist and motivate others to address seemingly insurmountable problems or conflicts by looking for common ground and shared interests. Third, these managers create "respectful, ethical, innovative, and productive work environments where everyone is encouraged to invent solutions for ongoing conflicts" (2011, p. viii). Those managers who thrive and who look forward to coming to work every day are those who proactively, respectfully, and thoughtfully address conflict rather than those who seek to ignore it or pass it on to another manager or department.

The question is not whether you are a conflict manager. The question is, "What kind of conflict manager are you?"

THE GOAL: CONTINUED GROWTH AND IMPROVEMENT

Even the best managers have room for improvement. The same is true for organizations as a whole. Whether your organization or work unit is highly functional or dysfunctional, there is likely room for improvement or a need to consider how did we get here and where do we want to be as an organization. Be sure you understand those behaviors, attitudes, policies, and elements of organizational culture that are serving you and your organization well. You certainly don't want to change those. This means some sort of benchmarking is needed for you as an individual and your work unit or organization as a whole. How does your performance stack up to what it could be, to those you consider to be great leader managers? What are some realistic goals for self-improvement that you can set and revisit periodically? Would a performance coach be a worthwhile investment during this effort? Or perhaps a mentor within the organization or at a similar one? Positive change will only come when your performance is monitored and goals for improvement are set. Only you can determine what those goals should be, the timeline for their achievement, and the rubrics by which your performance changes will be measured. Spend some time considering the goals you would like to work on this week, this month, and this year. Be sure to set up automatic reminders that will prompt you to take stock of your movement toward (or even away) from those goals. How will you know when your goals have been achieved?

SELF-REFLECTION FOR GOAL SETTING

In order to ensure your continual improvement, consider setting aside just a few minutes at the end of each day to reflect about what worked well, what didn't, and what changes you will make in order to learn from the day's challenges. Did you have a difficult conversation with an employee, customer, or regulator? How did that go? Did you use active listening skills, frame your comments constructively, remain open to feedback, and engage in interest-based negotiation to reach a solution that will work well for all parties? Which parts of your performance went well and which would you like to continue to work on in order to achieve even better results next time?

Setting aside time for self-reflection accomplishes at least two important goals: first, it helps you transfer the skills and knowledge from the written pages of this book to your actual working experience (called *transference* in pedagogical lingo).

Conflict management habits took years to create and won't be changed quickly or without conscious effort. Taking the time to reflect on your performance will ensure you are transferring what you are learning into behavioral changes. Second, self-reflection helps provide mental closure so you do not ruminate over situations that did not go as well as you had hoped. Rather than beating yourself up about what you should have said or done, self-reflection allows you to make an action plan to redress the situation or learn from the incident so it is not repeated. This allows you to mentally move on rather than dwelling on the problem or beating yourself up over missteps that are likely to occur as you attempt to implement changes to your old habits.

At the end of this chapter, there is a self-reflection assignment and questionnaire. Use this assignment to take stock of your current use of these techniques. Choose one or more areas to set an improvement goal. During the next month, focus on improving your performance in this area(s), then come back and take the survey again to look for improvement.

BUT I'M NOT A MANAGER YET . . .

No problem. If you have read this far, you surely intend to be a manager in the future. The skills and knowledge in this book can help you get there. Understanding your own communication style and how to communicate with others will help you as you work your way up in your organization or seek a new job. Active listening skills, self-reflection, and understanding the need for collaborative problem solving with unions, vendors, and customers will help gain you a solid reputation as someone with management potential. Building trust with your coworkers and managers, offering integrative solutions to problems that arise, and receiving and giving constructive feedback will help you achieve your goal of working in management. Apply the skills you can now, making note of those changes you would like to implement once you have greater decision-making authority. Self-reflection and goal setting are just as important for your continued growth as an employee as they are for managers.

DON'T MANAGE LIKE A DINOSAUR

Did you read this book and at least once or twice have a cynical reaction? You may have noted there still seem to be some managers who rule with an iron fist rather than a collaborative spirit. In spite of their authoritarian methods, some of these managers seem to survive, even thrive in their environments. What gives? If the best managers are proactive at managing conflict, if they seek integrative solutions and treat people respectfully and inclusively, then why do we still see some mean managers thriving, too? Kenneth Lloyd (1999) gave a name to these dictatorial, hostile, and often inappropriate managers: *jerks at work*. How do we explain their amazing staying power? Unfortunately, recent studies indicate that jerks at work earn more than nice guys on average but only if they are male (Rodgers, 2011). Men rated as less agreeable than their coworkers were found to earn more than others. The effect of disagreeableness didn't work for women. Although this isn't good news, the research indicates change is on the horizon.

There is some confusion as to why male managers who are disagreeable can still rise to the top in certain organizations or fields but there is more unanimity that they are a dying breed that can wreak havoc on an organization if not stopped. Perhaps those above and below them in the hierarchy simply seek to avoid confrontations with them, thereby allowing their bullying or rude behavior to continue rather than pursue their demotion or expulsion.

In any event, jerks at work can have a negative impact on the bottom line for their work units and entire organizations. "Disruptive behavior can impact engagement and there are absolutely mirroring characteristics that those bad apples can convey onto other people. Then, there is a downward spiral" (Rodgers, 2011). Organizations need to decide which behaviors they seek to foster and reward at work. Raises and promotions that are grounded in positive behaviors and the ability to play well with others are critical to rooting out bad behaviors, which in turn, reduces employee turnover and improves morale. Rodgers (2011) notes that it is more acceptable for women to be tough than for men to be perceived as nurturing. Getting rid of jerks near the top of the organizational food chain can mean changing the organizational culture and reward structures.

According to research by Davenport (2009) and others, jerks make poor decisions because they do not invite or welcome input from others, they see their own perspective as the only one that is valid, they believe they are always right, and they have difficulty thinking objectively and learning from mistakes. An interesting example comes from the debacles in the financial industry that arose in the mid- to late 2000s. For example, Joe Cassano came into power at the helm of AIG after his predecessor retired. By all accounts, Cassano was a jerk. "His crime was not mere legal fraudulence, but the deeper kind: a need for subservience in others and an unwillingness to acknowledge his own weaknesses"

(Davenport, 2009). He did not fully understand the complicated mathematics models being used or the changes in those models that led to poor decisions … and he refused to acknowledge that he needed help to understand them.

Similarly, Dick Fuld of Lehman Brothers is widely denounced as the jerk who let his bad personality get in the way of a bailout for his organization. He treated Hank Paulson, the secretary of the US Treasury, rudely, in plain view of many others during a dinner party in Spring 2008. Later, Paulson would decide to bail out Goldman Sachs but not Lehman Brothers. Although many factors likely influenced this decision, the poor treatment of Paulson has been noted by many as a factor that did not work in Lehman Brothers' favor. Clearly, treating others well not only makes it easier to sleep at night, it helps advance your career and your organization's mission. "Jerks often seem to get ahead in firms and advance through the ranks, but that's a dangerous phenomenon. If you want good decisions in your organization, don't hire, promote, or retain jerks" (Davenport, 2009).

The authoritarian approach to management was tolerated and even promoted during the twentieth century when factories and assembly lines were the mainstay of economic productivity. As North America has moved toward a service and knowledge-based economy the nature of work itself has changed, and workplace cultures have changed as well. Managers and supervisors are increasingly valued for their ability to support and motivate employees, removing obstacles to the fulfillment of their required tasks and duties along the way. The changes in the nature of work, along with emerging norms against bullying and disrespectful treatment, require a new kind of manager—a more collaborative manager. Managers who continue to use outdated methods will experience less success at work. Their organizations are more vulnerable to claims of discrimination, harassment, and the creation of a hostile work environment. Not only are these managers jerks at work, they are increasingly dated in their approach to management. Like the dinosaurs who roamed the earth millions of years ago, these managers are becoming extinct—they either adapt to new expectations and norms of respectful treatment or they die out. Although some of these old school managers remain, especially in industries in which competition and aggressive behavior are more common and hierarchies are entrenched (e.g., sales, banking and finance, professional sports and entertainment, factory settings), they are increasingly less common and less rewarded for these behaviors. They are a dying breed.

The techniques contained in this book are designed to support the changing expectations for managers in the twenty-first century. Through learning and adaptation to change, leaders and organizations can thrive even in the most challenging economic or political environments.

A SYSTEMIC APPROACH TO CONFLICT MANAGEMENT

This book has repeatedly argued for the use of a systemic approach to conflict. Your organization has preexisting systems for managing conflict but they might be invisible, informal, or outdated. A system approach is used to catalog the sources of conflicts, analyze their costs, create systems for the prevention of unproductive conflicts, and manage unpreventable conflicts to early and efficient resolutions. Through the conscious application of the techniques in this book, your ability to work successfully with your team, your customers, and within regulatory relationships will be greatly improved. But remember, it takes time and practice to change habits that have been deeply ingrained. Expect mistakes, invite feedback, and set goals for yourself and the organization or unit you manage. The larger the organization, the slower it may be to implement big changes in the processes used for handling conflict—yet the potential gains are bigger as well.

SUGGESTED SUPPLEMENTAL READING

The evolution of leadership, 2(9). Mind Resources Institute of Learning and Innovation. Retrieved from http://www.mindresources.net/web/institutejournal5/Article2.pdf

DISCUSSION QUESTIONS

1. Has your management style or approach changed since you began reading this text? If so, how and in what ways has it changed?

2. If you are not a manager yet, how can you use the concepts, processes, and skills found in this text to help you attain a management position or to move up in the ranks of your organization?

EXERCISES

1. Go back to Chapter One and retake the conflict skills inventory. Have your scores changed since you began reading and implementing the techniques contained in this book? Have you been able to consciously match your response to the problem or conflict at hand?

2. Self-reflection assignment: Answer the following questions. Once answered, set a goal for improving one or more of these measures within the next month. Then come back and retake the survey. Do this each month for one year. This is not an exhaustive list. Take a few minutes to add some questions that are customized to your managerial goals or your organizational needs.

   a. I get to know each employee as an individual, paying particular attention to his or her professional development goals and how I can assist in their professional development.

      ____Yes, definitely ____Somewhat ____A little bit ____Not really ____Unsure

   b. I use interest-based negotiation techniques with employees, superiors, clients, and regulatory agencies (or the regulated community) in order to ensure positive relationships and mutually beneficial outcomes.

      ____Yes, definitely ____Somewhat ____A little bit ____Not really ____Unsure

   c. I correctly identify those situations in which active listening is called for and apply it effectively, being sure to listen for understanding rather than listening to respond.

      ____Yes, definitely ____Somewhat ____A little bit ____Not really ____Unsure

   d. When conflict arises, I am able to identify potential cognitive biases at work in myself and take corrective actions (e.g., attribution bias, denial, reactive devaluation, etc.).

      ____Yes, definitely ____Somewhat ____A little bit ____Not really ____Unsure

   e. When providing feedback to employees, I use the EPM formula to empathize, pinpoint problems specifically, and suggest a constructive path forward together.

      ____Yes, definitely ____Somewhat ____A little bit ____Not really ____Unsure

   f. I receive feedback with an open mind, understanding that even poorly framed criticism may help me improve my management skills and understand the concerns of those around me. I refrain from becoming defensive and do not attack the person providing feedback to me.

_____Yes, definitely _____Somewhat _____A little bit _____Not really
_____Unsure

g. I build teams purposefully, train them to communicate effectively, and help them proactively manage challenges that arise during their collaborations.

_____Yes, definitely _____Somewhat _____A little bit _____Not really
_____Unsure

h. I understand that conflict can be a constructive and powerful force for organizational improvement and enhanced relationships. It is the way conflict is managed that determines whether its outcome will be positive or negative.

_____Yes, definitely _____Somewhat _____A little bit _____Not really
_____Unsure

i. I have conducted a needs assessment to catalog the sources and costs of conflict within my unit or organization.

_____Yes, definitely _____Somewhat _____A little bit _____Not really
_____Unsure or nonapplicable

j. My organization has created a system(s) for efficiently managing the conflicts we can reasonably expect to recur with employees and with our customers and clients.

_____Yes, definitely _____Somewhat _____A little bit _____Not really
_____Unsure or nonapplicable

k. I facilitate productive, efficient meetings that start and end on time. The goals for each meeting are clear to myself and to those in attendance and the goals are largely accomplished.

_____Yes, definitely _____Somewhat _____A little bit _____Not really
_____Unsure or nonapplicable

l. I make time to attend to, create, and sustain a positive organizational culture, including team building, intervening to stop bullying or disrespectful treatment, the explicit creation and dissemination of behavioral norms, and leading by example in my treatment of others.

____Yes, definitely ____Somewhat ____A little bit ____Not really ____Unsure

m. I understand the causes of employee turnover in my unit or organization and have taken appropriate steps to reduce unnecessary turnover.

____Yes, definitely ____Somewhat ____A little bit ____Not really ____Unsure

n. I am proactive and collaborative rather than competitive in my relationships with the union and its leadership. I understand that we survive and thrive together.

____Yes, definitely ____Somewhat ____A little bit ____Not really ____Unsure

o. I bring in external specialists as necessary to improve performance and reduce unproductive conflicts (i.e., performance coaches, mentoring programs, mediators, arbitrators, ombudsmen, dispute systems designers, etc.).

____Yes, definitely ____Somewhat ____A little bit ____Not really ____Unsure

p. I know which governmental agencies regulate or interact regularly with my organization and the individuals within those agencies with whom I need to work collaboratively. I proactively manage relationships and problem solving with regulators (or members of the regulated community).

____Yes, definitely ____Somewhat ____A little bit ____Not really ____Unsure

q. Positive or negative incentives for individual performance or behaviors are aligned with the organization's mission, goals, and values. What is good for the individual is also good for the team and organization and what is good for the organization is also good for individual employees.

____Yes, definitely ____Somewhat ____A little bit ____Not really ____Unsure

r. Everyone in my work unit can recite the organizational mission and is clear as to their role in the achievement of that mission.

____Yes, definitely ____Somewhat ____A little bit ____Not really ____Unsure

s. I regularly take time to reflect on my performance as a manager, taking stock of the actions that work well as well as those that need improvement. I invite feedback and input from my colleagues in an effort to continually improve my performance as a manager.

____Yes, definitely ____Somewhat ____A little bit ____Not really ____Unsure

GOAL SETTING

Using the list in exercise two, choose two or three questions in which you answered "a little bit" or "not really" and seek to improve your performance on those issues. Come back and take the test again in one month and see if your scores have improved.

GLOSSARY

Accommodative style: Occurs when individuals have a preferred outcome but are willing to sacrifice their preferences so the other negotiators can realize their own, conflicting preferences, thereby ensuring no harm comes to the relationship between them.

Acculturative stress: Occurs when culture change causes confusion and frustration, accidental transgressions, and then disharmony between workers. Acculturative stress is likely to be highest in new employees as they learn the cultural norms of the organization or during the process of mergers and acquisitions because cultural norms and expectations are in flux.

Accuser bias: A form of fundamental attribution error that is "the tendency for an observer negatively affected by an actor's behavior to attribute the behavior to causes under control of the actor" (Allred, 2000, p. 244).

Acquisition: Occurs when one company buys and assumes management of another, usually smaller, company.

Active listening: Occurs when listeners give the speaker all of their attention, listen to understand the speaker's meaning in content and in import, and confirm the meaning has been understood through summarizing back what has been said. Active listening serves multiple purposes: increased understanding on listeners' parts, building rapport and relationship between speakers and listeners, and making space for speakers to share something they consider important.

Adjudication: The formal process through which a judge renders a decision in a case before the court.

Administrative adjudication: Refers to the process through which agencies determine whether an individual or group is guilty of violating administrative rules.

Administrative law: "The name given to agencies' rule making and resolution of conflicts regarding their rules" (Harrison, Harris, & Tolchin, 2009, p. 479).

Administrative rule making: The "process by which upper-level bureaucrats use their administrative discretion and their expertise in the policy area to create rules, regulations, and standards that the bureaucracy will then enforce" (Harrison, Harris, & Tolchin, 2009, p. 480).

Agency capture: Occurs when governmental regulatory agencies begin to advocate for the industries or interests they are supposed to regulate rather than objectively ensuring they adhere to all applicable laws and rules.

Alternative dispute resolution (ADR): Refers to a host of processes that serve as alternatives to costly and adversarial litigation, including mediation, arbitration, the use of an ombudsman, and others.

Arbitration: An alternative dispute resolution process in which the parties hire a neutral, expert third-party decision maker to act as a private judge in their dispute. Arbitration is commonly used to resolve disputes in unionized workplaces, and arbitration decisions can serve as precedent for future similar cases within a union contract. Arbitration rulings do not set a legal precedent in the courts and cannot generally be appealed there except in cases of arbitrator misconduct.

Asking price: The first proposal shared by each party to the negotiation. Also called *initial offer*.

Assimilation: Occurs when the culture of one organization is imposed on, dominates, and replaces the original culture of the other organization.

Attribution theory: Explains the ways in which cognitive biases hinder our ability to accurately understand the motivations behind the behaviors of others.

Avoidant style: A common approach to conflict in which an individual ignores and refuses to acknowledge the presence of a conflict or significant problem. Typically, these individuals are uncomfortable with their ability to manage conflict proactively and successfully so they remain in a state of denial about the presence of conflict much longer than those with other preferred conflict styles. Once the conflict can no longer be ignored, these individuals sometimes blow up and overreact or become irrationally angry because they feel they should not have to address the conflict but are being forced to do so by others or by the situation itself.

Backcasting: A problem-solving technique in which the facilitator, mediator, or manager asks the parties to envision a future in which the problem is solved or the relationship is repaired. The parties are asked to describe what that looks like or feels like. Then, the parties are asked to describe the steps that each of them would need to take in order to reach that ideal future state. The parties are asked to focus on the actions that each person can take personally rather than focusing on the actions they wish the others would take.

BATNA: An acronym that stands for *best alternative to a negotiated agreement*.

Bias of the accused: Our tendency to downplay our own poor decisions or actions while attributing them to circumstances beyond our control.

Blue collar: Employees who work at jobs that are based on hourly pay and usually include manual labor. They may be considered **skilled laborers** or **unskilled laborers**.

Brainstorming: An important part of a problem-solving process. During brainstorming all parties agree to think broadly about any and all possible solutions to the problem at hand. It is critical to the success of the brainstorming process that the participants agree to separate the process of generating options from the process of evaluating those options.

Bullying: "Can be considered as a form of coercive interpersonal influence. It involves deliberately inflicting injury or discomfort on another person repeatedly through physical contact, verbal abuse, exclusion, or other negative actions" (Forsyth, 2006, p. 206). The behavior must be intentional, repeated over time, and have a negative impact on the target. Bullies wear down their victims over time, usually for more than a year in workplace settings (Einarsen & Skogstad, 1996).

Business-to-business (B2B): Refers to relationships in which the customer is another business.

Case evaluation: A process in which a neutral expert is hired to evaluate the strengths and weaknesses of each side's case and predict for the parties what would happen in court.

Claiming value: Occurs when a negotiator seeks to gain as much of a fixed resource as possible, leaving less for other negotiators.

Cognitive bias: A pattern of deviation in judgment leading to inaccurate conclusions, distorted perceptions of reality, illogical interpretation of facts or events, and often leads to irrational behaviors or thought patterns (Kahneman & Tversky, 1972).

Collaboration: Has four key constituent elements: interdependent stakeholders (i.e., those affected by a decision), the ability to constructively address differences, joint ownership of decisions, and collective responsibility for the future of the partnership. Collaboration occurs when multiple parties come together to accomplish a common objective because of a shared need, through authentic conversations in which people speak frankly and listen to one another, and under norms of reciprocity that require a cooperative give-and-take that enables the group to negotiate effectively.

Collaboration fatigue: The weariness that sets in among negotiators after talks have been ongoing for months or even years, especially if progress seems elusive or minimal. The signs of collaboration fatigue include falling meeting attendance, growing impatience or inattentiveness of representatives, and a decreased willingness to financially support the collaborative process.

Collaborative monitoring: Seeks to engage interested and affected stakeholders, public agencies, and scientific and technical experts in a more direct fashion to jointly gather data and information in an ongoing manner. This helps avoid the tendency for each group to gather information on its own, which supports its own preferred outcomes.

Collaborative public management: Defined as "the process of facilitating and operating in multi-organizational arrangements to solve problems that cannot be solved or easily solved by single organizations. Collaborative means to co-labor, to achieve common goals, often working across boundaries and in multi-sector-actor relationships. Collaborative public management may include participatory governance: the active involvement of citizens in government decision-making" (O'Leary & Blomgren Bingham, 2009, p. 3).

Collaborative style: Indicates a preference to work together with others to achieve outcomes that meet the needs of all negotiators. This style occurs when two or more individuals work together to share information and make joint decisions.

Collective bargaining: A process of negotiation between employers and the employees' representatives aimed at reaching agreements that regulate working conditions and pay.

Collective bargaining agreement: The agreement reached between an employees' union and the company outlining the terms of employment. This agreement covers the initial contract between a group of employees and company leaders as well as periodic renegotiation of that contract.

Collectivist societies: Where individual identities are based on ties to the group or community and one is expected to make decisions that take into account the best interests of the family, tribe, or community.

Competitive style: The competitive style indicates a preference to "win as much as you can," even at the expense of the other side or the relationship between negotiators.

Compromising style: Indicates a preference for splitting the difference between the negotiator's positions. Compromise can be a quick, efficient way to reach a solution. The compromising style is appropriate when a decision is not highly important, the time for negotiation and discussion is relatively short, and the process needs to be viewed as fair to all parties. One risk of using a compromise is that other styles, such as the collaborative style, might result in outcomes that create more value for both parties.

Conflict assessment: Helps to identify the issues of controversy in a given situation, the affected interests, and the appropriate form(s) of conflict resolution. Also called a *needs assessment*, this analysis is used to determine whether an ADR or collaborative process is likely to succeed.

Conflict avoidance: Occurs when an individual or group has evidence that a problem currently exists or will soon exist but no steps are taken to acknowledge and address the problem. Conflict avoiders refuse to acknowledge that the problem exists, in the hope that it will just go away.

Conflict coaching: "A process in which a coach and client communicate one-on-one for the purpose of developing the client's conflict-related understanding, interaction strategies, and interaction skills. Coaches help clients to make sense of conflicts they experience, help them learn to positively manage these conflicts, and help them master specific communication skills and behaviors" (Jones & Brinkert, 2008, pp. 4–5).

Conflict management (CM): Refers to the systematic prevention of unproductive conflict and proactively addressing those conflicts that cannot be prevented. Every workplace has existing conflict management methods but these methods have not usually been explicitly discussed, examined, and (re)designed for maximal efficiency and user satisfaction.

Conflict prevention: Occurs when an individual or group examines the sources of predictable and recurring problems and then takes reasonable steps to address the root causes of those problems so that they do not occur or recur.

Conflict styles inventory (CSI): A personality assessment tool designed to measure the conflict resolution reactions and habits of an individual. This information can be useful to understand one's basic approach to conflict as well as to learn how to match conflicts with effect response strategies.

Consensus: Occurs in matters of policy when "the parties have reached a meeting of the minds sufficient to make a decision and carry it out no one who could block or obstruct the decision or its implementation will exercise that power and everyone needed to support the decision and put it into effect will do so" (Arthur, Carlson, & Moore, 1999, p. 5).

Consensus building: Describes a number of collaborative decision-making techniques in which a facilitator or mediator is used to assist diverse or competing interest groups to reach agreement on policy matters, environmental conflicts, or other issues in controversy affecting a large number of people.

Contingent agreements: For example, if *x* happens by (insert date), then we both agree to do *y*. If *x* does not happen by this date, then we agree instead to do *z*. This allows both parties to react to changing future circumstances without needing to renegotiate the contract.

Convening: The process of bringing stakeholders together to design the process jointly and begin the dialogue or negotiation.

Creating value: When negotiators work together to ensure each of their needs are met by expanding existing value through collaboration, increased efficiency, or creativity.

Customer loyalty programs: A method for rewarding return customers by giving them, for example, a thirteenth night free or a free domestic airline ticket once they accumulate fifty thousand frequent flyer miles, and so on. These programs may help lure customers back to your business when there are others offering basically the same products and services at similar prices.

Customer recovery: Refers to the policies and practices put into place to address a disgruntled customer with the goal of winning back the customer's loyalty and business.

Customer satisfaction: Defined as "a measure of how a firm's product or service performs compared to customer's expectations" (Zondiros, Konstantopoulos, & Tomaras, 2007, p. 1086).

Customers as business partners: Means that organizations should evolve their mind-set from a worldview that sees each transaction as a one-time event to instead seeing each transaction as a chance to build a long-term, mutually beneficial relationship (Witschger, 2011).

Deculturation: Occurs when employees in one of the organizations or within some subunit of an organization reject the culture of the acquiring company but realize their old cultural behaviors and beliefs no longer work well in the new organizational environment.

Deliberative democracy: Refers to the underlying principle that for laws to have true legitimacy they must be subject to authentic deliberation prior to a majority vote. Authentic deliberation means that decision makers engage in discussion, debate, and analysis that is free from the influence of unequal power based on wealth, status, or other sources of inequality. The goal of deliberative democracy is to move toward consensus but decisions can be made based on majority vote once deliberations have occurred and all have had a chance to participate. Deliberative democracy is a founding principle of Western governmental systems, albeit incompletely achieved in practice.

Denial: Occurs when the reality of a situation is so overwhelming that it potentially causes an emotional breakdown. To avoid this potential, one refuses to acknowledge the reality of a situation in order to allow it to sink in slowly (if at all) rather than all at once.

Design team (DT): Composed of employees from different parts and levels of the organization who will assist in the development, implementation, and evaluation of the dispute system design.

Disassociation: Occurs when individuals are emotionally overwhelmed by a situation and therefore have difficulty focusing on that situation. Their minds may wander to more attractive thoughts, such as where to go on vacation or even drift toward making a mental grocery list—anything seen as safe or pleasant. In common terms, they daydream.

Displacement: Involves changing the topic as another way to avoid dealing directly with a problem or acting upset about one issue when it is really a different issue that has caused one's upset.

Dispute systems design (DSD): Refers to the strategic arrangement of dispute resolution processes within an organization (Costantino & Merchant, 1996). Disputing systems are commonly defined for internal employment disputes or disputes with external stakeholders such as clients, customers, or regulators (e.g., EEOC complaints within a federal agency or environmental enforcement cases with polluters). The goal of DSD processes is to track and reduce the occurrence and costs of disputes that can reasonably be predicted to occur within an organization and between the organization and external audiences such as customers, vendors, and regulators.

Distributive bargaining: Refers to negotiations between parties with perceived competitive goals. In distributive bargaining situations, resources are fixed and cannot be increased. Also called *win-lose* or *zero-sum negotiations*.

Distributive justice: Deals with perceptions that outcomes and payouts are fairly distributed. Perceptions of distributive justice generally hinge on one of three criteria for determining the fairness of an outcome: equity, equality, or need.

Diversity: Refers to all the ways in which individuals may differ: gender, race, ethnicity, age, technical abilities and backgrounds, sexual orientation, religiosity and religious affiliation, social class, work style, worldview, and so on.

Emotional intelligence (EI): Refers to the ability to perceive, control, and evaluate emotions in oneself and others. Emotional intelligence can be further broken down into four factors: the perception of emotion, the ability to reason using emotions, the ability to understand emotion, and the ability to manage emotions.

Employee turnover: Refers to the rate at which employees leave the organization and should be broken down by rank and location to better isolate the potential root causes. Average rates of employee turnover vary by industry and within organizations.

Environment and public policy conflict resolution (E/PP): Application of alternative dispute resolution methods to environmental and public policy issues.

Environmental conflict resolution (ECR): Refers to people with differing views and interests working together in a systematic and organized way to find workable solutions to shared problems about environmental issues, usually with the assistance of a neutral third party.

Equality principle: States that all group members should receive equal amounts of any good or benefit that comes from the labors of the group. Under this version of fairness, all employees would receive the same pay.

Equity principle: Denotes that benefits should be distributed based on each person or group's contribution; those who worked harder or contributed greater expertise to a project should receive a disproportionate amount of the fruits of that labor.

Ethnocentrism: The belief that one's cultural practices are inherently superior to those from other cultures.

Exit interview (exit survey): Used to gather information about the reasons why employees are leaving the organization, their perspectives about how the organization could improve as an employer and in the accomplishment of its mission, and various other points of information deemed vital to constant improvement. Employees who have made the choice to leave the organization may be in a position to be more honest about their observations than ongoing employees who may fear reprisals or retribution for speaking out.

External locus of control: Those who believe that they are controlled by factors external to themselves such as a higher power, the environment, political forces, and so on.

External stakeholders: Could include customers, vendors, shareholders, patients, the affected public, and regulators.

Facilitation: A group process in which either an inside or outside neutral leads the discussions in a neutral manner in order to assist in promoting an efficient and civil discussion process that stays on track.

Fairness: Fairness can be variably defined as the quality of being just, equitable, impartial, or evenhanded. Fairness can refer to the process by which decisions were made and the outcome of those decisions. Depending on one's perspective, there may be many contradictory viewpoints about what comprises a fair outcome depending on one's preference for equity, equality, or need-based outcomes.

Fallback offer: The offer made once the initial offer is rejected. It is somewhere in between the initial offer and the resistance point and it may lead to an agreement.

FourSight teams: Those teams that take a specific four-step approach to decision making: they define the problem, brainstorm solutions, sift out the best solution, and carry out their plan.

Framing: Refers to the ways in which facts or perceptions are defined, constructed, or labeled. "Framing is a process whereby communicators, consciously or unconsciously, act to construct a point of view that encourages the facts of a given situation to be interpreted by others in a particular manner. Frames operate in four key ways: they define problems, diagnose causes, make moral judgments, and suggest remedies. Frames are often found within a narrative account of an issue or event, and are generally the central organizing idea" (Kuypers, 2006, p. 7).

Framing effect: A cognitive bias occurring when the same option is presented in different formats or with different phrasing (i.e., it is framed differently) and the choice of format or phrasing unduly influences one's opinion or preferences on the matter.

Free riders: People who enjoy the benefit of a public good without paying their share for it. For example, someone who refuses to pay his taxes but still uses public roads, libraries, and emergency services is a free rider.

Fundamental attribution errors: Occurs when we incorrectly attribute peoples' behaviors to their dispositional or personality characteristics rather than attributing them to a situational factor.

Genius teams: Small teams of brilliant employees who benefit from lots of close contact while working with each other.

Great Recession: Refers to the period of negative and slow economic growth and high unemployment and underemployment that began in approximately 2007 and continues at the time of this writing (December 2011).

High-context cultures: When the majority of meaning is conveyed via nonverbal means such as eye contact, tone, the use of silence, and scripted conversations. *High context* refers to the degree to which one must understand the context of the conversation in order to understand the intended meaning. In high-context cultures the burden of understanding falls to the listener, not the speaker.

Impasse: (pronounced *im-pass*, not *im-pas-say*) Means the negotiation concludes with no agreement. Also known as a *stalemate*.

Improv teams: Highly adaptable and adjust well to rapidly changing circumstances. Team members are interchangeable and can tag team as necessary.

Individualistic societies: Those in which the needs, rights, and responsibilities of the individual are prioritized above those of the group or community. In these societies, it is generally considered positive for an individual to stand out from peers through individual achievements, whereas in collectivist societies it is less appropriate for individuals to stand out from the crowd.

Informal managerial mediation: Occurs when a manager acts as an informal mediator between two or more employees, supervisors, or managers in dispute. As an informal mediator, the manager listens to each party and encourages them to listen to each other. She engages the parties in a problem-solving discussion with the goal of reaching an agreement that meets the needs of all parties and is superior to continuing the dispute via more formal channels.

Informational justice: The quality of explanations about issues, outcomes, and procedures for decision making.

Inside counsel: Refers to attorneys who are employees of an organization and are salaried. As a salaried employee, their incentives for settlement may differ from outside counsel, who are typically paid by the hour to represent the organization.

Integration: Occurs when neither group involved in a merger or acquisition dominates the other. Although both cultures change because of their interactions, the resulting culture(s) are not dominated by either organization and both retain some distinct cultural aspects.

Integration manager: Helps the merger and acquisition process in four ways: speed it up, create a structure for it, forge social connections between the two organizations, and engineer short-term successes. This person can be thought of as an M&A ombudsman — managing conflicts and problems that arise during the M&A process and proactively working to minimize those conflicts.

Integrative bargaining: Those negotiations in which multiple negotiators can achieve their goals without necessarily leaving the others worse off.

Interests: Tell us of the needs that underlie the positions or demands being made during a negotiation, for example, the position "I demand a raise" and the interest "I need to earn more money in order to pay my student loans." Understanding the underlying interests of each party allows the negotiation to move away from a zero-sum discussion to one in which all parties leave the negotiation better off than they would be through the use of distributive bargaining techniques.

Internal locus of control: Means that individuals believe they are in control of events that affect themselves rather than being controlled by external forces such as God, the environment, or those in powerful positions. Individualistic societies are more likely to espouse a belief in an internal locus of control.

Internal stakeholders: Include employees at all levels and the legal and HR departments.

Interpersonal justice: Whether one is treated with dignity, respect, kindness, and honesty.

Joint fact finding: A process by which interested parties commit to building a mutual understanding of disputed scientific or technical information. Interested parties can select their own experts who presumably reflect differing interpretations of available information. Alternatively, they can also jointly decide on an unassociated third-party expert or a panel of experts. A facilitator or mediator works to clarify and define areas of agreement, disagreement, and uncertainty. The facilitator or mediator can coach the experts to translate technical information into a form that is understandable to all interested parties. The goal is to avoid adversarial or partisan science in which competing experts magnify small differences rather than focusing on points of agreement and creating a strategy to provide for a joint conclusion.

Leader-member exchange theory: A body of research that examines the types of relationships that form between leaders and organizational members as well as the benefits that accrue to leaders and members as a result of these relationships. This approach posits that the best managers develop positive relationships with organizational members based on "trust, respect, loyalty, liking, intimacy, support, openness, and honesty" (Wilson, Sin, & Conlon, 2010, p. 358).

Listening to respond: When people generally listen to figure out when they can jump into the conversation and get out their view, opinion, and thoughts rather than truly listening to understand.

Listening to understand: Requires the listener to suspend judgment and the need to drive the conversation. Instead of listening for the moment to jump into the conversation, the goal of listening to understand is to allow the speaker to completely share thoughts, concerns, or emotions with the listener, uninterrupted. This calls for active listening.

Litigation: The process of filing a court case and taking the necessary procedural steps to prepare that case for adjudication.

Low-context cultures: One in which most of the meaning is conveyed in the explicit verbal conversation as opposed to being implied through the context, nonverbal cue, or the use of scripted conversations. In low-context cultures the burden for understanding falls on the speaker. If the speaker is clear enough, then the listener will likely understand the intended meaning.

Mandatory arbitration clause: A binding predispute contract committing both parties to use arbitration for dispute settlement in the event of a future dispute. By signing a mandatory arbitration clause both parties give up their right to resort to resolution through the court systems.

Maslow's hierarchy of needs: Abraham Maslow was a psychologist who studied human motivations and behaviors. He is primarily known for his theory of a hierarchy of needs, which states that humans seek to satisfy their needs in order of importance. Primary needs included the need to breathe, eat, reproduce, and so on. The next most-pressing needs involve those related to safety—physical security of oneself and one's family, employment, and control over one's property. The third group of needs involves meeting the need for belonging in a community and feeling loved. Next comes the need to feel confident, respected, and have self-esteem. Finally, humans need to be able to express themselves as "self-actualized" individuals, including practicing creativity, moral choice, and problem solving.

Mediation: A process of facilitated negotiation in which the mediator does not act as a judge but instead assists the parties as they strive to have a civil, productive conversation about how to resolve the dispute and rebuild relationships (if appropriate).

Merger: A process through which two or more companies come together, with one retaining its corporate existence and the others losing theirs. The remaining company acquires all the assets and debts of the company it has acquired. From a conflict management perspective, mergers and acquisitions present myriad challenges related to organizational culture, change management, and communication that require proactive behaviors on the part of organizational leaders in order to achieve success.

Metacommunication: Occurs when people communicate about how they communicate. This information can avoid misunderstandings and attribution biases that often occur when one communicates with someone whose preferred patterns or methods of communication differ from his or her own.

Monochronic time orientation: Shows that one prefers to adhere to strict schedules and deadlines. Time is viewed as something tangible that can be saved, spent, or wasted. This orientation toward time is most common in countries such as Great Britain, Germany, Switzerland, the United States, Australia, and other cultures of Western European origin. People with this orientation may be somewhat less flexible and more driven by deadlines. They may also prefer to get right down to the task at hand rather than spend time building relationships. They tend to believe there is a right time for specific activities (e.g., arrive at work by 8:30 AM, take no more than a one-hour lunch, and so on).

Need principle: Asserts that more of the goods or benefits should go to those who need more. Therefore, a parent with three young children might receive greater pay or fewer taxes than someone with no children at all.

Need theories: Refer to those explanations for human behavior, including conflict, based on the unmet needs of individuals.

Needs assessment: See **Conflict assessment**.

Negotiated rule making: A multiparty consensus process in which a balanced negotiating committee seeks to reach agreement on the substance of a proposed agency rule, policy, or standard. The negotiating committee is composed of representatives of those interests that will be affected by or have an interest in the rule, including the rule-making agency itself. Affected interests that are represented in the negotiations are expected to abide by any resulting agreement and implement its terms. This agreement-seeking process usually occurs only after a thorough conflict assessment has been conducted and is generally undertaken with the assistance of a skilled, neutral mediator or facilitator. Also called *regulatory negotiation* or *reg-neg*.

Negotiation: Occurs between two or more interdependent parties who have a perceived conflict between their needs and desires yet believe a negotiated outcome is superior to the outcome they could achieve unilaterally.

Nonstructural sources of conflict: Occur one time or rarely, occurring generally as isolated events that could not have been predicted or avoided. These are generally resolved by taking action to resolve the individual problem rather than creating or changing policies across the organization.

Nonverbal communication: Includes many contextual cues that convey acknowledgment of power dynamics and emotional ties or lack thereof between individuals or groups. Nonverbal communication is conveyed through tone, body language, eye contact, and even such things as clothing, hairstyles, and demeanor, which convey relative social status and dominance or submission within a chain of command.

Ombudsman (ombuds): An organizational conflict management specialist who works to resolve either internal disputes with employees or external disputes with customers, clients, vendors, or business partners.

Open-door policy: When every manager is open to hearing from every employee. An open-door policy means that any employee with a problem can go to any manager in the organization for help to solve that problem. Although there is usually a preference to start lowest on the chain of command and work their way up, ultimately an open-door policy means employees can choose which manager to approach for help with a problem.

Organizational justice: Composed of four components: distributive justice (i.e., whether outcomes and payouts are fairly distributed), procedural justice (i.e., fairness in processes), informational justice (i.e., the quality of explanations about issues, outcomes, and procedures for decision making), and interpersonal justice (i.e., whether one is treated with dignity, respect, kindness, honesty, etc.). Perceptions of organizational justice are important because they are related to a host of behaviors within organizations that are crucial to mission achievement, including employee turnover, sabotage, or embezzlement by employees, shirking, absenteeism, presenteeism, and the commitment to caring for customers and clients.

Outside counsel: Refers to attorneys hired from outside the organization to which legal matters are referred for settlement or litigation.

Partnering: A long-term commitment between two or more organizations for the purpose of achieving specific business objectives by maximizing the effectiveness of each participant's resources (Anderson & Polkinghorn, 2008).

Patient care advocate (PCA): Someone who works either in the emergency department or in other parts of the hospital and is on call to manage patient complaints, to deescalate conflict when it arises, and to solve problems early whenever possible.

Peer review: A process most commonly used within organizational settings to deal with internal employment disputes such as claims of discrimination, wrongful termination, demotions, claims of favoritism or nepotism, or employee appeals of other disciplinary actions. The peer-review process is designed to allow employees to decide whether their peers are being treated fairly by the organization and its managers or supervisors.

Policy dialogues: Processes that bring together representatives of groups with divergent views or interests to tap the collective views of participants in the process. The goals include opening up discussion, improving communication and mutual understanding, exploring the issues of controversy to see if participants' different viewpoints can be distilled into general recommendations, and trying to reach agreement on a proposed policy standard or guidelines to be recommended by government. They are often used to address complex environmental conflicts or public policy disputes constructively.

Polychronic time orientation: Means one believes there are many right times to do different activities (e.g., arrive at work anytime between 8:30 AM and 10:00 AM, take a flexible lunch break, etc.). Polychronic cultures tend to arise nearer the equator, where seasonal differences are smaller (e.g., many Latino and Island cultures). Individuals from polychronic cultures tend to be more comfortable with flexible deadlines and spend time building relationships before attending to tasks.

Positions: Demands that have only one way to be met and lead to win-lose outcomes in which one party's gain comes at the other party's expense.

Positive conflict: The healthy sharing of differences of opinion and negotiation necessary to make tough decisions. Also called *cooperative conflict*.

Presenteeism: Occurs when an employee wishes to leave the organization but hasn't done so yet. Although remaining in the job, the employee is less committed to the organization, its customers, and its other employees. This lack of commitment is displayed through lower productivity and occasionally through acts of sabotage, theft, or embezzlement.

Primary stakeholders: Primary stakeholders are those most immediately affected by the policy outcomes.

Procedural justice: Deals with the fairness of the process used for reaching a decision or resolving a conflict. Individuals tend to perceive that a process is fair when it is transparent, respectful, and allows them to be heard during the decision-making process.

Process sponsor: The organization that convenes and usually financially supports the large-group process of decision making or information exchange. The sponsor is usually a governmental agency but it can also be a private or nonprofit organization or the process can be jointly sponsored by more than one organization. The sponsor generally conducts an assessment of the conflict or, ideally, hires an outside consultant to conduct an unbiased assessment.

Public disputes: Complex, multiparty, decision-making, or consensus-building processes on issues affecting the public interest or policy that involve complicated networks of interests, unequal accountability among stakeholders, strongly held values, and are highly influenced by governmental rules and regulations.

Public good: Something that, by its nature, is either supplied to all people or to none, regardless of whether or not each individual has paid his or her fair share for the enjoyment of that good. For example, national defense, clean air, public roads, and public libraries are all public goods: if they exist for anyone, then they exist for everyone.

Rationalization: Refers to the psychological tendency that individuals have to find rational reasons why their own behaviors make sense under the prevailing circumstances that were beyond their control.

Reframing: Refers to the language used to summarize, paraphrase, and reflect back what a party has said but using a different frame than originally intended with the goal of altering the course of the communication between two or more parties.

Regulatory agencies: Regulatory agencies are usually a part of the executive branch of the government at the federal or state level, or they have statutory authority to perform their functions with oversight from the legislative branch. Regulatory authorities are commonly set up to enforce standards and safety, regulate commerce, or to oversee public goods such as national defense or clean air. Regulatory agencies deal in the area of administrative law—regulation or rule making.

Relationship conflict: Occurs when two or more people experience nonstructural conflict stemming from a lack of rapport or personality conflicts between team members. Relationship conflict is associated with negative effects on the team's ability to accomplish its tasks (Farh, Lee, & Farh, 2010).

Relationship management: Refers to the specific techniques used to court and retain valued customers and partners over a long period of time.

Resistance point: Whereas the target point is the goal in a negotiation, the resistance point is the bottom line. The resistance point is the smallest amount the merchant will settle for and is sometimes referred to as the *reservation price* (Lewicki, Barry, & Saunders, 2010).

Revolving door: Refers to the fact that government bureaucrats often leave their government careers behind and go to work for the agencies they used to regulate. Similarly, members of Congress often become lobbyists when they leave elected office. The powerful ties among industry, Congress, and government regulatory agencies mean that a relatively small, tight-knit group of powerful decision makers are usually involved in rule making within each agency's issue area. This reduces the number and variety of voices heard when important decisions are being made and increases the public's distrust of many decision-making processes.

Secondary stakeholders: Individuals or groups who are indirectly affected by decisions or actions of an organization.

Separation: Occurs when little or no culture change comes to either organization, with each having little interaction with the other and no significant cultural changes resulting from the M&A process.

Settlement point: The spot within the settlement range where the negotiators reach agreement on settlement terms. The goal in distributive bargaining is to reach an agreement that is close to the other side's resistance point.

Settlement range: The space between two resistance points. For example, if the buyer's initial offer is $5,000 and her resistance point is $8,000 and the seller's initial offer is $9,000 but his resistance point is $6,000, then the settlement range will be between $6,000 and $8,000. Also called the *zone of agreement*.

Shared mental model (SMM): Those aspects of knowledge known by each team member are known collectively as a shared mental model.

Shirking: When employees choose not to do their share of the collective workload. As a result, other members of the team have to work harder to make up for those employees. Shirkers lead others in the organization to feel disgruntled, overworked, and taken advantage of. Also known as *social loafing*.

Sick-outs: Occur when unionized employees stage massive work stoppages by calling in sick for work to show their solidarity and bargaining strength. These sick-outs have sometimes been called the *blue flu* because police officers' unions have used them to overcome laws against labor strikes by first responders and other essential public employees.

Skilled labor: Those jobs that require special training, knowledge, and often an apprenticeship, such as plumbers, electricians, or carpenters.

Spoiler: Someone who uses his power to sabotage the group's progress in order to gain attention or further his own goals or gain attention. Spoilers usually hold significantly more extreme views than the majority of process participants and can use consensus processes to stall or sabotage outcomes they wish to avoid.

Stakeholders: Those who are directly or indirectly affected by a proposed change—they have a stake in the outcome.

Structural sources of conflict: Include unfair, unclear, or inefficient policies, procedures, organizational cultures, or ingrained practices that repeatedly give rise to disputes irrespective of personnel changes.

Summarizing: Occurs when the listener repeats back what he or she has heard the speaker say. In active listening, the summary focuses primarily on the emotional meaning and content of the speaker's message.

Summary jury trials (SJTs): Consists of trying the case in front of a judge and usually a mock jury. In advance of the mock trial, the attorneys and parties in the case reach agreements related to the types of evidence to be admitted, the length of the trial (usually one to three days), and whether the verdict will be binding or advisory. If the process is advisory, it is used as a settlement tool to enable both sides to see the weaknesses in their case and get the jury's objective perspective on the matter.

Sunshine laws: Refers to federal, state, and local laws that require regulatory meetings, decisions, and records to be open to the public.

Target point: The negotiator's end goal or preferred outcome for the negotiation.

Task conflict: Occurs when the group disagrees about the best ways to accomplish its tasks. Moderate levels of task conflict are associated with greater creativity and better outcomes, whereas relationship conflicts are associated with reduced productivity and morale.

Team cognition: The ability to think like a team.

Team mental models (TMMs): Jointly held information within a group.

The 10–80–10 percent rule: Means that 10 percent of employees won't steal under any circumstances. Another 10 percent are dishonest and nothing can be done to change their desire to steal so preventative accounting and other measures need to be in place. The other 80 percent will be influenced by the workplace climate and the thoughts of their peers on the matter. Therefore the key to reducing workplace theft or malfeasance is to create a workplace climate in which employees feel loyalty toward their organizations and where cultural norms mitigate against such behaviors.

Theory of relative deprivation: States that a sense of injustice can arise when one compares one's distribution to others in a competitive environment and sees that others are receiving more.

Transaction costs: Every negotiation entails transaction costs, which include the time, energy, and money necessary to facilitate the negotiation and the deal itself.

Transactive memory systems (TMSs): Mental maps disseminating the information held by individual members of a team and clarifying who knows what within the team.

Union grievance: Any alleged violation of the "contract, past practice, employer rules, previous grievance or arbitration settlements [which set precedence for the contract's interpretation], or any violation of laws such as Occupational Health and Safety, Americans with Disabilities Act, Family Medical Leave Act, or EEOC regulations on race, age or sex discrimination" (UE Information for Workers, 2011).

Union steward: The first point of contact for each rank-and-file union member when a grievance arises. The union steward is usually a position elected by the union members, someone who is generally liked and trusted by the employees. The steward can advise the union member as to whether the complaint is an actual violation of the union contract as well as offer information about the available dispute resolution options. The union steward may also accompany the employee to any grievance process such as mediation or arbitration and represent them in that process. The steward can provide information about the contents of the collective bargaining agreement and those issues that may or may not fall under its terms.

Unskilled labor: Used in those jobs that require little training and education, making workers easily replaced at a lower cost to employers. Traditionally, the labor market has had a larger surplus of unskilled rather than skilled laborers, making the former more vulnerable to poverty and at a bargaining disadvantage in terms of their ability to press employers for higher wages or better working conditions.

Virtual teams: Internet based and therefore members may come from anywhere on the globe and are unable or only infrequently able to meet in person.

White collar: A term used to describe skilled workers who do not usually wear uniforms, who undertake intellectual rather than physical work, and who have generally pursued education beyond secondary school (meaning they have attended college or university). These employees generally include supervisors and managers.

Zero sum: A negotiation concept indicating a winner-take-all scenario in which one negotiator receives everything sought and the other receives nothing. It is also used to show that one negotiator's gain comes at the other's expense.

REFERENCES

Abbasi, S. M., Hollman, K. W., & Hayes, R. D. (2008). Bad bosses and how not to be one. *Information Management Journal, 42*(1), 52–56.

Abramson, N. R. (2005). Building and maintaining effective buyer-seller relationships: A comparative study of American and Canadian expectations. *Journal of Promotion Management, 12*(1), 129–150.

Adler, P. S., & Fisher, R. C. (2007). Leading from behind: The un-heroic challenge of leading leaders. *ACResolution*, Summer, 18–21.

Alexander, M. (1999). *Transforming your workplace: A model for implementing change and labour-management cooperation.* Retrieved from http://irc .queensu.ca/gallery/1/cis-transforming-your-workplace-a-model-for -implementing-change-and-labour-management-cooperation.pdf

Allen, D. G. (2008). *Retaining talent: A guide to analyzing and managing employee turnover.* Alexandria, VA: The SHRM Foundation. Retrieved from http://www.shrm.org/about/foundation/research/Documents/Retaining %20Talent-%20Final.pdf

Allred, K. G. (2000). Anger and retaliation in conflict: The role of attribution. In M. Deutsch & P. Coleman (Eds.), *The handbook of conflict resolution: Theory and practice* (pp. 236–255). San Francisco: Jossey-Bass.

Amble, B. (2006, May 26). *Poor conflict management costs business billions.* Management Issues Ltd. Retrieved from http://www.management-issues.com /display_page.asp?section=research&id=3262

Anderson Jr., L. L., & Polkinghorn, B. (2008). Managing conflict in construction megaprojects: Leadership and third-party principles. *Conflict Resolution Quarterly, 26,* 167–198.

Angier, T. (2009, November 23). The biology behind the milk of human kindness. *New York Times*, p. D2.

Aronson, P. (2011). *How not to be sued.* Retrieved from http://www.private disputeresolutionservices.com/nottobesued.html

Arthur, J., Carlson, C., & Moore, J. (1999). *A practical guide to consensus.* Santa Fe, NM: Policy Consensus Initiative.

Ashkenas, R. N., & Francis, S. C. (2000). Integration managers: Special leaders for special times. *Harvard Business Review, 78,* 108–116.

Association of Certified Fraud Examiners (CFE). (2004). *2004 report to the nation on occupational fraud and abuse.* Retrieved from http://www.acfe.com /uploadedFiles/ACFE_Website/Content/documents/2004RttN.pdf

Austin, J. R. (2003). Transactive memory in organizational groups: The effects of content, consensus, specialization, and accuracy on group performance. *Journal of Applied Psychology, 88*(5), 866–878.

Babiak, P., & Hare, R. D. (2006). *Snakes in suits: When psychopaths go to work.* New York: HarperCollins.

Baghat, S., Brickley, J. A., & Coles, J. L. (1994). The costs of inefficient bargaining and financial distress: Evidence from corporate lawsuits. *Journal of Financial Economics, 35*(2), 221–247.

Bandura, A. (1973). *Aggression: A social learning analysis.* Englewood Cliffs, NJ: Prentice-Hall.

Barrett, J. T. (2007) Labor-management golden years: A foundation for today's ADR. *ACResolution,* Summer, 4.

Bass, B., & Bass, R. (2009). *The handbook of leadership: Theory, research, and managerial applications.* New York: Free Press.

Bass, B. M., & Avolio, B. J. (Eds.). (1994). *Improving organizational effectiveness through transformational leadership.* Thousand Oaks, CA: Sage Publications.

Bazerman, M. H., & Neale, M. A. (1992). *Negotiating rationally.* New York: Free Press.

Beierle, T. C., & Cayford, J. (2002). *Democracy in practice: Public participation in environmental decisions.* Washington, DC: RFF Press.

Beng-Chong, L., & Klein, K. J. (2006). Team mental models and team performance: A field study of the effects of team mental model similarity and accuracy. *Journal of Organizational Behavior, 27*(4), 403.

Bens, I. (2005). *Facilitating with ease! Core Skills for facilitators, team leaders and members, managers, consultants, and trainers.* San Francisco: Jossey-Bass.

Berry, J. W. (1983). Acculturation: A comparative analysis of alternative forms. In R. J. Samuda & S. L. Woods (Eds.), *Perspectives in immigrant and minority education* (pp. 66–77). Lanham, MD: University Press of America.

Bessette, J. M. (1980). Deliberative democracy: The majority principle in Republican government. In R. Goldwin & W. Shambra (Eds.), *How democratic is the Constitution?* (pp. 102–116) Washington, DC: AEI Press.

Bingham, L. B. (2002). Self-determination in dispute system design and employment arbitration. *University of Miami Law Review, 56,* 873–908.

Bingham, L. B. (2004). Employment dispute resolution: The case for mediation. *Conflict Resolution Quarterly, 22*(1–2), 145–174.

Bingham, L. B. (2008). Designing justice: Legal institutions and other systems for managing conflict. *Ohio State Journal on Dispute Resolution, 24,* 1–51.

Bingham, L. B., Hedeen, T., Napoli, L. M., & Raines, S. S. (2003). *A tale of three cities: Before and after REDRESS.* Unpublished manuscript.

Bingham, L. B., Kim, K., & Raines, S. S. (2002). Exploring the role of representation in employment mediation at the U.S.P.S. *Ohio State Journal on Dispute Resolution, 17,* 341–378.

Bingham, L. B., Nabatchi, T., Senger, J., & Jackman, M. S. (2009). Dispute resolution and the vanishing trial: Comparing federal government litigation and ADR outcomes. *Ohio State Journal of Dispute Resolution, 24,* 225–262.

Bingham, L. B., & Novac, M. C. (2001). Mediation's impact on formal discrimination complaint filing: Before and after the REDRESS program at the USPS. *Review of Public Personnel Administration, 21,* 308–331.

Birkinshaw, J., Bresman, H., & Hakanson, L. (2000). Managing the post-acquisition integration process: How the human integration and task integration processes interact to foster value creation. *Journal of Management Studies, 37*(3), 395–425.

Blackard, K. (2000). *Managing change in a unionized workplace: Countervailing collaboration.* Westport, CT: Greenwood.

Bland, V. (2004). Keeping customers (satisfied). *NZBusiness, 18*(8), 16–20.

Blodget, H. (2011, March 20). Eight habits of highly effective Google managers. *Business Insider.* Retrieved from http://articles.businessinsider.com/2011–03 -20/strategy/30006167_1_operations-managers-manifesto

Bough, V. (2011, June 21). Executive Q & A with Jim Bush of American Express. Victoria Bough's blog on Forrester.com. Retrieved from http:// blogs.forrester.com/victoria_bough/11–06–21-executive_qa_with_jim_bush _of_american_express

Brannen, M. Y., Gómez, C., Peterson, M. F., Romani, L., Sagiv, L., & Wu, P. C. (2004). People in global organizations: Culture, personality and social dynamics. In H. W. Lane, M. L. Maznevski, M. E. Mendenhall, & J. McNett (Eds.), *The Blackwell handbook of global management: A guide to managing complexity* (pp. 26–55). Malden, MA: Blackwell Publishing.

Bridges, W. (1991). *Managing change in a unionized workplace: Countervailing collaboration.* Westport, CT: Greenwood.

Brosnan, M., Turner-Cobb, J., Munro-Naan, Z., & Jessop, D. (2009). Absence of a normal cortisol awakening response (CAR) in adolescent males with Asperger Syndrome (AS). *Psychoneuroendocrinology, 34*(7), 1095–1100. Retrieved from http://opus.bath.ac.uk/13807/

Brown, J., & Isaacs, D. (2005). *The world café: Shaping our futures through conversations that matter.* San Francisco: Berrett-Koehler.

Bruner, R. F. (2005). *M&A lessons that rise above the ashes: Deals from hell.* Hoboken, NJ: John Wiley & Sons.

Bryant, A. (2011, March 13). The quest to build a better boss. *New York Times.* Retrieved from http://query.nytimes.com/gst/fullpage.html?res=9503E3DD 173EF930A25750C0A9679D8B63&scp=2&sq=Google%27s%20Quest%20to %20Build%20a%20Better%20Boss&st=cse

Bryson, J., & Crosby, B. (2006). Leadership for the common good. In S. Schuman (Ed.), *Creating a culture of collaboration.* San Francisco: Jossey-Bass.

Burns, M. (2010). *How American Express empowers call center employees to deliver great customer service experience: A report from Forrester's customer service forum 2010.* Retrieved from http://www.forrester.com/rb/Research /how_american_express_empowers_call_center_employees/q/id/57803/t/2

Bush, J. (2011, April 19). How American Express transformed its call centers. *Harvard Business Review.* Retrieved from http://blogs.hbr.org/cs/2011/04 /american_express_how_we_transf.html

Bush, R. A., & Folger, J. P. (1994). *The promise of mediation: The transformative approach to conflict.* San Francisco: Jossey-Bass.

Bush, R. A., & Folger, J. P. (2005). *The promise of mediation: The transformative approach to conflict* (2nd ed.). San Francisco: Jossey-Bass.

Carpenter, S. L., & Kennedy, W. J. (2001). *Managing public disputes: A practical guide for government, business and citizens' groups.* San Francisco: Jossey-Bass.

Cartwright, S., & Cooper, C. L. (1994). The human effects of mergers and acquisitions. *Journal of Organizational Behavior, 1*, 47–61.

Center for Public Integrity. (2008). *The Bush administration instituted a hiring freeze in 2001 and kept budget requests for the Equal Employment Opportunity Commission modest, even while the number of complaints increased. iWatch News.* Retrieved from http://www.publicintegrity.org/2008/12/10/6204/chronic-understaffing-eeoc

Chan, K. W., Huang, X., & Ng, P. M. (2008). Managers' conflict management styles and employee attitudinal outcomes: The mediating role of trust. *Asia Pacific Journal of Management, 25*(2), 277–295.

Charkoudian, L., & Wilson, C. (2006). Factors affecting individuals' decisions to use community mediation. *Review of Policy Research, 23*, 865–885.

Chaykowski, R., Cutcher-Gershenfeld, J., Kochan, T., & Sickles Merchant, C. (2001). *Facilitating resolution in union-management relationships: A guide for neutrals.* Society for Professionals in Dispute Resolution. Retrieved from http://digitalcommons.ilr.cornell.edu/cgi/viewcontent.cgi?article=1002&context=icrpubs

Cherry, K. (2012). *What is emotional intelligence? Definitions, history and measures of emotional intelligence.* About.com Psychology. Retrieved from http://psychology.about.com/od/personalitydevelopment/a/emotionalintell.htm

Children's Healthcare of Atlanta (CHOA). (2011). *Facts about Children's: A model for pediatric care.* Retrieved from http://www.choa.org/About-Childrens/Awards-and-Recognition/Facts-and-Figures

Cianci, R., & Gambrel, P. A. (2003). Maslow's hierarchy of needs: Does it apply in a collectivist culture? *Journal of Applied Management and Entrepreneurship, 8*(2), 143–161.

Citizens Against Lawsuit Abuse. (2007). *Litigation costs and opportunities lost: The fiscal impact of lawsuit abuse on California's largest counties and cities.* Retrieved from http://www.cala.com/docs/litigationcostsreport.pdf

Clermont, K. M., & Schwab, S. J. (2003). How employment-discrimination plaintiffs fare in the federal courts of appeals. *Employee Rights and Employment Policy Journal, 7*, 547.

Cloke, K., & Goldsmith, J. (1997). *The end of management and the rise of organizational democracy.* San Francisco: Jossey-Bass.

Cloke, K., & Goldsmith, J. (2003). *The art of waking people up: Cultivating awareness and authenticity at work.* San Francisco: Jossey-Bass.

Cloke, K., & Goldsmith, J. (2011). *Resolving conflicts at work: Ten strategies for everyone on the job* (3rd ed.). San Francisco: Jossey-Bass.

Coca-Cola Enterprises. (2011). *Corporate governance ombudsman*. Retrieved from http://ir.cokecce.com/phoenix.zhtml?c=117435&p=irol-govombudsman

Cole, M. S., Walter, F., & Bruch, H. (2008). The affective mechanisms linking dysfunctional behavior to performance in work teams: A moderated mediation study. *Journal of Applied Psychology, 93*, 945–958.

Coleman, D. (1992). How to achieve a productive partnership. *Journal of Accountancy, 173*(5), 113–118.

Colquitt, J. A., Conlon, D. E., Wesson, M. J., Porter, C., & Ng, K. Y. (2001). Justice at the millennium: A meta-analytic review of 25 years of organizational justice research. *Journal of Applied Psychology, 86*, 425–445.

Colvin, A. (2004). The relationship between employee involvement and workplace dispute resolution. *Relations Industrielles, 59*(4), 681–704.

Cooke, N. J., Gorman, J. C., Duran, J. L., & Taylor, A. R. (2007). Team cognition in experienced command-and-control teams. *Journal of Experimental Psychology, 13*(3), 146–157.

Costantino, C. A., & Merchant, C. S. (1996). *Designing conflict management systems: A guide to creating productive and healthy organizations*. San Francisco: Jossey-Bass.

Cox, D. (2010). *An examination of the impact of culture and human resources on cross-border M&A transactions*. Unpublished master's thesis. Kennesaw State University, Kennesaw, GA.

CPR Institute for Dispute Resolution. (2002). New skills and renewed challenges: Building better negotiation skills, *Alternatives, 20*(8), 1–22.

Crothers, L. M. (2009). Cliques, rumors, and gossip by the water cooler: Female bullying in the workplace. *The Psychologist-Manager Journal, 12*, 97–100.

Dana, D. (2001). *The Dana measure of financial cost of organizational conflict*. Retrieved from http://www.mediationworks.com/dmi/toolbox.htm

Darden Restaurants. (2011). *Dispute resolution procedures at Darden Restaurants*. YouTube. Retrieved from http://www.youtube.com/watch?v=Rs576 lPaov8

Darowski, M. (2009). The comfort of conciliation. *China Law & Practice*, p. 36.

Datamonitor. 2010. *UK consumer satisfaction index 2010: Sector summary*. Retrieved from http://www.datamonitor.com/store/Product/uk_consumer _satisfaction_index_2010_sector_summary?productid=DMVT0582

Davenport, T. (2009). Why jerks are bad decision makers. *Harvard Business Review*. Retrieved from http://blogs.hbr.org/davenport/2009/08/why_jerks _are_bad_decisionmake.html#.TuNaehTSNdU.email

DeChurch, L. A., & Marks, M. A. (2001). Maximizing the benefits of task conflict: The role of conflict management. *International Journal of Conflict Management*, *12*(1), 4.

DeChurch, L. A., & Mesmer-Magnus, J. (2010). The cognitive underpinnings of effective teamwork: A meta-analysis. *Journal of Applied Psychology*, *95*(1), 32–53.

DeCusatis, C. (2008). Creating, growing and sustaining efficient innovation teams. *Creativity and Innovation Management*, *17*(2), 155.

Deloitte. (2012). *The people's choice: Superior customer service in the public sector*. Podcast. Retrieved from http://www.deloitte.com/view/en_us/us /8ab4b44d3f0fb110VgnVCM100000ba42f00aRCRD.htm

Deutsch, M. (2000a). Cooperation and competition. In M. Deutsch & P. Coleman (Eds.), *The handbook of conflict resolution: Theory and practice* (pp. 21–40). San Francisco, CA: Jossey-Bass.

Deutsch, M. (2000b). Justice and conflict. In M. Deutsch & P. Coleman (Eds.), *The Handbook of conflict resolution: Theory and practice* (pp. 41–64). San Francisco: Jossey-Bass.

Deutsch, M., & Coleman, P. (Eds.). (2000). *The handbook of conflict resolution: Theory and practice*. San Francisco: Jossey-Bass.

Devasagayam, R., & DeMars, J. (2004). Consumer perceptions of alternative dispute resolution mechanisms in financial transactions. *Journal of Financial Services Marketing*, *8*(4), 378.

Dirks, K. T. (1999). The effects of interpersonal trust on work group performance. *Journal of Applied Psychology*, *84*(3), 445–455.

Drahozal, C. R., & Ware, S. J. (2010). Why do businesses use (or not use) arbitration clauses? *Ohio State Journal on Dispute Resolution*, *25*(2), 433–476.

Drucker, P. F. (2002). They're not employees, they're people. *Harvard Business Review*, *80*(2), 70–77.

Druckman, J. (2001). Evaluating framing effects. *Journal of Economic Psychology*, *22*, 96–101.

Duarte, M., & Davies, G. (2003). Testing the conflict—performance assumption in business-to-business relationships. *Industrial Marketing Management*, *32*(2), 91–99.

Duffy, J. (2010). Empathy, neutrality and emotional intelligence: A balancing act for the emotional Einstein. *Queensland University of Technology Law & Justice Journal, 10*(1), 44–61.

Duxbury, L., & Higgins, C. (2003). *Work-life conflict in Canada in the new millennium: A status report*. Retrieved from http://www.phac -aspc.gc.ca/publicat/work-travail/report2/index-eng.php

Einarsen, S., Hoel, H., Zapf, D., & Cooper, C. L. (2003). The concept of bullying at work: The European tradition. In S. Einarsen, H. Hoel, D. Zapf, & C. L. Cooper (Eds.), *Bullying and emotional abuse in the workplace* (pp. 3–30). London: Taylor & Francis.

Einarsen, S., & Skogstad, A. (1996). Bullying at work: Epidemiological findings in public and private organizations. *European Journal of Work and Organizational Psychology, 5*(2), 185–201.

Emerson, K., Orr, P. J., Keyes, D. L., & Mcknight, K. M. (2009). Environmental conflict resolution: Evaluating performance outcomes and contributing factors. *Conflict Resolution Quarterly, 27*, 27–64.

Engaging employees through social responsibility. (2007). *Leader to Leader, 46*, 56–58. Retrieved from http://www.sirota.com/pdfs/Engaging_Employees _through_Social_Responsibility.pdf

Equal Employment Opportunity Commission (EEOC). (2009). *EEOC mediation statistics FY 1999 through FY 2007*. The US Equal Employment Opportunity Commission. Retrieved from http://www.eeoc.gov/eeoc/mediation/mediation _stats.cfm

Equal Employment Opportunity Commission (EEOC). (2010). *EEOC reports job bias charges hit record high of nearly 100,000 in fiscal year 2010*. News release. Retrieved from http://www.eeoc.gov/eeoc/newsroom/release/1-11-11.cfm

Farh, J., Lee, C., & Farh, C. I. (2010). Task conflict and team creativity: A question of how much and when. *Journal of Applied Psychology, 95*(6), 1173–1180.

Farrell, L. U. (2002, March 18). Workplace bullying's high cost: $180m in lost time, productivity. *Orlando Business Journal*. Retrieved from http://orlando .bizjournals.com/orlando/stories/2002/03/18/focus1.html

Fedor, D. B., & Herold, D. M. (2008). *Change the way you lead change*. Stanford, CA: Stanford Business Books.

Fisher, R., & Ury, W. (1981). *Getting to yes: Negotiating agreement without giving in*. New York: Penguin Books.

Folger, J. P., Poole, M. S., & Stutman, R. K. (2000). *Working through conflict: Strategies for relationships, groups, and organizations* (4th ed.). New York: Longman.

Follett, M. P. (1942). Early sociology of "management and organizations." In M. Follett & L. Urwick (Eds.), *Dynamic administration: The collected papers of Mary Parker Follett.* (Vol. 3). New York: Taylor & Francis.

Ford, J. (2000). *Workplace conflict: Facts and figures.* Retrieved from http://www.mediate.com/articles/Ford1.cfm

Forsyth, D. R. (2006). *Group dynamics* (4th ed.). Belmont, CA: Thomson Wadsworth.

Fowler, E. (2011, July 28). *State attorney general questions Cobb School Board's emails.* SouthCobbPatch [website]. Retrieved from http://southcobb .patch.com/articles/state-attorney-general-questions-cobb-school-boards -emails-2

Friedlander, F. (1970). The primacy of trust as a facilitator of further group accomplishment. *Journal of Applied Behavioral Science, 6*(4), 387–400.

Garland's Digest. (2012). *Hooters of America, Inc. v. Phillips,* 173 F.3d 933; 4th Cir. April 8, 1999. Retrieved from http://www.garlands-digest.com/cs/4th /1990s/99/040499ho.html

Garrison, J. & Keller, L. (2008). *Southwest Airlines case study.* Retrieved from http://www.thomashauck.net/pdfs/1southwest.pdf

Gault, D. (2011). *Creating respectful, violence-free productive workplaces: A community level response to workplace violence.* Ramsey County Department of Public Health. Retrieved from http://www.tandfonline.com/doi/abs/10.1300 /J135v04n03_08#preview

Gerzon, M. (2006). *Leading through conflict.* Cambridge, MA: Harvard Business Press.

Gevers, J. M., & Peeters, M. (2009). A pleasure working together? The effects of dissimilarity in team member conscientiousness on team temporal processes and individual satisfaction. *Journal of Organizational Behavior, 30*(3), 379–400.

Gillespie, B. M., Chaboyer, W., & Murray, P. (2010). Enhancing communication in surgery through team training interventions: A systematic literature review. *AORN Journal, 92*(6), 642–657.

Gilly, M. C., & Gelb, B. D. (1982). Post-purchase consumer processes and the complaining consumer. *Journal of Consumer Research, 9*(3), 323–328.

Gittell, J. H., Von Nordenflycht, A., & Kochan, T. A. (2003, March). *Mutual gains or zero sum? Labor relations and firm performance in the airline industry*. MIT Sloan Working Paper No. 4298–03. Institute for Work and Employment Research Working Paper No. 01–2003. Retrieved from http://ssrn.com/abstract=395447

Godt, P. T. (2005). Additional tips for dealing with "difficult" people. *Illinois Reading Council Journal*, *33*(3), 57–59.

Goudreau, J. (2011). Disappearing middle class jobs. *Forbes*. Retrieved from http://www.forbes.com/sites/jennagoudreau/2011/06/22/disappearing-middle-class-jobs/

Gray, B. (1989). *Collaborating: Finding common ground for multiparty problems*. San Francisco: Jossey-Bass.

Greenberg, J. (1990). Looking fair vs. being fair: Managing impressions of organizational justice. In B. M. Staw & L. L. Cummings (Eds.), *Research in organizational behavior* (Vol. *12*, pp. 111–157). Greenwich, CT: JAI Press.

Greengard, S. (2003). Keeping the customer satisfied. *CIO Insight*, *109*, 32–35.

Greenhouse, S. (2010, June 4). Report warned Wal-Mart of risks before bias suit. *New York Times*, p. B1. Retrieved from http://www.nytimes.com/2010/06/04/business/04lawsuit.html?pagewanted=1&_r=1&src=mv

Gunnar, M. R., & Fisher, P. A. (2006). Bringing basic research on early experience and stress neurobiology to bear on preventive interventions for neglected and maltreated children. *Development and Psychopathology*, *18*(3), 651–677.

Hallberlin, C. J. (2001). Transforming workplace culture through mediation: Lessons learned from swimming upstream. *Hofstra Labor & Employment Law Journal*, *18*, 375–383.

Hamilton, W. D. (1964). The genetical evolution of social behaviour I and II. *Journal of Theoretical Biology*, *7*, 1–52.

Harms, P. D., & Credé, M. (2010). Emotional intelligence and transformational and transactional leadership: A meta-analysis. *Journal of Leadership & Organizational Studies*, *17*(1), 5–17.

Harrison, B. C., Harris, J. W., & Tolchin, S. J. (2009). *American democracy now*. Boston: McGraw-Hill.

Harrison, O. (2008). *Open space technology: A user's guide* (3rd ed.). San Francisco: Berrett-Koehler.

Hasson, R. (2006). How to resolve board disputes more effectively. *MIT Sloan Management Review*, *48*(1), 77–80.

Hayes, J. (2008). Foreword. In CCP GLOBAL, *Workplace Conflict and How Businesses Can Harness It to Thrive.* Retrieved from http://img.en25.com /Web/CPP/Conflict_report.pdf

Haynes, C. (2009). *Conflict management for mergers, acquisitions and downsizing.* Unpublished master's thesis. Kennesaw State University, Kennesaw, GA.

Health Canada. (1998). *Workplace health system.* Ottawa, Ontario: Canadian Fitness and Lifestyle Research Institute. Retrieved from http://www .hc-sc.gc.ca/ewh-semt/pubs/occup-travail/absenteeism/index-eng.php

Hempel, P. S., Zhang, Z., & Tjosvold, D. (2009). Conflict management between and within teams for trusting relationships and performance in China. *Journal of Organizational Behavior, 30*(1), 41–65.

Hickok, T. A. (1998). Downsizing organizational culture. *Journal of Public Administration and Management, 3*(3).

Hippensteele, S. K. (2009). Revisiting the promise of mediation for employment discrimination claims. *Pepperdine Dispute Resolution Law Journal, 9,* 211.

Hirsch, B. (2006). Wage determination in the US airline industry: Union power under product market constraints. Bonn, Germany: Institute for the Study of Labor. Retrieved from http://ftp.iza.org/dp2384.pdf

Howard, W. M. (1995). Arbitrating claims of employment discrimination: What really does happen? What really should happen? *Dispute Resolution Journal,* October–December, 40–50.

Hughes, S., & Bennett, M. (2005). *The art of mediation* (2nd ed.). Washington, DC: National Institute for Trial Advocacy.

Illinois Legal Aid. (2010). *How to represent yourself at an EEOC mediation.* Retrieved from http://www.illinoislegalaid.org/index.cfm?fuseaction=home .dsp_Content&contentID=5346

The incredibly shrinking U.S. middle class. (2011). *The Day.* Retrieved from http://www.theday.com/article/20110905/OP01/309059972

International Court of Arbitration. (nd). *Sample arbitration clauses.* Retrieved from http://www.dispute.it/?page_id=7

Ito, S., Toshihiko, T., & Fujimura, S. (2010). Effects of cultural assimilation in a cross-border M&A. *Transactions on Engineering Technologies, 4,* 389–402.

Jehn, K. A., Greer, L., Levine, S., & Szulanski, G. (2008). The effects of conflict types, dimensions, and emergent states on group outcomes. *Group Decision & Negotiation, 17*(6), 465–495.

Jones, T., & Brinkert, R. (2008). *Conflict coaching: Conflict management strategies and skills for the individual*. Thousand Oaks, CA: Sage Publications.

Kaboulian, L., & Sutherland, P. (2005). *Win-win labor-management collaboration in education: Breakthrough practices to benefit students, teachers and administrators*. Bethesda, MD: Education Week Press.

Kahneman, D., & Tversky, A. (1972). Subjective probability. *A judgment of representativeness. Cognitive Psychology, 3*(3), 430–454.

Katz, T. Y., & Block, C. J. (2000). Process and outcome goal orientations in conflict situations: The importance of framing. In M. Deutsch & P. Coleman (Eds.), *The handbook of conflict resolution: Theory and practice* (pp. 279–288). San Francisco: Jossey-Bass.

Kaufman, B. (2001). An interview with Lynn Williams. *Journal of Labor Research, 1*, 145–171.

Keyton, J. (1999). Analyzing interaction patterns in dysfunctional teams. *Small Group Research, 30*(4), 491–518.

Kim, Y. (2011). Confucianism-based organization value & post-merger syndrome in cross-border M&A: How family-system principles hinder communications in cross-border M&A. *International Journal of Business Management, 6*(2), 49–63.

King, E. B., Hebl, M. R., & Beal, D. J. (2009). Conflict and cooperation in diverse workgroups. *Journal of Social Issues, 65*, 261–285.

Klimoski, R. J., & Karol, B. L. (1976). The impact of trust on creative problem solving groups. *Journal of Applied Psychology, 61*(5), 630–633.

Knight, J. (2004, August 17). Bullied workers suffer "battle stress." *BBC News Online*. Retrieved from http://news.bbc.co.uk/2/hi/business/3563450.stm

Kochan, T. A., Von Nordenflycht, A., McKersie, R. B., & Gittell, J. H. (2003). *Out of the ashes: Options for rebuilding airline labor relations*. MIT Sloan Working Paper No. 4301–03. Retrieved from http://ssrn.com/abstract=395452

Kohli, J. (2010). *Happy workers are better workers: Improving labor-management relations in the federal government*. Center for American Progress. Retrieved from http://www.americanprogress.org/issues/2010/04/happy_workers.html

Kotter, J. P. (1996). *Leading change*. Cambridge, MA: Harvard Business School Press.

Kozlowski, S. W., & Ilgen, D. R. (2006). Enhancing the effectiveness of work groups and teams. *Psychological Science in the Public Interest, 7*(3), 77–124.

Kuypers, J. (2006). *Bush's war: Media bias and justifications for war in a terrorist age*. Lanham, MD: Rowman & Littlefield.

Kyckelhahn, T., & Cohen, T. H. (2008). *Civil rights complaints in U.S. District Courts, 1990–2006*. NCJ 222989. Washington, DC: United States Department of Justice, Office of Justice Programs, Bureau of Justice Statistics.

Langan-Fox, J. (2004). Mental models, team mental models, and performance: Process, development, and future directions. *Human Factors & Ergonomics in Manufacturing, 14*(4), 331–352.

Larson, E. (1996). The economic costs of sexual harassment: Expansion of a crime's definition obscures genuine instances of it. *The Freeman, 46*(8). Retrieved from http://www.thefreemanonline.org/features/the-economic -costs-of-sexual-harassment/

Lebedun, J., & Kantola, R. (1996). *The art of criticism: Giving and taking*. Mill Valley, CA: Kantola Productions.

Lee, M. (2010, April 28). *Finding, minding, binding and grinding*. Retrieved from http://www.bookmarklee.co.uk/2010/04/28/finding-minding-binding -grinding/

Legal Information Institute. (2012). *Gilmer v. Interstate/Johnson Lane Corporation*. Cornell University Law School. Retrieved from http://www.law .cornell.edu/supct/html/90–18.ZS.html

Lencioni, P. (2002). *The five dysfunctions of a team: A leadership fable*. San Francisco: Jossey-Bass.

Lewicki, R., Barry, B., & Saunders, D. (2010). *Essentials of negotiation*. New York: McGraw-Hill.

Lewicki, R. S. (2006). Trust, trust development, and repair. In M. Deutsch, P. T. Coleman, & E. C. Marcus (Eds.), *The handbook of conflict resolution: Theory and practice* (2nd ed.). San Francisco: Jossey-Bass.

Lewis, M. (2007). System design means process precision, but emphasizes culture, value and results. *Alternatives to the High Cost of Litigation, 25*(7), 113–119.

Linden, R. (2003). The discipline of collaboration. *Leader to Leader, 29*, 41–47.

Lloyd, K. (1999). *Jerks at work: How to deal with people problems and problem people*. Franklin Lakes, NJ: Career Press.

Luke, J. (1998). *Catalytic leadership: Strategies for an interconnected world*. San Francisco: Jossey-Bass.

Lutgen-Sandvik, P., Tracy, S. J., & Alberts, J. K. (2007). Burned by bullying in the American workplace: Prevalence, perception, degree and impact. *Journal of Management Studies, 44*, 837–862.

MacBriade-King, J. L., & Bachmann, K. (1999). *Solutions for the stressed-out worker*. Ontario: The Conference Board of Canada.

Maden, C. (2011). Dark side of mergers & acquisitions: Organizational interventions and survival strategies. *Journal of American Academy of Business, 17*(1), 188–195.

Magee, J. C., Galinsky, A. D., & Gruenfeld, D. (2007). Power, propensity to negotiate, and moving first in competitive interactions. *Personality and Social Psychology Bulletin, 33*(2), 200–212.

Malin, D. M. (2004). Johnson & Johnson's dispute resolution program: A new formula for achieving common ground. In S. Estreicher & D. Sherwyn (Eds.), *Alternative dispute resolution in the employment arena*. The Hague, Netherlands: Kluwer Law International.

Mallick, D. L. (2007). Don't think twice, mediation's alright: U.S. corporations should implement in-house mediation programs into their business plans to resolve disputes. *Harvard Negotiation Law Review*. Retrieved from http://www.hnlr.org/2009/03/us-corporations-should-implement-in-house-mediation-programs-into-their-business-plans-to-resolve-disputes/

Malveaux, S. M. (2009). Is it the "real thing"? How Coke's one-way binding arbitration may bridge the divide between litigation and arbitration. *Journal of Dispute Resolution*. CUA Columbus School of Law Legal Studies Research Paper No. 2009–11. Retrieved from http://papers.ssrn.com/sol3/papers.cfm?abstract_id=1472045

Manning, H. (2011). *Call center customer experience transformation at American Express—and that's the way it's done*. Forrester.com. Retrieved from http://blogs.forrester.com/harley_manning/11–07–08-call_center_customer_experience_transformation_at_american_express_and_thats_the_way_its_done

Markey, S. (2003, September 17). Monkeys show sense of fairness, study says. *National Geographic*. Retrieved from http://news.nationalgeographic.com/news/2003/09/0917_030917_monkeyfairness_2.html

Marks, M. L., & Mirvis, P. H. (2010). *Joining forces: Making one plus one equal three in mergers, acquisitions and alliances*. San Francisco: Jossey-Bass.

Maslow, A. (1954). *Motivation and personality*. New York: Harper and Row.

Matthiesen, S. B., & Einarsen, S. (2007). Perpetrators & targets of bullying at work: Role stress and individual differences. *Violence and Victims, 22*(6), 735–753.

McDermott, P., Obar, R., Jose, A., & Bowers, M. (2000, September 20). *An evaluation of the Equal Employment Opportunity Commission mediation program.* EEOC Order No. 9/0900/7632/2. Retrieved from http://www.eeoc.gov/eeoc/mediation/report/index.html

McEwen, C. (1994). *An evaluation of the Equal Employment Opportunity Commission's pilot mediation program.* Washington, DC: Center for Dispute Settlement.

McGown, A. (2009). Keeping customers satisfied. *Retail Merchandiser, 49*(3), 66–67.

Merecz, D., Drabek, M., & Mościcka, A. (2009). Aggression at the workplace — psychological consequences of abusive encounters with coworkers and clients. *International Journal of Occupational Medicine & Environmental Health, 22*(3), 243–260.

Meyer, C. B., & Altenborg, E. (2008). Incompatible strategies in international mergers: The failed merger between Telia and Telenor. *The Journal of International Business Studies, 39*(3), 508–525.

Monahan, C. (2008). Faster, cheaper, and unused: The paradox of grievance mediation in unionized environments. *Conflict Resolution Quarterly, 25*:479–496. doi: 10.1002/crq.218

Moore, C. (2003). *The mediation process: Practical strategies for resolving conflict* (3rd ed.). San Francisco: Jossey-Bass.

Moorman, R. H. (1991). Relationship between justice and organizational citizenship behaviors: Do fairness perceptions influence employee citizenship? *Journal of Applied Psychology, 76,* 845–855.

Moye, N. A., & Langfred, C. W. (2004). Information sharing and group conflict: Going beyond decision making to understand the effects of information sharing on group performance. *The International Journal of Conflict Management, 15*(4), 381–410.

Nabatchi, T., & Bingham, L. B. (2010). From postal to peaceful: Dispute system design in the USPS REDRESS program. *Review of Public Personnel Administration, 30*(2), 211–234.

Nahavavandi, A., & Malekzadeh, A. (1988). Acculturation in mergers and acquisitions. *Academy of Management Review, 13*(1), 79–90.

Namie, G., & Namie, R. (2003). *The bully at work: What you can do to stop the hurt and reclaim the dignity in your job.* Naperville, IL: Sourcebooks.

Neuberger, O. (1989). Mikropolitik als Gegenstand der Personalentwicklung [Micropolitics as object of personnel development]. *Zeitschrift fuer Arbeits und Organisationspsychologie, 33*(1), 40–46.

Neuliep, J. W. (2009). *Intercultural communication: A contextual approach* (4th ed.). Thousand Oaks, CA: Sage Publications.

Nielson, L. B., & Beim, A. (2004). Media misrepresentation: Title VII, print media, and public perceptions of discrimination litigation. *Stanford Law & Policy Review, 15,* 237.

Nowak, M., & Sigmund, K. (2005). Evolution of indirect reciprocity. *Nature, 437*(7063), 1291–1298.

O'Donovan, E. (2007). *Dealing with difficult people. District Administration, 43*(9), 70.

O'Leary, R., & Blomgren Bingham, L. (2011). *The collaborative public manager: New ideas for the twentieth century.* Washington, DC: Georgetown University Press.

Orr, P. J., Emerson, K., & Keyes, D. L. (2008). Environmental conflict resolution practice and performance: An evaluation framework. *Conflict Resolution Quarterly, 25,* 283–301.

Overman, S. (2011). Can a hybrid union/professional association give white-collar employees a voice at work without the power of collective bargaining? *Fortune.* Retrieved from http://finance.fortune.cnn.com/2011/09/02/not-quite -the-union-label/

Palmer, E. J., & Thakordas, V. (2005). Relationship between bullying and scores on the Buss-Perry aggression questionnaire among imprisoned male offenders. *Aggressive Behavior, 31,* 55–66.

Pearsall, M. J., Christian, M. S., & Ellis, A. J. (2010). Motivating interdependent teams: Individual rewards, shared rewards, or something in between? *Journal of Applied Psychology, 95*(1), 183–191.

Pelusi, N. (2006). Dealing with difficult people. *Psychology Today, 39*(5), 68–69.

Phillips, D. T. (1990, December). The price tag of turnover. *Personnel Journal,* p. 58.

Pikula, D. A. (1999). *Mergers & acquisitions: Organizational culture and HR Issues.* Kingston, Ontario: Industrial Relations Center.

Preston, P. (2005). Dealing with "difficult" people. *Journal of Healthcare Management, 50*(6), 367–370.

Quinn, R. (2004). *Building the bridge as you walk on it: A guide for leading change* (2nd ed.). San Francisco: Jossey-Bass.

Rafenstein, M. (2000). Dealing with difficult people on the job. *Current Health 2, 26*(5), 16.

Raines, S. (2002). Unheard voices in international environmental relations. Doctoral dissertation. Bloomington: Indiana University.

Raines, S., & O'Leary, R. (2000). Evaluating the use of alternative dispute resolution in U.S. Environmental Protection Agency enforcement cases: Views of agency attorneys. *Pace Environmental Law Review, 18*(1), 119.

Raines, S. S. (2005). Can online mediation be transformative? Tales from the front. *Conflict Resolution Quarterly, 22,* 2.

Raines, S. S., & Kubala, D. (2011). Environmental conflict resolution by water utilities: Applications and lessons learned. *Journal of the American Water Works Association, 103*(6), pp. 61–70.

Rains, J. (2011, April 18). Unconventional measures of customer service excellence. Wise Bread. Retrieved from http://www.openforum.com/idea -hub/topics/managing/article/unconventional-measures-of-customer-service -excellence

Rajagopal & Rajagopal, A. (2006). *Trust and cross-cultural dissimilarities in corporate environment.* Retrieved from http://papers.ssrn.com/sol3/papers.cfm? abstract_id=916023

Rigge, M. (1997). NHS—Keeping the customer satisfied. *Health Service Journal, 107*(5577), 24–27.

Robbennolt, J. K. (2003). *Apologies and legal settlement: An empirical examination.* 102 Mich. L. Rev. 460.

Rodgers, K. (2011, November 3). *Why being a jerk could pay off.* Fox Business News. Retrieved from http://www.foxbusiness.com/personal-finance/2011 /11/03/workplace-jerks-make-more-money/?cmpid=cmty_%7BlinkBack%7D _Why_Being_the_Office_Jerk_Could_Pay_Off

Rohlander, D. G. (1999). Effective team building. *IIE Solutions, 31*(9), 22.

Salovey, P., & Mayer, J. (1990). Emotional intelligence. *Imagination, Cognition & Personality, 9,* 185–211.

Sandy, S. V., Boardman, S. K., & Deutsch, M. (2000). Personality and conflict. In M. Deutsch & P. Coleman (Eds.), *The handbook of conflict resolution: Theory and practice* (pp. 289–315). San Francisco: Jossey-Bass.

Sarrio, J. (2011, March 19). School calendar dispute brings Cobb school board dissension. *Atlanta Journal-Constitution*. Retrieved from http://www.ajc.com /news/cobb/school-calendar-dispute-brings-878302.html

Schweiger, D. M., & Goulet, P. K. (2000). Integrating mergers and acquisitions: An international research review. *Advances in Mergers & Acquisitions, 1*, 61–91.

Scott, G. (2008). Take emotion out of conflict resolution. *T + D, 62*(2), 84.

SHRM. (2011). *Employee recognition programs survey findings*. Retrieved from http://www.shrm.org/Research/SurveyFindings/Articles/Pages/Employee RecognitionProgramsSurveyFindings.aspx

Sipe, N., & Stiftel, B. (1995). Mediating environmental enforcement disputes: How well does it work? *Environmental Impact Assessment Review 15*(2), 139.

Skilton, P. F., & Dooley, K. J. (2010). The effects of repeat collaboration on creative abrasion. *Academy of Management Review, 35*(1), 118–134.

Solomon, R. C., & Flores, F. (2001). *Building trust in business, politics, relationships and life*. London: Oxford University Press.

Stafford, D. (2011, September 4). Union organizing shifts to white collar jobs, especially in hospitals. *Kansas City Star*. Retrieved from http://www.kansascity .com/2011/09/04/3121350/organized-labor-goes-to-the-hospital.html

Thompson, L., & Nadler, J. (2000). Judgmental biases in conflict resolution and how to overcome them. In M. Deutsch & P. Coleman (Eds.), *The handbook of conflict resolution: Theory and practice* (pp. 213–235). San Francisco: Jossey-Bass.

Tidwell, A. (1997). Problem solving for one. *Mediation Quarterly, 14*, 309–317.

Tierney, J. (2010, March 22). Moral lessons, down aisle 9. *New York Times*. Retrieved from http://www.nytimes.com/2010/03/23/science/23tier.html

Tierney, M. (2011, April 16). Executive Q & A: The best in business. *Atlanta Journal-Constitution*. Retrieved from http://www.ajc.com/business/topwork places/executive-q-a-911507.html

Tiffan, B. (2009). Dealing with difficult people. *Physician Executive, 35*(5), 86–89.

Tjosvold, D. (2008). The conflict-positive organization: It depends upon us. *Journal of Organizational Behavior, 29*, 19–28.

Trevarthen, D. S. (2011). *Toro, Byers and his ADR legacy*. Retrieved from http://www.cpradr.org/Resources/ALLCPRArticles/tabid/265/ID/738/Toros -Byers-and-his-ADR-Legacy-Dec-7.aspx

Trivers, R. L. (1971). The evolution of reciprocal altruism. *Quarterly Review of Biology 46*(35), 57.

Tuchman, B. W., & Jensen, M. A. (1977). Stages of small-group development revisited. *Group & Organization Studies, 2*(4), 419.

Tversky, A., & Kahneman, D. (1981). The framing of decisions and the psychology of choice. *Science, 211*, 453–458.

UE Information for workers. (2011). *Step one of the grievance procedure.* Retrieved from http://www.ueunion.org/stwd_grstep1.html

Ullrich, J., & Van Dick, R. (2007). The group psychology of mergers & acquisitions: Lessons from the social identity approach. In C. L. Cooper and S. Finkelstein (Eds.), *Advances in mergers and acquisitions* (pp. 1–15). New York: Emerald Group Publishing.

University of Chicago Medical Center. (2000, January 20). Low levels of salivary cortisol associated with aggressive behavior. *ScienceDaily.* Retrieved from http://www.sciencedaily.com /releases/2000/01/000120073039.htm

University of Iowa. (2011). *Child labor public education project.* Retrieved from http://www.continuetolearn.uiowa.edu/laborctr/child_labor/about/us_history .html

Ury, W., Brett, J., & Goldberg, S. (1988). *Getting disputes resolved: Designing systems to cut the cost of conflict.* San Francisco: Jossey-Bass.

US General Accounting Office. (1997). *U.S. Postal Service: Little progress made in addressing persistent labor-management problems.* Washington, DC: Author.

USIECR. (nd-a). *Federal ECR policy: OMB and CEQ joint memorandum on ECR.* Retrieved from http://www.ecr.gov/Resources/FederalECRPolicy/FederalECR Policy.aspx

USIECR. (nd-b). *Types of ECR processes.* Retrieved from http://www.ecr.gov /Basics/SampleProcessOutline.aspx

Vaaland, T. I. (2006). When conflict communication threatens the business relationship: Lessons from the "balder" story. *Journal of Business-to-Business Marketing, 13*(2), 3–27.

Vaaland, T. I., Haugland, S. A., & Purchase, S. (2004). Why do business partners divorce? The role of cultural distance in inter-firm conflict behavior. *Journal of Business-to-Business Marketing, 11*(4), 1–22.

Van den Steen, E. (2011). *Organizational beliefs and managerial vision.* MIT Sloan Working Paper No. 4224–01. Retrieved from http://ssrn.com/abstract=278200

Varettoni, W. (2005). Success overdue at the Quincy library group. *PERC Reports,* *23*(2).

Vedantam, S. (2007). If it feels good to be good, it might be only natural. *Washington Post.* Retrieved from http://www.washingtonpost.com/wp-dyn /content/article/2007/05/27/AR2007052701056.html

Vogel, G. (2004, February 20). The evolution of the "golden rule." *Science,* *303*(5661), 1128–1131.

von Neumann, J. (1944). *The theory of games and economic behavior.* Princeton, NJ: Princeton University Press.

WarrenShepel. (2005). Research-based database. Retrieved from http://www .shepellfgiservices.com/research/iresearch.asp

Watson, C., & Hoffman, R. L. (1996). Managers as negotiators: A test of power versus gender as predictors of feelings, behavior, and outcomes. *Leadership Quarterly,* *7*(1), 63–85.

Westwood, C. (2010). Managing difficult behavior. *Nursing Manager,* *17*(6), 20–21.

Wiedmer, T. L. (2011). Workplace bullying: Costly and preventable. *The Delta Kappa Gamma Bulletin,* *77*(2), 35–41.

Wilmot, W. W., & Hocker, J. L. (2001). Interpersonal conflict (6th ed.). New York: McGraw-Hill.

Wilson, K. S., Sin, H., & Conlon, D. E. (2010). What about the leader in leader-member exchange? The impact of resource exchanges and substitutability on the leader. *The Academy of Management Review,* *35*(3), 358.

Winter, G. (2000, November 17). Coca-Cola settles racial bias case. *New York Times.* Retrieved from http://www.nytimes.com/2000/11/17/business/coca -cola-settles-racial-bias-case.html

Wissler, R. L. (2002). Court-connected mediation in general civil cases: What we know from empirical research. *Ohio State Journal on Dispute Resolution,* *17*(3), 641–703.

Witschger, J. D. (2011). Our customers, our partners. *American Salesman,* *56*(4), 27–30.

World Bank. (2011). *Respectful workplace advisors program.* Retrieved from http://web.worldbank.org/WBSITE/EXTERNAL/EXTABOUTUS /ORGANIZATION/ORGUNITS/EXTCRS/EXTRWA/0,,contentMDK: 20573730~menuPK:840468~pagePK:64168427~piPK:64168435~theSitePK: 840430,00.html

World Bank. (2012). *Welcome to the World Bank administrative tribunal.* Retrieved from http://web.worldbank.org/external/default/main?pagePK= 7333373&contentMDK=22956391

Yarn, D. H. (2010). *Conflict resolution as evolution.* Gruter Institute Squaw Valley Conference: Law Institutions & Human Behavior; Georgia State University College of Law, Legal Studies Research Paper No 2010–13. Retrieved from http://ssrn.com/abstract=1608250

Yerkes Primate Research Center at Emory University. (2003). *Yerkes researchers first to recognize sense of fairness in non-human primates.* (2003). Atlanta, GA: Author. Retrieved from http://www2.gsu.edu/~wwwcbs/pdf/Senseoffairness .pdf

Zapf, D., & Einarsen, S. (2003). Individual antecedents of bullying. In S. Einarsen, H. Hoel, D. Zapf, & C. L. Cooper (Eds.), *Bullying and emotional abuse in the workplace* (pp. 165–184). London: Taylor & Francis.

Zondiros, D., Konstantopoulos, N., & Tomaras, P. (2007). A simulation model for measuring customer satisfaction through employee satisfaction. *AIP Conference Proceedings, 963*(2), 1086–1089.

Zullo, R. (2011). *The effect of interest arbitration on fire fighter wage increases: Evaluating Michigan's Act 312.* Institute for Research on Labor, Employment and the Economy. Kalamazoo: University of Michigan.

ABOUT THE AUTHOR

Susan S. Raines has a PhD in public policy from Indiana University, 2002; an MA in political science from the University of Idaho, 1995; and a BA in government from California State University, Sacramento, 1992. She is a professor of conflict management at Kennesaw State University in Georgia and the editor-in-chief of *Conflict Resolution Quarterly*. She mediates employment disputes, designs conflict management systems for government and corporate organizations, and provides training within the United States and abroad. She frequently facilitates public meetings and decision-making processes for various US government agencies including the Army Corps of Engineers.

INDEX

Bakeries, 227–228, 263; and non-profit sector, 255–259; in public policy process, 337–338; sample private sector, 246–251; sample public sector, 251–255; six principles of, 232–237; in small organizations, 259–260; supplemental reading on, 264; and values, 230–232

Distributive bargaining: integrative bargaining versus, 72; steps in, 73–74

Distributive justice, 53

Diversity, 167

Dooley, K. J., 168

Downsizing, organizational, 189–190

Drabek, M., 145

Drahozal, C. R., 286

Druckman, J., 46, 125

Duarte, M., 270

Duffy, J., 102

Duran, J. L., 170

Duxbury, L., 135, 136

E

Einarsen, S., 144, 145, 146

Elementary school discipline trap, 63–64

Ellis, A. J., 152, 177

Emerson, K., 371

Emotional intelligence (EI), 26–27, 147

Emotional investment, and clouded judgment, 88–89

Employee Free Choice Act, 217

Employee lawsuits, increase in, 137–138. *See also* Dispute systems design (DSD)

Employee turnover: conclusions on, 160; cost of, 135–138; and difficult employees, 140–144, 191–193; exercises related to, 162–163; and feedback, 148–151; and goal setting, 163; and hiring process, 140; at Main Street Bakeries, 133–134; 160–161; and managers, 154–160; and performance reviews, 151–154; reasons for, 138–139; supplemental reading on, 162; and workplace bullying, 144–148

Employees: difficult, 140–144; dissatisfied, 134–135; empowered, 277–279, 302–303; hiring great, 140. *See also* Difficult employees

Empowered employees, 277–279, 302–303

Environment and public policy conflict resolution (E/PP): conclusions on, 348; description of: 319, 330–336; and errors in collaboration, 344–348; and partnering, 340–344; process options, 336–340

Environmental conflict resolution (ECR), 330

EPM (empathize, pinpoint problems, move forward) formula, 148, 149, 150

Equality principle, 53, 54

Equity principle, 53, 54

Erdman Act of 1898, 216

Executive Order 10988, 217

Executive Order 13522, 220

Exit, evaluation, and diffusion phases, 237, 244–246

Exit interview, 136

External locus of control, 56

F

Facilitation skills, 111–112, 390

Facilitators, large-group: characteristics of successful, 374–375; habits of effective, 375–380

Fairness: across cultures, 55–57; defined, 51; three types of, 53–54

Fallback offer, 83

Farh, C. I., 176, 179

Farh, J., 176, 179

Farrell, L. U., 145

Federal Arbitration Act of 1925, 285

Federal Register, 322, 327

in, 170–172; conflict versus dysfunction in, 176–179; during mergers and acquisitions, 179–189; roles and duties within, 174–175; and "snakes in suits," 191–193; types of, 169–170

Teamwork: best practices for, 167–168; at Bureau of Reclamation, 165–166, 193–194; conclusions on, 193; and goal setting, 197; need for, 166–167; phases of, 173–174; supplemental reading on, 195; and time management, 172–173; and trust, 175–176

Technical skills of managers, importance of, 156, 157

10–80–10 percent rule, 137

Thakordas, V., 146

Theft or embezzlement, 137

Theory of relative deprivation, 52

Third party, bringing in a, 90

Tidwell, A., 115

Tierney, J., 35

Tierney, M., 137, 138, 139, 140, 154

Tiffan, B., 143

Timber wars, 328

Time management, cultural preferences for, 172–173

Time pressures, 89

Timing, of conflict interventions, 59, 61

Tjosvold, D., 6, 14, 91, 175, 176, 177, 178

Tolchin, S. J., 323, 326

Tomaras, P., 270, 271, 303

Toro (outdoor maintenance equipment), 299–302

Toshihiko, T., 279

Town hall meeting, 380–381

Tracy, S. J., 144, 145, 146

Transaction costs, 82

Transactive memory systems (TMSs), 170, 171

Trevarthen, D. S., 299, 300

Trials, summary jury, 113–114

Trivers, R., 35

Trust, and teamwork, 175–176

Trust repair, in negotiations, 91–93

Tuchman, B. W., 173

Turner-Cobb, J., 36

Turnover, employee: conclusions on, 160; cost of, 135–138; and difficult employees, 140–144; exercises related to, 162–163; and feedback, 148–151; and goal setting, 163; and hiring process, 140; at Main Street Bakeries, 133–134; 160–161; and managers, 154–160; and performance reviews, 151–154; reasons for, 138–139; supplemental reading on, 162; and workplace bullying, 144–148

Tversky, A., 42, 125

Twenty-first century town hall meetings, 381

U

Ullrich, J., 182

Unhelpful behaviors, in work environment, 142

Union grievance process, 207–212

Union steward, 209

Unionization, trends in, 203–207

Unionized environments: collaborative leaders in, 215–216; and collective bargaining, 200–201, 216–218; conclusions on, 222–223; examples of conflict management in, 212; historical background of unions, 201–203

United Nations (UN), advice from, 374–375

United Parcel Service (UPS), peer review process at, 103

United States Postal Service (USPS) REDRESS mediation program, 251–255